THE CATHEDRAL 'OPEN AND FREE'

LIVERPOOL HISTORICAL STUDIES

1. Patrick J. N. Tuck, *French Catholic Missionaries and the Politics of Imperialism in Vietnam, 1857–1914: A Documentary Survey*, 1987, 352pp. (Out of print)

2. Michael de Cossart, *Ida Rubinstein (1885–1960): A Theatrical Life*, 1987, 244pp.

3. P. E. H. Hair, ed., *Coals on Rails, Or the Reason of My Wrighting: The Autobiography of Anthony Errington, a Tyneside colliery waggon and waggonway wright, from his birth in 1778 to around 1825*, 1988, 288pp.

4. Peter Rowlands, *Oliver Lodge and the Liverpool Physical Society*, 1990, 336pp.

5. P. E. H. Hair, ed., *To Defend Your Empire and the Faith: Advice on a Global Strategy Offered c. 1590 to Philip, King of Spain and Portugal, by Manoel de Andrada Castel Blanco*, 1990, 304pp.

6. Christine Hillam, *Brass Plate and Brazen Impudence: Dental Practice in the Provinces 1755–1855*, 1991, 352pp.

7. John Shepherd, *The Crimean Doctors: A History of the British Medical Services in the Crimean War*, 1991, 2 vols, 704pp.

8. John Belchem, ed., *Popular Politics, Riot and Labour: Essays in Liverpool History 1790–1940*, 1992, 272pp.

9. Duncan Crewe, *Yellow Jack and the Worm: British Naval Administration in the West Indies, 1739–1748*, 1993, 352pp.

10. Stephen J. Braidwood, *Black Poor and White Philanthropists: London's Blacks and the Foundation of the Sierra Leone Settlement 1786–1791*, 1994, 336pp.

11. David Dutton, *'His Majesty's Loyal Opposition': The Unionist Party in Opposition 1905–1915*, 1992, 336pp.

12. Cecil H. Clough and P. E. H. Hair, eds., *The European Outthrust and Encounter: The First Phase c.1400–c.1700: Essays in Tribute to David Beers Quinn on His 85th Birthday*, 1994, 380pp.

13. David Dutton, ed., *Statecraft and Diplomacy in the Twentieth Century: Essays Presented to P. M. H. Bell*, 1995, 192pp.

14. Roger Swift, ed., *Victorian Chester: Essays in Social History 1830–1900*, 1996, 263pp.

15. P. E. H. Hair, ed., *Arts · Letters · Society: A Miscellany Commemorating the Centenary of the Faculty of Arts at the University of Liverpool*, 1996, 272pp.

16. Susan George, *Liverpool Park Estates: Their Legal Basis, Creation and Early Management*, 2000, 176pp.

17. Alex Bruce, *The Cathedral 'Open and Free': Dean Bennett of Chester*, 2000, 304pp.

The dean in his renovated cloister garden, c. 1928

THE CATHEDRAL 'OPEN AND FREE'
Dean Bennett of Chester

ALEX BRUCE

LIVERPOOL UNIVERSITY PRESS

Liverpool Historical Studies no. 16
Series Editor: P. E. H. Hair

First published 2000
by Liverpool University Press
4 Cambridge Street, Liverpool L69 7ZU

Copyright © 2000 Liverpool University Press

British Library Cataloguing in Publication Data
A British Library CIP record is available

ISBN 0 85323 924 X

Typeset by Frances Hackeson Freelance Publishing Services, Brinscall, Lancs.
Printed in Great Britain by Redwood Books Ltd, Trowbridge, Wilts.

Contents

Abbreviations		*viii*
Acknowledgements		*ix*
Series editor's note		*x*
Preface		*xi*
I	The new dean	1
II	Parish priest: apprentice to master craftsman	26
III	Through Welsh Disestablishment to English deanery	58
IV	The nation's cathedrals adopt the Chester model	74
V	The cathedral restored	100
VI	The nature of a cathedral	122
VII	The New World: 'cathedrals and other things'	143
VIII	Robust theology, educational philosophy, ecclesiastical politics	170
IX	Harmony and discord: a dean and his two communities	204
X	Private lives, last lap, and journey home	232
Epilogue	Today	244
Appendix	Was Bennett ever considered for a Bishopric?	258
Bibliography		*265*
Index		*276*

The illustrations appear between pp. 99 and 100

Abbreviations

Cathedrals Commission	*Report of the Cathedrals Commission appointed in pursuance of a resolution of the National Assembly of the Church of England, Parts I and II, Report and Appendices* (1927)
Chap. Bk.	Cheshire Record Office, Diocesan Archives, 'Chapter Book (1894–1941)'
Ches. Chr.	*Chester Chronicle*
CDG	*Chester Diocesan Gazette*
CEMS	Church of England Men's Society
Coué	F. S. M. Bennett, *M. Coué and his Gospel of Health* (1922)
CPB	Cheshire Record Office, Diocesan Archives, 'Commonplace Book'
CRO	Cheshire Record Office
Crockford	*Crockford's Clerical Directory*
ECU	English Church Union
Howe, *Report*	*Heritage and Renewal: The Report of the Archbishops' Commission on Cathedrals* (1994)
HPM	*Hawarden Parish Magazine*
ICF	Industrial Christian Fellowship
Official Report	*Official Report of the Proceedings of the Convention of the Church in Wales* [1919]
PP	Parliamentary Papers
TLS	*Times Literary Supplement*
VCH	*Victoria County History of Cheshire*

Acknowledgements

Over the dozen years in which I have been researching the life and career of Dean Bennett, I have been assisted by a large number of institutions and individuals. I have been encouraged by the courtesy shown in the former to me in person or in reply to my often extended postal inquiries, and by the kindness and patience of the latter, many providing me with oral or written recollections or seeking out material of relevance. I name the following, although there are others who did not name themselves to me, and to all express my deep indebtedness.

Miss Melanie Barber; J. W. Barker; The Rt. Revd. Allen L. Bartlett, Jr.; Miss C. M. Baxter; The Revd. Guy Bennett; Dr Nicholas Bennett; Robert Bennett; E. G. W. Bill; Ms E. V. Bligh; Ms Claire Breay; A. Brien; Dr A. C. Bruce; R. J. Childs; Mrs Gordon Clark; Jeff Clew; Mrs Caroline M. Cloutte; Clive W. Cornell; Dr M. W. Cornish; Miss Vanessa Corrick; Ms Sarah Costley; Professor J. S. Cunningham; Ms Jay Curtis; Geoffrey Dryland; Mrs Deirdre Dunn; Brian Dutton; Miss D. Dyer; Mike Eddison; Canon T. E. P. Edwards; Miss Suzanne M. Eward; Ms Cathy Franks; Dr Richard Gem; R. J. Goulden; Canon T. R. K. Goulstone; J. A. S. Green; Canon J. Harris; Simon Harrison; Canon S. Higham; S. D. Hobbs; Ms Brenda Hough; Nevil James; Gwyn Jenkins; Marian Keyes; Ms Alice Laird; The Revd. D. J. Lanel; Arthur Leggatt; Mrs Margaret Lewis; Marilyn Lewis; Charles S. Longley; C. L. Marsden; Mrs Christine Mason; R. McDonald; Miss Sally McInnes; The Revd. Lyn Morris; Richard Mortimer; Ms Christine Mosser; Yoshitaka Nishimiya; Roger Norris; Miss Anne M. Oakley; Miss Sharon Orton; Dr D. M. Owen; Richard Palmer; Jonathan Pepler; Miss E. L. Pettitt; D. T. W. Price; The Venerable T. W. Pritchard; Professor Keith Robbins; Canon J. Rogers; D. M. M. Shorrocks; Eileen Simpson; Dr David Smith; R.J. Stratton; Peter S. Thring; Hamish Todd; Jeffrey Veysey; Canon K. Walker; David Wall; Miss R. Watson; Dennis Whiting; J. S. Williams; R. R. Williams; The Revd. Graham Wolfenden.

The illustrations are mainly from a family photograph album in the possession of a great-granddaughter of Bennett, Mrs Caroline M. Cloutte of Ashstead, Surrey; I am indebted to her for allowing selected photographs to be reproduced.

I am grateful to the Publications Committee of the Department (now School) of History for including this work in the series of Liverpool Historical Studies, and to Liverpool University Press and its Secretary, Robin Bloxsidge, for organizing its publication. I am indebted to Dr Sheridan Gilley of Durham University for the extremely valuable suggestions and recommendations he made when acting as outside reader for the series. The final preparation of copy has been undertaken by the Editor of the Series, Emeritus Professor Paul Hair, whose guidance and care in detail have much improved my text.

Alex Bruce
1 August 1998

Series editor's note

Alex Bruce died while this book was in press. A retired headmaster, living in Chester, he maintained a wide range of public and church interests and commitments, as well as a consuming interest in history. He published many articles on local history, and a nationwide guide, *Monuments, Memorials and the Local Historian* (1997). We had not discussed a dedication for the present book, but had he lived and agreed to frame one, I believe it would have acknowledged the support of his family during his long researches, and so would have been addressed to his wife, Margaret, and his son, Alasdair.

P. E. H. H.

PREFACE

Frank Selwyn Macaulay Bennett, appointed Dean of Chester in 1920, within a few months of his 54th birthday, is remembered in accounts of the Church of England in the twentieth century principally for the reforms he effected at Chester Cathedral during his 17 years as Dean, and for the impact these reforms had on the other Anglican cathedrals of England and Wales. One by one, the others followed Chester's example in abolishing entry charges and generally in making the cathedral church more welcoming and open to visitors.

Bennett has not been forgotten. The best brief account of his work at Chester and its significance is given in Roger Lloyd's *The Church of England, 1900–1965* (1966).[1] A concise summary of important aspects can be found in the *Victoria County History of Cheshire* (vol. III, 1980).[2] Elma Paget, widow of Bishop Paget of Chester, in her memoir of her husband (1939) offered some impressions of relations between bishop and dean.[3] An American church historian, Horton Davies, in his wide ranging *Worship and Theology in England* (1965), when discussing cathedrals and their functions gives place of honour to Bennett:

> The pioneer in their revival was Dean Bennett of Chester, who changed Chester Cathedral from a museum for curious visitors into a home for pilgrims. His pioneering example, in domesticating a cathedral, was widely but not quickly followed.[4]

More recently, Michael De-la-Noy, in *The Church of England: A Portrait* (1993), has paid tribute to Bennett, who 'demonstrated the possibility of using a cathedral as a major centre for worship and ministry'.[5] Again, Keith Robbins in his contribution on 'The Twentieth Century' to the 1995 collaborative *A History of Canterbury Cathedral*, refers to Bennett's influence on Canterbury.[6]

But there are several elements of Bennett's work at Chester which have received little attention, and his activities during 28 formative years of active ministry before he came to Chester have received scant notice. His writings, though now largely forgotten, were highly regarded in the 1920s and 1930s, at least in some religious quarters, and they provide important insights into his thinking and thus into his approach to practical problems. Furthermore, Bennett's writings illustrate many aspects of the history of the Church of England in the period between two world wars, as well as on occasion testifying to the 'spirit of the age' in 'Anglo-Saxon' Christianity and in the popular religious – and religiose – writing of the time.[7]

As regards detailed sources for this study, the Deanery files for the Bennett years do not seem to have survived, but there is material in the Cathedral Chapter minutes, in the Cathedral 'Commonplace Book', in *Chester Diocesan Gazette*, and in the press, local and national. Scattered correspondence exists in Lambeth Palace Library, the Church of England Record Centre, the British Architectural Library, and Flintshire Record Office. Diocesan archives in the USA, notably those of Washington diocese, contain valuable material for his three-month trans-Atlantic visit. Newspapers in the United States and Canada carry accounts of the visit, and American and Canadian archivists and librarians have been most helpful. The printed minutes of the 1917 Convention of the Church in Wales and of the Governing Body indicate the part Bennett played in Welsh Disestablishment. In the final Report of the Cathedrals Commission (1927), Bennett's reservations make explicit those issues in connection with reform on which he felt strongly.

His early work as parish priest is less well documented, but the local press gives some help. For Portwood and Christ Church parishes the *Chester Diocesan Gazette* provides pointers; Stockport and Chester newspapers are useful. I have not discovered any copies of Portwood parish magazine; those of *Christ Church Messenger* are scarce, but Cheshire Record Office has a few 1908 numbers. For Hawarden parish, the main source is *Hawarden Parish Magazine*; St Deiniol's Library at Hawarden has bound volumes of issues up to 1916. There is other material in Flintshire Record Office, but no Parochial Council minutes for Bennett's period as rector. For Bennett's latter years in retirement, there is material in Somerset Record Office.

Sherborne School magazine and class lists provide clues to Bennett's schooldays. There is nothing for his four years at Oxford except the printed Keble College Register. However, for personal reminiscence and family details I am much indebted to Bennett's two grandsons, the late Roderick Macaulay Bennett (1930–1990), and his brother, the Reverend Guy Bennett. I have especially appreciated Guy

Bennett's generosity in sending me a copy of his father's typescript 'Memoir' describing, as he knew it, the life and career of Dean Bennett, as well as a tape recording of his own boyhood recollections of his grandfather, the Dean. I am indebted to him, also, for arranging for me to see the complete Bennett 'Family History', a typescript text written by his late brother, Roderick, and now in the possession of Roderick's daughter. Another relative, Mr R. L. S. Bennett, has also been helpful. Canon Owen Conway, a member of Chester Cathedral Chapter, generously provided me with a copy of a Report on the 1989 sabbatical leave which he spent visiting English cathedrals, a survey of more or less contemporary practice which has greatly helped me to assess Bennett's lasting influence.

I now acknowledge the invaluable assistance generously provided by record office staff, librarians, deans, cathedral clergy, and private individuals, in England, Wales, the United States of America, Canada, and Japan. The discussion following a paper I gave on Bennett to *The Historic Society of Lancashire and Cheshire* in 1996 was a useful stimulus to further investigation. Margaret Lewis, of Washington Cathedral Archives, who had provided a wealth of information, kindly read and checked the chapter on Bennett's American visit. Above all, I am deeply indebted to Professor Paul Hair of the Department of History of the University of Liverpool for advice, criticism, and encouragement.

Notes

1   Roger Lloyd, *The Church of England, 1900-1965* (London, 1966), 45, 392–402 (for the lady visitor comforted in the Cathedral, 399). Before becoming Canon of Winchester in 1937, Lloyd had served in Lancashire parishes for 13 years, and therefore could hardly have failed to know at first hand Bennett's work in neighbouring Chester. See also J. H. R. Moorman, *History of the Church of England* (London, 1953; 2nd edit., 1967), chapter 22; C. K. Francis Brown, *A History of the English Clergy 1800-1900* (London, (1953), 71–2.

2   B. H. Harris (ed.), *Victoria County History of Cheshire, III* (Oxford, 1980), 194.

3   Elma K. Paget, *Henry Luke Paget* (London, 1939), 224–39.

4   Horton Davies, *Worship and Theology in England*, 5 vols (Princeton/London, 1961–5), 5 ('The Ecumenical Century 1900–65'): 51 (the index reference to Bennett is wrong).

5   Michael De-la-Noy, *The Church of England: A Portrait* (London, 1993), 75–6.

6   Keith Robbins, 'The Twentieth Century', in Patrick Collinson *et al* (eds.), *A History of Canterbury Cathedral* (Oxford, 1995), 310–11. Surprisingly, in *Heritage and Renewal: The Report of the Archbishops' Commission on Cathedrals* (London, 1994), Bennett is merely credited with 'what Bishop Wand of London once called "the spiritualisation of the tourist traffic" (he put up notices telling people what they were looking at)'. Thus the Dean was 'merely updating a very traditional service of the cathedrals: the provision of "history in stone"'. There is no mention of Bennett's role in initiating the 'Open and Free' movement (*op. cit.*, 195).

7   Religion and belief in the period is sharply and sociologically analysed in a recent study, Ross McKibbin, *Classes and Cultures: England 1918-1951* (Oxford, 1998), 272–96.

I

The new Dean

1

On 3 April 1920, the *Chester Chronicle*, announcing the appointment of Frank Bennett, a parish priest, as Dean of Chester, described it as 'highly original and unexpected'. The upper ecclesiastical ranks were normally recruited from amongst those who had spent some time in a cathedral close or in academia, and so there was undoubtedly a marked element of originality in this appointment. The 'unexpected' hints broadly at the speculation that must have been rife in City and clerical circles during the four-month vacancy. But Bennett was no stranger to Chester. As a young man, he had served an ecclesiastical apprenticeship as secretary to a bishop of Chester, and had then worked as priest in local parishes before moving to Hawarden, in the neighbouring Welsh diocese, where he was currently Rector. It seemed that New Dean was indeed to be Old Parish Priest writ large. With the journalistic rhetoric of the time, the *Daily Mail* hailed him as 'The Cheery Dean', whose 'working capacity' shamed most men of thirty; whose parochial organisations ran 'like clockwork', and who was possessed of 'a heart flaming with idealism and the disposition of a schoolboy on holiday'. The eulogy continued:

> Without fuss or pride he never poses as learned or superior. He appeals straight to the heart in simple language, with homely simile and undoubted sincerity. In debate he reduces difficulties to utter simplicities. He visualises big ideals rather than the petty problems through which they are attained. He is the embodiment of the Church's need – vitality, reality and humanity ... Above all he preaches the gospel of cheerfulness.[1]

2

During the three months between his appointment to Chester and his installation, on 2 June 1920, Bennett thought and read a great deal about the task ahead of him. He was sufficiently in touch with Chester to know that there were pressing problems. Cathedral finances were in a shaky state; restoration of the fabric was required; a somewhat moribund Chapter, presided over until recently by an eighty-nine year old dean, needed revitalising. He admitted that, as a parish priest, he had 'oddly enough ... never felt that, as such, I had much to do with the Cathedral, or it with me'. However the 'altogether unexpected offer' of the deanery had launched him on a detailed study of the Statutes of Chester Cathedral. From these he had gone on to read 'all I could lay hands on about Cathedrals in general and their Chapters – their purposes and possibilities'. Out of this 'immense' reading he had acquired 'a whole crop of new ideas and ideals'.[2]

On 6 June, only four days after his installation, Bennett set out what we should today call his strategic plan, though in 1920 it took the form of a sermon, subsequently published in full. The pattern owes something to the first few of his series of 'Rector's Notes', which he had started to publish in *The Hawarden Parish Magazine* as soon as he became rector.[3] As at Hawarden, he now articulated his own rights and duties and made clear the reciprocal rights and duties of others. On paper, as the dean of a 'New Foundation' cathedral he was a virtual autocrat; his duties minimal.[4] This, however, was not how he intended to operate.

The High Churchman in Bennett fastened on aspects of his statutory and other duties which reflected his own style of high-churchmanship. He must appoint a sacristan, not only 'to visit the sick', but to 'hear their confessions'. The dean should be available, when required, to give private spiritual counsel and absolution to others, an early indication of the relationship he intended to develop with worshippers and visitors. The principal service on week-days and Sundays should be the Eucharist, celebrated by a dean, appropriately attended and attired in a cope. He spoke of deans who did otherwise, but he tactfully refrained from citing his predecessor's firm rejection of the cope.[5] But the Church embraced a range of tastes and attitudes. Some preferred services devoid of ceremonial and plain celebration of communion; some were instead 'uplifted by the combined beauty of sight and sound and movement with celebrant, deacon and sub-deacon, with vestments, lights and incense and music'. Bennett's choice of words signalled his own preference, about which he proceeded to be specific. Described by some as a High Churchman he had 'no wish to deny the gentle impeachment'. He would respect the views of those who differed from him, but expected a similar respect and tolerance for those who thought as he did.

The cathedral, he reminded listeners, was the bishop's home; the cathedral body his household. A cathedral estranged from its bishop was a contradiction in terms. In fact Bennett and the recently appointed Bishop Paget thought alike on churchmanship and the role of the cathedral, but it was common knowledge that Bennett's predecessor, Dean Darby, and Paget's predecessor, Bishop Jayne, had not been on speaking terms, after being locked in lengthy litigation over their respective rights.

The cathedral had a duty of hospitality, proclaimed Bennett. The old Day Room would be furnished for visitors, the cloisters glazed, and the cloister garth developed as 'the most beautiful garden of the most hospitable and friendly cathedral in the world'. Bennett hoped to restore the old refectory so that 'all who exercise any ministry in this Cathedral may meet for that greatest bond of friendliness – the Masonic Fourth Degree – a common meal'. His reference to Masonry gave clear notice of attachment to the ideals of a society he had joined at Hawarden (and whose local members greeted him on his arrival at the cathedral).[6] There was also 'external' policy. He would not poach on the preserves of the local parish clergy, but as a parish priest of twenty-five years standing his inclinations were pastoral, and he hoped to establish with those who attended cathedral services, 'something warmer and more personal than a Sunday evening acquaintance'. Cathedral and neighbouring Town Hall belonged together 'in all that makes for the City's welfare'. He would seek, too, to establish (as he had done at Hawarden) a forum for regular discussion with ministers of other denominations. Cathedral and Diocese belonged together, too. Church societies (such as those which flourished at Hawarden) should have their corner – even altar – within the cathedral. There would also be 'a very special place for children'. Prayer should be another link between diocese and cathedral. Parishes should ask for intercession at cathedral services for their own special needs. 'Where', he concluded, 'shall we find experts at intercession if not in our cathedrals, and in what Cathedral, if not here?'

Embedded, however, in the heart of the sermon is Bennett's key to linking Cathedral and outside world. Accessibility (and, by extension, Openness, in a variety of contexts) were to be keynotes of his policy. The cathedral should be accessible to all on Sundays and week-days, with staff and voluntary guides to assist, and should have within it a chapel for private devotions. Above all, however, he said he wanted to be accessible to everyone, from archdeacon to choir-boy. Friendliness was the 'chiefest of the virtues'.

On 24 November, Bennett followed up his sermon with a paper read to the cathedral's Great Chapter, comprising the four 'residentiary' canons and two dozen or so 'honorary' canons. The 'residentiaries' were, in effect, the cathedral management, presided over by the dean, though the description 'residentiary' is misleading as each was only required to 'reside' for a three-month period.[7] The 'honoraries', who were parish clergy, had the honour of an empty title but no noticeable duties or rights, except the privilege of occupying a stall in the cathedral. Basing his case on an essay by the historian E. A. Freeman, in a collection, *Essays on Cathedrals* (1872), edited by a former Dean of Chester, J. S. Howson, Bennett argued that, sadly, the Great Chapter was merely the attenuated relic of what in early medieval cathedrals had been the bishop's *'familia'*, his spiritual bodyguard and council. Chester was simply one specimen of the whole cathedral system. Bishops and deans had drawn so far apart that it was no surprise that they sometimes fell out. 'The wonder', he added, 'is that they ever agree at all', though, he hastened to add, at Chester they did work 'harmoniously together'. The Bishop presided at the present meeting but (ironically) 'by invitation of the Dean!'. It was a 'nice point in law' whether the Bishop could even preach in the cathedral without the dean's permission. As three of the residential canons lived in Chester and the fourth hoped to spend his university vacations there, his comment that 'Our own little Chapter has been able to meet only once for any sort of service together since I became dean six months ago' may be interpreted as a gentle admonition to his close colleagues. Bennett's three proposals 'to restore the honorary canons to some status of reality as well as of title' were 'most cordially received'. They would follow the custom of cathedrals of the 'Old Foundation', and as part of the bishop's spiritual bodyguard each would say daily a portion of the Psalter, arranged so that each portion included 'praise, penitence and prayer'; the Great Chapter would meet twice yearly and would make suggestions to the Little Chapter which would meet the following day; and each canon would have the opportunity of preaching, once a year, in the cathedral. All this would also help to unite diocese and cathedral.[8]

Significantly, Bennett had steered clear in his sermon and his paper of direct reference to finance, and many of the changes he had mentioned would cost nothing or very little. He had been privately warned, before he became dean, that the cathedral finances were 'in a sad way'.[9] Financial probity was the hidden agenda.

3

Bennett's account of the separation of bishop and chapter may be set in context by relating it, first, to the development in the twelfth century, an age of increasing self-awareness, of groups of men forming communities through which to advance their own interests. Bishops, with expanding diocesan and governmental work, needed a level of wealth to sustain them and their household. Hence arose a division of the *mensa* – the property and income of the ecclesiastical body. It is unrealistic to suppose, furthermore, that the bishop could necessarily be much about his cathedral, which might not even be sited strategically for communications. Over the last fifty years, studies have given a clearer picture of the role of the medieval bishop as ecclesiastical officer *vis-à-vis* the chapter, and as tenant-in-chief *vis-à-vis* the king. However, 'dramatic conflict' was not the unavoidable rule in cathedral churches. Periods of harmony between bishop and chapter were probably greater than the 'fractious episodes' which attracted attention. Nor was the chapter 'a monolithic structure, but an association composed of factions' concerned with material and practical concerns. Fundamental to changes in the capitular constitution of cathedrals was 'the control of wealth which, when translated into political terms, meant power'.[10] In the later Middle Ages, bishops were readier to admit that a cathedral church could not exist unless allowed certain privileges and customs. As to the definition and extent of these, the many canon lawyers of chapters were, however, only too eager to engage in negotiation and lengthy lawsuits.[11]

Post-Reformation Tudor monarchs, notably Elizabeth, in control of a weakened English church, took the opportunity when vacancies arose of stripping bishops of a proportion of their assets, for the ever-expanding requirements of sixteenth-century government. Protestantism might logically have done without cathedrals. Nevertheless, despite reformers' calls for disendowment, they survived – apart from their institutional eclipse during the Cromwellian era. This might seem surprising when some, Norwich in the seventeenth century, Winchester in the early nineteenth, were uninspiring performers (Cobbett visited Winchester in 1825 and roundly castigated it for its deficiencies). While there were outstanding individual cathedrals within the system, the continuing pressure from without for reform in the relationship between cathedral and society is readily understandable.[12]

4

Bennett's efforts at reform should be set, too, in their broader context. By the early nineteenth century, the affairs of the Church of England were a matter of intense public concern within the country and the Church as it was had enemies both within and without. The assault gathered momentum in the 1820s and 1830s and extended into the 1840s and beyond. For long it has been argued by historians that the combined efforts of Evangelicals and Tractarians rescued the Church from extinction. This is perhaps to accept the claims of these two protagonists at their own valuation. Recent research suggests that it was equally the exercise of enlightened and discriminating patronage by conservative Old High Churchmen, notably the 'Hackney Phalanx', which helped to rescue the Church of England from threatened disendowment and disestablishment during the 'greatest onslaught on Anglican privileges and property since the Civil War'.[13]

Trollope, then, chose well in selecting the community of the Close as a theme for his novels. Though Jane Austen, Charlotte Bronte, Thackeray, and others incidentally portrayed clerical attitudes, none dealt with church issues as Trollope did.[14] He portrayed a structure deserving of criticism, yet he deplored the press attacks on honest and honourable clergy who inhabited it and derived income thereby. Trollope's sympathies lay with the Old High Churchmen, the scholars and gentlemen of the Close; he had acquired his anti-Evangelical attitudes from his mother, Frances Trollope. A prolific and successful writer, with an eye to the market, she had already grasped that a novel about church issues would sell. Similarities between characters in her *Uncle Walter* (1852), and in her son's first succesful novel, *The Warden* (1855), and in the subsequent *Barchester Towers* (1857), can be noted.[15]

Some changes to the Close came about early. At Salisbury – Trollope's 'Barchester' – in the 1840s and early 1850s the Precentor, Walter Kerr Hamilton (1808–1869), a devout Tractarian, promoted important reforms with the strong support of a new dean. He carefully scrutinised previous Chapter rulings and precedents regarding the bishop's use of the cathedral and his role therein. He addressed a variety of problems: residence, property, preaching, the duties of Dean, Chapter and Vicars Choral, and the education of choristers, in the last case establishing thereby a pattern for all future British choir schools. Hamilton's report to the dean was published and widely circulated throughout the Church. His work has been hailed as heralding 'an epoch in Cathedral reform'.[16]

Ecclesiastical reform in the latter part of the nineteenth century may be perceived as an ecclesiastical parallel to the Victorian revival and adaptation of other great institutions, not least the endowed schools. A good dean, working in harmony with his chapter, could overcome many obstacles and achieve a great deal. One such dean, regarded by a modern ecclesiastical historian as 'the greatest of all Victorian deans', was Richard William Church (1815–1890) – who, as it happened, married one of Bennett's aunts.[17] After ordination in 1852, Church left Oxford for a country rectory, where he remained happily until persuaded by Gladstone in 1871 to become Dean of St Paul's, a post to which he then devoted the remainder of his life. At that date, St Paul's had become 'a byword for slovenliness and neglect'. From the start Church clearly outlined his three aims: winning from the Ecclesiastical Commissioners the revenues necessary for the needs 'of the *reformed* [*sic*] cathedral'; restoring the fabric, for which he demanded £250,000; and reducing to order a refractory staff of singing men entrenched in chartered rights.[18] Transmitting his vision of a reformed cathedral to the gifted chapter he assembled and with whom he established a harmonious relationship, Church achieved outstanding success in the reform of St Paul's and 'gradually achieved his object of turning it into a model cathedral'. Where St Paul's had led, the public expected other cathedrals to follow. By 1900 their expectation of deans was markedly higher than it had been a century earlier, and deans of a new generation were exercising successful ministries and promoting a different atmosphere in several provincial closes.[19] Increasingly, congregational services, special services, sung eucharists, and more professionally effective choirs, became features of cathedral worship and activity.[20]

It is possible to speculate on the influence which Church's career as a reformer may have exercised on Bennett's thinking. Church had served in the Somerset rectory of Whatley (1852–1871), where in 1853 he married Helen Frances Bennett (1826–1905), Frank Bennett's paternal aunt. Although we have no documentary evidence about contacts between Church and his nephew by marriage, it is highly unlikely that Frank Bennett, aged twenty-four by the end of Church's life, would have been unaware of his uncle's reforming activities at St Paul's. Indeed, if Church was the nineteenth century 'quintessence of a dean', his nephew can justly be claimed as the twentieth century version.[21]

5

The problem of the relationship between, on the one hand, bishop and diocese, and on the other, chapter and cathedral, was addressed directly by Edward White Benson (1829–1897). The first headmaster of Wellington College (which he fashioned after Arnold's Rugby), Benson in 1872 became Diocesan Chancellor of Lincoln, where he established a theological college, started night schools for working men, founded a society of mission preachers, and gave sermons regularly in the cathedral which attracted many of the humbler citizens of Lincoln.[22] A cathedral, he argued, should be the centre for an evangelism reaching out into all the world.[23] His ideal cathedral required five canons, who were, in effect, to be diocesan officials with additional cathedral responsibilities. Appointed Bishop of the newly created see of Truro in 1877, Benson built a cathedral and then published his views on reform, contending that the weakness of the cathedral system derived from the drawing apart of Bishop and Chapter.[24] At Truro he remedied this by making himself dean of his new cathedral, thereby emphasising the 'diocesan' role of the chapter.[25] The Benson model for the diocesan employment of cathedral canons was widely copied to a greater or lesser degree, but there was no enthusiasm for bishops becoming their own deans.[26] His scheme linked cathedral and bishop (whose officials were on the cathedral pay roll), and provided a positive role for canons. At Durham, however, Dean Hensley Henson questioned the whole enterprise, as tending, eventually, to destroy the *raison d'être* of cathedrals. But no seemingly viable alternative emerged in a Church which saw its priority as outreach into parishes in such key areas as mission work and education, with diocesan supervision of these.[27]

The new Dean of Chester in 1920 thus stood at the end of a long line of critics and reformers, lay and clerical, conservative and radical, variously motivated by a range of concerns both secular and religious. In placing the significance of Bennett's work in context it cannot be overlooked that, following the clamour for change in the 1830s, piecemeal reform had already been taking place and that much progress had been made in the later decades of the nineteenth century and up to 1920. A modern historian's verdict, after revisiting 'Barsetshire', is that 'the revitalization of English cathedrals was one of the most impressive achievements of the Victorian Church' and that this produced a 'growing perception' of the distinctive role that cathedrals might have in the life of the Church. He argues that it was harder to 'reform an institution with a long history' than to make 'important new initiatives'.[28] Whether Dean Bennett was a 'reformer' or an 'innovator' may be a matter of debate, even semantics, but the overall new spirit which he infused into cathedral life was hailed in his day (and after) as innovative, even to the point of 'revolution'.

6

The extensive changes which Bennett effected in his seventeen years at Chester were made possible because, above all else, he possessed the qualities of the good administrator, the individual who who can analyse problems, reduce them to their elements, and assess realistically the means at his disposal to resolve them. Equally important, he was always able to involve others, secure their support, and infect them with his own enthusiasm and drive, all qualities of the successful leader. The skills which Bennett deployed at Chester were, however, largely those which he had developed and employed as a parish priest. Furthermore Bennett was a good learner. The lessons he had learnt in his several parishes were not forgotten. He did not repeat those mistakes which – as he was the first to admit – he had made from time to time.

Foremost amongst Bennett's natural strengths was his effectiveness as a communicator. By the time he became dean he was already skilled in public relations, whose techniques he had perfected and used with notable success both in his Chester parish of Christ Church and at Hawarden. Bennett always believed that the way to carry people along with him was to keep them fully informed. He had been christened 'Frank', he once characteristically remarked, and, 'like his name' he 'liked things out in the open'.[29] Fortunately, the *Chester Diocesan Gazette* had recently been revived, and Bennett used it, as he had used his parish magazines at Hawarden and Christ Church, to float ideas, announce plans, report progress, and laud success. His 'Dean's Notes', one of his first innovations, reached an extensive audience throughout the diocese, and attracted the attention of the local press, and sometimes even the national newspapers, as had his writings in the Hawarden magazine. He presented issues simply, was lavish in his praise for the efforts of others, and sought no credit for himself. Generally he kept his major current project to the fore, coming back to it, with variations on the theme, month by month, until it was completed. Then he would start on the next important one. His own letters to the press, when he felt them to be necessary, are models of clarity and reasonableness.

In his personal relations with worshippers, visitors, and members of the public, Bennett adopted an easy informality which won him a wide circle of friends and admirers of all ages and social groupings. To many of his young friends – and older ones, too – he was simply 'The Very Rev.', a title he rather enjoyed.[30] He retained a schoolboy-like sense of fun. He is said to have been well-known at the counter of the 'joke' department in the local Woolworths store, where the staff would gather round to offer advice on the latest tricks available, sometimes to try out on his wife on 1 April. Bennett's secretary, occasionally his agent in obtaining his joke-packs and later to become his daughter-in-law, together with one of her friends accompanied him on a particular occasion to a meeting of cathedral deans. Bennett disliked dull meetings, and after lunch he told the two girls that as it would be a boring afternoon he would instead show them the attractive garden of the dean who was hosting the gathering. The meeting, however, ended sooner than expected and down the garden path came the procession of gaitered deans. 'Quick', he cried, 'here they come! Hide behind this bush!'. The august procession passed, unaware that the Dean of Chester was holding his breath, hiding behind a bush with two young women.[31] Characteristic, also, is the saga of Cocklebun, the pet parrot which Bennett had brought with him from Hawarden. The bird became as famous in cathedral circles as it had been around the Rectory. In Hawarden it had been wont to sit on a signpost and offer salutations to passers-by, until one day a furious inhabitant hit it over the head with a stone. Taken for dead, it was brought back in a paper bag to Bennett who revived it with chocolate soaked in brandy. After the move to Chester Cockelbun was lost for some time, until it reappeared in a children's ward at the Infirmary. It was not generally known outside the deanery that whenever the telephone rang Cocklebun would shriek repetitively and disgracefully, 'Let the devils ring'.[32]

Totally devoid of pomposity, Bennett sought above all else to avoid being thought of as a remote and impersonal ecclesiastical dignitary. Not that he did not know the value and role of ceremonial, in its proper place and on the appropriate occasion.³³ When ceremonial was called for, he would give considerable time and thought to it. Inserted loosely in the cathedral 'Commonplace Book' is a sheet of paper setting out in detail the arrangements for the procession at the 1931 St Werburgh Day Festival: clergy, Bishop, visiting Bishop of London, banners of the different chapels, Dean with cope, boys. The hand-writing is almost certainly that of Bennett, who (if it is he) has endorsed it, 'A very impressive procession'.³⁴ (Werburgh was the patron saint of the medieval monastery to which the cathedral succeeded, and Bennett's borrowing of the name to give the dignity of distant heritage to cathedral events was also typical, in this case of his acuity.)

Bennett had a considerable charm of manner, which greatly assisted in winning powerful supporters to his causes and not least in encouraging them to dip deeply into their purses. The skills which had earned him a reputation at Hawarden for being able to talk money out of the influential and affluent he deployed more widely, and with even greater success, at Chester.

7

Early days are often critical in setting the direction and pace of reform, and Bennett moved swiftly to deal with what he considered to be the most important issues.³⁵ He immediately opened the cathedral to all, 'without let or hindrance', and abolished the traditional sixpenny entrance fee which almost all cathedrals then charged.³⁶ At a stroke, Bennett had started the process which would change Chester Cathedral 'from a museum for curious visitors into a home for pilgrims'.³⁷ Perhaps predictably, not all members of the cathedral staff were immediately convinced of the merits of the change. At Bennett's first Chapter meeting, on 23 June 1920, the Precentor reported 'on the question of the crowds that now frequent the Cathedral', and the dean was asked to prepare some form of notice as to the freedom of the Church and the observance of proper behaviour, while the vergers were to be instructed 'to always have someone present in the Choir when there are any people in the building'. The result must have been the notice which the local press reported shortly afterwards. This announced that:

> Free access to the whole Cathedral both on Sundays and weekdays is given to visitors, in the confidence that they will, in return (1) be reverently appreciative of this holy and beautiful House of God and of all that is in it; (2) be still and quiet during the time of service; (3) say one prayer for themselves and one for those who minister and worship here; and (4) put into the boxes some contribution towards the stipends of the vergers and the care and upkeep of the building and its services. May the Peace of God go with you.[38]

No further complaints are recorded, and within two months of his installation Bennett was reporting progress on this and other changes he had effected, and relating these to the objectives he had set out in his installation sermon, his 'strategic plan'.[39]

The most important development was that the cathedral, open without charge since June, had become 'the one wholly hospitable Cathedral in England, open everywhere to everybody on Sundays as well as weekdays'. Throughout that second summer after the 'Great War' it drew large crowds of visitors, in Bennett's words, 'orderly, reverent and most appreciative'. The dean was often in the cathedral himself to assist with the visitors, including a number of Americans, who flocked to Chester.[40] The local press welcomed the dean's new policies, believing that 'the citizens will warmly support his action', an action which must in itself have helped to attract tourists to the town and prolong their stay, with consequent benefits to local traders. Visitors to the cathedral responded well to Bennett's appeal. Soon the voluntary offerings were producing more income than the old charges – in September and August, £148, compared with £48 in the same months of the previous year – and the income steadily mounted. A handy brief guide book was shortly available, enabling 'the mere visitor' to transform himself into a pilgrim. It was entitled, appropriately, *A Little Handbook for Pilgrims to Chester Cathedral*, and was written by Bennett's son, Frank Livesey Macaulay Bennett (who later published an authoritative work on the cathedral). The *Little Handbook*, at twopence, sold extensively. By 1935 it was running into its 172nd thousand and was taken by one in seven of all visitors.[41]

8

Bennett's career after his installation as Dean of Chester and his early days in the office is the subject of most of the rest of this study. But the child is father of the man. What stages of process, what influences, what dispensations brought Bennett to Chester Cathedral? The remainder of the present chapter deals with his early years, the next two chapters with his previous clerical ministries.

Bennett sometimes spoke of his 'native Devon', and indeed by birth he was a Devon man, having been born in Torquay, on 28 October 1866, where his parents were temporarily residing.[42] He was christened there, in St Luke's, as Frank Selwyn Macaulay Bennett, on Holy Innocent's Day, by the Reverend Joseph Hemington Harris. Harris was a former Principal of Upper Canada College, and there may well have been some link with Frank's grandfather, Sir James Macaulay, once Chief Justice of the Canadian Court of Common Pleas, who gave his surname to the boy.[43] When Sir James was given the task of codifying the laws of Canada, Henry Bennett had gone out as his secretary, and then married the Judge's daughter, Louisa. Frank was their second surviving son.[44] The Canadian connection was eventually to be of use to Bennett.

Though a Devon man by birth, it was to the Somerset of his family home that Frank was always most closely attached. There is an apocryphal story that, as a boy, when taken unwillingly one year on holiday to Normandy he was filled with enthusiasm by the sight of an orchard, but only because it reminded him of his Somerset home. In later life he returned from time to time to Somerset, 'where', he said, 'everything is timed by the cows – an ideal holiday county', and it was to Taunton in his beloved Somerset that he retired in 1937, after his seventeen years as Dean of Chester, there to spend the remaining ten years of his life.[45]

The Bennetts were minor Somerset gentry (their original merchant fortunes sprung from the East India trade), and 'Bennett of Sparkford Hall' was listed in *Burke's Landed Gentry* until the edition of 1921, by which time the house and estate had been sold. Bennett's father, Henry Edward Bennett, was patron of Sparkford church, and as the local squire performed those duties expected of one of his position, appearing regularly on the County Bench and serving as Captain in the Somerset Militia. Bennett's early upbringing at Sparkford Hall almost certainly had a strong influence on him in relation to easy personal relationships.[46] Conscious of his gentry origins, the assumption of authority came easily to him. As head of his house at his public school, he had practised it early. At the same time he was endowed with that characteristic sense of *noblesse oblige*, an obligation to serve, which accompanied – at least not infrequently – social privilege.

At Sparkford, Bennett was on terms of easy friendship with local gentry and servants alike.[47] Sparkford was a happy, easy-going household, albeit one faced with a measure of financial stringency. When Lady Macaulay came to live there after the Judge died, Frank was always her favourite grandson, perhaps because the boy took after his mother and her Macaulay forebears, inheriting even their long eyebrows. There could, however, be Victorian sternness when the occasion seemed to warrant it. As a punishment for drawing on a freshly painted wall Frank had to stand behind his father's chair at meals.[48]

9

Little of significance survives about Bennett's schooldays. He seems to have been educated at home until the age of ten, when he went to his preparatory school, Walton Lodge, in Clevedon.[49] This appears to have been an exclusive establishment, recently opened, and Bennett was one of the original pupils.[50] In September 1880 he entered Sherborne School, a residential 'public school' situated not far from his home, and was allocated to Mr Rhoades' house. The space in the Register for 'proposed pursuit in life' is blank for most of the boys in the 1880 entry, but against Bennett's name it reads, unequivocally, 'Clergyman'.[51] His vocation had thus been settled early, strongly influenced, it would seem, by family tradition. In later years, he said that had he not felt called to the priesthood he would have been a doctor. His paternal grandfather, Henry Bennett (*ob.* 1874), had been Rector of Sparkford, and was succeeded on his death by one of his younger sons, Charles William, who was incumbent there until 1899. A second Bennett uncle, James Arthur (Frank's godfather), was Rector of South Cadbury, of which an elder branch of the Bennett family were patrons.[52] Bennett's younger brother, George (1873–1954), to whom he was very close throughout his life, was also ordained.[53]

The Sherborne staff of the 1880s were an exceptionally able body.[54] With their help, Bennett seems early to have shown himself to be a capable classicist. Just before his sixteenth birthday he was promoted to the sixth form, where he spent the next nine terms, winning prizes successively for Divinity and Greek Testament. He became Head of his house, played in Rhoades' XV, won more prizes for botanical and entomological collections, and participated in musical and dramatic performances at Commemoration Day. He was active in the Debating Society, to which select body he had been elected in 1883, eventually becoming vice-president and a member of the 'cabinet' which ordered the debates. Little can be deduced from the side he took in the various debates, but the subjects chosen are interesting in reflecting those issues of the day which exercised the minds of sixth formers of the 1880s. He supported compulsory military service and fagging at public schools, but opposed the total freedom of the press and the extension of the franchise; he applauded Napoleon I, found the character of Oliver Cromwell to be worthy of the 'highest approval', yet asserted that a barbarian was happier than a civilized man.[55]

Bennett concluded his schooldays by winning a classical open scholarship to Keble College, Oxford, in 1885 – one of the three Oxford scholarships secured by Sherborne sixth formers that year. He chose as his school prize the *Commentaries* of Bishop Lightfoot, whose exposition of the overtones and nuances of words of New Testament Greek exercised a considerable fascination for him.[56] His choice suggests that he was still determined on ordination. Bennett read Greats, the exacting four-year course in classical languages, literature, philosophy, and history, and graduated with a second in 1889.[57] While participating in sport at Oxford he sustained an injury to one of his eyes, which left him with a permanent minor disability.

10

Bennett's first job was as secretary to Francis John Jayne, Bishop of Chester, and tutor to his sons. A good administrator, appointed Bishop in 1889, Jayne needed an efficient secretary, and Bennett was given the post.[58] As this was the beginning of an association with the Diocese of Chester which would extend over forty-five years, the background to the appointment is worth examination.

When was Bennett appointed? It is likely that Jayne wished to have a secretary as soon as possible. No relevant correspondence survives and Jayne ordered his letters to be destroyed on his death.[59] According to Bennett's 'Obituary' in *The Times*, he was appointed in 1892, the year of his ordination as deacon, and his grandson, Roderick Bennett, gives the same year.[60] This is, however, almost certainly incorrect. If Bennett was not secretary to Jayne prior to 1892, it is difficult to account for the years between graduation and employment in Chester. He is most unlikely to have been at a theological college and I have found no evidence to suggest that he was otherwise occupied.[61] There is also firm evidence that by 1891 he was already acting as Jayne's secretary.[62] Moreover, Bennett's only son, Francis, records that Jayne made the appointment as soon as Bennett graduated, and he is most likely to be correct in this. He also claims that Bennett, at this stage, had thoughts of becoming a doctor, and had taken the job with Jayne to help finance subsequent medical studies. This, however, must be considered in the context of Bennett's own statement, thirty years later: 'No other profession but my own ever attracted me except that of a doctor, and a doctor I should certainly have tried to be had I not thought that I was truly called to the Priesthood'.[63] His interest in healing and in biology during his long clerical ministry lends substance to this statement.

11

Why was Chester an attractive proposition to Bennett? If he hoped for ordination, it is not inconceivable that preliminary work as a lay secretary to a bishop would be valuable experience and provide some opportunity for appropriate reading. On the other hand, why did he not look towards his home diocese, that of Bath and Wells?[64] In his account of his father, Bennett's son claims that when Bennett graduated Jayne was a tutor at Keble, and links this with Bennett's appointment. In fact, Jayne had been a tutor at Keble only from 1871 to 1879, and so had left six years before Bennett went up. Since then Jayne had held appointments as Principal of Lampeter College, and Vicar and Rural Dean of Leeds, where he was serving when appointed bishop.[65] Nevertheless, he may have known of Bennett by repute, or may have particularly wanted a Keble man and so made enquiries of the College. Bennett's antecedents for such a post were impeccable, and he could not have been wanting in recommendations from relatives well placed in the Church. Chester may also have attracted Bennett because Arthur Gascoigne Child, his friend and near contemporary at Keble, was ordained at Chester in 1889 and had been appointed to a curacy at St John's, Chester.[66] Child had graduated in 1888, the year before Bennett, and had spent a year at Sarum Theological College. The two friends were now able to share St John's Cottage, located at the gate of Jayne's palace by the River Dee.

Bishops' secretaries and private chaplains (Bennett became a private chaplain after his ordination) are expected to be self-effacing, and it is not surprising that little evidence of Bennett's early days in Chester has survived.[67] He would work in the century-old house overlooking the Dee, which a recent predecessor of Jayne's had had remodelled and renovated as Bishop's residence, in place of the old, dilapidated palace adjoining the cathedral.[68] Bennett did some part-time teaching, as an honorary assistant master at The King's School, which had a constitutional link with the adjoining cathedral, and the bishop was an important member of the Governing Body. The school was in financial difficulties and an 'honorary' teacher, with sound academic qualifications, must have been doubly welcome.[69]

Bennett's field of activity was further extended in 1896, when he became curate at Eccleston, on the Duke of Westminster's Cheshire estate, and he acted also as librarian to the Duke whose library he catalogued. He was further called on to 'teach his catechism' to the Duke's sixteen-year old heir.[70] As Bennett was still secretary and chaplain to the bishop while he was working at Eccleston, he must have been kept fairly fully occupied. Jayne was a vigorous opponent of the Liberal proposals for Welsh Disestablishment between 1893 and 1895, and Bennett must have heard rehearsed those arguments which he would reiterate, twenty years later, as rector of a Welsh parish. Another of Jayne's concerns was the role of the Victorian public house, which he wished to see transformed from a mere drinking house into a proper place of real refreshment and food supply. On these issues he frequently figured in the correspondence columns of *The Times*. Bennett shared Jayne's social concern, and so, in due course, when the People's Refreshment House Association was established under the direction of Jayne, Bennett arranged to put the Sparkford Inn, which was owned by the Bennett family, at the disposal of the new Association, the first property it acquired.[71]

In 1894 Bennett was ordained priest, and in 1897, after eight years of varied experience in a range of jobs very much at the heart of the Diocese and in close and confidential association with his bishop, his extended apprenticeship was completed. He had had exceptional opportunities for insight into the affairs of the diocese and in 1897 Jayne appointed him to his first incumbency, St Paul's, Portwood, in Stockport. That Bennett had spent as little as twelve months in a curacy, and that 'part-time', is indicative of Jayne's confidence in him. Did the bishop remember that the present Dean of Chester, Darby, had started as chaplain to a bishop of Chester?[72]

Notes

1 Quoted in *Chester Chronicle* [hereafter *Ches. Chr.*], 17.4.1920. The Chapter was concerned about the cost of the four-month vacancy and asked Bennett about his contribution to the cost (not more than £150) of carrying on the dean's work since November 1919. There is no record of his response (Cheshire Record Office [hereafter CRO], Diocesan Archives, 'Chapter Book (1894–1941)' [hereafter Chap. Bk.], 93, 5.4.1920).

2 'A Sermon Preached in Chester Cathedral ... June 6th 1920'; *Chester Diocesan Gazette* [hereafter *CDG*] (monthly to 1936, copies in CRO), June 1920, 83–90.

3 'A Sermon'; *Hawarden Parish Magazine* [hereafter *HPM*], Nov. 1910, Jan., Mar., Apr., 1911.

4 'New Foundation' cathedrals were those converted by Henry VIII from pre-existing monasteries; those already in existence in 1541 were of the 'Old Foundation'.

5 Darby did not celebrate Communion in a cope, though 'the dean ought to have worn a cope in the cathedral, by law' (*The Report of the Royal Commission on Ecclesiastical Discipline*, Cd. 3040, *Parliamentary Papers* [hereafter *PP*], 1906, xxxiii), 271, qq. 4119, 4120. Bennett's grandson, Guy Bennett, Rector of Oxted, has his grandfather's cope which, he says, is reputed to be the first cope worn in the Church of England in modern times but agrees that the claim is probably exaggerated. He used his grandfather's cope himself until it became too worn. On Bennett's cope, see also the Reverend T. C. Teape-Fugard, *Ches. Chr.*, 5.5.1972. There is good evidence that Bishop Jayne, in his earlier 'high church' phase, attended ordinations, and inaugurated diocesan conferences, wearing cope and mitre (B. H. Harris, ed., *Victoria County History of Cheshire, III* [hereafter *VCH*] (Oxford, 1980), 76).

6 In the 1920s Freemasonry had a significant clerical following. Indeed, Bennett was later to found St Anselm Lodge, for those connected with the cathedral.

7 Out of his period of actual residence the canon might be working elsewhere – in a university post or a parish.

8 *A Cathedral Chapter: A Paper read before the Great Chapter of Chester Cathedral, On Wednesday Nov. 24th 1920 by the Dean* (privately printed, Chester, 1920). A Foreword by Bennett acknowledged the kindness of the Chapter in assisting him with the cost of printing, although 'some members would probably dissent' from

his 'statements or sentiments'.

9   CDG, Apr. 1923.

10   I am indebted for this section to Crosby Everett, *Bishop and Chapter in Twelfth-Century England* (Cambridge, 1994); see esp. 1–9; 394–5. For bishop and cathedral church, see also Kathleen Edwards, *The English Secular Cathedrals in the Middle Ages* (Manchester, 1949), 97–135, 331–2.

11   Edwards, *English Secular Cathedrals*, 114.

12   David Marcombe and C.S. Knighton, (eds.), *Close Encounters: English Cathedrals and Society since 1540* (Nottingham, 1991), 1–3, 53–8, 115.

13   A detailed study of the patronage exercised by the Lyall connection notes that Tractarian polemic deliberately marginalised the Phalanx's work and Tractarian indebtedness to Old High Churchmen (Clive Dewey, *The Passing of Barchester* (London, 1991), esp. 1–6); and for the place of Tractarianism within the context of a continuing and varied High Church tradition, see Peter B. Nockles, *The Oxford Movement in Context: Anglican High Churchmanship, 1760-1857* (London, 1994).

14   Jane Austen (1775–1817), of an earlier generation than Trollope, despite her close clerical connections and the many references to the clergy in her novels and letters, significantly displayed very little interest in bishops and none whatever in cathedrals (Irene Collins, *Jane Austen and the Clergy* (London, 1994), *passim*; bishops, 32).

15 See Teresa Ransom, *Fanny Trollope: A Remarkable Life* (Stroud, 1995), 132–3, 162–3, 200–5. In a Foreword, Victoria Glendenning underlines the legacies of 'energy, endurance and application' which Trollope acquired from his mother and notes the resemblance between the eponymous Vicar in Frances Trollope, *Vicar of Wrexhill*, and Mr Slope of *The Warden* and *Barchester Towers* (xii). Ransom speculates 'that Uncle Walter may have been one of the foundation stones upon which Barchester was built'. Trollope claimed that when he conceived the story of *The Warden* he had never lived in any cathedral town, and had had no previous knowledge of the Close or the clergy (Anthony Trollope, *An Autobiography* (1941 edition, 85). Pamela Neville-Sington, *Fanny Trollope: The Life and Adventures of a Clever Woman*, dismisses this as 'somewhat disingenuous', pointing out that he knew the clergy through his mother. Fanny's father had been a clergyman; family holidays were often spent in the cathedral town of Exeter visiting Fanny's cousin; and Fanny's clashes with the Evangelical cleric, the Reverend John Cunningham, were famous throughout Harrow. 'The Trollopean realm for which he would become famous was his mother's before him'. Neville-Sington cites an 1851 critic who pointed out that the English clergy, from poor country curate to 'haughty, dictatorial, heartless Bishops and preferment-seeking Rectors' had been recognised as her province since the publication of *The Vicar of Wrexhill* in 1837 (356, citing a review of *Second Love*, in *The Critic*, 15.4.1851, 566). The evidence supports her claim that 'without Fanny Trollope we would have had no

Barsetshire or Palliser novels' (371).

16   Arthur E. Bridge, 'The nineteenth ccentury revivication of Salisbury Cathedral: Walter Kerr Hamilton, 1841–1854', in Marcombe and Knighton, *Close Encounters*, 137–60; Francis Brown regards Hamilton's 'ideals of cathedral reform' as 'much closer to those of modern pioneers like Dean Bennett than they were to those of the planners on the cathedrals commission' (C. K. Francis Brown, *A History of the English Clergy 1800-1900* (London, 1953), 120); the direct quotation is from W. H. Hutton, *Robert Gregory* (London, 1912), 162 (as quoted in Bridge, 'Revivication', 141, note 23).

17   Philip Barrett, *Barchester: English Cathedral Life in the Nineteenth Century* (London, 1993), 52.

18   ibid., 52–3.

19   ibid., 55–6.

20   ibid., 115–215, *passim*.

21   ibid., 55. The impression of Guy Bennett, the dean's grandson, is that R. W. Church was revered as something of a cult-figure in the Bennett family.

22   E. Carpenter, *Cantuar: the Archbishops in their Office* (London, 1971), 360; for Benson at Lincoln, see David M. Thompson, 'Historical survey, 1750–1949', in Dorothy Owen, (ed.), *Lincoln Minster* (Cambridge, 1994)), 210–318; and for a recent biography, Geoffrey Palmer and Noel Lloyd, *Father of the Bensons: The Life of Edward White Benson, sometime Bishop of Canterbury* (Harpenden, 1998).

23   D. L. Edwards, *Leaders of the Church of England, 1828-1944* (London, 1971), 195.

24   E. W. Benson, *The Cathedral: its Necessary Place in the Life of the Church* (London, 1878).

25   Beyond the diocese, Benson thought on the grand scale, after the manner of the great Victorians. The Church was 'charged with the world's Christianity, and must make herself truly Christian first'. It was an imperialist vision, in line with the aspirations of the age. He was to present it again in 1894, now as Archbishop of Canterbury (Edwards, *Leaders*, 195; Roger Lloyd, *The Church of England, 1900-1965* (London, 1966), 388; Adrian Hastings, *A History of English Christianity, 1920-1985* (London, 1986), 92).

26   Lloyd, Church of England, 391.

27   Hensley Henson, *Retrospect of an Unimportant Life* (London, 1942), 151–2, quoted in Lloyd, *Church of England*, 391. Bennett later availed himself of a unique opportunity to study the Truro system at first-hand when his friend and mentor, Walter Frere, became Bishop of Truro in 1923. Bennett had become acquainted with Frere in his first parish, at Portwood (see Chapter II, note 55).

28   Barrett, *Barchester*, 311.

29   Report of his farewell gathering at Hawarden, in *Ches. Chr.*, 29.5.1920.

30   Bennett refused to be over-impressed by the mighty. On returning home after showing the Crown Prince of Japan around the cathedral, he was asked, 'What did you do with him?'. 'I gave him two picture postcards', he replied, and quite failed to see why his wife and son thought this funny. To the Princess Royal, reputedly stiff and formal, but probably really shy, he showed a picture of St Werburgh, commenting, 'Here is another pretty princess'. Her entourage were thunderstruck, but she was delighted ('Memoir'; 'Family History').

31   The story of the jokes is in the 'Memoir'; I owe the account of the deans' meeting to Bennett's grandson, Guy Bennett, who probably had it from his mother, the dean's former secretary. Significantly, this story is not included by Dean Bennett's sedate son in his 'Memoir' of the dean.

32   'Memoir', except for the telephone story which Guy Bennett provided.

33   Cf. Bennett's approval of masonic ceremonial.

34   CRO, Diocesan Archives, 'Commonplace Book [2 vols., 1908–22, 1922–32]', 1922–32, 227–8.

35   *CDG*, Aug. 1920, 138–9.

36   *ibid.*, 123, 138–9.

37   Horton Davies, *Worship and Theology in England* (5 vols., Princeton and London, 1961–5), 5: 51.

38   CRO, Diocesan Archives, 'Chapter Book 1894–1941' [hereafter Chap. Bk.]., 23.6.1920, 197; *Ches. Chr.*, 24.7.1920.

39   *CDG*, Aug. 1920, 138–9. However, the Archdeacon of Chester, Canon Paige Cox, continued to be displeased with the 'free and open cathedral' (Peterborough Cathedral Archives, letter from Paige Cox to a Canon of Peterborough (no name given), 30.8.1926).

40   *CDG*, Aug. 1920, 138–9: July 1921, 107–8; Aug. 1921, 122.

41   *ibid.*, Oct. 1920, 148; Dec. 1920, 184; Oct. 1935, 154–5.

42   Given incorrectly as 1865 in *Burke's Landed Gentry* (1897).

43   For baptism and officiant, Devon Record Office, parish registers of Tormohun (St Luke's did not have its own registers at that time). Harris had been Principal of Upper Canada College immediately prior to appointment as incumbent of St Luke's in 1848 (*Crockford's Clerical Directory* [hereafter *Crockford*]. There seems to be no reason for supposing any connection with Lord Macaulay, though Frank's somewhat forbidding Macaulay aunts, when asked if they were related, would reply that he had always claimed to be a member of their family ('Memoir'). The 'Selwyn' name was given to Frank because of his father's admiration for the great George Augustus Selwyn, consecrated first Bishop of New Zealand, in 1841, and translated to Lichfield the year after Frank was born. For Selwyn, see G. H. Curteis, *Bishop Selwyn of New Zealand and Lichfield* (London, 1889), 32–3, 183; J. H. Evans, *Churchman Militant* (London, 1961); *Crockford* (1872), 529. Both the 'Macaulay',

and the 'Selwyn' names are borne by different members of the Bennett family today. An accessible summary of the history of the Bennett family, from 1795 to 1897 (the year of the death of Bennett's father), is now available in Jeff Clew, *Sparkford: Memories of the Past* (Sparkford, 1997). This makes use of extracts from Roderick Bennett's 'Family History' provided by Guy Bennett, but contains only brief passing references to Frank Bennett and his brothers and sisters.

44 'Memoir'; 'Family History'; information from Guy Bennett. Frank's elder brother, Harry Macaulay Bennett (1863–1920; Winchester and Cambridge) eventually ran into problems over alcohol and money, abandoned his wife (m. 1901) and family, and emigrated to Canada where he remained for the rest of his life (buried Sachett, British Columbia). Frank was thus responsible for the care of his sisters after his parents' deaths (his mother in 1892; his father in 1897). His Canadian connection showed up in his 1946 will, his modest portfolio of company shares including shares in the Canadian Pacific Railway which may have been inherited.

45 *CDG*, Sep. 1923, 216. Bennett's last house, The Orchard, still stands at the corner of Middleway and Fons George, at Wilton, to the south of Taunton. He is buried in the family plot, in Sparkford churchyard.

46 This, at any rate, was the opinion of his grandson, Roderick, who, being born in 1930, was acquainted with his grandfather in his later years, and undoubtedly would also hear stories about him from his own father, Frank Livesey Macaulay Bennett (1902–1973), the dean's only surviving son, and from his mother, Margaret Hilda (nee Blain) (1902–1973), who had been Bennett's secretary.

47 In 1891 there were four female servants, three of them born locally and one from Manchester. The butler was Frederick Shire, aged 18 (Somerset Record Office, Census 1891, 'Enumerators' Returns', Sparkford, mc122, f. 131, 10). I am much indebted to Mr R. Stead, Secretary of the Somerset and Dorset Family History Society for this and other information from the 1891 Census. Bennett is said to have been sympathetically aware of the long hours worked by the domestic staff at Sparkford, and their poor recompense. In later life, when servants were scarcer, and their wages higher, he is said to have remarked, with some approval, that they were at last getting their own back.

48 'Memoir'.

49 The school closed in 1971.

50 Information from the only copy of the School Register, in possession of L. Gordon Holmes, last headmaster of Walton Lodge.

51 Sherborne School, 'Sherborne School Admission Register for the Year 1880', 20.

52 Bernard Burke, *A Genealogical and Heraldic History of the Landed Gentry of Great Britain and Ireland*, 2 vols. (London, 1898), 97; *Crockford*, 1872, 1902, 1918, 1932. Three clerical uncles by marriage were James Baker, R. W. Church (Dean

of St Paul's and historian of the Oxford Movement), and C. M. Church (Prebendary and subsequently Sub-Dean of Wells). For good measure, Bennett's eldest sister, Emily Louisa (1858–1937), later strengthened the clerical connection by marrying another Rector of Sparkford, Trevor Griffiths, who had served as curate to Bennett. After Sparkford Hall was leased, on the death of Henry Bennett in 1897, his wife having predeceased him, the Bennett family gathered for holidays at the Rectory ('Memoir').

53 *Crockford* (1932). The tradition was continued by Frank's son (1902–1973) and grandson, Guy Bennett (b. 1933), Rector of Oxted who, as a boy, drew great inspiration from his much loved grandfather.

54 See A. B. Gourlay, *A History of Sherborne School* (Sherborne, 1971), 177–8, 181. Edward Mallett Young, appointed Headmaster in 1877, former Fellow of Trinity, had been a brilliant teacher of the Classical Sixth at Harrow; Bennett's housemaster, James Rhoades, published *The Georgics of Virgil translated into English Verse* (Kegan Paul, London, 1881) and *Timoleon: a Dramatic Poem* (Kegan Paul, London). The latter work was highly praised by reviewers in the *Saturday Review* and the *Graphic*, and Rhoades is represented in *The Oxford Book of Mystical Verse*.

55 *The Shirburnian*, 1880–81, 1884–5; *Sherborne School Lists*, 1878–91. I am grateful for invaluable help given by the Registrar of Sherborne School, J. R. Tozer, the Librarian, John Warmington, and his assistant, Linda Best.

56 'Memoir'.

57 *The Shirburnian*, 1884–5; O.C.C. Nicolls, *A Register of the Alumni of Keble College, Oxford from 1870 to 1925* (Keble Association, Oxford, 1927), 154, 160; B. St G. Drennan, *The Keble College Centenary Register* (Keble College, Oxford, 1970), 56, 60. The College records give no details of his involvement in College or University activities, and the Keble Register has nothing to add, except that he played for the College XV in 1888–89.

58 For Jayne, see *Crockford* (1918), 270; *Who was Who 1916-1953*; *VCH*, 69.

59 *Ches. Chr.*, 24.9.1921.

60 *The Times*, 15.11.1947; 'Family History'.

61 In the published list of those ordained deacon in 1892 there is no mention of a theological college against Bennett's name (*The Times*, 28.9.1892, 10). I have enquired of all the colleges which Bennett might have attended, and none has any record of him. Such training was not *de rigueur* in Bennett's day.

62 The 1891 census enumerator's return for Sparkford lists him as Bishop's secretary. Bennett may have been in Sparkford on holiday, or have gone there deliberately to be included in the census, though it could equally be argued that he had just been appointed and had not yet taken up the post.

63 F. S. M. Bennett, *M. Coué and the Gospel of Health* (London, 1922), 11–12.

64 Bennett's 'squarson' grandfather, Henry Bennett, had been ordained priest

in 1823, by George Henry Law, Bishop of Chester, 1812–1824 (*Crockford*, 1872, 63). However, Law was about to be translated to Bath and Wells (*VCH*, 52; R. V. H. Burne, *Chester Cathedral* (Chester, 1958), 258). All Henry Bennett's subsequent incumbencies were in Bath and Wells diocese (*Crockford*, 1872, 63).

65   *Crockford (1918)*, 270.

66   *Crockford* (1965–6): Child's last entry. Virtually all Child's later ministry was to be in the Chester Diocese, where he was an Honorary Canon 1919–1936 and thus a member of the Great Chapter for almost all of Bennett's time as dean. Their association continued over the years, and Child, his 'very kind friend', reviewed two of Bennett's books in *CDG*. As one who had known Bennett personally for so long, he could, in 1923, speak of 'that remarkable success which, without flattery, must be acknowledged to have attended him' (*CDG*, Jan. 1923, 14–5; May 1924, 122–4).

67   Ordained deacon, 1892; priest, 1894.

68   In 1876 the King's School, then occupying the Refectory, moved to a new building, designed by Blomfield, on the site of the old palace (Brian Harris, *Chester* (London, 1979), 161). When the school moved to its present 'greenfield' site on Wrexham Road, in 1960, Barclays Bank took over the former King's building.

69   Bennett later recalled, how, as a beginner in the classroom, he had 'endeavoured to teach history', though he 'didn't understand very much about it ... but fortunately a little more than the boys' (*Ches. Chr.*, 31.7.1920). We know virtually nothing about Bennett's role as tutor to the bishop's five sons. The respective ages of the boys were 16, 14, 13, 11, and 8. The eldest, Francis, might have been at some public school, and home for Easter Vacation, but if so, it was not Rugby – Jayne's old school ('Rugby Admissions Register' – kindly checked for me by the Headmaster's Secretary). The next two may have been at prep school; the two youngest may have been educated at home for their earlier years, as Bennett had been. There were two infants, Grace (aged one), and an unbaptised baby. Apart from Bennett, as tutor, there was also a governess, Laura E. May, assisting with the education of the younger boys. Nurses looked after the two infants (Chester Record Office, Census 1891, Chester, 'Enumerators' Returns', entry 197, Bishop's Palace).

70   'Memoir'. There is little information about Bennett in the Westminster archives. The papers of the first and second Dukes contain no references to him, nor does a catalogue of the library, printed in 1897, and probably compiled by Bennett. His name appears from time to time in the Housekeeper's Journal (1894–1900), as one of the 'casuals' to whom meals were served, probably on days when Bennett was working at Eccleston. On one occasion (21.9.1896) he was accompanied for tea by 'Mr Jayne', presumably the Bishop's eldest son (Eaton Estate Office, Estate Volume 912, 'Housekeeper's Journal, 1894–1900'). I am indebted to the Eaton Estate Archivist for supplying me with copies of the relevant pages of the Journal, and for other assistance.

71   For Sparkford Inn, see Clew, *Sparkford*, 22–8. Later, when Bennett was Rector of Hawarden, the Glynne Arms in the town was controlled by the PRHA; Bennett's 1946 will showed that he still held shares in the PRHA.

72   *VCH*, 193.

II

Parish priest: apprentice to master craftsman

1

His apprenticeship completed, the fledgling priest spent the next thirteen years mastering his pastoral craft in parochial service. At both Portwood and again in his next parish, Christ Church, Chester, he was experimenting, moving sometimes too boldly, but always with an eye to implementing the style of churchmanship to which he was committed; developing those interpersonal, organisational, and administrative skills for which he had a bent; and endeavouring to build cohesive parishes. He gained, also, some 'political' feel for sensitive local issues, and (though not always without ruffling some feathers) for contentious ecclesiastical matters – doubtless assisted by his clerical background. However, his natural sympathy with people, a flair for informality, and his open frankness were assets which won him allies and made him the successful pastor which he became. Above all, however, Bennett was learning. A good learner, he admitted to mistakes and did not repeat them. Later, at Hawarden, he would show that he could deploy, in a more complex and challenging situation, the skills he had by then mastered, which would ultimately bring him back to Chester as dean.

The year Bennett went to Portwood, 1897, was the year of Queen Victoria's Diamond Jubilee. It was marked all over by the erection of statues of the Queen or other monuments and by local celebrations. In Chester the elegant clock set up in 1898 on the Eastgate, an arch across the principal thoroughfare, was a gift from a prominent citizen. This was the late afternoon of imperial confidence and grandeur, and it seemed that the sun would never set on the British Empire. The imperial mission of the Church, proclaimed by Archbishop Benson in 1894, echoed the same self-confidence: 'The Church of England is now charged with the world's Christianity'. The reality, though not generally perceived, was that the decline in both imperial and Church dominance had already begun to set in.

This was the Golden Age of the Victorian and Edwardian parish when it was still possible for a good priest to attract and hold together a large and enthusiastic congregation in a working class parish, despite the rivalry of Chapel and secular influences. In urban areas cohesion was strengthened by the dense networks of clubs, Scouts, Boys' Brigades, Church Lads' Brigades, football clubs, men's and women's societies, and the powerful integrative influence of a common workplace and of the immediate community itself. Priests promoted clubs and societies within their parish to help weld a congregation together. Nevertheless, despite the built-in advantages, a priest had to work hard, and be seen to do so, to achieve results. In a predominantly middle class parish there was normally an assured congregation. But none of Bennett's three parishes was predominantly middle class, and his final parish, Hawarden, exceptional as a 'rural' parish in its series of industrial and semi-industrial settlements, was also exceptional in the variety of its partly segregated social strata.

The first parish, Portwood, part of Stockport, was a cultural shock for Bennett. He had had no experience of the industrial north and had not previously encountered plain blunt-speaking Lancashire folk, not slow to express themselves forcibly. Most of the parishioners of St Paul's were factory workers, who spent long hours in the cotton mills whose chimneys dominated the landscape, spreading a layer of smog across the town. The early morning clatter of clogs on cobbled streets came as a strange sound to Bennett's ears. Nor was a murky November afternoon the ideal time for an initial visit and first view of the scene. The door of St Paul's was locked and when Bennett eventually gained admission to the church he sensed 'a curious grimness about the walls'.[1] Nevertheless, Stockport had a sense of community, with its local Lancashire customs such as 'Walking Days' – occasions for great outdoor processions – and, of course, brass bands. Among people bred to hardship there was a close bonding and mutual understanding. Inevitably, a southerner arriving to replace an incumbent who had served the parish for 34 years and died in the post was viewed at first with a measure of reserve. Bennett never came to love Portwood, and he would return from holidays in Somerset with a sinking heart; but he overcame the obstacles and developed a flourishing parish. There seems to have been genuine regret at his departure in 1907. Bennett retained a wry affection for the place and its people and in after-years would remark, 'They're rude, and they call it being good-hearted'.[2]

He was only the third vicar of St Paul's, a parish formed in the middle of the nineteenth century to cater for the mushrooming industrial population of Stockport.[3] The congregation had become used to his predecessor, the long-serving, bearded and patriarchal Jeremiah Coombes, and inevitably the innovating ways of the newcomer were viewed with suspicion by the cautious Portwood folk. By the 1890s High Church doctrines and practices had gained a foothold in Chester Diocese. Diocesan ceremonial was conducted with added dignity. Before Bennett came to Portwood, Jayne had carried out ordinations in Stockport in cope and mitre, and had opened diocesan conferences, similarly attired, with a solemn Eucharist, though during the course of his 27 year episcopate he was to veer sharply to the protestant wing. Ritualism was, however, by 1897 firmly established at two Stockport churches, St Peter's and St Thomas's. Indeed, Stockport was regarded as the most important Anglo-Catholic locality in the diocese.[4]

Jayne doubtless expected Bennett to move St Paul's in the same direction. Bennett was very much in sympathy with such practices. Though not of the most advanced wing, he was always an avowed high-churchman, and at Portwood his approach contrasted with that of his more evangelically inclined predecessor. Bennett was not the man for compromises on what he regarded as central issues, but with the enthusiasm of a young man in his first incumbency, he innovated faster than was prudent. Indeed, he later 'admitted having made mistakes, and was sorry for any offence he had given'. His practice with regard to ritual was, as he admitted ten years later, 'very much criticised and looked upon with suspicion'.[5] Bennett insisted that his duty was to follow scrupulously the rubrics of the Book of Common Prayer, and, perhaps less high-mindedly, the requirements of diocesan policy. The Eucharist assumed a central place in the pattern of worship; baptisms were carried out monthly at the service where the greatest number were present, and not privately, a diocesan policy initiated by Jacobson, Jayne's predecessor.[6]

Other changes followed. The 'grim' interior of the church was improved, and pew rents tardily abolished, so that parishioners 'could go anywhere they liked', with 'no distinction ... made between one and another'.[7] The congregation was knit together in a range of church societies, organised separately, in the fashion of the day, for boys, girls, women, and men. The Church of England Men's Society was one of Bennett's special and abiding interests. While at Portwood Bennett became acquainted with Father Walter Frere, Superior of the Community of the Resurrection. These were the great days of parochial missions and Bennett persuaded Frere and another priest of the Community, Father Horner, to conduct a successful mission in Portwood.[8]

In Rural Deanery debates Bennett adopted a moderate, conciliatory, and convincingly practical view against extremists. He was a cogent debater, as is apparent in reports of his contribution on issues such as education, relations with Nonconformist clergy wishing to conduct burials in consecrated parts of the local cemetery, competing claims of the three church missionary societies, charitable work (help only 'our own', or others also?) and inter-parochial priestly squabbling about 'poaching' of parishioners. He deplored the divisiveness caused by the use of the exclusive terms 'catholic' and 'protestant', with which individuals 'adorn themselves or label others with whom they disagreed'. He reiterated that the Church of England was both. It was part of the catholic church, but was protestant in resisting 'additions to, or substractions from the Catholic faith'.[9]

Within a couple of years, Bennett's undoubted sincerity, and his ability to win people over, enabled him to establish himself, to the extent that he was able – to the delight of his parishioners – to mock himself, and his 'high church guile', at a parish concert, by singing, in the music-hall style of the day, a self-composed ditty. He repeated the performance at his farewell parish gathering in 1907, but with a new verse, in which he proclaimed, to applause, that Portwood was now 'agate' and 'up-to-date'.[10] When two candles appeared on St Paul's altar, the 'protestant' Church Association in Manchester posted mini-candles to a selection of Bennett's parishioners. But the attack misfired because the packages were understamped, and so were returned to the Association, to the delight of Portwood, much conscious, whether high church or low, of its local pride and sense of community.[11]

2

Bennett came to Portwood as a bachelor. Because he lacked the support of the almost mandatory vicarage wife to manage the household and lead the ladies of the parish, Bennett's sisters rallied round their brother. Emily, the eldest (b. 1858), kept house, Edith and Marion saw to the parish work. The youngest Bennett, George (b. 1873), after graduating at Lincoln College, Oxford in 1897, was ordained deacon the following year, and in 1898 came to Portwood as second curate. When the first curate, Trevor Griffiths, became Rector of Sparkford in 1899, and subsequently married Emily, George became principal curate. Thus the ways of Sparkford became part of the Portwood round. For the brother and sisters, Portwood must have been as much a cultural shock as it had been for Bennett, but his sisters made a considerable impact and were long remembered, while George was to succeed Frank as Vicar in 1907. In the meantime, Bennett's marriage, on 15 November 1900, effected something of a change in the pattern of life both at the vicarage and in the parish.

Ida Clegg Livesey was the daughter of Clegg Livesey, a local magistrate, a strong Conservative supporter, and a prosperous coal owner, but nevertheless, one who is said to have had a real concern for the welfare of the work force which operated his medium-sized mining enterprise.[12] The wedding on 15 November 1900 was a great occasion for Portwood. Crowds turned out in streets decked with bunting and set out with placards proclaiming good wishes and happiness. The bells of Bredbury and the adjoining St Mary's rang out with those of St Paul's. On the one hand, all this may be seen as a tribute to a respected pastor and the daughter of a good employer; on the other, it may be regarded as reflecting, in microcosm, the deferential, class-structured nature of late Victorian and Edwardian society in this part of Lancashire. It serves also also a reminder of the prestige of the Anglican clergy in that society. No similar marriage, even if celebrated by a diocesan bishop, would today occasion such public interest and demonstration. Bishop Jayne conducted the ceremony, assisted by Bennett's uncle, Charles William Bennett, formerly Rector of Sparkford, and now Vicar of Pilton. Bennett's parishioners presented gifts.[13] In 1902 the Bennetts' first and only surviving son was born. Frank Livesey Macaulay Bennett would, in due course, follow his father into the ministry.

Bennett had achieved considerable success at Portwood, but in 1907 Jayne brought him back to Chester, as Vicar of Christ Church. The generous farewell tributes which parishioners accorded to him, to his sisters, and to Ida are some indication of the place he and his family had won in Portwood hearts, and of the support for the changes he had brought about. *The Stockport Express* of 31 January 1907 carried a full report. Bennett returned the compliment, and 'thanked heartily all those who had co-operated with him'. Portwood had, indeed, 'learnt a thing or two', and, as for the vicar, and his family – 'we've learnt a lot'. Bennett, always a quick learner, never spoke more truly. The lessons he learnt at Portwood would contribute significantly to the success of his later ministries. Similarly, the pattern of services and the organisation of parish societies which Bennett had worked out at St Paul's would reappear in his next two parishes, and finally at the cathedral.

3

Christ Church, Chester, was an urban, working class parish, though the worshippers included a middle class element, drawn partly from within the parish boundaries and partly from other parts of Chester.[14] The vicar of Christ Church was also responsible for an outlying church and a mission hall.[15] The parish church, originally built in 1838, had been rebuilt during the last quarter of the nineteenth century.[16] But, unlike St Paul's, at least as Bennett had first seen it, the church was 'filled with beautiful things'.[17] Outside, however, the scene was as drab as Portwood had been, for the church lay amidst terraced housing near the the railway sidings of a massive coalyard, where many of the menfolk worked. Nevertheless, the parish enjoyed a splendid community spirit which had been nurtured by Bennett's popular predecessor, James Francis Howson. During his seventeen years at Christ Church Howson had maintained a large and active congregation, with whom he could relax at social gatherings, and, as Bennett had at Portwood, sing self-composed ditties.[18]

Bennett inherited, then, a more flourishing and well-organised parish than had fallen to his lot in 1897. Jayne, wanting continuity, had consulted Howson, who had recommended Bennett as his successor, and Bennett accepted although he had already rejected another invitation (not from Jayne) to go elsewhere.[19] The new vicar was received with considerable good-will, and during his incumbency (1907–1910), Bennett had no difficulty in retaining Howson's large congregation. He introduced a number of innovations, developed further the structure he had inherited, and in the process further enhanced his reputation. At the same time, he was, characteristically, learning much from what he saw and heard and from reactions to the changes he was making.

At Christ Church Bennett had further scope to exercise those skills which would attract wider attention later at Hawarden, and which he would finally employ as Dean of Chester. Much of the Portwood pattern was repeated. One of his first tasks was to reorganise and up-date the administration of the several branches of Church work. The Women's Help Society (there was no Mothers' Union), the Church of England Men's Society, the Girls' Friendly Society, and the Church Lads' Brigade, all grew steadily in membership.[20] These societies, which he described as 'our four strong arms for active work in the parish',[21] were a cohesive force, and provided, in an Edwardian parish, an inexpensive focus for socialising. The annual Sunday School outing to

Rhyl by special train was an exciting event for children, many of whom rarely moved much beyond the local streets. The Infants' Department had its own 'treat' – the children carried to a neighbouring field in ribboned and gaily decked coal-carts, proudly driven by fathers, uncles, and elder brothers.[22] Bennett found the parish teas, Howson's innovation, much after his own heart, and he was later to carry the custom with him to Hawarden. He saw a common meal not merely as a social occasion but as a means of binding a group together. In the 1920s, as Dean of Chester, he was to develop the idea a stage further. At Christ Church, District Visitors provided the food and presided at the tables. Afterwards, the choir and various church societies performed, and Bennett himself invariably provided some amusing item.[23]

An unhappy aspect of the parish, however, was the blight of recurring unemployment. With the Guild of Help (on whose committee he served) Bennett set up a labour yard to occupy the unemployed, restore morale, and provide a minor source of income. Bennett had little time for the easy 'charity hand-out' approach. and 'urged that the underlying principle of the Guild was to get persons into contact with persons as being the only way to help them', his own method.[24] Bennett's concern with social problems, already manifest at Portwood, led to his appointment to the Chester Board of Guardians.

The arrangements for worship, however, were Bennett's prime concern. Remembering the early days at Portwood, Bennett moved cautiously. The 'said' monthly celebration of communion became weekly.[25] More significantly, a weekly eight o'clock sung eucharist was established 'as a tentative experiment', but soon became permanent when numbers of communicants steadily increased, as demonstrated by Bennett's novel registration system.[26] He now tactfully persuaded the organist to 'allow me to reckon it [this 8 a.m. service] amongst [his] official duties'.[27] At Christ Church we see emerging, in clearer outline, the pattern of services which Bennett would operate at Hawarden, and finally introduce, confidently, at the cathedral.

Music, for Bennett, was an important feature of worship. He was fortunate in having in charge of the choir an expert musician, Aubrey Baxter, a minor canon of the cathedral and a former choral scholar of King's College, Cambridge.[28] Hence the ease with which Bennett raised £800 for a new organ. Bennett's informal style made him a popular preacher both in the parish and beyond. Eager for seats, people filled the church well before Evensong began, and so Bennett organised 'community singing', he himself leading the congregation in well-known hymns, which he said were the Englishman's form of popular worship. Later, as dean, he would encourage similar singing by groups of visitors to the cathedral.[29]

Bennett knew that praise was a key to successful management. He carried the volunteer Sunday School teachers along with him by giving 'warmest thanks' for their 'extraordinary forebearance in putting up with and putting into effect my various dodges' – a registration system, introduction of written work, a combined class for 'girls and lads' between the ages of fourteen and seventeen, and a 'little school', under Ida Bennett, at another end of the parish.[30] Shortly after Bennett arrived the parish day school, no longer able to meet requirements for an official grant, had closed. He converted the empty building into a parish hall, expressing 'universal satisfaction' that pupils and staff were to be transferred *en bloc* to the same Council school.[31] The sweeping Liberal electoral victory of 1906, however, had projected religious education to centre stage. Bennett pursued the case for denominational instruction through two organisations which embraced parents, the Church of England Mens Society and the Women's Help Society, and sponsored a branch of the Parents' League, whose aim was to secure for parents the right to decide the character of their children's religious education.[32]

4

Following Bennett's experience at Portwood, it is not surprising that his high church practices at Christ Church attracted the attention of local members of the Church Association, a body which had attacked even Howson's modest ceremonial.[33] In 1908, Bennett proposed, with the support of his parochial parish council, to start using, ceremonially, a beautiful processional cross surmounted by a seventeenth-century crucifix, which had been presented to Christ Church in 1902 but never used. To obtain a faculty for use, he had first to seek approval at a Vestry meeting of inhabitants of the parish. He brought forward at the same time two non-controversial proposals (the new organ and a replacement bell), a good tactic. The contingent opposed to the cross was led by Robert Foulkes, who spent his time uncovering 'popish' practices in Chester, and had previously harried Howson. Because he was a non-resident, the Vestry voted against allowing him to speak.[34] However, others entitled to speak did so, hinting ominously at the idolatry of 'figures on crosses'. Foulkes had also written to the bishop, seemingly in defence of a chorister who had refused to sing 'Gloria in Excelsis'. Now, confronting his opponents head on, Bennett told the meeting that if 'the mass of his people wanted a new vicar' they could soon have one. The response was, 'Not for one moment', and 'There is no question of that'. A vote was taken, and the request for a faculty approved by a clear majority. Bennett's characteristic 'few conciliatory words', hoping that the audience 'would leave the room as good friends as before', was greeted with applause, and cries of, 'Hear, hear'.[35]

After a prolonged hearing, during which a Buckingham solicitor, W. B. Etches, spoke on behalf of 83 objectors resident in the parish, the Consistory Court granted the faculty. The Chancellor found the processional cross legal, following the precedent of practice in the cathedral, where Henry VIII had ordained that a ceremonial cross should be carried before the bishop and the dean when either of them entered the cathedral. What was lawful there was not unlawful in a parish church.[36] However, he advised Bennett (who had said that he would abide by any suggestion the Chancellor might make) to lock the cross in a cupboard, 'and wait for kindlier times'. It was a compromise solution. Bennett locked the cross away, and, in fact, never used it. Within a year he had moved to Hawarden. Perhaps he was unwise to push his case as far as he did. The 83 objectors represented a sizeable minority, though there is no proof that most of them actually attended Christ Church.[37] Bennett doubtless registered the incident as one more lesson learnt.

On leaving Christ Church, Bennett told his parishioners that his years with them had been 'the very happiest of my whole life'. He had 'met with unbounded kindness, confidence and affection on every side' – a more fulsome tribute than he had paid Portwood on his departure. His brother George would come from Portwood to succeed him. Thus, said Bennett, 'you have got the man you wanted'. In his final sermon, on Sunday, 26 November 1910, Bennett was equally effusive. He spoke of the 'happy homely church life' they had enjoyed together. He was going to Hawarden only because 'I could not help feeling I was called there, and ought to go'.[38] But Christ Church would continue developing and gaining further strength. Christ Church had been another formative experience for Bennett, as he frankly admitted in his closing words: 'If by God's help I have been able to teach you anything while Vicar of Christ Church, you have taught me a great deal more'.

5

The extensive parish of Hawarden, which immediately adjoined Chester diocese, measured some thirty square miles, and included both rural and industrial areas.[39] The parish church (St Deiniol's) was in residential Hawarden, and the rest of the area was served by district churches, at Shotton (St Ethelwold's), Broughton (St Mary's), Pentrobin (St John's), and Sealand (St Bartholomew's), with a developing church centre in the school at Sandycroft. Services were also held in a club room at the Garden City, adjoining Queensferry; at Mancott Royal, in a large building, put up when the factory and village were being built; at Ewloe (St Winifred's); and at Pentre (Holy Innocents). This extent of pastoral activity necessitated the employment of a staff of eight assistant clergy, and later using the services of two licensed lay readers, in addition to those of a Church Army captain. The large rectory was expensive to keep up. But its great library, built by a former rector, had been converted into a parish room by Bennett's predecessor, Canon Harry Drew; and the extensive garden was used, in Bennett's time, for various functions.

Bennett displayed a clear strategy for the parish. He stressed its unity, not least by preaching regularly at district churches, by attending their functions, and by convening joint meetings of all district parish councils on common issues. To establish direct communication with a population of some 10,000 in his 'mini-diocese', he used the *Hawarden Parish Magazine*, which circulated monthly throughout the area and carried reports of district church activities.[40] Drew had rarely contributed but Bennett immediately inaugurated 'The Rector's Letter', a front page feature, often quoted by local newspapers. In technique and informal style we can discern the origins of the 'Notes by the Dean', which Bennett in 1920 began to write, for a similar purpose, in the *Chester Diocesan Gazette*. Finance was a pressing problem, but within less than a year he had devised means of tapping the resources of his parishioners, targeting especially the better off, in a grand version of the Free Will Offering scheme he had employed at Christ Church. Again, we see him practising the techniques which he would exploit in a much wider field, at Chester. Finally, there were liturgical concerns – again a foretaste of Chester – with echoes of Portwood and Christ Church. Indeed, Bennett's whole ministry must be thought of as a steady development. Like Hawarden's most famous past resident, W. E. Gladstone, he prided himself on being a great learner.

Bennett's appointment came about unexpectedly. The benefice had been vacant for some time, following the sudden death, in April 1910, of Canon Harry Drew. Drew had been Rector for the previous five years, and before that, apart for a one year in South Africa, had served in the benefice since 1883. When he died, W. G. C. Gladstone, grandson of the late Prime Minister and 'the young squire' to Hawarden people, was abroad, and therefore unable to act until he arrived home in July, when he put the living 'on offer'. By late August it had been refused 'more than once' and was still unfilled. The deterrent was that the net income of the benefice was only such that any incumbent with a family needed 'considerable private means'. Gladstone told the parish that he had 'persevered in his endeavours to find a man whose private means would not make an appeal to the parish necessary', but failed. He would welcome any 'helpful thoughts' from readers of his letter. The probable cost of being Rector of Hawarden was daunting. Although nominally one of the richest livings in Britain, there were considerable outgoings. The upkeep of district churches, payment of their clergy, and maintenance of the enormous Rectory, were some of the charges. In addition there were parish schools, church furniture, taxes and insurance. Drew was estimated to have spent some £20,000 over five and a half years, and to have been £8,000 out of pocket by 1910.[41]

Though Bennett's financial situation had improved because Ida had brought Livesey money to the marriage, he was not a rich man. During their ten years in Hawarden, he and Ida seem to have dipped into their personal resources. When in 1920 they left for Chester, one who knew them well said publicly that 'they had literally spent themselves, both physically and financially, to further the interests of the parishioners'.[42] Indeed, in his family, Bennett had a reputation for being extremely generous to all and sundry.

Equally, however, in Gladstone's mind, was a concern to find a man of the suitable quality, and probably appropriate churchmanship. Further, he needed a man with administrative skills as well as pastoral and other qualities.[43] We do not know who suggested Bennett, but someone must have told Gladstone of Bennett's reputation. To find out for himself how Bennett conducted worship and performed in the pulpit, Gladstone cycled to Chester and, unannounced, attended the early morning service and matins. The presence of a stranger in the congregation aroused suspicions, and fearing that they had a 'Kensitite' in their midst, ready to stage a demonstration, the church officers kept a vigilant watch on him.[44] Gladstone's offer of the living to Bennett followed immediately, conveyed, it is said, in a note left at the vicarage after the service.

Immediately after his induction to the Hawarden benefice on 26 November 1910, Bennett set out the broad lines of his strategy in his first 'Rector's Letter'. This was written in his conversational style which was, according to his son, the mark of his sermons at Hawarden.[45] Knowing by now how any new incumbent was viewed, Bennett disarmed criticism by introducing himself in homely simile: 'a new Rector must be something like a new pair of shoes, only worse!' He was a 'south countryman', from 'another Province and Diocese', and would have to be put up with 'for a bit ... in the hope that presently you'll find him as easy as the proverbial old shoe'. But please, he asked 'be patient with me and my queer ways, and I'll be going round and getting to know you, and before long we shall settle down comfortably all right'.[46]

Parishioners, he went on, had certain rights. They would expect him to endeavour to understand their ways, and to preserve continuity and traditions, to add to their 'treasure', and 'get to know and love your parish and yourselves'. The Rector, also, had rights. He was entitled 'to make great claims upon you', having given up the 'most delightful parish in all England' and a beautiful modern church, with big congregations and a Parish Council which raised funds to pay his assistant clergy and finance parish organisations. He came to Hawarden, despite misgivings, because he believed it was right to do so, though 'no sensible man could undertake to become Rector of Hawarden with a light heart'. Bennett stressed the problems of the 'little Diocese'. It was no 'soft job'. Apart from paying assistant clergy, he had to occupy a house 'large enough to accommodate a large public institution',[47] His 'modest wage' would barely pay for upkeep of his 'embarrassingly large garden'. Moreover, Welsh Disestablishment and Disendowment threatened, with likely dire financial consequence, not least for himself. But he would devote himself to Hawarden, and if the day ever came for him to leave, it would be as sorrowful as leaving Christ Church had been. Meanwhile, he wanted them to introduce themselves and 'pass the time of day'. They would find him 'one of the homeliest and friendliest of people you ever met, and you will find Mrs Bennett even more so'.[48]

To succeed, innovation required support. The key lay people in each district were the members of the parish councils.[49] To these councils he unfolded his first plans, and would continue to consult and involve them directly, and soon, collectively. He similarly consulted his district clergy at regular, friendly meetings in the Rectory. Bennett's right hand man was W. Bell Jones, whom he appointed as his Warden. Hawarden's printer and stationer, its postmaster, its member of the local Council and later the Council's Chairman, Bell was an influential figure.[50] The two became firm friends, and kept in touch into Bennett's declining years.

Bennett laid down two main principles for worship: loyalty to the spirit of the Prayer Book, and, as far as possible, to its letter; and recognition that the Church comprised 'the blessed company of all faithful people', defined as those baptised and, when old enough, confirmed, and regularly in communion.[51] Liturgical practice at Hawarden was already much closer to his own than that of his previous parishes had initially been. Drew had been blacklisted by the Church Association for adopting the eastward position, for ceremonial mixing of the chalice, for wearing sacrificial vestments, and for burning candles on the altar in daylight.[52] A previous incumbent, Stephen Gladstone, had been a member of the Anglo-Catholic order, the Confraternity of the Blessed Sacrament.

Bennett proposed two further changes. First, Baptism should be carried out, as the Prayer Book required, at the service to which most people came, Sunday Evensong. When he had introduced the change at Portwood and Christ Church, 'everyone liked it', but 'it is not a question of likes, but of orders'. There was an early response to his, 'Who will be the first to provide the all important infant?'.[53] Secondly, he wanted, at St Deiniol's, a large Eucharist Choir, working on roster, to sing the liturgy at 8 a.m. and on one or two Sundays each month. It was soon recruited and Choral Eucharists became firmly established at Hawarden, and soon, also, at the district churches, where similar choirs were formed. By July 1911 Bennett was organising a United Choirs Festival, and had written to all 14,000 parish communicants on his lists.[54] Walter Frere, with whose churchmanship Bennett was aligned, proved again supportive, as, through him, was the Community of the Resurrection. In 1913, recalling the week's preaching Frere did at Portwood as 'one of the great events of my life', Bennett persuaded him to give a week-long series of addresses to communicants, aimed to 'strengthen and enrich religious life'. All other events were cancelled, to ensure a full attendance.[55]

Bennett wanted lay people to be actively involved. He set out his ideas for a common pattern of organisation, on the Christ Church model. Each district would form branches of 'the four great societies', cooperating with branches in other districts, and each linked also to its national network. He brought in national speakers to promote interest. Ida organised these meetings for the Girls' Friendly Society, and headed the central organisation.[56] The Christ Church contingent of the Church Lads' Brigade gave a display. Bennett devised what we would now call a 'logo' for the joint societies, symbolising unity, based on his Christ Church design. He promoted classes in each district for the 'post-Sunday School group',[57] thereby ensuring the retention of young parishioners, and he established Visitors (Christ Church, again) in working-class Shotton.[58]

Parish councils, he held, existed to work. Bennett therefore asked each to organise a Parish Tea, on Christ Church lines; to promote pressure from below, he broadcast his ideas in his 'Rector's Letter'. The Church, he wrote, was a household, not 'stiff and starchy', and at such functions those from 'big houses' and 'little houses' would meet 'on terms of affection' – though we may be sure that, as at Christ Church, the ladies from the 'big houses' would preside at the teapot. The clergy would meet everybody; wardens would make speeches; children would entertain; and there would be singing. Bennett devised a Parish Song, to the tune of 'Men of Harlech', and asked the teachers to teach children the words – now, sadly lost. The teas were soon under way, and Bennett attended them all.[59]

Within months, Bennett had set the parish on the lines he wished. In the past Hawarden had offered more limited opportunities for socialising and so his various societies and classes became as popular as they had been at Christ Church. Peer-pressure acclimatised members to the ethos of the societies and so to the Church itself. It was now time to address the problem of finance.

6

At the end of March, 1911, the benefice had an income of £1,085.6s.5d, of which £841.16s.8d had been expended on stipends of assistant clergy. Repairs, insurance, payment to a tithe collecting agency, and postage, absorbed the balance. Bennett had received no stipend. He summoned a meeting of all churchwardens and indicated the need for urgent action. The wardens immediately agreed to allocate a third of the Easter Offering to the Rector, with the remainder to be divided among the assistant clergy, who had in fact received their full stipends. Bennett published the accounts in the *Hawarden Parish Magazine* – not, as in Drew's day, as a separate leaflet – and thereafter did so each year, with his comments. In 1911, he stressed (in homely agricultural metaphors) the need for new sources of income.[60]

His solution was a Free Will Offering Scheme, on the Christ Church pattern, where 500 subscribers had between them contributed £250 a year. Hawarden should aim at 1,000, to produce an income of £500.[61] 'Some could and ought to give big sums', while others would be doing their duty at a penny a week. This was a new and daring message but Hawarden responded to his frankness. Within a month of the scheme's inauguration, 426 subscribers had contributed £537.[62] At Bennett's urging, Church Councils organised fund raising parties, pageants, and dances. Bennett's 'shaming' technique was to publish names of subscribers, and, semi-anonymously, the individual amounts, making it relatively easy for a parishioner to work out what others had contributed. He advertised the names of those 'manifestly blessed with this world's goods' giving more than £10, but reminded 'humbler subscribers' that it was a 'many a Mickle' fund. Even 'Master F. Bennett' (aged 9) appears in the Hawarden list – but not in the £10 class. The tardy were urged on with *bis dat qui cito dat*, a sentiment later repeated in Bennett's cathedral appeals.[63]

In 1912–1913, Bennett at last received a stipend of £500, which he now continued to receive regularly. District parsons received between £150 and £190.[64] Bennett budgeted carefully each year for stipends, consulting parish councils regularly and ensuring that they were fully informed. By 1914–1915 the Stipend Fund was running into deficit, and as the Free Will Offering Scheme was not providing sufficient, Bennett had to increase the subsidy from the Benefice Account (which he controlled). It was thus, he pointed out, 'doubly important' to solve the problem, because the Church in Wales was now disendowed. The Bill, against which he had campaigned, had become law, and its operation had merely been suspended for the duration of hostilities. Unless Parliament changed its mind, all that would be left to him would be his life interest in the benefice.[65] The problem was likely to be exacerbated because the population of the parish was increasing, and more staff would be needed.[66] This stirred the more affluent to increase their giving.

The population of the parish had increased, largely because of the growing influx of industrial workers engaged on war work including munitions manufacture, many of them from South Wales. However, as the Army had a growing need for chaplains, it became less easy to find assistant clergy and retain them for long periods, thereby doubtless diminishing the demands on the Stipend Fund. Between 1913 and the end of 1916, the total paid out to assistant clergy remained generally steady at around £1,100 a year. The financial situation would seem to have been stable.[67] It is a tribute to Bennett's far-sightedness and clear thinking, and above all leadership, that he had rescued the parish from the perilous financial situation in which he found it.[68]

7

At Sandycroft, Bennett brought to conclusion the church project which had begun in 1872 when Helen Gladstone started a Sunday School in the vaults behind the Lifeboat Inn. When day schools were erected, public worship was celebrated there from 1876, so that by 1900 church life was flourishing. In 1907 Drew had launched an appeal for funds to build a church. Bennett saw the project through to a successful conclusion in 1913.[69] Gladstone provided a site and his household contributed £70. Bennett's target was £3,000. At Bennett's invitation, Colonel Henry Platt, C.B., laid the foundation stone, on 26 October 1912, with Church and Masonic ceremony.[70] At Bennett's request, Sir Charles Nicholson (1867–1949), who had a reputation for the dignity of his low-cost churches, designed a building with a broad ceiling, on the lines of Bennett's beloved Christ Church.[71] Dedicated to St Francis, the church was opened in December 1913.[72] The Hawarden benefice now had six churches.[73] Bennett planned a seventh, for the industrial population of Garden City, on Deeside, but war supervened. However, by 1915 a flourishing church centre had developed, with full-time clergy.[74] Similarly, at Mancott Royal, a building was converted for use as a temporary church.[75] At Shotton, on Deeside, an extensive church hall was erected behind the church, and a canteen provided. Bennett also successfully pressed for the erection of a Church Army hut at Sealand Aerodrome.[76] Bennett always thought of his benefice as a single entity. Whereas Drew had merely 'attended all churches at intervals',[77] Bennett regularly officiated or preached at all the churches and church centres in his extensive benefice, sometimes driving to two on the same day.[78]

For most of Bennett's parishioners the main language was English. In 1907, according to Drew, none of the people in the parish spoke Welsh and only 'a few of the elderly people ... know Welsh, but they are a mere handful, and they speak English also'.[79] There were, in consequence, no calls on Bennett to preach in Welsh, but he regarded it as his duty to understand the language and he became a fluent reader. He occasionally prefaced his 'Rector's Letter' with a few flourishes in Welsh. Traditionally, the St David's Day service in St Deiniol's was conducted in Welsh, and Bennett always took part, usually securing a Welsh speaker to officiate, but Bennett saying a collect and giving the blessing in Welsh.[80] On St David's Day, 1914, he gave his 'maiden speech' in Welsh.[81]

Bennett established excellent relations with free church ministers by forming a 'ministers' fraternal', where church and Nonconformist clergy met to discuss religious topics – previously a 'no-go' area – and he became an officer of the non-sectarian British and Foreign Bible Society. This open approach won Bennett allies in the mounting conflict over Disestablishment. As dean, he would establish similar links with Chester Nonconformists.[82] However, politics and religion did become an issue in the Hawarden Rural District Council over cemetery policy – an echo of Portwood – and Bennett could hardly avoid becoming involved.[83]

Education continued to be an abiding concern of Bennett's ministry. He successfully completed Drew's programme of school building and extension at Broughton, Sandycroft, Pentrobin, Shotton, and Ewloe. To meet Hawarden's need he built the Drew Memorial Schools (opened September 1912).[84] Religious education was Bennett's special concern. He himself was a successful teacher, and almost daily was present in one or other of his nine church schools to assist with religious teaching. His later writings on the subject, revealing insight into practicalities and grasp of the learning process, undoubtedly owe something to his classroom experience. He took care to study the publications of the Welsh Education Department, and was quick to condemn ill-informed advice on religious teaching and history.[85] He was anxious that the schools should maintain a right tone, and his regular presence there was an undoubted influence on this, and on their religious education.[86] Bennett regularly reported in his 'Rector's Letter' individual successes in the County Scholarship examinations, sometimes commending individual schools. Significantly, children from the residential areas of Hawarden and Broughton performed particularly well, both in the examination, and afterwards at secondary school.[87]

Always up-to-date on day school classroom methods, Bennett campaigned tirelessly against outworn practices in Sunday schools. He urged superintendents to group children 'scientifically' by age in order to create 'the right atmosphere'; and also to train older pupils as future teachers. They should emulate day schools, where methods improved 'every year'. He set up a training week (12–15 May, 1914) for Sunday School teachers, and then planned classes to train 16-year olds as future teachers.[88] Sunday School led to confirmation. Bennett told parents that fourteen was the right 'psychological moment'; of those confirmed later, only around 10% became regular communicants; of those confirmed below thirteen, a mere 10% failed to be such.[89] His institution of a special Children's Eucharist at Hawarden and Sandycroft was aimed at showing children that the Eucharist was not a 'rather awful thing to which the very pious sometimes go' but was the service of services for everyone, every Sunday, and that Confirmation was the door in to it.[90] A further innovation at Hawarden, later repeated more obviously at the cathedral, was the creation of a special space in the church for the sole use of children. 'Children's Corners', so termed, came to be introduced widely, not only in Britain but in the United States. The concept will be discussed below in this wider perspective, in Chapter VII, section 5.

Bennett's early introduction of an annual excursion to Rhyl (a grander version of the Christ Church model) was related to his general strategy. No fewer than 790 children took part in the first excursion, the train picking up contingents at stations on the way. The charge for an individual child depended on his or her number of attendances at Sunday School. From Rhyl, the newly-formed Hawarden contingent of the Church Lads' Brigade went off to camp. Soon CLB. companies were established in the other districts, Hawarden itself, as in most innovations, having been the pace-setter.[91]

8

On 3 August 1914, Gladstone hosted a splendid fête at Hawarden Castle. In high summer sunshine, the Balkan conflict seemed remote. Bennett's luncheon speech included the hope that 'the lamentable crisis' would soon be resolved and peace restored.[92] With Britain's subsequent declaration of war, however, his tone changed, and it eventually matched the patriotic, shrill, and unthinking exhortations issuing from numerous other pulpits. No able-bodied unmarried man under 35 could 'without shame' hesitate to volunteer. Even the married should ponder earnestly before remaining behind. 'Go', he urged, 'and God go with you', an injunction which parents, wives, and children should echo bravely.[93] He announced that he would place in the porch, in St Deiniol's, lists of the names of all those in the parish who were serving and he sought details from relatives. Soon lengthy lists were on display. 'The young Squire' was among the first to join. When a Church Lads Brigade battalion was recruited by the King's Royal Rifles, Bennett proudly named five members of the parish who had joined. He urged present members to volunteer as cyclists, messengers, patrollers, guards of railways and other installations. All this was much to the taste of the local boys.[94] People at home could visit hospitals, comfort the bereaved, and pray. Every day, at 7.50 a.m. he offered the Eucharist for all engaged in the war, and he read out the names of those serving, immediately before the Prayer for the Church Militant. Soon, as casualties mounted, the roll sounded a more sombre note, and in 1915 Bennett inaugurated Friday intercession services.[95]

Although Bennett contemplated 'the ... futility of keeping the peace by everlasting preparations for war', he saw 1915 as a year of hope for a 'universal brotherhood of Christians', and trusted that 'when this war is over and the cross replaces the crescent on the Cathedral of St Sophia in Constantinople', the Orthodox and Anglican communions would unite and greater ecumenical possibilities emerge.[96] In their own terms, Bennett's ecumenical hopes (dispelled by the subsequent disastrous Dardanelles campaign) paralleled the equally unrealistic idealism of the young men who rushed to volunteer in 1914. Among them was W. G. C. Gladstone, who, promptly commissioned, but semi-trained and inexperienced, became an easy target for a German sniper, three weeks after going to the front in France. He was buried in Hawarden with full military honours. Bennett felt the loss deeply, and at a solemn Eucharist spoke of the close understanding between himself and Gladstone. At Bennett's suggestion, his mother provided a rood in the parish church designed by Giles Gilbert Scott.[97]

War did not divert Bennett's attention from the round of the Christian year, and he saw his own prime role of priest and pastor as more important than ever. During Lent of 1915, he was available daily in church to offer private spiritual counsel, and he wrote two pamphlets, *Helps to Self Examination* and *How to make a first Confession*. He believed that 'many a soul in Hawarden' needed Absolution.[98] As his later writings indicate, Bennett regarded Anglo-Catholic practice as sound psychology. Inevitably, the war affected Sunday observance in the parish, especially on industrial Deeside, where production became increasingly geared to the urgency of military needs. But

Bennett was uncompromising and categorised all Sunday labour as a loss, 'spiritually, domestically, and, I believe, economically'. He held up his brother George's model for Christ Church as the pattern for Hawarden: make pre-breakfast communion once a month, gradually increasing this, and aiming at every Sunday; add Holy Days, if possible, and Eucharist, 'as often as you can'. To those who derided the futility of this spiritual regime in current conditions, he presented a motoring metaphor: 'A motor car will run for a week or two without greasing, but you don't get a larger mileage out of it in consequence!'.[99] However, Deeside workers knew that Sunday working would gain them a larger pay-packet.

Bennett's message for 1916 mingled religion and patriotism. There was 'more to be done than to beat the Germans, essential ... as that ... is'. Through war, God was addressing a world which had forgotten him, lost the sense of sin, and neglected worship. The practical recipe was: pray, repent, give service ('The lads at the front are doing their bit. Ask, am I doing it?'), and save. The nation needed to save £1,000 million a year. Invest in War Loan, Bennett urged, and avoid waste.[100] At the end of 1916, as the agony of the Somme drew to a close, the parish, led by Bennett (assisted by four visiting priests, including two Anglo-Catholic Cowley Fathers), joined in the National Mission of Repentance and Hope.[101] There was a profound difference in mood from that of the heady days of August 1914.

9

Following the 1918 Armistice, parish social activities revived. The Hawarden Carol Singers were out; two local families gave a 'select party', with dancing and a supper at the rectory on 21 January 1919; the next day the first post-war Parish Tea was held, followed by a fancy dress ball, attended by 400, Bennett in costume as a long departed predecessor. At the Sunday School 'Treat' in the school hall, he entertained with lantern slides and tales of 'comic situations'. On another occasion, Bennett's 16-year old son produced 'Everyman'. Convention dictated solemnity – final prayers instead of applause.[102] In July 1919, to mark the signing of the Treaty of Versailles, Hawarden joined with most other places in holding 'Peace Celebrations' and a service of thanksgiving. On 6 July 1919, Bell Jones, now Chairman of the Council, proudly headed the civic procession to the church, where his Rector conducted the service according to the special 'Form of Thanksgiving and Prayer'.[103] On 19 July, national 'Peace Day', Hawarden celebrated with music, entertainments, and sports for the children, the citizens responding generously to the appeal for funds. Hawarden councillors voted themselves specially designed medals.

A War Memorial Committee, of which Bennett was a member, agreed that the Hawarden memorial should be a cross in the churchyard, and supported Bennett's proposal that this should be based on the fourteenth- century cross at Bishop's Lydeard, in Somerset. As Rector, Bennett was entitled to rule on additions to the churchyard. The well-known Giles Gilbert Scott, now much in demand for war memorials, was to be 'consulting architect', and Haswells of Chester were to execute the memorial.[104] The cross was never executed, nor is there any drawing of it in the Scott files in the British Architectural Library.[105] There may have been some local feeling that the churchyard was not the place to commemorate men, not all of whom were necessarily Anglicans – or even Christians. The explanation, however, probably lies with the architect. Scott, who could afford to be particular, always insisted that an artist was not a mere copier of old models, and seems (according to Bennett's son) to have treated the idea of the Bishop's Lydeard cross with 'a not unnatural disdain'. This rebuff to Bennett (who had enthused about Bishop's Lydeard) may have have affected some of his later dealings with Scott when dean.[106] Eventually, a memorial, by Scott, in his characteristic style (and in no way based on the Bishop's Lydeard cross) was executed by Thompsons of Peterborough, his usual stonemasons, and erected, in the event, at a road junction near the church.[107]

10

Throughout his ten years at Hawarden, amid all the varied concerns of a complex parish, Bennett was always clear that his central role was the conduct of worship and administration of the sacraments. He never disguised his high-church attachment, and was always ready to defend his convictions, which were 'quite definite, and written out plainly in the whole look and feel of Hawarden Church'. In March 1920, an anonymous writer summed up Bennett's innovations. Services had been 'more ornate', and 'ritual more elaborate', with 'coloured vestments' and 'lights and incense on ceremonial occasions'. Two innovations were the 8 a.m. Sung Eucharist (attended by 70 to 80 people), and a Children's Eucharist at 10 a.m.[108] Bennett was building on an existing high-church tradition, and though not all necessarily liked his changes, his charm and sincerity, combined with the 'innovation-management' skills he had acquired at Portwood and Christ Church, ensured their acceptance. Nevertheless, there were always supporters of the Church Association ready to spring to the attack. Their utterances had little practical effect. Three examples are typical.

In December 1913, the hawk-eyed Robert Foulkes of Waverton, who had crossed swords with Bennett at Christ Church and was still a prolific writer to the newspapers, fastened on a Hawarden innovation. 'The dedication of a crucifix in front of the rood screen on Saturday', he protested, 'is another step nearer the Papacy'; furthermore, 'the ECU [the English Church Union, of which Bennett was not a member] favours image worship and mariolatry'.[109] A dreary correspondence continued for some weeks in the *Chester Chronicle*. In February 1920, 'Evangelical Churchman' objected to the 'tableaux' used at Hawarden 'to illustrate incidents of divine truths'.[110] In mid May, 1920, on the eve of Bennett's departure, a group of North Wales opponents attempted to influence the choice of a successor, by attacking Bennett's liturgical practices in letters to the press. When Bennett read the 'extraordinarily rude letter' saying that 'the right place for him was the Church of Rome', he woke 'laughing in his sleep'.[111]

What was the real extent, in the parish of Hawarden, of dissatisfaction with Bennett's innovations? Before the 'protestant' letter writing campaign started, the anti-ritualists had organised a secret petition to the new (but as yet not enthroned) Archbishop of Wales, Bennett's diocesan bishop, A. G. Edwards. It aimed at influencing the choice of a new Rector. Bennett spoke about it, before starting his farewell Whitsun sermon. It was claimed, Bennett said, that the petition had been signed by 'a vast number of church people against the present practices of the church'. However, with a parish population of between fifteen and twenty thousand, to call 300 a vast number was 'a very picturesque description'. He disliked the furtiveness of the move. 'He had been christened Frank, and like his name, he liked things out in the open'. People had a right to differ, but not to quarrel. Now that the Church was disestablished, there was appropriate machinery for such matters, which (doubtless sensing the outcome) he confidently set out. The report that the Whitsuntide communion was sung with full festal ritual, and 300 communicants, may be taken as sufficient comment.[112] Despite the petition, the parish tradition of worship, strengthened by Bennett, continued under his successor.

11

At the end of May 1920, parishioners from St Deiniol's itself, and from all the outlying district churches and church centres in the whole large parish, gathered in the Rectory garden at Hawarden to bid farewell to Bennett and Ida. There were eulogies, and expressions of sadness at their departure, and a range of presentations from the various groups and organisations in the parish, which between them they had fostered. The most magnificent gift, and one which gave Bennett very considerable pleasure, was the return to him, splendidly refurbished and renovated, of his beloved old Buick car, with a dashboard inscription, 'To the Dean of Chester and Mrs Bennett with every good wish from Hawarden, and happy and affectionate memories of 1910 to 1920'.[113] Characteristically, Bennett spoke lightheartedly of his new appointment. As a parish priest, he had always regarded deans as the most useless form of any minister in the Church of England. Now, by a piece of 'Gilbertian irony', he was a dean himself. But perhaps he would regard a dean in another light when he 'put on those different clothes'. He might even come to regard a dean as 'the most valuable of all the servants of the church'.[114] Sure enough, four years later he was telling the newly appointed Dean of Canterbury that a deanery 'seems to me the greatest opportunity in the world a man could have'.[115]

Notes

    1   *Stockport Advertiser*, 16.11.1900, 4.
    2   'Family History'.
    3   For photographs of the incumbents to 1936, see *Parish Church of St Paul's, Portwood, Stockport Centenary Brochure* (copy in Stockport Central Library). Stockport Library has an unpublished history of St Paul's Church, by Joseph Holmes, giving dates of major events occurring during Bennett's incumbency. I am indebted to Anne Brien, a Local Studies librarian, for much assistance in my quest at the library for evidence about Bennett's Portwood years.
    4   B. H. Harris, (ed.), *Victoria County History of Cheshire, III* [hereafter *VCH*] (Oxford, 1980) 76–7.

PARISH PRIEST

5   *Stockport Express*, 31.1.1907; *Stockport Advertiser*, 8.2.1907.
6   *VCH*, 76.
7   *Stockport Advertiser*, 8.2.1907.
8   In 1898 the Community of the Resurrection had moved North, from Radley to Mirfield, not far from Stockport.
9   *Cheshire Diocesan Gazette* [hereafter *CDG*], Aug. 1898, 131–2.
10 *Stockport Express*, 31.1.1907. Bennett repeated the song at this farewell gathering; 'agate' = 'on the way' or 'afoot' (M.F. Wakelin, *English Dialects: an Introduction* (London, 1977).
11 Incident recounted in 'Memoir.'
12 'Memoir'.
13 *Stockport Advertiser*, 16.11.1900, 4.
14 Some of the more affluent and leisured ladies acted as District Visitors, each serving as counsellor and adviser to parishioners living in one area of the parish.
15 St Luke's Church was at the distant end of the parish and the mission hall in Back Brook Street.
16 The architect was a local man, John Douglas. Subsequently, Sir Charles Nicholson renovated the chancel, in what has been described as 'a curious chunky neo-Perp' (N. Pevsner and E. Hubbard, *The Buildings of England: Cheshire* (Harmondsworth, 1978), 150).
17 'Memoir'.
18 Reprinted in *Chester Team Parish News*, May 1988 (items collected by Janet Thorp, a member of the congregation).
19 *Cheshire Chronicle* [hereafter *Ches. Chr.*], 9.2.1907.
20 Bennett reported a steady growth in membership. By the end of 1907 their respective rolls stood at 150, 80, 135, 67 (*Christ Church Parish Messenger*, Jan. 1908, 2, copy in CRO).
21 *ibid.*
22 'Memoir'. Bennett's account is based on his childhood recollections.
23 Bennett's son was at the parish teas. He also remembered Chester's Pageant of 1910, another opportunity for collective activity, when Christ Church was the only parish to take part. Bennett participated, as Archbishop Baldwin preaching the Third Crusade, improbably clad in chain mail and mitre, and Ida organised the vicarage sewing party which provided all the costumes ('Memoir').
24 *Ches. Chr.*, 5.11.1910.
25 But as a compromise, at 7.15 a.m., instead of 7.00 a.m.
26 Bennett used a system of tickets, which also registered names; in 1907 there were some 75 weekly communicants and he easily attained his 1908 target of 150. Nearly 600 attended communion on Christmas Day, 1907 (*Christ Church Parish Messenger*, Jan. 1908).

27   ibid.; *Chester Team Parish News*, July 1988.

28   B.A., 1894; M.A. 1900; d., 1896; p. 1897; curacy, Lond., 1896–1900; tutor, Ches. Trg. Coll., 1927; Hon. Canon, 1939 *(Crockford*, 1963–4, his last entry). Though Baxter ceased to be a member of Christ Church staff at the end of January 1908, he enjoyed the work so much that he stayed on as Choir Master. Bennett wrote that this was 'good news to the choir and everyone else' (*Christ Church Parish Messenger*, Jan. 1908).

29   'New Dean of Chester' (newspaper report pasted in CRO, 'Commonplace Book' [hereafter CPB], March 1920, 389); for singing in the cathedral, *CDG*, Aug. 1921, 122; July 1929, 103.

30   *Christ Church Parish Messenger*, Jan. 1908.

31   *CDG*, Jan. 1908, 2; for the value of the site and buildings, maintenance contributions etc., see *CDG*, Apr. 1907, 71; Nov. 1908, 163.

32   For a concise account of the religious issue, in its political context, see E.R. Norman, *Church and Society in England, 1770–1970* (Oxford, 1976), 262–6.

33   Church Association, *The Disruption of the Church of England by More than 9000 Clergymen who are Helping the Romeward Movement in the National Church* (London, 1900), 71. Howson was listed as one of the 9,000; on Foulkes, who led the attack, see *Royal Commission on Ecclesiastical Discipline, Minutes of Evidence*, Cd 3069, 3070 (1906), 21 July 1904, Mr Robert Foulkes, qq 4098–4121.

34   *Ches. Chr.*, 8.12.1908. The cross is now kept in the Lady Chapel, where a plaque explains its origins (identification of this as the cross in question has been deduced from reports in *Christ Church Messenger*, July 1988, and from information given to me by a former choirboy of the 1930s). The text of Foulkes's unspoken speech, printed in the local newspaper, is a tendentious pseudo-historical tract about the role of a cross in ritual, which the meeting may have found some difficulty in following (*Ches. Chr.*, 8.12.1908).

35   *Ches. Chr.*, 8.12.1908. Bennett had merely told the choirman, a Mr Thomas, that he should not come to the service where 'Gloria in Excelsis' was sung. Thomas had construed this as dismissal, and stalked off. Bennett had sent him messages saying that he 'had only to walk back, and his robes were on the peg, waiting for him'.

36   *CDG*, Feb. 1909, 20; May 1909, 58–9.

37   *ibid.*

38   *Ches. Chr.*, 26.11.1910. Bennett would be aware that his words would be noted at Hawarden, to which he may have been sending a signal that he had not been seeking a move, a message implicit in his early remarks to his new parishioners.

39   It stretched from Shotton, in the north, with the John Summers steelworks (established 1896) and the rapidly expanding Deeside industrial villages of Sandycroft, Pentre, and Queensferry, through country areas, to Hope in the south.

40   The population of the parish was given as 11,539 in *Crockford* (1918); in a sermon of 1920, Bennett spoke of 'ten to fifteen thousand'; in 1923 he referred to '14,000 communicants' ('Parish Notes', *Hawarden Parish Magazine* [hereafter *HPM*], July, 1913).

41   *The Times*, 27.8.1910, 14, for a brief report; *Ches. Chr.*, 27.8.1910, 6, giving the text; 'Parish Notes', *HPM*, Sept. 1910. For the expense of maintaining the rectory, *Ches. Chr.*, 31.7 1920. The 'young squire', William Glynne Charles Gladstone (1885–1915), educated Eton and New College, Oxford, was the son and heir of W.H. Gladstone, the great W. E. Gladstone's son and heir. He was elected M.P. for the Kilmarnock Burghs in 1911, and was sometime Honorary Attaché at the British Embassy in Washington (*Who was Who*, 1897–1915).

42   Mr Toller, making a presentation to Bennett on his departure in 1920 (*Ches. Chr.*, 29.5.1920).

43   CPB, 28.3.1920, 389.

44   *ibid.*; 'Appreciations of W. G. C. Gladstone', *Ches. Chr.*, 24.4.1915. John Kensit started the practice of interrupting divine service where there was ritual, by standing up and making a public protest (G. K. A. Bell, *Randall Davidson, Archbishop of Canterbury* (2 vols., Oxford, 1935, 1938, cited 3rd. ed., single vol., 1952), 295, 328, 322, 467–8; J. R. H. Moorman, *A History of the Church of England* (London, 1953; 2nd. edit., London, 1967), 399–400).

45   CRO, CPB, 20.3.1920. 389; 'Parish Notes', *HPM*, Oct. 1910. His son believed that Bennett's preaching style achieved its best at Hawarden.

46   *HPM*, Dec. 1910.

47   An apt description: it became the Record Office of the County of Flintshire (later Clwyd, now again Flintshire).

48   *HPM*, Dec. 1910; Jan. 1912; Flintshire Record Office, D/BJ/466, Bennett to Bell Jones.

49   These bodies had, as yet, no legal status; they were established constitutionally by the Church Assembly in 1919.

50   Bennett called him 'the King of Hawarden' (Flintshire Record Office, D/BJ/466).

51   *HPM*, Jan. 1911. During the war, when baptism at Evensong was less convenient, Bennett added two Sunday afternoons a month and Monday evenings (*ibid.*, May 1915).

52   *ibid.*, May 1915. For Drew and Gladstone, and the Church Association, see *Disruption of the Church of England*, 40, 54.

53   *HPM*, Jan. 1911.

54   *ibid.*, Jan. 1911; July 1911.

55   *ibid.*, 'Rector's Letter', Sept., Nov., and Dec., 1913; June 1914. At Hawarden Bennett took on two assistant clergy, members of the Community of the

Resurrection and he probably learnt a more advanced ritual from them (*ibid.*, Oct. 1912; 'Memoir').
    56   *ibid.*, Jan. 1911; Mar. 1911.
    57   *ibid.*.
    58   *ibid.*, Mar. 1911.
    59   *ibid.*, Jan. 1911. Cf. Bennett's introduction at the cathedral of suppers for the cathedral community. A roneo-produced, hand-written and illustrated Toast List, for proceedings after the meal on 13.1.1921 (probably the first Bennett organised) gives the order of proceedings: toasts and respondents (interspersed with songs) to 'Church and King' (followed by the singing of the National Anthem), to 'The Lord Bishop', to 'The Chapter, to the Chapter Clerk, to the Deputy Chapter Clerk', to 'Professor Joseph C. Bridge and the Cathedral Choir', to 'The Precentor, Minor Canons, Choir School and School Masters', and finally to 'The Dean and the remaining members of the Cathedral body including the Bedesmen' (proposed by the Lord Bishop) – a comprehensive list. The evening ended with the singing of 'Auld Lang Syne', and 'Pax vobiscum'.
    60   *ibid.*, Apr., May 1911; the benefice's income accrued from glebe rents, tithes, investments, and fees.'The poor old cow of the Hawarden benefice has been milked over dry in the effort to make it support sustenance for a parish which has altogether outgrown its unaided capacity. We must get some more cows' (*ibid.*, June 1911).
    61   *ibid.*, June 1911.
    62   *ibid.*, June, July, 1911.
    63   *ibid.*, July, Aug. 1911; Aug. 1912; Aug. 1913.
    64   *ibid.*, May 1913.
    65   *ibid.*, Apr., May, June, 1915.
    66   In 1916 he saved a few pounds in subsidy to the Parish Magazine by raising the annual subscription from a shilling to one shilling and sixpence, adopting his usual technique of floating the idea well in advance of implementation. The magazine cost just over one penny a copy to produce. Circulation was 1,300; advertisement revenue paid for 1,000 (*ibid.*, May and Nov., 1915) – so Bennett gained.
    67   My account of the finances is necessarily telescoped; the detailed accounts (1911–1916), with Bennett's comments, give a fuller picture (*ibid.*, May issues).
    68   *ibid.*, May, July, Aug., 1915; June, Aug., 1916.
    69   *ibid.*, Dec. 1913.
    70   Platt was Provincial Grand Master of the Freemasons of Wales, and Bennett had joined the Hawarden Lodge soon after coming to the Principality (*ibid.*, Nov. 1912; *Ches. Chr.*, 1.4.1911, 8, reported 'the initiation ... of the Rev. F. S. M. Bennett, the already popular Rector of the parish', at a meeting of St Deiniol's Lodge'). Later, the North Wales Freemasons presented a font.

71 Jill Lever (ed.), *Catalogue of the Drawings Collection of the Royal Institute of British Architects (L- N)* (Farnborough, 1973), 145. 'The man who cannot build a cheap church well', he had once written, 'is not to be trusted to build a costly one'.

72 *HPM*, Dec. 1913.

73 Support for church building extended overseas. In 1912, Harry Bucklee, the Anglo-Catholic Vicar of another Hawarden, in Saskatchewan, appealed to the Hawarden CEMS. for help in erecting a church, to be dedicated to St Deiniol. The society's successful fund-raising efforts included organising a well-attended lecture on the needs and opportunities of the Church in Western Canada. Gladstone and the parish also responded generously to the appeal. The church was built, and Bucklee and Bennett continued to correspond (*ibid.*, Nov. 1912, Apr. 1913).

74 *ibid.*, Dec. 1913; July 1914; Aug. 1914; *Ches. Chr.*, 27.6.1914.

75 CPB, 1920, 391.

76 A private airfield, established shortly before the First World War, in 1916 it became a Royal Flying Corps station (R.A.F. in 1918) – see a pre-First World War photograph in *Clwyd in Old Photographs, 32* (Flintshire Record Office, 1975); CPB, 1920, 391).

77 Canon Drew to Welsh Church Commission (*Ches. Chr.*, 18.5.1907).

78 'Family History'.

79 See note 77 above.

80 *HPM*, Jan. 1914; Feb. 1915; Mar. 1915.

81 *ibid.*, Mar. 1914.

82 'New Dean of Chester', *Ches. Chr.*, 3.4.1920; *CDG*, Dec. 1920, 184. In 1933, at a public farewell meeting for the Reverend Alfred Hill, minister of a Chester Congregationalist Church, who had been secretary of the joint Church-Nonconformist group which Bennett organised, he spoke of Hill as being 'the kind of man' he 'would like to have as a Canon of Chester Cathedral (CRO, 942.2, W. E. Kay, 'Queen Street Congregational Church, Chester: Historical Notes from its foundation to 1942', typescript, n.d.).

83 The parish churchyard was almost full and the Hawarden Rural District Council therefore provided its statutory public cemetery. Local authorities were not obliged to have ground within such cemeteries consecrated, but could do so on payment of a £10 fee. Many families (not only Church people) preferred consecrated ground. This had to be clearly marked, an Established Church chapel built, and an officiating chaplain appointed, who would receive the burial fees. Non-conformist clergy might officiate only with permission. In consequence a divided Council resolved not to consecrate. Remembering the acrimony in Portwood, Bennett offered to pay the £10 fee himself. The Council, however, was adamant, and so Bennett responded to need by extending the churchyard, as urged by Vestry meetings, so providing for all, 'irrespective of politics and religion'. Meanwhile, the new cemetery remained

unused. The Council attacked Bennett, who replied, reasonably, that 'Church people ... had as much right to wish to have part of the cemetery consecrated, as others had to have some of it unconsecrated'. Rival factions disputed at Council sessions; the cemetery remained unused; the argument turned to the question of erecting a chapel; and finally, the matter was dropped. Logistically, the cemetery was bound to be needed eventually (Flintshire Record Office, 'Hawarden Parish Vestry Book', Easter Vestry, 1911; *HPM*, May 1911, June 1912; *Ches. Chr.*, 8.4.1911, 17.6.1911, 15.6.1912).

84   *HPM*, Dec. 1911. A memorial window to Drew was placed in the church in December 1911 (*The Times*, 25.12.1911, 9); Flintshire Record Office, W. Bell Jones, 'History of Hawarden Parish', unpublished typescript, n.d., 73–4; *The Times*, 18.11.1911, 8; 16.9.1912, 12. The contract price was £3,700 (*HPM*, Sept. 1912). The architects were Willinck and Thicknesse 89 (*ibid.*). who had recently designed an elegant new building for Wallasey Grammar School. The Drew classrooms were placed around a central hall – a more modest version of Wallasey's (Pevsner and Hubbard, *Cheshire*, 372).

85   On St David's Day in 1915, Bennett tilted at the Welsh Department of the Board of Education, which had recently published a booklet, *Some things every child in Wales should know*, which included the suggestion that St David was 'some kind of local preacher with a splendid enthusiasm for total abstinence'. The truth was somewhat different. Bennett told readers that David was the founder of twelve monasteries; a Churchman 'learned in the scriptures and devoted to the religious life'; the 'famous protagonist of the Catholic faith against Pelagius' (*HPM*, Mar. 1915).

86   In August 1914, the Diocesan Inspector, after a four day inspection of the nine schools, had reported that great pains were being taken with Religious Education, which the pupils enjoyed. He was 'much more than satisfied with the knowledge of the children and the tone of the schools themselves' (*ibid.*, Aug. 1914).

87   Children brought their secondary school reports for Bennett's perusal (*ibid.*, Aug. 1915; Feb. 1916).

88   Bennett said he would take the Hawarden and Queensferry classes himself. Without other evidence we cannot be certain what took place (*ibid.*, Sept. 1913; Apr. 1914; June 1914).

89   *ibid.*, Mar. 1915. He gives no basis for these statistics. They may have been an impressionistic estimate, based on his experience in previous parishes, or derived from his Christ Church registration scheme.

90   *ibid.*, Mar. 1915.

91   *ibid.*, June 1911; July 1911; Aug 1911; July 1913.

92   *Ches. Chr.*, 8.8.1914

93   *HPM*, Sept. 1914. In agricultural areas of Britain farm-workers did not necessarily rush to enlist; soldiering took second place to the harvest. Later, it was sensed that farmers at home grew rich whilst conscripted labourers and upper-class

junior officers suffered. Labourers who had served came back with a broader outlook and a more critical attitude (Nick Mansfield, 'Class Conflict and Village War Memorials, 1914–24', *Rural History* 6, 1995, 68–87). We do not, however, have detailed evidence of the situation in the Hawarden benefice.

94   *HPM*, Sept. 1914; Oct. 1914.

95   *ibid*. We do not know if he ever volunteered as a chaplain, but it is unlikely. In 1914, he was aged 48, and had an eye defect, caused by an accident sustained as an undergraduate. In 1925, writing about army chaplains, he referred to himself as having been 'too old to share their experience' (F. S. M. Bennett, *The Nature of a Cathedral* (London, 1925), 33.) Nevertheless, men who were determined to serve succeeded in being accepted, despite being over (or under) age.

96   *Ches. Chr.*, 16.1.1915, 6; *HPM*, Jan. 1915. Turkey's entry into the war, in October 1914, and the British bombardment of the Dardanelles forts on 3 November 1914, constitute the background to Bennett's pronouncement (T. Wilson, *The Myriad Faces of War* (Oxford, 1986), 108–21; cf. 'Cross against Crescent', in M. Moyniham, *God on our Side* (London, 1983), 80–115). The acquisition of Constantinople was a long-standing Russian ambition, and the restoration of St. Sophia, desecrated in 1453, was an age-old dream of the Orthodox (R. Guerdan, *Byzantium: Its Triumphs and Tragedy* (London, 1956)).

97   *HPM*, Apr. 1916; executed by Frank Haswell, son of the Chester Cathedral surveyor; dedicated on 13.4.1916, the anniversary of Gladstone's death (*Ches. Chr.*, 24.7.1915, 8.4.1916; K. Goulborn, R. Welch and P. Welch, *Hawarden, a Portrait in Old Picture Postcards* (Loggerheads, 1990), 33). It was inscribed, 'It is not the length of existence which counts, but what is achieved during that existence, however short'. Despite Joffre's prohibition in March 1915 of wartime exhumation, Gladstone's body was disinterred, under fire, at Poperinghe, and sent home 'in obedience to pressure from a very high quarter'. Consequently, in April 1915, to prevent further abuse of privilege, the Adjutant-General specifically banned British exhumations (P. Longworth, *The Unending Vigil* (London, 1967, rev. ed., 1985), 14). Bennett led a successful parish appeal to provide, as an additional memorial to Gladstone, an opthalmic theatre and wards at Chester Royal Infirmary, perhaps drawn to this particular cause by his own disability (*HPM*, Feb. 1916).

98   *HPM*, Mar. 1915.

99   *ibid.*. The wartime problems on Deeside of overcrowding, lack of amenities, and consequent rampant spread of disease, also exercised Bennett. The state, he asserted, 'which has brought workers here by the thousand should make some proper provision for their housing' (*ibid.*, Dec. 1915). In 1916, as the demand for munitions became more imperative, and the numbers of workers moving into the area increased, the Housing Branch of the new Ministry of Munitions started a building programme in Queensferry, which provided houses, hostels, a hospital, and a church hall for meet-

ings and social occasions (E. Hubbard, *The Buildings of Wales: Clwyd* (London, 1986), 421). The Girls Friendly Society gave its attention to girls, and Bennett started a boys' club for Hawarden and Ewloe, which met for 'games and company', twice a week (*HPM*, Dec. 1915).

100   *HPM*, Jan. 1916.
101   23.11.1916 – 3.12.1916 (*ibid.*, Sept. 1916).
102   'Hawarden' column, *Ches. Chr.*, 25.1.1919.
103   Thanksgiving Sunday, 6.7.1919. Copies of the special *Form of Thanksgiving and Prayer to be used in all Churches and Chapels in England and Wales, and in the Town of Berwick-upon-Tweed*, together with the hymn sheet, are preserved in the 'Parish Council Minute Book' in Flintshire Record Office.

104   For the service and Peace Celebrations, 'Council Minute Book 16.11.1910 – 5.3.1923', 302, 304; for the war memorial, *HPM*, 7.6.1919 (also quoted in *Ches. Chr.*); for the joint meeting with West Saltney Parish Council and the future maintenance of the memorial, 'Minute Book', 16.4.1919, 288; 11.10.1920, 335.

105   For the Bishop's Lydeard cross, see A. Vallance, *Old Crosses and Lychgates* (London, 1920), 17.

106   'Memoir'. For Bennett and Scott in disagreement over the Chester War Memorial, see J. A. Bruce, 'Giles Gilbert Scott and the Chester War Memorial Project', *Journal of the Chester Archaeological Society*, 73, 1994/1995, 99–114.

107   It was unveiled and dedicated on Sunday, 14.11.1920, by which time Bennett had left Hawarden (see 'Council Minute Book, 16.11.1910 – 5.3. 1923', 335. The late Edward Hubbard's reference, in his excellent *The Buildings of Wales: Clwyd*, 367, to another war memorial (1919–1924) by D.T. Fyfe inside the church, is an error based on a misreading. There never was any such memorial. Hubbard, who had misread his notes, would have corrected the error in a future edition (conversations and correspondence with him). For the war memorial dedication, see the copy of a poster, 'Hawarden Parish War Memorial', in 'Parish Council Minute Book, 16.11.1910 – 5.3.1923'.

108   Chap. Bk., 28.3.1920, copy of local newspaper article, 'Prominent High Churchman', 391.

109   *Ches. Chr.*, 27.12.1913. The crucifix was probably the one shown, in a post–1918 photograph, on the pillar adjoining the south end of the rood screen. The ECU could be equally forthright but it did not represent the views of all Anglo-Catholics; nor did the Church Association represent those of all evangelicals (Roger Lloyd, *The Church of England: 1900–1965* (London, 1966), 128, 139–40).

110   *Ches. Chr.*, 20.4.1920. 'The Gospel, not tableaux, performances, and images, conveyed God's word. If these other things were appropriate, why did St Paul's and Westminster Abbey not use them?'.

111   Bennett to parishioners, at a farewell gathering (*Ches. Chr.*, 29.5.1920).

His dismissive response provoked a further outburst from Robert J. Hughes of Wrexham, who had probably written the original letter: 'no clergyman – presbyter or Dean' had the right to adopt ritualistic practices 'whilst receiving the emoluments of the State Church' (*Ches. Chr.*, 26.6.1920); and 'as for Dean Bennett, it is a case of hors de combat – R.I.P.' (*Ches. Chr.*, 5.8.1920). Another polemicist equated ritualism with Rome and Rome with contemporary ills: 'During the war the Pope kept perfectly silent (not a word of protest when priests and people were massacred in Belgium and elsewhere) – while on the other hand the whole Protestant Church was in the ascendant of protest. The present state of Ireland is not very encouraging for moral law and order under Rome' (B. Ellis, of 22 Mold Road, Buckley, in *Ches. Chr.*, 26.6.1920). The letters of Bennett's defenders stressed his sincerity and energy; his opponents, wrote one, displayed not 'one particle of the sportsman's spirit Englishmen [*sic*] pride themselves upon' (*Ches. Chr.*, 3.7.1920).

    112   *Ches. Chr.*, 29.5.1920.
    113   *ibid.*
    114   *ibid.*
    115   Lambeth Palace Library, Bell Papers (193), 23, Bennett to G. K. A. Bell, 18.2.1924.

III
Through Welsh Disestablishment to English Deanery

1

The name of the Liberal leader, Lloyd George, is inseparably associated with the story of the disestablishment of the Church in Wales, against which Bennett tirelessly campaigned from the time of his arrival at Hawarden. To Livesey, Bennett's father-in-law, stalwart Conservative, erstwhile chairman to Balfour, the Conservative leader, Lloyd George was 'beyond the Livesey pale'.[1]

On one occasion, years before Ida Livesey met Bennett, the Livesey family had been holidaying in Llandidrod Wells. 'I always', Livesey told Ida and her sisters, 'like you to be on friendly terms with our fellow guests but there is one young man staying at this hotel to whom I must ask you not to speak. His name is David Lloyd George'.[2] Little could Ida have guessed that this young man would one day appoint a future husband to the Deanery of Chester. Nor, indeed, could Bennett himself, when he went to Hawarden in 1910, have foreseen that a decade later he would be an elected member of the Governing Body of a disestablished Church in Wales, and planning the arrangements for the enthronement of his bishop, A. G. Edwards, an indefatigable opponent of Lloyd George's disestablishment bills, as Archbishop of Wales.[3] Lloyd George would not only be present, but, Nonconformist as he was, would, at the early service, have received communion at the hands of the new archbishop – a striking ecumenical gesture, and public sealing of peace, underlined, later in the day, by the presence at the enthronement of official representatives of the Nonconformist churches.[4] How did all this come about?

2

Disestablishment, linked with Disendowment, was very much a live issue when Bennett came to Hawarden in 1910. He inherited a tradition of cooperation between Church and Nonconformity in social matters, and on this he built, establishing good relations with Nonconformist clergy in Hawarden itself and in the rest of his extensive benefice. Having gained trust and made personal friendships, he won Nonconformist backing for his own opposition to the Liberal government's proposals. In 1911, the 'young squire' was elected as Liberal member for a Scottish constituency. In congratulating him on entering his parliamentary career 'with flying colours', Bennett disclosed his own political leanings, as they were in 1911. 'I am probably the most double-dyed old Tory in the Parish, but am sure that, irrespective of our different political convictions we all do so heartily congratulate him.'[5] He was even more delighted when Gladstone, contrary to the general Liberal consensus, did not hesitate to come out against the Bill and voice his firm support for the *status quo* of the Church in Wales.

The Church in Wales was organised into four dioceses: St David's, Llandaff, Bangor, and St Asaph, in the last of which Bennett's parish of Hawarden lay. All four were within the Province of Canterbury, and so the question of disestablishment in Wales could not really become a live political issue at Westminster until Parliament recognised that Wales could, for legislative purposes, be dealt with separately from England. During the 1880s both Conservative and Liberal governments, by legislating for Wales on other issues, had, in effect, recognised this, and during the same period the movement for disestablishment in Wales became less of a straight religious issue, and developed into a nationalist campaign, focusing on the Church as an endowed and – a somewhat unjust accusation – alien institution.

Disestablishment loomed large in most speeches and election addresses of Liberal candidates in Wales, and by 1892, Liberals held, with large majorities, all but three of the thirty four Welsh seats. They were ultimately able to induce the Liberal party as a whole to adopt Welsh disestablishment as part of its programme, leading to the setting up, in 1904, of a Royal Commission, to examine the position of the established church and other religious bodies in Wales. Between 1894 and 1914, there were four Welsh disestablishment bills, but for the Liberal politicians involved with them they became increasingly a matter of producing a case to satisfy their Welsh colleagues. Indeed, as time went on, even for Lloyd George himself, Welsh disestablishment became of less importance, as more pressing issues, social problems, industrial relations, and the House of Lords, took centre stage, though he wisely did not say so in public.

Bennett regularly used his 'Rector's Letter', in the *Hawarden Parish Magazine*, to marshal his arguments against government proposals and to predict, in stark terms, the likely outcome for Hawarden. Understandably, he opposed any move to sever the historic link with Canterbury. At this time, he also opposed a break in the link between Church and State, though not, it would seem, as a principle, but because of the motive which he suspected lay behind it. Years later, he would have been willing to support disestablishment in England, against a Parliament which thwarted the Church's clearly declared wish to revise the Prayer Book. In 1912, however, he saw Disestablishment in Wales as 'a great question going to the very roots of our national life', which was being settled as a piece of political gerrymandering, in that, following the 1910 election, the Liberal Government, with a reduced majority, now depended for survival on the support of the Irish Nationalist members.[6] He wrote

> If the life long relationship between the Church and the State in our land is to be altered, it ought to be dealt with soberly, deliberately, and as a whole, and not piecemeal as part of a political bargain. Could anything be more grotesque than the rending asunder of Church and State in Wales as a convenient preliminary to doing the same in England by means of a majority almost wholly consisting of Irish Roman Catholic votes[?][7]

But the force of Bennett's attack was directed at the disendowment clauses, which, he predicted, would have disastrous consequences for his parish. The alleged benefits which would flow from the 'great wrong' which was to be perpetrated were illusory. Attempts to stop it might fail, but should not be allowed to fail because 'we sat with folded hands when we should have been up and doing'. Hawarden would lose its rectory and its land. The number of clergy would have to be cut. Regular services would cease in the district churches, with the possible exception of St Ethelwold's; the Church Army centre would have to be abandoned; and plans for a church at Sandycroft, and for a Church Army Mission at Pentre would go. Tithes would still be levied, but the County Council would get the proceeds. Of course, disestablishment and partial disendowment had been effected in Ireland, but against those Liberals who quoted the Grand Old Man who had carried the Irish measure, Bennett reminded his readers that Gladstone had pointed out, in 1868, that the case of Wales was quite different from that of Ireland. 'We in Hawarden',

Bennett said, 'revere the memory of our greatest parishioner', and concluded, 'Is it not time that Churchmen began to make a bit of a row, and a good sizeable row, too?' He urged them all to write to their M.P. immediately.[8]

In January 1913, as the proposed terms became clear, Bennett spoke out bitterly against the 'injustice of the whole thing'

> With me, amazement, shame, resentment have been jostling one another for the first place, while pretty well every sentiment and conviction that I have learned to hold dear – not so much as a churchman, but as an ordinary British citizen – have been rudely jarred ... I verily believe that if the mass of people understood what is being done in their name by their Government, we would have such an outburst of national resentment as this country has not seen for many a hundred years.

He went on to castigate the whole principle of the Bill:

> The idea that if any number of people want what belongs to somebody else, they thereby have the right to take it if they can, is utterly intolerable; no one outside Bedlam could suggest it as a principle for all sound legislation, but it is the main idea, all the same, that underlies the Welsh Church Bill.

People, he continued, often asked why a meeting on the subject had not been called.

Bennett made clear where the responsibility lay. It was 'the business of the laymen of the parish to get it up and not mine'.[9] In fact, as he probably knew, his loyal churchwardens, W. Bell Jones, and William Edmunds, already had the matter in hand. On their initiative, a Church Defence meeting was held in Hawarden on 14 February 1913, timed to take place two days after the National Day of Prayer for the Church, called for by the four Welsh bishops. For this, Bennett organised a chain of unbroken intercession, on a fifteen-minute rota basis, but made clear that political action must follow prayer.[10] Under Bennett's leadership, Hawarden people (including Nonconformists) signed petitions, bombarded their Member of Parliament with letters, and supported Church Defence meetings. Bennett was immensely cheered to hear one brave voice speak out at Westminster on the government benches, in 1913. The squire of Hawarden had 'the pluck to stand up and say a good word for his Mother Church, while most of the Liberal [*sc.*, Liberal Party] Churchmen in the House seemed to be, like the conies, "a feeble folk"'.[11]

It was, of course, the disendowment clauses, rather than actual Disestablishment, which Bennett and his fellow clergy found particularly odious. We are fortunate in having a report of Bennett's precise views at a critical stage. In October 1913 he debated with Councillor John Owens of Chester, the question whether the changes were 'just and fair', at a public meeting organised by Chester Debating Society. Bennett and Owens already knew each other, having worked together in Chester Guild of Help during Bennett's Christ Church days. In consequence, the debate was conducted in a friendly and tolerant spirit, and attracted widespread interest. A few weeks earlier Chester had witnessed a great protest meeting, held in Chester Market Square, followed by a procession to a special service in the cathedral. Hawarden people had attended, and Bennett himself was well known in the City.[12] At the debate, Bennett, in responding to Owen, opened by professing not to be a 'diehard'. He would make sacrifices for peace in Wales, and, if he believed the Bill would lead to peace, he, too, would be for it, but (his favourite homely area of analogy) you would not smash up a car because the air inlet was wrong. Owens had concentrated on the principle of disestablishment, and Bennett agreed with much of what he said. There was, however, no logical reason why disendowment should go with disestablishment. No arguments were adduced, and he had never come across any explanation as to why, because relations between Church and State were altered, the Church should be disendowed. Indeed, Bennett had 'come to wonder if the justification for Disendowment was not dependent upon the principle of saying a thing often enough to make people believe it was true'. He mocked at the alleged value of Establishment as such. It had two advantages only: the presence of four bishops in the House of Lords, and the State's payment of Church of England parsons as chaplains in 'lunatic asylums'. There would be nothing unjust about turning the bishops out of the Lords, but levelling up was better than levelling down. It would be a pity, in some ways, to remove representatives of religion from the Constitution, and he would as soon have seen representatives of the great Nonconformist bodies included in the Lords, alongside the bishops.

He protested at the injustice of disendowment. The Church in Wales had an income of £260,000; the Bill would take away £100,000. Hawarden would be £1,500 a year poorer; it would lose its churchyard. Such things, he contended, could be justified only if it could be shown that the Church was over-endowed, or doing positive harm, and nobody suggested that. As far as other religious bodies were concerned, 25 years possession was regarded as sufficient title:

> If George-street Chapel possessed what we possess in Hawarden, and she had had it for 25 years, it could not be touched. In Hawarden I can show you a list of the men who have had it without any kind of a break since 1180. Why, if 25 years would secure it absolutely to George-street Chapel, should the period since 1180, or 300 years, be insufficient for a title in Hawarden? It is not justice. (Applause) Justice means you should deal with all parts of the community alike. Under this Bill you have one law for George-street and another for Hawarden.

In a further shrewd concession to his Nonconformist clergy friends who supported him, he conceded that there was a strong case to be made out for sharing ancient endowments with other bodies, but stressed that this constituted no case for taking endowments away, and spending them on something else. It was not customary, in 1913, nor is it today, to take a vote at meetings of Chester Debating Society. Both speakers were thanked, and it is clear from the reports of appreciative applause, that Bennett had made his case very effectively.[13]

Support by some North Wales Nonconformists for Bennett in his opposition to the disendowment clauses was made manifest in 1914, in the months immediately prior to the passing of the Bill.[14] By 1914, however, Welsh Liberal M.P.s, expressing the determination of hard line Nonconformity, were able, partly by the turn of political events, to press through the fourth bill, which despite its rejection by the House of Lords became law in 1914, under the Parliament Act, though its operation was, in due course, suspended for the duration of the war. Bennett now drew topical parallels between German 'Hymns of Hate and imprecatory salutations', and the embittered attitude of 'political [sic] Nonconformists' who opposed the suspension.[15] The Act ended state sanction for ecclesiastical law in Wales, removed Welsh bishops from the Lords, abolished the existing system of patronage, and passed to the Church in Wales control of ecclesiastical appointments, discipline, services, and doctrine. The Church was also partially disendowed. It was left with its church buildings and other property, valued at £102,000 per annum, while other property, valued at £157,000 per annum, went mainly to the county councils, for charitable purposes, with a smaller proportion to the National Library and the

University of Wales. The Church was to frame its own constitution and to set up a representative body to manage its property and finances.[16]

3

Common prudence now dictated that Welsh churchmen, while not prejudicing any movement for repeal, should take early steps to prepare for the coming into operation of the Act. Bennett's bishop, A.G. Edwards, chaired the Joint Committee of Clergy and Laity (1914–1915).[17] Though Bennett was not one of the six clergy elected from his diocese, he took part in the consequent discussions within the diocese, which he later represented as a clerical delegate to the subsequent Convention, held in Cardiff, 2–5 October 1917, where Edwards, as the senior bishop, again presided.[18]

Bennett made an important and characteristic contribution to the debate on the proposed constitution of the Representative Body, which would administer the property and finances of the Church in Wales, an aspect which interested him closely. Laymen were to predominate on this body and the debate and amendments had largely concerned numbers. Bennett saw a role for women, who had not been mentioned in the male-dominated debate. His amendment was 'to delete the word "male"'. Displaying that tact and sweet reasonableness which, having already won him friends and supporters at Hawarden, was to serve him in such good stead later, at Chester, and which contrasted with some of the blunt speaking which had preceded him in the debate, Bennett moved his amendment, 'not because I do not fully appreciate the care with which these draft schemes have been drawn up, but from the mere fact that [when] we meet together it is assumed that there are omissions and mistakes. I venture to think that the addition of the word "male" is the first of these mistakes.'[19] The war had shaken traditional views of the role of women.

> The labours of the last three years have completely altered in most of our minds the status of women and their value to the Government. That is a value that you must multiply by at least 500 if you want to get at what is the claim of women with regard to our Church ... Their claim is more obviously strong with regard to the Governing than to the Representative Body, because some of us feel that women have

not much to do with finance, but there are just three things I would press upon this body.

These were (1) The Church had, in the past, 'existed enormously' on women as leading 'givers' and organisers of fund raising. It would need them even more in the future. To expect this help, yet to exclude them from the financial body, was 'absurd'. (2) Women were to vote in the election of the Representative Body. It was thus 'an anomaly' to exclude them from membership of it. (3) Women entrusted with management of properties did it 'exceedingly well'. Some of them could give 'very real advice', be 'of great value', and 'extremely useful'. He concluded, in ringing tones:

> Let us not hereafter give under coercion almost grudgingly, what every feeling of appreciation bids us do now. If hereafter the State decides that women shall be electors to and members of Parliament, we shall be able to say that the Church in Wales gave the lead to the whole community.[20]

Bennett was seconded by a member of his patron's family, Miss Helen Gladstone, one of the five women lay representatives included in the St Asaph delegation.[21] She would speak, she said, not of women's rights (of which perhaps too much was heard), but of women's duties. Women needed the 'stimulus' of being involved in 'public questions', and 'events of recent years had suggested that women offered 'resources hitherto untried'. A lively debate extended into the second day when Convention finally agreed to a modification, accepted by Bennett and Helen Gladstone, that 'communicants of either sex', but with a restriction on the number of women, would be admitted to the Representative Body.[22] The decision as to whether it would be canonically acceptable to include women in the Governing Body was left to that Body to decide, when it had been set up. Women, albeit in limited numbers, were admitted to both. Bennett's intervention had been significant and was clearly attuned to the now growing 'Church feminist movement'. Some leading churchwomen had played an important part in the campaign for women's suffrage, through such bodies as The Church League for Women's Suffrage, which also sought to draw out 'the deep religious significance of the women's movement'; during the war women's role was vital to the economy; within the Church their generally increasing importance led to pressure for their admission to hitherto 'male only' spheres of activity.[23]

Bennett intervened again in the proceedings on three occasions, twice to seek clarification of technical but important points in the wording of resolutions, and once, briefly to contribute to the debate on the composition of the Governing Body, on which the larger southern dioceses sought to have stronger proportional representation.[24] Skating round the heated arguments about numbers, he urged: 'Looking to the future, would it not make it much simpler to have the Diocese as the unit, and not have everlastingly fresh calculations and discussions every time there is a new Diocese to be created?'[25] A compromise was eventually agreed whereby equal representation of all dioceses was accepted, in return for Bangor's withdrawing its opposition to the creation of the Governing Body at that meeting.[26] Two new dioceses were soon formed in the south.

That Bennett, at Cardiff, had enhanced his reputation may perhaps be indicated by his being asked to second a vote of thanks, proposed by the Bishop of Bangor, at the end of the Convention. He did it, characteristically, 'with the greatest of pleasure, and as briefly as I can' (unlike some of the other seconders). Bennett's subsequent election to the new Governing Body, as one of the twenty-five elected clerical members representing St Asaph's diocese is, perhaps, a further indication of his standing. Significantly, his is the only English (that is, non-Welsh-sounding) name among the eleven names listed as representing the Archdeaconry of Wrexham.[27] The formal printed minutes cannot give the flavour of the discussions which must have taken place, and of Bennett's contribution to them. He is recorded as seconding the adoption of the Report of the Committee on the Training of Ordinands, a subject which was to interest him later at Chester, and was appointed to the committee responsible for making arrangements for the enthronement of A. G. Edwards, as the first Archbishop of Wales.[28]

This was the end of Bennett's membership of the Church in Wales. His last official duty, as Rector of Hawarden, was to attend the enthronement in St Asaph Cathedral, on 1 June 1920. The next day he was installed in Chester Cathedral as Dean, the date delayed so that he could play his final role in Wales at the great ceremony in St Asaph Cathedral, where both Lloyd George and his wife were present. Bennett was to serve Edwards again at least once, when in 1928, he acted as his Commissary at Monmouth Diocesan Conference, where Bennett trenchantly contributed to the discussion on the erection of a new cathedral.[29]

It is a tribute to Bennett's practicality – if not to his foresight – that his views on Disestablishment changed radically after the event. By the time his appointment to Chester was announced, in March 1920, Bennett was convinced that 'nothing but good' would come from Welsh Disestablishment, though he thought that the financial clauses of the Act 'dealt hardly with the Church'. The Chester press believed, probably on the strength of a few words at an interview, that 'he would not break his heart if the Church of England followed suit!'.[30] The passage of time only strengthened his conviction that Disestablishment was right for Wales. In 1930, he articulated his last recorded perception of the Disestablishment experience and its aftermath:

> I was a member of the Welsh Church Governing Body during the throes of Disestablishment. We none of us, I think, foresaw how great was going to be the gain, especially in the direction of sweetening relationships with other bodies and of facilitating co-operation for manifold good purposes. No one in their senses wants Establishment back in Wales today.[31]

4

How did Lloyd George fasten on Bennett as his candidate for the Deanery of Chester? Tradition in the Bennett family attributes the appointment to a chance remark by A. G. Edwards. The story is recounted in a section of the Bennett 'Family History', a typescript written by Bennett's grandson, Roderick Macaulay Bennett (1930–1990), who had a special interest in genealogy and family history.

> The vacancy at the Chester Deanery was on Lloyd George's mind whilst he was staying under the same roof as the Bishop of St Asaph. As the two men were making their way to bed Lloyd George remarked, 'Just one more thing before we say goodnight. I have to find a Dean for Chester; any suggestions?' The Bishop rubbed his nose, as he always did when thinking or about to give the blessing. 'Hmm. hmm. I think the Rector of Hawarden would do'.[32]

Se non vero e bene trovato. The circumstantial detail may be coloured – or fictitious – but it may well be true that Lloyd George sought some informal advice from A. G. Edwards, and then acted on it. While this may seem an unlikely and casual way for a Prime Minister to set about making an ecclesiastical appointment, in the case of Lloyd George the behaviour is plausible, as we shall see.

Darby, who had been Dean of Chester since 1886, died on 6 November 1919, within a fortnight of his 89th birthday.[33] An interregnum of some three months followed. Chester, like all other cathedrals of the New Foundation, had a dean appointed by the Crown, that is, in practice, by the Prime Minister. The appointment of the new dean was not officially announced until 31 March, but Bennett, who was preaching in the cathedral on 23 March, informed the scribe of the cathedral 'Commonplace Book' of his appointment, in confidence, and told him that the only other person who knew was the bishop. However, within a few days the news was leaked, and it seems to have given satisfaction in cathedral circles. 'We are all', the Commonplace Book records, 'so thankful for the appointment'.[34] Had there been dark speculation about some undesirable candidate? The choice of Bennett by Lloyd George was hailed in the local press as 'a highly original and unexpected appointment'.[35] That it was unexpected may be judged from the fact that Bennett had only recently been made Rural Dean of Mold, an office which, under the recently approved Constitution of the Church in Wales, had a more important role than in the past.

How did a Prime Minister of that era proceed in such matters? Lloyd George's predecessor, Asquith, had been keenly interested in ecclesiastical appointments and patronage. For appointments to bishoprics, a private secretary produced a short list and Asquith scrupulously weighed the claims of those on it, but was ready to receive advice from Davidson, the Archbishop of Canterbury, with whom he was on intimate terms. The final choice, however, was Asquith's 'own unbiased selection', and he endeavoured, as had his predecessors, to keep a balance amongst the different schools of thought in the Church. But in the handling of ecclesiastical affairs by Asquith's successor, Lloyd George, 'no greater contrast could be imagined'.[36] According to Davidson, Lloyd George admitted 'quite frankly that he had no time for it [the making of ecclesiastical appointments], or adequate knowledge, and is not at all averse to the idea of getting some advice regularly given by those who can be regarded as representative churchmen'. He did from time to time have access to advice, though his methods caused some concern in higher ecclesiastical circles and among certain Churchmen in Parliament. Lloyd George's knowledge of Church life and affairs was scant, and he was more interested in preaching ability than academic record. Bennett, from his performance at Hawarden, would have scored highly for his preaching; he had a sound enough university record – and with no published works yet to his name could not be dismissed as an academic!

It is possible that the Prime Minister sought advice from E. H. Pearce, Bishop of Worcester, who had been recently appointed to the see by Lloyd George. Pearce wielded considerable influence, having had, as a Canon of Westminster before his translation, access to the Downing Street ecclesiastical patronage correspondence. He had assisted Asquith with church appointments and was certainly consulted at times on such matters by Lloyd George. It would, however, not have been out of character for Lloyd George simply to have taken one or two soundings in connection with Chester and then to have made up his own mind.

Is it, however, feasible that Edwards, the doughty opponent in speech and writing of disestablishment in Wales, could have been one of those sounded out by Lloyd George? Certainly the two had crossed swords openly in the 1890s.[37] Yet there was, from 1903, a growing rapprochement occasioned in part by Lloyd George's increasing concern with a wider political horizon and in part by a common interest in the development of the North Wales University College and the operation of Balfour's Education Act in Wales.[38] Furthermore, the grievances of Welsh Nonconformists seemed no longer as real as they had done twenty years previously.[39] The death in 1907 of a much loved daughter of Lloyd George drew him closer to Edwards, who had suffered a recent bereavement of his own.[40] Finally, the two found common ground in cooperating over the arrangements for the 1911 investiture of the Prince of Wales, not as traditionally in the House of Lords but at Carnarvon.[41] It is, therefore, not implausible, and is perhaps even likely that Lloyd George did speak informally with Edwards about the Chester appointment following Darby's death in November 1919. An informal discussion would not, of course, have precluded consultation with others on the subject. With Welsh Disestablishment now assured, Lloyd George may even have favoured an appointment from within the Church in Wales into the Church of England, as raising the prestige of the former.

Bennett had first got to know Edwards through his brother George, who, after coming down from Oxford, had spent several years working in the Palace at St Asaph.[42] Later, when Bennett came to Hawarden, he and Edwards became firm friends. As Bennett's bishop, Edwards must soon have become well aware of Bennett's worth. Ten years in a large parish, with several churches and a large staff of clergy to manage, were recommendations in themselves. Indeed, he had already marked Bennett out for promotion within the Diocese.[43] Bennett had recently demonstrated administrative and diplomatic skills in connection with Welsh Disestablishment, skills which Edwards was in a unique position to assess, and he had displayed, in his parish, and often beyond it, an undoubted ability to get on well with people of all sorts. Tact was not the least of Bennett's qualities. Furthermore – a not unimportant consideration – his general background and undoubted ability to resolve problems equipped him well for the role of cathedral dean in 1920. Finally, he knew Chester, and was already well known there. If Edwards was, in fact, asked by Lloyd George for a name, Bennett's must have sprung most readily to mind. If Edwards admired Bennett, it is clear that the admiration was mutual. In 1926 Bennett dedicated his book, *Expecto: a Biology of the World to Come*, to Edwards, 'in token of gratitude for long friendship and of admiration for his work for the Church in the Principality'.[44] Was the 'gratitude' also for Edwards' word in the P.M.'s ear?

Notes

    1   'Memoir'.
    2   *ibid.*
    3   *List of Members of the first Governing Body of the Church in Wales. 1918*, 'Elected Members. Diocese of St Asaph. Archdeaconry of Wrexham', 4; *The Governing Body of the Church in Wales* [Minutes], 6.1.1920, 2; *Minutes of the Governing Body of the Church in Wales*, 7.4.1920, 14; 5.10.1920, 1 (Bennett, still seemingly a nominal member, named among 19 apologies for absence).
    4   Lloyd George's wife accompanied him to the early service and the pair were welcomed by both Davidson (Archbishop of Canterbury) and Edwards. But, in those less than ecumenical days, the Georges' presence, Davidson wrote, raised 'a teapot storm in ecclesiastical circles, of the *Church Times* sort'. Davidson, however, saw Lloyd George coming, not 'to triumph' but as 'a religious man' (G. K. A. Bell, *Randall Davidson, Archbishop of Canterbury* (Oxford, single vol. edit., 1952), 990). See also *Ches. Chr.*, 5.6.1920; Roman Catholic representatives were also present at the enthronement (Kenneth O. Morgan, *Rebirth of a Nation: Wales 1880-1980* (Oxford, 1981), 185.

5   *Hawarden Parish Magazine* [hereafter *HPM*], Oct. 1911.
6   R. C. K. Ensor, *England, 1870-1914* (Oxford, 1936), 418. On the Church in Wales, see also John Davies, *A History of Wales* (West Drayton, 1993), 537–9.
7   *HPM*, Oct. 1911
8   *ibid.*, Nov. and Dec. 1911. The M.P. was Henry Lewis (Liberal).
9   *ibid.*, Jan. 1913.
10   *ibid.*, Feb. 1913.
11   *ibid.*, Sept. 1913.
12   *ibid.*
13   *Ches. Chr.*, 11.10.1913. Glebes – their loss a sore point with all clergy – were a private gift. Hawarden had half a dozen fields in different places (their total extent recorded in the 1905 *Crockford* as 90 acres but in the 1918 as 93 acres). The state had nothing to do with them, Bennett argued: their current value was dependent on the development carried out by such as Stephen Gladstone and Canon Drew.
14   Bennett reported that a number of Nonconformists in and around Denbigh had expressed 'conscientious disapproval' of the disendowment clauses. A meeting with leading Nonconformist laymen of Hawarden and Sandycroft had been held, and a letter to the Prime Minister, protesting at the proposal to take away endowments worth £157,000 per annum, was to be circulated throughout the Diocese. 1,000 signatures had been hoped for; the total number would probably be nearer ten times that figure (*HPM*, Feb. 1914; *Ches. Chr.*, 14.2.1914).
15   *HPM*, Dec. 1914, Apr. 1915.
16   P. M. H. Bell, *Disestablishment in Ireland and Wales* (London, 1969), 258–9.
17   *Official Report of the Proceedings of the Joint Committee of the Church in Wales No.1* (Oxford?, n.d.), 12.1.1915, 10–11.
18   *Official Report of the Proceedings of the Convention of the Church in Wales* [hereafter *Official Report*] (Cardiff?, n.d.), 2.10.1917 – 5.10.1917.
19   *ibid.*, 69.
20   *ibid.*, 69–70; for women as churchwardens, and members of the vestries in the late Victorian Church, see Owen Chadwick, *The Victorian Church* (2 vols., London, 1966, 1970), 2: 201; for women's position in Church and society, see Adrian Hastings, *A History of English Christianity 1920-1985* (London, 1986), 19–22, 42–5.
21   *Official Report*, 257. There were 61 men, including Bennett's churchwarden, W. Bell Jones.
22   *ibid.*, 79; *The Times*, 5.10.1917, 4.
23   See Brian Heeney, 'The beginnings of church feminism: women and the councils of the Church of England', *Ecclesiastical History*, 33, 1982, 89–109; for the Church League for Women's Suffrage and the Suffragist Women's Protest Committee, and their impact on ecclesiastical issues, *op. cit.*, 100–3.

24 *Official Report*, 165, 181, 191.
25 *ibid.*, 165.
26 Bell, *Disestablishment*, 303.
27 *List of Members of the First Governing Body and of the Representative Body of the Church in Wales and of Committees.*
28 RBCW, *Minutes of the Governing Body of the Church in Wales*, 6.1.1920, 2; 7.4.1920, 14.
29 *The Times*, 7.11.1928. The conference was in Newport.
30 CRO, 'Commonplace Book', 28.3.1920, 389.
31 F. S. M. Bennett, 'Integration', in H.R.L. Sheppard (ed.), *My Hopes and Fears for the Church* (London, 1930), 83–95.
32 'Family History' (typescript now in possession of the daughter of the late Roderick Bennett; photocopy held by present writer), chap. XII, 51. How did the story originate? It does not appear in the 'Memoir', written by Bennett's son, F. L. M. Bennett (Roderick's father), though much of the other information about the dean in the 'Family History' is drawn from this source. Assuming that the story is not a complete fabrication, it could have come from the dean himself, via his son, or have been recounted by him, in his latter years, direct to his elder grandson, Roderick. This leaves open the question as to how Bennett himself came by it. Alternatively, Bennett's son, himself a member of the clergy, could have got it from a third source, the bishop's chaplain, or some other cleric who might have been present. However, it is significant that he does not mention it in his 'Memoir'. The circumstantial detail (direct speech and 'rubbed his nose') could, of course, be colourful devices, added, in recounting the tale, either by the dean himself (always a good raconteur), by his son, or by a third person. Roderick Bennett's mother had been Dean Bennett's secretary, and she too could have contributed to the account, as of course could Bennett's brother, George (in 1920 vicar of Christ Church), who might have had the story from Edwards, whom he had known since the days when he worked in the Palace at St Asaph.

The story may have had some local currency in Chester, because Bernard Wall, retired schoolmaster, former official City guide, and writer of popular local history, recounts a version of it in his *Tales of Chester, II* (1992), without indicating a source.'In 1920 a new Dean for Chester was needed. Prime Minister Lloyd George didn't know whose name to put forward. One night, so the story goes, he found himself staying at the same house as the Archbishop of Wales and, on his way to bed, asked for advice. At Hawarden, twelve miles into Wales from Chester, the Rector, Frank Bennett, was considered eccentric. The Archbishop nevertheless recommended him for the post.' Wall's qualifying phrase, 'so the story goes', suggests hearsay or cathedral gossip. The description of Edwards as 'Archbishop' is an anachronism. He was consecrated archbishop the day before Bennett was installed as dean. I have spoken with Wall, and he cannot recollect where he heard the story. He tells me that he talks with many people who pass on their personal recollections and comments.

The story, in whole or in part, must have originated from someone who was present. Clearly the future dean would not be there; the bishop would not have recounted the story in such terms, though he might have subsequently told Bennett about some enquiry by Lloyd George. Lloyd George himself, always loquacious, might, of course, have told someone the bare facts, but he can have attended few services where Edwards, as bishop, had pronounced the blessing ('rubbed his nose, as he *always* [my italics] did when ... about to give the blessing'), though he was present at Edwards' consecration in 1920 (Bell, *Randall Davidson*, 990).

33   CRO, 'Commonplace Book 1908–22', 6.11.1919, 372.
34   *ibid.*, 388.
35   *Ches. Chr*, 3.4.1920.
36   Bell, *Randall Davidson*, 1240. For the contrast between the handling of ecclesiastical appointments by Asquith and Lloyd George, and the advice each received, see *ibid.*, 1240–6. See also J. A. Spender and Cyril Asquith, *Life of Lord Oxford and Asquith* (2 vols., London, 1932), II, 378–9 (quoted by Bell, 1240): 'No branch of Asquith's activities as Prime Minister interested him more than that which relates to ecclesiastical appointments'.
37   Peter Rowland, *Lloyd George* (London, 1975), 88, 108, 109.
38   *ibid.*, 167, 171.
39   *ibid.*, 191.
40   *ibid.*, 197
41   *ibid.*, 248.
42   'Memoir'. George Bennett read Modern History at Lincoln College, Oxford, 1891–1894, but could not take his degree until his debts (many of them to his sisters) had been paid. He therefore took a post, probably as secretary, with Bishop Edwards of St Asaph, to earn money to settle his debts. He was thus able to graduate in 1897, and was ordained (d. 1898, p. 1899). The work at St Asaph was congenial, but George responded to Frank's urgent request that he come to Portwood as his second curate. George came in 1898, and became first curate in 1899, when Trevor Griffiths left to become Rector of Hawarden ('Family History').
43   As Rural Dean of Mold, a post which, under the new Church in Wales, would have increased importance. 'It is said that Archbishop Edwards wanted to get a bishopric for Bennett' (Bennett, 'Memoir'). No indication is given as to by whom 'it is said'. For an examination of whether Bennett was ever considered for a bishopric, see the Appendix.
44   F. S. M. Bennett, *Expecto: an Essay Towards a Biology of the World to Come* (Chester/London, 1926), (ii).

IV

The nation's cathedrals adopt the Chester model

1

Bennett's policy of opening up the cathedral, without charge, was only one aspect, albeit a very important one, of his general policy of making the cathedral not merely a centre of diocesan usefulness but a welcoming, spiritual home, for all manner of people. A cathedral, he later contended, could not begin to do its real work until visitors' fees were replaced by pilgrims' offerings. Even had this had involved loss, he would have stuck to his policy of a free, open cathedral. He trusted everyone, and would lock up nothing – except the safe.

In July 1924, *The Times*, under the heading 'A Cathedral in Use: New Methods at Chester', published an appreciation of 'the revolutionary changes effected by Dean Bennett', and this helped to bring his achievement to national attention. The writer found the cathedral different from every other cathedral, in the warmth of its welcome. A visitor might, indeed, wonder if he had run into a family party, but 'a little perseverance' would reveal that he had been invited, too. Furthermore, the cathedral had become – and this was Bennett's vision of a cathedral – the 'complete household of the bishop'. In every house 'that is at unity in itself', there were two bonds: the practical and the spiritual and emotional. Bennett had ensured that both were provided. The remaining fragments of the monastic house helped to induce a common ambience. In the Refectory, 'now refurbished', Simon of Whitchurch's lovely Early English pulpit was there for any member of the Chapter to remind those feasting that 'all meals eaten in love and joy are sacramental'. The newly glazed cloisters offered opportunity for 'reflection and rest'. In the Church, all was 'open and free', with a chapel set aside for private prayer. A globe showed mission fields. Religion was made to seem 'quite natural'.[1] The correspondence sparked off by the article was a clear indication that the Chester model was being seriously studied elsewhere, and was already being emulated by some chapters.

Fortuitously, Bennett had arrived at the cathedral at an opportune moment for developing a cathedral ministry and providing 'free and open' opportunities for visitors. The relative decline of the urban parish in the wake of the First World War was, paradoxically, the cathedral's opportunity. The confidence and community cohesion of late Edwardian communities had waned, with consequent problems for parish priests in many parts of the country. The sort of organisations and societies which Bennett had nurtured as a parish priest were – though this was not immediately apparent – everywhere past their prime.

The 'Memoir' of the dean written by his son (ordained priest in 1927) shows that as a parish priest he became aware of the changed situation. Bennett's attempts to repeat his parochial successes with such organisations on a grander scale at the cathedral were less successful than he had hoped. But the growth of the leisure industry after 1918, which in its Sunday aspects was causing additional problems for parish priests, made recourse to the cathedral attractive and more possible and may well have represented a loosening of ties to the parish. The cathedral's reverential atmosphere, soaring vaults, excellent music, and sense of place where worship had been celebrated over centuries gave a touch of transcendence which the parish church could not match. Bennett's efforts to involve the parishes in cathedral fund-raising, visits, and direct involvement of their clergy were consequently less successful than he had hoped. To parish priests the cathedral must have seemed to be something of a rival super-parish.

However, in his amusingly satirical book *Barchester Pilgrimage* (1935), Ronald Knox expressed the view that compared with pre-war days fewer people attended cathedral worship, but that these, presumably the devout, attended more often. Since the war, there had been 'a rallying of forces within the Church, accompanied by, and producing, a kind of moral disestablishment'.[2] We do not know exactly who comprised the regular cathedral worshippers and though Bennett said that he had no intention of 'poaching' from parishes, he had little control over who came. The cathedral clearly had a regular following, but this was augmented by increasing numbers of tourists – including Americans en route from Liverpool to the south. That this popular response to the new spirit of the cathedral at Chester bore some relationship to wider contemporary social trends was proved when other cathedrals with their own worshippers and visitors adopted the Chester model.

2

Although we have evidence as to when various chapters abandoned admission fees in the 1920s and 30s, it is more difficult to discover exactly when charges were introduced at English cathedrals. We might have expected Bennett to have evinced some interest in the origin of the charges – or, at the very least, at Chester – but he never mentions the matter. His silence, however, merely emphasises that his role was that of proselytiser, not historian.

It is also surprising that Bennett, who had served for ten years in the Welsh diocese of St Asaph, when regularly reporting in the *Chester Diocesan Gazette* on other cathedrals adopting the Chester model, makes no mention of Welsh cathedrals. In 1924, he claimed that, since he had become dean, he had 'visited every cathedral in England and Wales ... except three or four which I hope to see another day'.[3] St Asaph Cathedral was not a tourist atraction, and there is no evidence of charges being in existence there, either when Bennett was at Hawarden, or previously. Bennett must have been aware of the situation. Of the other Welsh cathedrals, St David's probably attracted nineteenth century visitors, but there is no evidence of entry fees. Llandaff Cathedral was not fully restored until 1869, and was not a tourist attraction. The Chapter Act books and other likely sources make no mention of charges. The Diocese of Swansea and Brecon (created 1923) made the Priory Church of St John the Evangelist, Brecon, its Cathedral, and although the adjoining set of medieval buildings attracted many visitors, there is nothing to indicate entry charges. Until recently, Bangor, which George Gilbert Scott considered the poorest cathedral he had ever seen, has attracted few visitors, and did not attempt to charge. Nor does it do so now. Monmouth Diocese had been created only a year before Bennett was writing his seminal work, *The Nature of a Cathedral* (1925) and, at that time, had no cathedral (some years later, Bennett advised on the establishment of one).

Perhaps Bennett considered it inappropriate to comment on cathedrals outside the English provinces (he never mentions Scotland); perhaps he considered that, as Welsh cathedrals were generally so little frequented by tourists, they did not merit mention; he may even have felt that the situation in Wales might confuse his argument. Nor did Bennett mention cathedrals in England outside the Anglican communion. No charges were ever levied for admission to Roman Catholic cathedrals. Visitors have always been assumed to be on a spiritual quest, and there were no historical monuments or pre-nineteenth century architectural features such as those which visitors to Anglican cathedrals had sought. Nor do admission charges seem to have been made at the Orthodox Cathedral in London.[4]

3

At the start of the nineteenth century, English cathedrals were generally open only at specific times (other than actually during infrequent divine services), and they normally levied a charge on visitors at those times. The visitors came, and had done so throughout the eighteenth century (and perhaps even earlier), not as religious pilgrims but largely as antiquarians, in quest of that 'history in stone' with which cathedrals were well endowed.[5] Architectural aspects were especially attractive to some; monuments to others. When he was a schoolboy, Thomas Arnold (1795–1842) frequently visited cathedrals, and kept detailed notes and drawings of what he had seen. Cathedrals varied in their practices regarding charges. Generally, vergers collected the money, which constituted and was usually recognised as an important part of their pay. At cathedrals where I have evidence about fees, this link with pay is underlined by the fact that when charges were abandoned, the salaries of vergers and sextons were frequently increased. In return for payment, vergers conducted visitors around, pointing out features deserving special attention. Cathedral authorities regarded the presence of vergers and their custodianship of visitors as some assurance of good order and a protection against damage. Fees were also a means of control. Normally, only serious visitors were willing to pay, and the more generous perhaps contributed something extra via the offertory box.[5]

The 1994 Report of the Archbishops' Commission on Cathedrals claims that cathedrals abolished charges in the nineteenth century, as an aspect of 'Victorian idealism', manifested elsewhere in the form of free access to public libraries, reading rooms, art galleries, and – more specifically – public buildings previously 'reserved to the privileged'; renting of church pews was also 'mostly swept away'.[6] By the middle of the nineteenth century, however, all cathedrals were not 'open and free'. The final report of the 1854 Cathedrals Commission had urged a 'free' regime: 'We are glad to find *in some places* the Cathedral is open to the public free, and we recommend that this should be the case as to all cathedrals at seasonable hours' (my emphasis). Not all cathedrals, however, seem immediately to have heeded this advice, and the need for revenue, combined with a concern to protect property, appears sometimes to have taken precedence over 'Victorian idealism'. In 1872, M. E. C. Walcott claimed that 'most' cathedrals were, by then, open daily, without charge.[7] There is, however, adequate evidence that charges for entry to most parts of some cathedrals (e.g., choir, tower, chapter house etc.) remained in force, even if naves were 'free'. The writer of the 1994 Report seems to have been unaware of this. Furthermore, in many cases where charges were for a time abandoned, there is clear evidence that they had been reintroduced at some date before 1920.

In the Cathedral Chapter minutes of post-Reformation Chester I can find no mention of the introduction of admission fees. However, the dean of a cathedral of the New Foundation had considerable powers, and did not need to consult the Chapter on such a matter. Indeed, Bennett, on his own authority, made Chester a 'free and open cathedral' some three weeks before his first Chapter meeting. An earlier dean may simply have decided to levy official charges, or allow vergers to augment their small stipends by pocketing a fee/gratuity – not an uncommon practice elsewhere. The minutes of Bennett's first Chapter (23 June 1920), under the heading 'The throwing open of the Cathedral to the public', merely record that the Precentor reported on 'the question of the crowds that now frequent the Cathedral', with a request that there be a notice 'as to the freedom of the church, and the observance of proper behaviour'.[8]

The only hints of charges occur in 1884: '5. That the whole of the Box money be retained towards current expences [*sic*] instead of a moiety as at present'; and (a more direct hint at a charge) '9. That the Vergers be admonished not to accept any fees for their own benefit'.[9] Curiously and regrettably, the 1994 Report on cathedrals does not recognise Bennett's role in the twentieth century abandonment of entry fees in English cathedrals, and merely credits him with posting 'notices inside the Cathedral telling people what they were looking at', and thereby 'updating a very traditional service of the cathedrals'.[10] In reality, he was giving it a very different direction.

Evidence regarding entry charges from most other cathedrals is sparse and often difficult to interpret. A few examples may illustrate the situation. At Chichester, in answers to the bishop's questions at his 1798 Visitation, 'admission fees' are specifically mentioned as being used to defray the cost of repairs. However, these fees seem eventually to have become part of the remuneration of two sextons and the dean's verger, because in 1860 the Chapter decided that these officials should cease to receive the pew rents and fees for admission, by then a major part of their income. Instead, each was now to be paid an annual salary of £30.[11] As there is no reference to an alternative destination for rents and fees, this decision could imply either their abandonment, or their diversion to cathedral funds.

At Lincoln, by the 1700s it was accepted that visitors should give money to the verger conducting them, and there is evidence that this system was still operating in 1866. However, in 1883, the practice seems to have been stopped, and a Visitors' Fund was set up to receive payments for visiting the choir, chapter house, cloisters, and tower; the nave, presumably, being now free. The Fund proved to be a useful source of revenue, subsequently providing, in 1886, £200 towards the restoration of the nave; from 1914, £200 annually towards restoration of the north-west tower, and later contributing to reduction of an overdraft.[12]

At Gloucester, in 1858, two vergers were to be on duty to receive and guide visitors round the building, a fee being required only for the choir, chapter house, cloisters, and tower.[13] At Wells, in 1873, the sacrist or principal verger was ordered to 'show the Cathedral without charge or fee at such hours and subject to such regulations as the Dean and Chapter may prescribe'. Visitors wishing to see the quire, Lady Chapel, chapter house, and tower were to give sixpence to the fabric fund, and write their names in a visitors' book. A verger was to be on duty as guide, from 10 a.m. to 4 p.m. during the summer.[14] The visitors' book was perhaps devised to discourage any dishonesty by the verger. In 1806, a visitor to Winchester Cathedral had complained about the 'avaricious propensity' of those deputed to show the nave. By 1889, however, vergers had been forbidden to receive gratuities. A notice warned visitors of this, and a box was provided into which they could put money, which was used to supplement vergers' stipends, augment the fabric fund, and pay for inserting new statues into the Great Screen.[15]

Until 1841, 'virgers' of Durham Cathedral had derived profit from admission charges. There is no evidence as to when this practice began. In July 1841, however, the Dean and Chapter ordered free admission to the nave and aisles from May to the end of October, and, in December 1841, extended this provision to the Chapel of the Nine Altars. One virger was to be present and would receive five shillings weekly for this extra work. Six months later – the summer season presumably in full swing – virgers asked for compensation for loss occasioned by free opening. The Chapter rejected the request. In November 1860, in response to representations by virgers, the chapter made regulations about climbing the dangerous central tower (open daily for four hours only), and prescribed a virger-escort; for this work the virgers each received an extra £10 per annum. There seems to have been no charge for access during the first two decades of the twentieth century, and today the only charge is for the tower (no escort needed).[16]

At Norwich, in 1893, monies raised by an admission charge of sixpence per visitor were augmenting the funds of Dean Lefroy's restoration appeal. The charge must, therefore, have already been in force. Lichfield Cathedral told the Cathedrals Commission, in 1925, that it had 'always' been open without fee.[17] However, as visitors were allowed to go round 'unaccompanied' only from April 1925, gratuities to the conducting verger may well have been regarded as part of his normal remuneration. Subsequently, money formerly paid in gratuities may now have found its way into offertory boxes. This supposition is strengthened by the fact that, in September 1925, details of such offerings for the previous twenty-four weeks only (i.e., from April 1925) were reported to the Cathedrals Commission.[18] Also significantly, during the course of the 1920s correspondence in *The Times* about admission fees, when cathedrals were either justifying their existing practices or advertising their changes – proposed or actual – Lichfield made no claim to have pre-empted Chester in becoming truly 'free'.

4

Undoubtedly there were reformers before Bennett, although never perhaps as generally successful or as wide-ranging in their reformation. Peterborough Cathedral has a claim to have been the pioneer of 'free and open cathedrals'. In July 1926, the Reverend Herbert Hall wrote that he was 'empowered to state ... that both the nave and choir of Peterborough Cathedral had been freely open to visitors every day during the period from 1853 to 1878', and [Peterborough] was thus the pioneer in 'free and open cathedrals'.[19]

Hall's statement implies a 'fee regime' both before 1853 and after 1878. Yet in February 1926, when the Cathedrals Commission team (including Bennett) visited Peterborough a charge for entry was being levied. How correct

THE CHESTER MODEL 81

was Hall's assertion? Peterborough was (like Chester) a cathedral of the New Foundation, and so the dean had considerable powers. It is significant that the years 1853–78 coincide with the period of office, as dean, of the reforming Augustus Page Saunders.[20] He certainly seems, according to the evidence, to have presided over 'a 'free and open cathedral' during these years. Wisely, perhaps, he involved the Chapter in his decisions. On 26 October 1853, the Dean and Chapter resolved, 'That as soon as the Sextons and Vergers receive their increased pay the Cathedral be open within certain hours and under certain regulations to be fixed by the Dean each Verger or Sexton taking his turn and share in the duty of pointing out its beauties etc. to visitors'. The *Peterborough Advertiser* congratulated its 'fellow citizens' on 'the liberality which characterises the regulations of the present Dean and Chapter'; gave the times of daily opening fixed by the dean: 10.00 a.m. to 4.00 p.m.; and noted that vergers were 'strictly forbidden' to receive fees for conducting visitors round the cathedral.[21] Indeed, there was little need, as 'printed cards explaining the various objects of interest' were provided, 'thus enabling every one to act as his own Verger'.[22] In certain respects Saunders indeed seems to have been a precursor of Bennett. His emphasis, however (as in cathedrals generally), was on architectural aspects; unlike Bennett, he gave no hint of visitors being guided round 'religiously'.

Three years after Saunders' death, however, there were modifications. On 17 October 1881, Chapter resolved to charge sixpence for admission to the Tower; any visitor who required a verger to show him round the cathedral was now to pay sixpence, but a party of three, 'not less than 1/-. [one shilling]', the money being deposited in a special box, and (presumably as a check) a note made by the Sextons in a book. It is thus clear that no compulsory charge for admission was to be made from 1853; from 1881, however, although there was to be a charge for a conducted tour, there was none for actual admission and the freedom to wander at will. The 1881 charges for admission to the Tower were a completely new feature. A resolution of 26 June 1888 makes the position clear: 'That a notice be be placed in the Cathedral stating that all parts of the Cathedral except the Tower are open to the public free of charge'. However, some six weeks later, there was a change. Chapter resolved to make charges for entry to the Choir: 'not less than sixpence' per individual, with graduated charges for different-sized parties, those of between twelve and forty (the maximum number allowed in any one party) paying five shillings; all visitors were to sign the book, and place the money in a collecting box. These charges of 1881 and 1888, were to help finance essential repair and renovation to both Tower and Choir. By August 1888 this work had begun in the Choir, and seems to have attracted visitors, thus probably leading the Chapter to combine control over numbers with tapping a welcome source of potential revenue.[23] The foregoing suggests that (reluctantly or not) the Dean and Chapter were not unreservedly committed to 'Victorian idealism' for free access.

At Salisbury, Walter Kerr Hamilton, Precentor 1841–1854, and subsequently Bishop, was another notable reformer, and he had close support from a new dean, Francis Lear, who was much in sympathy with Hamilton's policies. Hamilton firmly believed that the cathedral, as the Mother Church of the Diocese, should be open daily, and be accessible to everyone who wished to enter it. During a visit to Europe, in 1849, he was greatly impressed by the great numbers of ordinary people he saw in the naves of cathedrals, and when he returned to Salisbury he made himself personally responsible for ensuring that the cathedral was open each day between Matins and Evensong, with a canon on duty. His 'open door' was only one aspect of his general programme of reform.[24] Nevertheless, later in the nineteenth century visitors were being charged sixpence, collected by vergers as part of their remuneration for showing visitors around.[25] A charge was still being made in 1920.

5

The cathedrals of London and Canterbury (little is known about York) should perhaps be regarded as special cases. At St Paul's Cathedral charges were initially introduced as early as 1709, a year before the final completion of Wren's new church. The proceeds, known as 'stairsfoot money', were for the relief of men injured during the course of the long building operation.[26] It may well be that, after the need for this had ceased, the charge persisted, but there is no sure evidence of eighteenth century practice. We have, however, precise details of the arrangements which were in place by 1837. The cathedral was open to visitors from 8.00 a.m. to 8.00 p.m. in the summer, and from 11.00 a.m. to 3.00 p.m. in the winter. There were separate charges for each part of the building: the monuments and body of the church, 2d; whispering gallery, outside galleries, library, model room, geometrical staircase, and great bell, 1s 6d; clock, 2d; ball and cross, 2s 0d; and the crypt, 1s 0d. The complete tour therefore cost 4s 10d.[27] There seems to have been no shortage of visitors keen to view the interior of Wren's masterpiece, and inspect the many monuments.

By the beginning of the nineteenth century, St Paul's was more than a London cathedral; it was a national building, virtually a second national shrine, since Westminster Abbey had been unable, by the end of the Napoleonic Wars, to accommodate the growing crop of monuments to national heroes. The Whig government of 1837, the year of Victoria's accession, therefore requested (via the Home Secretary, Lord John Russell), that the cathedral should henceforth be open free of charge, 'like any other national building ... containing works of art, historical or literary monuments, or objects of national history'[28] As the cathedral had been rebuilt mainly through parliamentary legislation, and the work financed by the proceeds of the coal tax, the request must have seemed not unreasonable.

However, by 1837, the entrance fees largely covered the salaries of vergers who admitted visitors and kept decent order. The Dean and Chapter firmly rejected the request, arguing, in detail, that, despite public financing of Wren's work, central Government had no more authority over the new building than it had had over the old; furthermore, charges assisted the necessary preservation of good order, by limiting the numbers of visitors. There was no additional charge for viewing the monuments; in any case, a church was not 'a gallery of art or a place of public exhibition'. Peel's government repeated the request (again without avail) in 1842, following a Report by a Commons committee on National Monuments. Eventually, in 1851, on the eve of the Great Exhibition, under the leadership of a new dean, the famous Henry Milman (appointed 1849), the Chapter abandoned charges.[29] They perhaps sensed that they might excite unwelcome controversy if they did not fall into line with the spirit of 1851, but doubtless also hoped for voluntary largesse from the hordes of visitors expected in the capital during Exhibition year. How long this state of affairs continued is not known. The Cathedrals Commission Report of 1927 made no mention of freedom of admission to St Paul's. Had admission been free, it is likely that the Report would have mentioned the fact. It is probably reasonable to suppose that that, by then, along with virtually every other English cathedral, St Paul's charged for admission.

It might be assumed that when Russell had made his 1837 request to St Paul's that it allow free admission, 'like any other national building ... containing works of art, historical or literary monuments, or objects of national history', one 'public building' he would have had in mind as offering free admission would have been the main national shrine, Westminster Abbey. This is not a cathedral, but a Royal Peculiar, directly under the Crown, and thus more obviously a 'public building' than St Paul's. The Abbey did, however, levy charges, having been accorded the right to do so by its Charter of 1560. The collection of entry fees was originally farmed out, as Elizabethan dues normally were.

This arrangement continued until around 1700, when the Dean and Chapter granted the right of collection to the Choir, who in return were to arrange to keep the Abbey's increasing stock of monuments clean. Later, it was found more convenient for the Treasurer to make arrangements for this work to be done, charging the cost against receipts of entry fees, the balance being retained by the Choir as an element of their pay. In 1697, the admission charge was 3d; in 1723 it was doubled; at the end of the century it became 9d. In the early nineteenth century, it was replaced by detailed charges for viewing different parts: tombs in Henry VII Chapel, 6d; the models, 3d; wax figures and north crossing, 6d; west end, 6d; gratuity for 'tomb-shewer', 2d. The 'all-in' charge was thus 1s 11d. However, as complaints arose at the pressure from the 'tomb-shewer' for supplementary 'tips', the twopenny gratuity was abolished, and the Dean and Chapter instituted a compound charge fee of 2s 0d, divided thus: south transept, 9d; chapels, north transept, west end, and models, 1s 3d. A notice was prominently displayed, stating the charges, and making it clear that 'the persons employed to shew the Church being sufficiently remunerated', they were forbidden to request anything from visitors, who were to send any complaints to the resident Prebendary. The Chapter allocated one eighth of the takings to the three regular tomb-shewers; payment of the 'extraordinary shewers', employed in the summer season, was left to the choir's discretion.[30]

Public complaints at having to pay to view national monuments at Westminster Abbey began to mount in the press and elsewhere. Members of Parliament took up the matter, and in response to a letter from a leading member, the Chapter, on 29 May 1823, detailed their position. The monuments, they asserted, did not belong to the public, who hence had no right of access to them; this applied even to those erected by parliamentary grant, as these occasioned a financial loss to the Dean and Chapter because no fine was levied on them. The only right of admission was to divine service. Furthermore, entry fees were necessary to control access, thereby protecting the fabric and the monuments from 'profanation or injury'. However, if Parliament would provide a regular allowance to the Abbey, the Dean and Chapter (now seemingly discounting 'profanation and injury') would consider 'more easy admission of the Publick'.

Nevertheless, conscious of continuing criticism, on 6 May 1825 they compromised. Poets' Corner (south transept) and the nave now cost 3d, and the rest of the church 1s 0d. However, complaints continued, fuelled by the dissatisfaction of the Minor Canons and singing men of the choir, who collectively drew only £1,400 as income supplement from the fund which had been allocated to them, the Abbey retaining other amounts, ostensibly to pay for the cleaning of the monuments – one old lady dusting the pavements. In this general climate of feeling, after Joseph Hume, M.P. for Middlesex, had raised the matter in 1826, the House of Commons asked the Chapter for details of charges for viewing 'the public monuments', and the amount collected over the previous five years. The Chapter replied that there was no separate charge for viewing the public monuments, as distinct from the private ones; however, they gave full details of receipts.[31] Still not satisfied, Hume moved that the Dean and Chapter be ordered to lay their Charter before Parliament. Peel discouraged this, and the matter rested for the meantime, though Parliament remained critical. The Dean and Chapter made appropriate financial arrangements to resolve internal disputes about pay of choir and tomb-shewers.[32]

In that 'age of reform', the changes instituted by the Dean and Chapter did not quieten criticism amongst members of Parliament and the public. In 1837, when the Government tackled St Paul's over admission fees, they asked Westminster for a report on fees for burials and monuments, and details of the amounts collected for showing the tombs. The Chapter's reply was largely a reiteration of their 1826 letter. Finally, in 1841, they gave way. Admission fees were abolished. Plans describing the monuments were displayed and notices posted warning against touching the monuments. To view the nave and north transept now cost 3d, and the royal chapels an extra 3d.[33] The proceeds were allocated to 'ornamental improvements' – interpreted very loosely.[34] By 1926. the nave was free of charges, but fees (producing a good income) were levied for entry to the royal chapels and undercroft.[35]

At Canterbury, after the Interregnum, the cathedral began, once again, to attract visitors. In 1660 the Dean and Chapter had returned to a cathedral 'sad, forlorne and languishing ... more like a ruined Monastery than a church'.[36] Thanks, however, to a satisfactory cash-flow from accumulated entry fines on repossessed property, they were able to start the work of restoring the fabric and furnishings. The first record of payment occurs as early 1665, when visitors such as John Evelyn could, of they wished, pay a verger to show them round. Evelyn enthused that 'the Cathedral is the finest sight here'.[37] In the early eighteenth century, there does seems to have been no control over visitors by means of entry charges, since the Dean and Chapter found it necessary to instruct their officers to prevent noise and disorder, the carrying of 'any Burden' through the cathedral, and its use as a 'common thoroughfare'.[38]

Situated on the London to Dover road, Canterbury was a popular stopping-off place for visitors to and from Europe. The races on the nearby Downs also drew crowds to the city, where the cathedral, which dominated it was an unrivalled attraction.[39] Vergers must have had a continuing income from charges levied for their services as guides. In response to the growing tourism, the cathedral authorities helped finance histories and guide books.[40] In the 1850s, official guides were appointed, and tours were popular, though complaints were heard about the garrulousness or incompetence of individual guides. In 1870 the Dean and Chapter ruled that not more than thirty people should be shown round at one time. It may be assumed that charges were made (if only to remunerate guides), because in 1879 'free days [*sic*] for visiting the Cathedral were fixed for Whit Sunday, Whit Monday, and the last Thursday in every month'.[41] By the twentieth century, charges had been formalised into the standard sixpence fee, which was, by then, levied by cathedrals generally. All monies collected in admission fees, 'after payment of the necessary guides', were allotted to the fabric fund.[42]

6

In assessing the significance of Bennett's work, it is relevant that, from the 1830s, piecemeal reform of cathedrals had occurred. As noted earlier, the verdict of a modern historian is that 'the revitalization of English cathedrals was one of the most impressive achievements of the Victorian Church', with a 'growing perception' of the 'distinctive role' that cathedrals might have in the life of the Church.[43] Nevertheless, much remained to be done when the twentieth century arrived, and the work of Bennett between the wars was a vital new initiative. While the importance of his impact, beyond his own cathedral, has been recognised, the detail of his influence on the 'open door' movement

– the precondition of real reform – which spread from cathedral to cathedral, has not been examined.

The contact between deans themselves, when they met at their regular formal meetings at different cathedrals and took turns in providing hospitality, was one obvious channel of communication. After the 1934 annual general meeting, held at Canterbury, Bennett reported his impressions in the August issue of *Chester Diocesan Gazette*. From all he had heard, cathedrals had in recent years clearly become 'invigorated'. His own contributions to the discussions at the meeting, and the example, on the spot, of Canterbury itself – open and free, 'all day and every day' – must have inspired any laggards. Direct contact between individual deans was another line of communication, though except for the occasional letters which have survived, it cannot be evidenced, but may reasonably be inferred from Bennett's own remarks about other cathedrals.

The publicity Bennett received in the national press was an important factor. There was also an element of competition amongst cathedrals in an age of expanding post-war tourism, fostered by excursion trains, charabanc-trips, and the private motor-car. Bennett's grandson recounts an amusing story (known only in the family, and referred to briefly in the 'Memoir' by Bennett's son) concerning one of Bennett's typically unorthodox methods of encouraging cathedrals to open their doors. He would attend Mattins, incognito, in some unregenerate cathedral, quietly hide when the doors were locked, and emerge later to sound the bell or raise a clamour. When released he would plead ignorance of the arrangements, express great surprise at finding himself locked in, and finish up with something like, 'I never dreamt that a cathedral would lock its doors like this'. Doubtless his hope that the message would reach the appropriate quarter was occasionally realised. At the end of his book, *The Nature of a Cathedral*, Bennett himself refers in more sober terms to being locked in ('Once or twice ... I chanced to forget that the public were excluded ... ').

By 1921, Chester was regularly open till eight in the evening, members of the Church of England Mens' Society 'invigilating' on rota, and Bennett could announce, at the end of his first year, that 'other great cathedrals' were turning 'a flattering eye' on Chester. Bristol, he reported, was 'frankly following our example', and opening without fee. This claim is confirmed in a work on the cathedral, published in 1924: 'For the "summer time" doors remain open till 7 or 7.30 p.m.' Nevertheless (as in so many cathedrals) this 'open' regime was qualified by charges for entry to specialised areas. Bristol charged sixpence for admission to the library, chapter house, and vestry, 'for reasons of control'.[44] Exeter, Bennett reported, was debating the issue. However, it seems that fees were still being charged in 1926, when four boxes in the cathedral were in position for 'visitors' *fees*' [my emphasis].[45] Wells, he went on, was enquiring 'as to how we have fared with the annoying sixpenny fee abolished. It is good to be able to tell them, that we are doing excellently well'. Wells took note, and the Cathedrals Commission's representatives, visiting in April 1926, reported that there was a charge now of sixpence only for the portion east of the nave and the tower. On Sundays, the nave was open until 6.00 p.m.[46] By the Autumn of 1922, Ely and Salisbury had followed Chester. Within two years, Salisbury, in response to an enquiry from another cathedral, was enthusiastically reporting an improved general atmosphere and increased revenue.[47]

As regards Ely, it is surprising to find that the Czech, Karel Capek, in his *Letters from England*, reported that cathedral as unwelcoming: 'The sacristan comes up and enjoins the tourist not to look at the ceiling and the pillars, but to sit down in a pew and listen to what is being sung in the choir'.[48] Capek's book was first published in England in 1925, but there is no indication as to the actual year of his visit. In fact, from 1 January 1922, entry fees were suspended for an experimental period of one year, on the initiative of J. F. Kirkpatrick, who, as dean of a cathedral of the New Foundation, had considerable powers.[49] The experiment was so successful that the arrangement was continued, with no term fixed.[50] In October 1925, the Cathedrals Commission reported that 'great facilities are given', and 'no fees are charged except for mounting the tower'.[51] (Charges for towers were not uncommon.) Fees were not reintroduced until the mid–1980s. Capek was equally uncomplimentary about York, Durham, and Lincoln, where sacristans variously watched him 'with enmity', said he 'should desist' from looking around, as 'a service would be held shortly', and sought even larger tips than their Catholic counterparts in Italy.[52] He generalised on English cathedrals from this limited experience, and did not visit Chester, which by 1925 was widely acknowledged as the exemplar and in 1926, was warmly commended by the Cathedrals Commission.[53] It is not unlikely, therefore, that Capek's actual visits were much earlier. Certainly, by 1925 nobody could expect any comments about English cathedrals which ignored Chester to be taken seriously.

St Alban's claimed that poverty precluded its opening up free, and affirmed the need of the sixpenny fee. However, in the spate of correspondence following the publication of *The Times* article about Chester, a letter from 'A Layman' had insisted that, despite its poverty, St Alban's was trying to follow Chester. The Chapter had resolved to suspend the fee for a trial period of a year, and had inaugurated a guarantee fund, from the Diocese, to cover the estimated £900 obtained from fees, though hoping that, as at Chester, voluntary offerings would justify this 'venture of faith'.[54] St Alban's seems to have been pleased with the results, and there was no need to call on the guarantors. When representatives of the Cathedrals Commission visited St Alban's, in November 1925, they reported that admission fees had been abolished nine months previously (i.e., February 1925), and that the income from voluntary contributions, £650, now amounted to a little more than that obtained previously from admission fees. Bennett, delighted to add another cathedral to his list, had already, in April 1925, announced St Alban's decision and had congratulated the Dean and Chapter.[55]

Developments regarding charges at Lincoln were less decisive, and the hesitancy displayed may be more typical of other cathedrals than the evidence about their changes always reveals.[56] It was not until 1934 that the cathedral considered whether to continue charging visitors to chapter house, choir and cloisters, admission to the nave and great transept being, in fact, already free; or else to invite voluntary contributions. York, Winchester, Gloucester were consulted about the tax position regarding such contributions. No change was made, however, until September 1939, when the whole Minster (with the possible exception of the chapter house) was thrown open as a shelter for evacuated students and children. Charges ceased and voluntary contributions were sought, but in April 1940 charges were resumed, with remission for H.M. forces and persons in official uniform.

Bennett had a very direct influence on Canterbury. George Bell, appointed dean in 1924, immediately sought advice from Bennett and visited him in April 1924, to study the whole range of developments at Chester, and Bennett paid a return visit to Canterbury during the summer. The two deans developed a friendly relationship, continuing to correspond, from time to time, over the next five years, and meeting at the regular gatherings of cathedral deans. It gave Bennett great pleasure when Bell's success at Canterbury led to his appointment as Bishop of Chichester, in 1929.[57] In January 1925, in a confidential report to his Chapter on 'the practicality and desirability of opening all parts of the Cathedral without charge', Bell quoted the example of

Chester, where voluntary contributions now produced £1,200 a year, as against £150 previously. Furthermore, Bell reported, the Dean of Bristol had told him that, since fees had been abolished there 'four or five years ago', they 'have had no loss and have no reason to be dissatisfied with what the public contributes'. 'Salisbury', he reported, 'has been similarly open for two years and the Dean writes that their experience has been quite satisfactory, that no damage has been done, and there is a different atmosphere in the Cathedral, while the amount raised by voluntary contributions was practically double, £600 instead of £300'. Finally, 'Worcester has been open since about last Easter and the Dean tells me that there, too, the results have been most satisfactory, and they have had no loss, rather the reverse'.[58] By the following spring, Canterbury was open, without charge, though the Chapter took the precaution of establishing a guarantor fund, which in the event proved not necessary to call upon.

Soon Bennett was offering congratulations to the latest newcomers to the club: 'With our Chester experiment behind us, we congratulate heartily the great cathedral of St Alban's and the still greater Metropolitan Cathedral of Canterbury on freeing themselves from the obnoxious visitors' fees ...' The opportunity, however, which now presented itself, for prodding York into action was too good to be missed, and Bennett concluded: 'and [we] can hardly help hoping that the magnificent metropolitan Minster of our Province won't for long let the South monopolise the spirit of good adventure in this direction'.[59] York, however, had been aware of the changes at Chester since shortly after Bennett arrived there. In the early autumn of 1920, the Chapter Clerk of the Minster had been in correspondence with J. T. Wickham, Deputy Clerk at Chester. He was anxious to know the financial consequences of free admission. Wickham's figures, showing the immensely increased revenue via voluntary offerings he found 'astonishing'; they 'will lead to much discussion by my dean and canons', he commented sagely. Significantly, he also sought information about arrangements for explaining the architecture and history of the building – the 'history in stone', traditionally provided by cathedrals. Nevertheless, discussion did not result in action until 1927, when York finally followed Canterbury.[60] However, charges for visiting the central tower continued. It seems, also, that certain other charges (still in operation) also continued. Free admission applied mainly to the eastern part of the Minster which, of course, most tourists wished to see.[61]

Meanwhile, from Canterbury Bell was soon in touch with Bennett again, about practical details relating to an 'open' cathedral. His queries may be deduced from the numbered paragraphs of Bennett's reply, dealing with (1) costs of electricity for lighting and power; (2) gratuities to vergers; (3) Chester's opening and closing times.[62] As regards vergers, Bennett had raised their stipend from £100 to £160, which could be afforded only if 'from their side they would "play the game"'. He had told them that it was not unreasonable 'to accept a coin from well-to-do visitors on whom they had spent half an hour or more showing them round', but that they must not 'pocket the small sums which the mass of pilgrims would drop into our boxes'. Notices forbidding tips to vergers were 'horrid'.

Other instances of the influence of Bennett can be traced. At Worcester, on 23 February 1922, the Chapter resolved that 'the Chester experiment of free admission of visitors to the Nave, Choir and Chapels of the Cathedral be tried during the month of June'. But, worried about possible financial loss, the Chapter had second thoughts, suspending the arrangement, and instead ordering a notice to be displayed stating that admission fees would be devoted to care of the fabric.

It was not until 1924 that the Chapter considered the matter again. The dean was asked to find out how free and open access had worked at Salisbury (which had followed the example of Chester), and, following a satisfactory report, fees were abolished, except for the crypt and tower where, for safety reasons, visitors had to be accompanied by a verger. During the first year, according to a report in the *Worcester Echo* of 28 June 1926, 'the contributions placed in the pilgrims' boxes exceeded in amount that formerly received from a sixpenny charge'. However, in 1926 there was a temporary setback, with 'a considerable falling off due to the decrease in the number of visitors consequent on the bad weather in the early part of the year and then the [General] strike'. By June 1926, the Dean and Chapter were 'satisfied that the abolition of fees has been of very great advantage, because it creates a different atmosphere and encourages private devotions'.

Worcester followed the Chester practice of trusting visitors to put their three pence for the Guide Book in a box. Nearly 30,000 copies were sold in the first fifteen months, and it was reported that around one visitor in five took the booklet. The same proportion was reported by Bennett for Chester (where the booklet cost two pence), which by the summer of 1926 had just ordered its 110th thousand.[63] The 'one in five' (if correct) would mean that Worcester had more visitors than Chester, but the proportion must have been, in both cases, only a guess.[64]

Peterborough in 1926 informed the Cathedrals Commission that charges were still in operation, although certain kinds of visitors, estimated by the Dean and Chapter at some 50 per cent of the total, were admitted free. The cathedral authorities, for reasons which they hoped were temporary, regretted that they could not open the whole cathedral freely, every day of the week, though they hoped, eventually, to do so. They eventually opened without admission charge, wholly and at all times, in 1931, after cautiously consulting other cathedral chapters. There was no mention in February 1926 of any claim by the Dean and Chapter to have pioneered reform in an earlier day. Perhaps they were unaware of Saunders' reform.[65]

Norwich continued to levy selective fees for entry to the choir and east end of the cathedral until 1948, but even in that early post-war year, voluntary offerings, plus proceeds from sales of postcards and publications, matched those from fees. In April 1993, however, when the Chapter applied for state-aid to fund massive and unexpected repair costs, there were thinly-veiled warnings that a grant might be conditional on a general reintroduction of admission fees. Bravely, the Chapter resolutely set its face against such a step and nevertheless secured grants covering 60 per cent of the work. In an echo of Bennett, one of the cathedral's historians comments – 'There is all the difference between being a paid-up sight-seer and going into our parental home'.[66]

7

In July 1925, Bennett summed up some the results of his crusade. 'Five years ago we stood alone, to some cautious minds a dubious experiment'. To date, Bristol, Ely, Salisbury, Worcester, St Alban's, Gloucester, Canterbury, Rochester had followed; Winchester was preparing to do so.[67] Bennett, who had won special praise for recognising that Sunday was the only day when the majority of people 'who love fine architecture' could visit, regretted only that 'none of these are open between the services on Sundays'. He was a member of the Sub-Commission which visited and reported on Ely, in October 1925, and so it is not surprising to read in the Report that it 'seems a pity that the church should be closed on Sundays, even in Summer, between 4 and 6.30 p.m.' The new dean noted the comments and, the following year, opened the cathedral on Sundays from 2.30 p.m. until Evensong.[68]

It is clear that, within the new 'free' regime, many cathedrals retained some residual charges for admission to certain areas, partly as a measure of control, but also, of course, as a still welcome source of income. The main point, however, is that admission to the central, important part of the great church was free, or would soon become so. In his reports in *Chester Diocesan Gazette* Bennett does not mention the residual charges which some cathedrals still made (and were to continue to make, in some instances to the present day). Perhaps he regarded them as of less importance; perhaps he felt that to do so would diminish the force of his 'free and open cathedral' crusade. It seems unlikely that he was unaware of them. Nevertheless, because cathedrals were now in general open and largely free, the model of the 'welcoming cathedral' was being adopted. Bennett proclaimed that the position 'is won for England', and the only point of interest left was 'who is going to come in last?'[69] Within a month, he was congratulating the Dean of Manchester – 'whom Cheshire recently gave to Manchester' – on its open door.[70] The roll continued to increase, and Cheshire's man in Manchester was not the last. Although the Dean of Gloucester had reservations, Aubrey Lawrence, Chancellor of the Diocese of Worcester, a man not noted for exaggeration, expressed his perception of the new mood:

With singular unanimity and enthusiasm, Dean after Dean pays tribute to the new spirit of visitors, the increase of reverence and the desire to take part in some form of worship, formal or informal. The public as a whole begins to realise that a cathedral is not primarily for sightseers, but to appreciate its true function as the mother church of the whole diocese, the property of all its people, and the centre of all spiritual activities. Hand in hand with this goes the spirit of order and respect. 'No special precautions are needed', 'no damage is done', 'the privilege is not abused' are typical reports'.[71] Bennett's achievement, then, was considerable.

Within five years, by example and exhortation, he had set in motion a process which ultimately would affect every cathedral in the country. The Chester 'open door' model, and all that it implied, had come to stay – at least until recent years, when financial problems of a different order have caused some chapters to review their policies. Chester, however, has continued to set its face firmly against any reversion to a charging regime. With some justification, Roger Lloyd described Bennett as 'the greatest dean of his generation'.[72] His fame, by now, had spread to the United States, and, in July 1925 he told the Diocese that he had accepted an invitation to visit Washington, to talk about cathedrals.[73]

Notes

1 *The Times*, 24.7.1924, 15.
2 Ronald Knox, *Barchester Pilgrimage* (London, 1935), 184–5.
3 F. S. M. Bennett, *The Nature of a Cathedral* (London, 1925), 71.
4 I am indebted to the deans of St Asaph, Bangor, Brecon, Llandaff, and Monmouth, to Mr Nevil James (Honorary Archivist of Llandaff), Mr D. J. Llewellyn (of the Representative Body of the Church in Wales), and to Ms Sally McInnes (Assistant Archivist, The National Library of Wales), for information on cathedrals in Wales. Archbishop's House, Westminster, has confirmed that charges have never been a feature of Roman Catholic cathedrals. I am indebted also to Mr A. Bond, of the Orthodox Information Office, Prebend Gardens, London, who has been most helpful. When people enter an Orthodox church the first thing they do is to venerate an ikon. In doing this they buy and light candles, so generating revenue.
5 *Heritage and Renewal: The Report of the Archbishops' Commission on Cathedrals* (London, 1994), 147, 195. For instance, William Cobbett, who in 1830 claimed to have seen all the English cathedrals except Chester, Carlisle, York, and Durham during the 1820s, frequently contrasted (sometimes exaggeratedly) the run-down state of cathedrals with the wealth and indolence of their higher clergy, but he made no mention of entry charges. This, however, does not prove their non-existence in cathedrals he saw, or, necessarily, in the four he did not encounter (*William Cobbett's Rural Rides* (2 vols., London, 1957), 2: 260; William Cobbett, *Rural Rides*, ed. G. D. H. and M. Cole (3 vols., London, 1930), passim).
6 *Heritage and Renewal*, 147.
7 M. E. C. Walcott, *Traditions and Customs of Cathedrals* (London, 1872), as cited in Philip Barrett, *Barchester: English Cathedral Life in the Nineteenth Century* (London, 1993), 268.
8 CRO, Chap. Bk., 197, 23.6.1920.
9 CRO, Diocesan Archives, 'Chapter Book November 1816–May 1894', 436–7, 28.11.1884.
10 *Heritage and Renewal*, 195.
11 Mary Hobbs (ed.), *Chichester Cathedral: An Historical Survey* (Chichester, 1994), 117, 122 (based on West Sussex Record Office, Cap. 1/3/7, 20.1.1860).
12 Dorothy Owen (ed.), *A History of Lincoln Minster* (Cambridge, 1994),

216–7, 281, 294, 297. See also Barrett, *Barchester*, 108, 353, notes 261, 262; Church of England Record Centre, 'Returns to Cathedrals Commission Questionnaire (1926)', file CBF/CC/D. Cobbett described Lincoln Cathedral as 'magnificent', and considered it 'the finest building in the whole world' (*Rural Rides*, (1957), 2: 260).

13 Barrett, *Barchester*, 106; note 244 does not relate to Gloucester, and seems to be be misplaced.

14 *ibid.*, 108.

15 *ibid.*, 108–9; 353, note 263.

16 University of Durham Library (Archives and Special Collections), Durham Chapter Muniments, 'Chapter Acts', 20.7.1841, 18.12.1841, 18.6.1842, 20.7.1842, 20.11.1860, 24.11.1860. Free opening in 1841 was fixed at 10 a.m. to 5 p.m. (May–October); 10 a.m.to 12 noon, and 3 p.m.to 5 p.m. (November-April). Tower opening (1860) was 11 a.m.to 3 p.m. I am indebted to the Archivist, Patrick Mussett, for his generous response to my enquiries about Durham.

17 *Report of the Cathedrals Commission appointed in pursuance of a resolution of the National Assembly of the Church of England, Parts I and II: Report and Appendices* (London, 1927), Report of Sub-Commission VI.

18 *ibid.*.

19 *The Times*, 9.7.1926, 10.

20 Formerly Headmaster of Charterhouse; *ob.* in office at Peterborough, 1878 ('Obituary', *The Times*; H. Isham Longden, *Northamptonshire and Rutland Clergy* (16 vols., Northampton, 1938–1952), 12: 59). For much assistance in investigating Peterborough, I am indebted to Miss Rachel Watson, County Archivist, and Canon Jack Higham, Canon Chancellor of Peterborough.

21 *Peterborough Advertiser*, March 1853.

22 Peterborough Cathedral Archives, printed card headed 'Explanatory Remarks', dated August 1854, setting out general arrangements.

23 *ibid.*, 'Chapter Act Book', 26.10.1853, 17.10.1881, 26.6.1888, 3.8.1888 (this last resolution mentions, specifically, 'Visitors to the works going on in the Choir', and makes clear that the money collected was 'for the Restoration Fund'). For restoration, etc., see W. D. Sweeting, *The Cathedral Church of Peterborough: A Description of its Fabric and a brief History of the Episcopal See* (London, 1932), 28–33.

24 Arthur E. Bridge, 'The nineteenth century revivication of Salisbury Cathedral: Walter Kerr Hamilton, 1841–1854', in David Marcombe and C. S. Knighton (eds.), *Close Encounters* (Nottingham, 1991), 141. See also C. K. Francis Brown, *A History of the English Clergy* (London, 1953), 120–21. Brown regards Hamilton's 'ideals of cathedral reform' as being 'much closer to those of modern pioneers like Dean Bennett than they were to those of the cathedrals commission' (*ibid.*, 120).

25 Suzanne M. Edward, Keeper of the Muniments and Librarian at the Cathedral, has informed me that such charges went back to the seventeenth century.

26   Probably collected at the foot of the stairs (OED gives only 'stairfoot', from *Avenger's Tragedy*, as one arranging illicit liaisons).

27   George Godwin, *A History and Description of St Paul's Cathedral* (Thames Ditton, 1837), 47, quoted in Peter Burman, *St Paul's Cathedral* (London, 1987), 170.

28   Burman, *St Paul's*, 170.

29   *ibid.*, 170–1. For Milman, see F. L. Cross and E. A. Livingstone (eds.), *The Oxford Dictionary of the Christian Church* (Oxford, 1958, rev. ed. 1983), 916–7; for a fuller account, see *DNB*. It is significant that Milman had been appointed by Lord John Russell, then Prime Minister, who, as Home Secretary, had made the 1837 request. Russell was backed in his quest for 'liberal minds to rule the church' by Prince Albert (Owen Chadwick, *The Victorian Church* (2 vols., London, 1966–1970), 1: 235).

30   Edward Carpenter (ed.), *A House of Kings: The History of Westminster Abbey* (London, 1966), 252.

31   Receipts were: 1821, £648 11s 11d; 1822, £2,317 9s 3d; 1823, £1,664 13s 9d; 1824, £1,529 0s 5d ; 1825, £1,585 1s 0d. The royal coronation of 1822 accounts for the discrepancy between 1821 (preparations going on in the Abbey), and 1822 (influx of visitors for the coronation) (*ibid.*, 254).

32   *ibid.*, 254–5.

33   *ibid.*, 288.

34   A retirement gratuity for the Clerk of Works, and a slate slab for a urinal are amongst the more unusual items (*ibid.*, 289).

35   *Cathedrals Commission*, 57.

36   C. Robertson, 'The condition of Canterbury Cathedral at the Restoration in AD 1660', *Archaeologia Cantiana*, 10 (1876), 93–8, quoted in Patrick Collinson *et. al.* (eds.), *Canterbury Cathedral* (Oxford, 1995), 203.

37   Collinson, *Canterbury Cathedral*, 237–8.

38   *ibid.*, 234.

39   *ibid.*, 237.

40   *ibid.*, 238–9.

41   *ibid.*, 285.

42   Although the amount received was – as described in 1912 – 'considerable', nevertheless 'it would have been quite insufficient for the general upkeep, had not outside aid been invoked from time to time' (Eveleigh Woodruff and William Danks, *Memorials of the Cathedral Church and Priory of Christ in Canterbury* (London, 1912), 370). In 1892, the dean and canons accepted a halving of their stipends, in order to assist. Happily, their private means made this gesture possible (Collinson, *Canterbury Cathedral*, 269).

43   Barrett, *Barchester*, 311.

44   E. A. Burroughs, ed., *Education and Religion: A Course of Lectures given in Bristol Cathedral ...* (London, [1924]), 50. 'A short informal service' was to be 'the

normal climax' to visits.

45   Church of England Record Centre, CBF/CC/D, 'Replies to Cathedrals Commission questionnaire'.

46   *CDG*, June 1921, 88; *Report of Cathedrals Commission*, Sub-Commission VII, 306.

47   Lambeth Palace Library, Bell Papers, 193 (1919–25), ff. 227–33.

48   Karel Capek, *Letters from England* (Popular Edition, London, 1927; first publ. 1925).

49   Canterbury Cathedral Library, 'Chapter Book', 25.11.1921. I am indebted to Dr D. M. Owen for this reference.

50   Letter from Dr Dorothy Owen to A.B., 21.7.1989.

51   *Report of Cathedrals Commission*, 150.

52   Lincoln's reply to the Cathedrals Commission questionnaire (1925) states: 'for Choir and Cloisters names are signed and 6d paid. Clergy of Diocese free. A fee for the Great Tower', seeming to imply that entry to the nave was free (Church of England Record Office, CBF/CC/D). I am indebted to Ms Brenda Hough, of the Church Records Centre, for tracing this reference. See also note 56 below.

53   *Report of Cathedrals Commission*, 234–5.

54   *The Times*, 31.7.1924. 8.

55   *Report of Cathedrals Commission*, Sub-Commission I, 44; *CDG*, Apr. 1925, 54.

56   In detail, the developments are as follows.

In the eighteenth century: visitors paid conducting verger.

In 1883: payments by visitors to choir, chapter house, cloisters and tower to be made to new Visitors Fund (see note 12 above).

In 1890: nave and great transept free; choir, chapter house, and cloisters a fee of not less than 6d in return for which a plan of the Minster, with a summary of its features, was supplied (Murray's *Handbook to Lincolnshire* (1890), 34).

In 1900: as in 1890 (*Illustrated Lincolnshire* (1900)).

In 1907: as in 1900 with addition as below; whole cathedral free admission after 2 p.m. on last Saturday of each month (*Boots Guide to Lincoln* (1907 edn)).

In 1925: nave and transept not mentioned (implying no change); choir and cloisters, visitors' names to be signed and 6d. paid, clergy of diocese free; Great Tower, fee (unspecified amount) charged (Reply to Cathedrals Commission questionnaire (1925), section XVI, qu. 2: 'Is a fee charged during [opening hours] for admission to (a) any part of the Cathedral; (b) any building or buildings in the precincts?')

In 1934: debate as to whether to continue charging or to invite contributions in lieu, no decision to change.

In 1939: charges abandoned; contributions invited in lieu (p.c. Dorothy Owen); 'for the present no charge is made for admission to the choir and cloisters' (*Lincoln

Cathedral Notes, October 1939).
In 1940: charges resumed. H.M. Forces, and others in official uniform free (David M. Thompson, 'Historical survey, 1750–1949', in Dorothy Owen (ed.), *A History of Lincoln Minster* (Cambridge, 1994), 307).
I am indebted to Dr Nicholas Bennett, Vice-Chancellor and Librarian of Lincoln Cathedral, for much guidance and assistance in connection with Lincoln.

57   Lambeth Palace Library, Bell Papers, 193 (1919–25), f. 23, Bennett to Bell, 18.2.1924; f. 25, Bennett to Bell, 14.4.1924. For other correspondence, see, e.g., ff. 61, 91, 251, 252, 370.

58   *ibid.*, 193 (1919–25), f. 227–33.

59   *CDG*, Mar. 1925, 35. That there were no 'extra' charges at Canterbury seems to be confirmed in Bell's rhyming jingle of 1928 (quoted in R. C. Jasper, *George Bell, Bishop of Chichester* (London, 1967), 55), recalling that 'we enabled all nobodies to see / The Whole Cathedral without fee'.

60   York Minster Library, H 12/3/ 'Minutes etc.' and D 4/11 'Letter Book, 1920–3', 123, quoted in G. E. Aylmer and R. Cant, *A History of York Minster* (Oxford, 1977), 544.

61   Information from Ms S. Costley, Archivist, York Minster, 16.2.1995.

62   Bennett sent him a copy of his 1924 accounts. and pointed to the £120 for lighting, and £31 for power and organ. At the end of his letter he mentioned that the annual cost of repairing the lights varied, but he had no figures. Chester opened at 7 a.m., and closed at 9 p.m. on light evenings, earlier on dark evenings, or when there were too few visitors to justify keeping on the lights. In the summer the organ would be playing for an hour, with no collection (Canterbury Cathedral Archives, 'Deanery Papers', Box 7). I am indebted to Professor Keith Robbins for a copy of this. For further changes effected by Bell, see Jasper, *George Bell*. See also the invaluable account of the modern cathedral in Keith Robbins, 'The Twentieth Century, 1898–1994', in Collinson, *Canterbury Cathedral*, 297–340.

63   *Worcester Echo*, 28.6.1926; *CDG*, Aug. 1926, 126.

64   Worcester Cathedral Library, 'Chapter Minutes', 23.2.1922, 25.5.1922; 15.3.1924, 16.4.1924, 29.5.1924, 23.6.1924; 'Minute Book of the Worcester Cathedral Council', 23.6.1921; 16.6.1922; 17.7.1926. I am indebted to R. R. Stratton of Worcester Cathedral Library for tracing these references.

65   *Cathedrals Commission*, Report of Sub-Commission III, 162. For consultations with other cathedrals, see correspondence in Peterborough Cathedral Archives.

66   Peter Burbridge in I. Atherton *et. al.* (eds.), *Norwich Cathedral* (London/ Rio Grande, U.S.A., 1996), 'Epilogue', 752, 754–5.

67   Rochester informed the Cathedrals Commission in April 1926 that it had not found the results of abolishing charges immediately 'financially encouraging', but did not report a loss and did not reverse its decision (*Cathedrals Commission*, Report

of Sub-Commission II, 70). However, charges were retained for the crypt, treasury, and chapter room. The Chapter's reply to the Cathedrals Commission questionnaire (1925) stated: 'A charge of 6d per person for viewing the Crypt, and 1/- extra per person for viewing the Treasury and the Chapter Room' (Church of England Record Centre, CBF/CC/D). Similarly, Bristol still charged sixpence for the library, vestries, and chapter house (Burroughs, *Bristol Cathedral*, 50; *Cathedrals Commission*, Report of Sub-Commission VII, 312).

68 *The Times*, 30.7.1924, 8; *CDG*, July 1925, 107–8; *Cathedrals Commission*, Report of Sub-Commission III, 150, 151.

69 *CDG*, July 1925, 107–8.

70 *CDG*, Aug. 1925, 124. Bennett had been a member of the Cathedrals Commission team which visited and reported on Manchester, in June-July 1925 (*Cathedrals Commission*, 93–113).

71 'Free Cathedrals', *Worcester Echo*, 28.6.1926. Aubrey T. Lawrence, as a nominee of the Ecclesiastical Commission, had been a member of the Cathedrals Commission's Sub Commission V which visited and reported on Chester Cathedral, 21–23.4.1926 (*Cathedrals Commission*, 9, 228).

72 Roger Lloyd, *The Church of England: 1900–1965* (London, 1966), 393; see also, 45, 387, 392–9, 401–2.

73 *CDG*, Aug. 1925, 124.

Frank Selwyn Macaulay Bennett, c. 1935

above Family gathering, Sparkford Rectory, 1927, including (back row) Bennett's brother George and sisters Edith, Mildred and Evelyn Bennett; Frank with his wife Ida and son Frank; (front row) Bennett's brother-in-law Trevor Griffiths; his wife Emily and daughters Violet, Florence and Isabel; the rector, Bennett's uncle, Charles Bennett

left The title-page from Bennett's most important book, *The Nature of a Cathedral*, published in 1925

The Nature
of a Cathedral.

"Look unto the rock whence ye are hewn, and to the hole of the pit whence ye are digged."—*Isaiah* li., 1.

F. S. M. BENNETT,
Dean of Chester.

CHESTER:
Phillipson and Golder Ltd.
LONDON:
A. R. Mowbray & Co., Ltd.,
28, Margaret Street, Oxford Circus, W. 1.
OXFORD: 9, High Street.
1925.
Printed in Great Britain.

above The new car, December 1926, with Bennett, his wife, Ida, and his two younger sisters

left Fancy dress: Bennett as Archbishop Baldwin, Chester Pageant, 1910

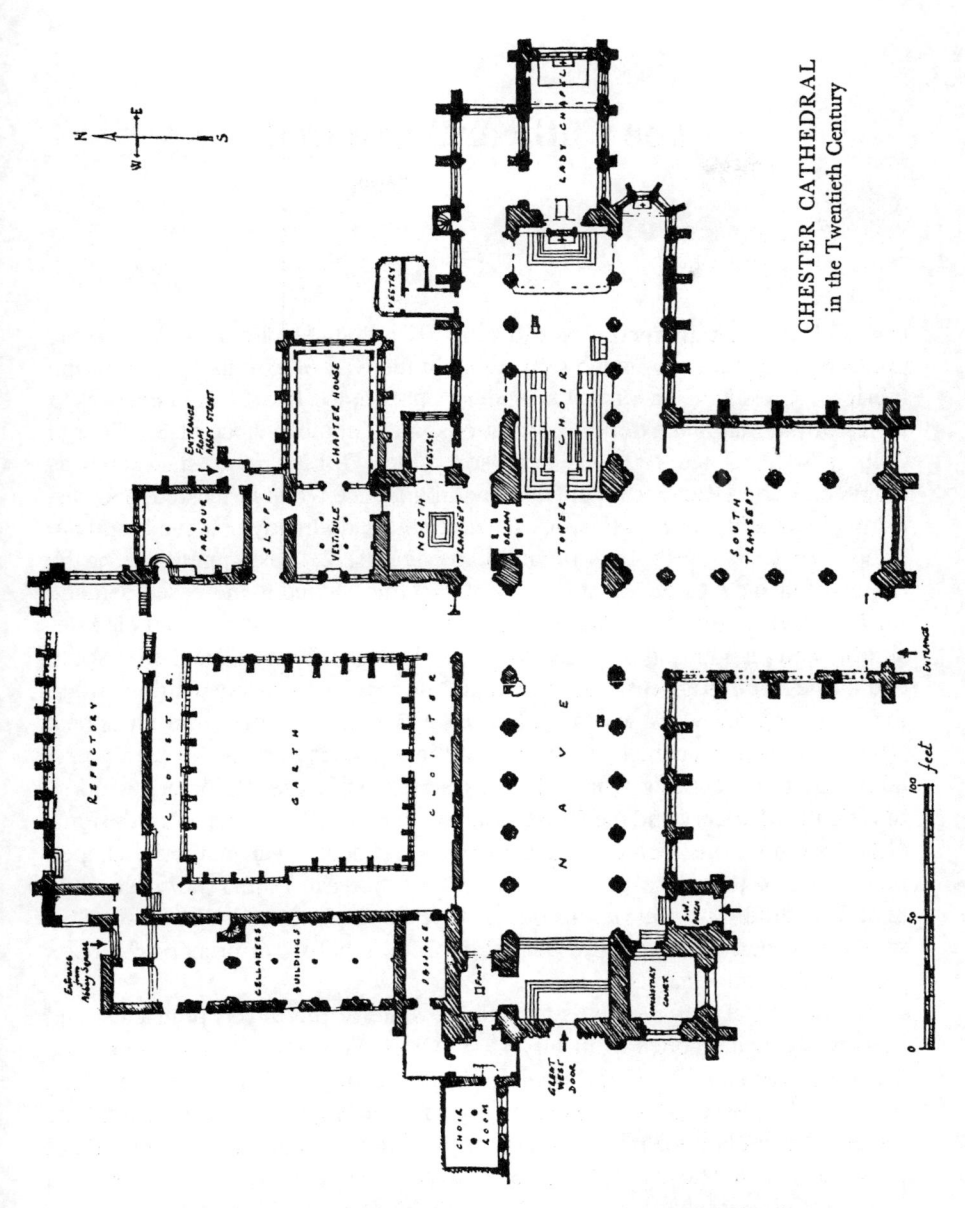

Plan of Chester Cathedral, 1958. The 'vestry' adjoining the north transept is Bennett's 'sacristy', with the St Anselm window at the east

V

The Cathedral restored

1

It was clear, when Bennett took office in 1920, that, despite the efforts of his predecessors, there was much to be done in the way of essential repair to the fabric of Chester Cathedral. Its modern appearance had been shaped by a series of internal and external restorations, most notably those of Sir George Gilbert Scott. Since 1907 his grandson, Giles Gilbert Scott, had acted as architect to the Dean and Chapter, providing advice when requested, and carrying out specific work when instructed. Scott had already achieved national fame, four years earlier by winning at the age of 22, the competition for the design of the new cathedral at Liverpool, and this had led to increased demand for his services by other clients. His early work at Chester had included designing and planning 'the rebuilding of the doorway, buttress &c. at the South end of the South transept', the dean and four canons each contributing £40 to the cost, and the work to start when £4,000 was available from an appeal which had been launched.[1] Scott had continued, over the next thirteen years, advising, and executing work when instructed. The great Refectory window of reticulated tracery and the Rood, both executed in 1913, were to his designs. Other commissions included the Cheshire Regiment's war memorial chapel, restoration of the monastic buildings, and of the east, north, and west cloisters. The building firm, Thompsons of Peterborough, carried out most of his work, and their surveyor often acted on Scott's behalf in preparing reports requested by the Chapter.

On the eve of Bennett's arrival, the state of the tower, pinnacles, and bells was causing concern. In July 1919, when the bells of Chester churches had rung out to celebrate the signing of the Treaty of Versailles, those of the cathedral had been silent because to sound them might have endangered the tower.[2] But money for repairs was at a premium, and the aged dean did not press for action. Shortly after his death, in November 1919, the Chapter asked Scott to find out what was needed to make the tower and pinnacles safe, 'at the least possible cost'.[3] By February 1920 there had been no progress, and so

Scott was asked to 'put forward his survey ... and to obtain definite estimates for this and such work as is necessary to be done to the bells with a view to having everything in order to present to a new Dean'.[4] However, Scott does not seem to have visualised acting until the new dean arrived – perhaps in order to have his personal instructions – and he therefore wrote to Thompson as follows. 'I hear that the new Dean is to be Mr Bennett of Hawarden, and I gather that the appointment will be definitely made at an early date, so I hope that before long we shall be able to proceed with the lowering of the turrets, and with the urgently required works of repair and restoration to the tower, and its abutments.'[5]

But Bennett had far-reaching plans for the cathedral, which required the detailed attention of an architect who would initiate constructive thinking, and make recommendations, rather than be reactive. By mid-August – and probably earlier – he had decided to dispense with Scott's services. On 18 August, R. T. Wickham, the Deputy Clerk to the Chapter, wrote to Scott: 'while nothing is settled ... [the Dean] finds a feeling among the Canons, which he shares, that you are so very busy that you are not always available and that they ought to have an architect with whom they can more often be in close touch'.[6]

Scott was in the USA when the letter arrived, thus lending point to Bennett's remarks, but his staff immediately endeavoured to reassure Wickham: 'There will be no danger of Mr Scott's not being available at any time to visit Chester and to attend to any work which it may be intended to carry out there'. They pointed out that, as Scott had not held any formal appointment as architect, he had never suggested carrying out work unless his advice was specifically sought. This attitude, they said, might have been misunderstood by the Chapter.[7] Bennett would not be side-tracked. On 27 September 1920, the Chapter formally resolved to appoint David Theodore Fyfe, of 2 Gray's Inn Square, London, as 'Practical Architect to the Cathedral', and Professor W. R. Lethaby (1857–1931) was appointed as consulting architect.[8]

On his return from America, Scott was dismayed to learn of his curt dismissal. Bennett wrote to him, immediately after the chapter meeting, quite agreeably but firmly. He offered grateful thanks for the 'care and skill' with which Scott had carried out 'not a few' very important pieces of work, and set out his reasons for the change. A man of experience and skill was needed, but one 'not involved in too many great works and undertakings to allow his making the repair of our fabric a first interest, giving it his frequent and personal supervision'. The Chapter had selected Fyfe, of whom Bennett had formed a high opinion before he came to Chester (he had done work for Bennett at Hawarden). The change would not affect work which Scott already had in hand, for instance, St Leonard's Chapel.[9] Scott wrote at once to seek a meeting with Bennett.[10]

But Bennett was adamant: Fyfe's appointment 'as our permanent architect' had 'been before the Chapter, and quite deliberately decided. I cannot discuss it personally'. Scott believed that there had been 'lack of consideration' for which he clearly blamed Bennett. He knew that he had not held an appointment as 'official architect', but had 'not unreasonably' expected that if such a post were to be created, he would receive the appointment, and would have then kept the whole building constantly under supervision. His relations with Dean and Chapter, for the last 13 years, had been 'most cordial and friendly', and he was at a loss to understand the reason for the treatment he had received. In the amendments to his scribbled draft, for his typist, one senses his bubbling resentment.[11]

It must be said that there is no evidence, in the correspondence between Scott and the cathedral, between 1907 and 1920, of dissatisfaction with him. In 1920, however, there was a new dean, with new expectations. Indeed, Scott, with his mounting Liverpool and other commitments, might have not found it easy to meet Bennett's heavy demands on his time. Fyfe's appointment, not surprisingly, gave rise to some acrimony between Scott and Fyfe.[12] Bennett must have approached Fyfe even before Wickham wrote to Scott on 18 August, because Fyfe wrote to Scott on 25 August, seeking some sort of approval from him, mentioning that he had known of his possible appointment 'for some weeks', and had 'only a few days ago' learned from 'my friend F. S. M. Bennett' that 'he was practically certain that there would be no difficulty as far as the Chapter were concerned'.[13] The designation of Bennett as 'my friend' is significant, and Wickham's initial comment on the Chapter's role indicates Bennett's ascendancy. There had been no hints at a need for change in Darby's day, but Scott's lack of response over the bells, during the vacancy in the deanery, may have antagonised the Canons, doubtless keen to impress a new dean.

The new architect, David Theodore Fyfe, was aged 45, slightly senior to Scott, younger than Bennett, and with useful experience behind him. Educated at Albany Academy in Glasgow, he had served his articles with John (later Sir John) Burnet, and had been in Crete with Sir Arthur Evans' team investigating the site of Knossos. When Bennett appointed him, he was in practice in London. Two years later, he was appointed to the prestigious post of Director of Cambridge's new School of Architecture, where he remained until he retired, but he continued to serve the cathedral.[14] In correspondence with Scott, anxious to play down any jealousies, he had compared himself disparagingly with Scott, whose metier was 'positive architecture ... not the more hum-drum clerk of working that I would expect to get' – the ultimate in would-be self-effacement.[15] In fact, The Chapter had acquired a man well placed in his profession.[16]

Even before the Chapter had formally appointed Fyfe and Lethaby, Bennett had arranged for Lethaby to inspect and report on the cathedral. His report is dated 14 September. Bennett was in a hurry. Scott learned of what was going on in Chester, and resented the slight: 'other architects are called in to inspect the building even before the Chapter have dispensed with my services'.[17] Bennett was merely adopting a position entirely consistent with what he always regarded as his first duty, to serve the cathedral. He was under no obligation to Scott, with whom the Chapter had no formal contract or agreement. Fyfe's own report is dated 20 October 1920. There is no evidence to show whether he had inspected the cathedral prior to 27 September, despite Scott's comments about 'other architects'. However, as late as 20 October, the date on his report, he was still eagerly trying to convey to Scott that he would not accept the appointment without some concurrence from him. Scott's curt 'do as you wish regarding the appointment', of 21 October, concluded the affair.[18] There can be little doubt that Fyfe served the Chapter well. He had clearly been anxious to secure the appointment, and Bennett, who usually knew his man, had been determined to have him. Fyfe would have preferred to have been able to accept without antagonising Scott, who had upbraided him bitterly, saying that if architects did not stick together, they would never ensure their position as a profession.

2

Lethaby's report, dated 14 September, suggested that the north-west prospect of the cathedral buildings should be considered as a whole, to make all 'pleasant and orderly'. This called for tidying up and planting. Work on the roof of the the Refectory, only partly complete, should be continued. With the necessary repairs, the Refectory could be made into 'a magnificent hall'. He considered, too, the general repairs necessary in many parts of the cathedral itself, for example, the north clerestory, the walls of the tower, the parapet of the south transept, whose repair was 'urgently required'.[19]

Fyfe's report of 20 October was very thorough. It described work which should be done to the walls, the Tower, clerestory external stonework, and the external walls of the south transept. Particularly urgent was the North wall, which was 'in a lamentable state and leans over in such a way which might become serious if not attended to'. The wall from the new Choir School was also 'in danger of collapse in places'. The existing roof of the Refectory needed 'complete overhaul'.[20] Fyfe was quite categorical about the bells. The platform in the Tower 'in its present state is quite unsuited for such use'.[21] This perhaps prompted Bennett's rueful reflection that he 'came on the scene too late', to get the re-hanging of the bells adopted as the Chester war memorial.[22] The East and West external walling of the South Transept, 'though possibly not in a dangerous condition ... is liable to rapid deterioration in its present state, and is very unsightly'.

The total cost of urgent repairs Fyfe estimated at between £20,000 and £30,000, but this included no provision for either the re-seating of the bells, nor the provision of a 'completely usable refectory'. It was the first modern report, in this sort of detail, on the cathedral's fabric, though, of course, the Chapter had not, prior to the advent of Bennett, commissioned such a survey, and seem to have been daunted by possible financial implications. Nor was Darby, latterly, able to provide strong leadership. Fyfe concluded justly that 'buildings of the magnitude and historical importance of Chester Cathedral require continued supervision if they are to be kept in a proper state'.[23]

In his 'strategic plan' Bennett had made his first objectives the glazing of the cloisters and the refurbishment of the Refectory. These he regarded as the basic essentials, if his vision of the cathedral, as it should be, were to be realised. The self-financing cloister project he had already launched. It was merely a matter of continuing to advertise it to the Diocese, from time to time, via his 'Dean's Notes'. The Refectory was a bigger proposition. Its renovation was not a new idea. For example, at the end of 1919, Honorary Canon John H. Thorpe of Stockport, floated the idea of restoration 'as a "war" or "peace" memorial ... because we do not appear as churchmen of a great and wealthy Diocese to be able to meet under one roof in the Cathedral City. How long is this to continue?'[24]

In 1920, the restoration of the Refectory was not, as we have seen, from a purely structural point of view, the most urgent work required. Available finance was the key factor in the decision. As Fyfe put it, 'under ordinary circumstances it would have been a nice question if it should obtain precedence over the north wall of the Nave Clerestory, that priceless piece of work which escaped whole from the hands of nineteenth century restoration. Mr Rigby's bequest [specifically for the refurbishment of the refectory] fortunately settled the question, and work on the Refectory was begun'. The cathedral, after all, though in urgent need of repair in parts was wholly usable, whereas Bennett's ultimate priority, the Refectory, was only partially usable. Moreover, a restored Refectory, 'potentially a great hall', would be of service, not only to the cathedral and the diocese, but to 'the community as a whole'.[25] It would thereby help to achieve another of the objectives set out in Bennett's plan, the linking of Cathedral and City. By the end of 1922, the Refectory had been put into 'a thoroughly sound state'.[26] At the same time the Undercroft was renovated, and it was eventually fitted with a 'serve-yourself' counter. Bennett had heard the term 'caffeteria' (*sic*) in the United States, and so the cathedral must have one.[27]

The total cost of the work was £9,662, the major item being 'Stonework and General Works', at £6,150 – roughly the size of the Rigby bequest.[28] In a footnote, Bennett reported his satisfaction. The total cost of the work (including architects' fees, and a memorial window to Rigby) was £11,760, a sum virtually covered by monies received to date. Work on the North Wall would await further cash flow. Finally, he had reduced the £3,000 debt he had inherited as dean to £2,000.[29] After Bennett's day, F. H. Crossley designed the present ceiling of the refectory, and the work was executed on the eve of the Second World War.

One 'welcoming' change which happily cost very little may be briefly mentioned here. This was the introduction into the cathedral of a Children's Corner – a furnished space for the sole use of children – a concept Bennett appears to have evolved at Hawarden. This innovation was widely copied elsewhere, and hence is discussed later in this study, in Chapter VII, section 5.

In the space of two and a half years, Bennett had materially improved the amenities of the cathedral. Indeed, he now published a priority scale by function for each of the parts. From the most sacred, the Church itself, there was a descending order via Cloisters, Chapter House, Refectory, to the Parlour (now supplied with magazines and notepaper), where 'it will be permissible to smoke a cigarette'.[30] All were in use for the 1922 Diocesan Conference, and were clearly appreciated by delegates. Bennett enthused at the success of this event. 'As never before in its long history', he wrote, 'the Diocese occupied the Cathedral for its Conference and obviously found the doing so wholly enjoyable'.[31] One who was present recorded his impressions. The Diocese now had – 'A home of its own. A mind of its own. A very beautiful home and a very lively mind'. There was a spirit of 'charity', even between opponents, perhaps 'caught from the great buildings which the dean's imagination had provided'.[32] So it was to continue over the next fifteen years, and beyond. The open cathedral was now manifestly the welcoming cathedral, and increasingly other deans took note.

3

Meanwhile, the Chapter's rising salary bill was causing concern; increases in lay ministers' salaries alone cost an extra £700 per annum. Accordingly, at the end of 1923, the Chapter reviewed Fyfe's fees. Fyfe was now installed in his Cambridge post, a situation not visualised in 1920. Nor can the Chester consultancy have been a disadvantage to him in his application to Cambridge. On 27 November 1923, the Chapter Clerk was instructed to write to say that as he was 'living so far from Chester' (shades of Scott!), and as the 'expenditure of £10,000 which was contemplated when he was appointed had been exceeded,...and that as the expenditure must of necessity be much less', he was asked to accept a retainer of £50, 'with a commission of 5½ per cent on such works as shall be definitely be brought under his superintendance ... but this percentage is not to accrue unless definitely so arranged by the Dean'. The whole arrangement was to be reviewed annually.[33] At the same time, the local Clerk of the Works, Haswell, was given increased authority, with an annual fee of £50, plus commission of 12½ per cent on work done by him in his own trade – stonemasonry. He was to superintend all work done in the cathedral, and was empowered to order such work, when authorised by the Dean or Chapter Clerk. Apart from saving money, the new joint arrangements for Architect and Clerk of Works would make for prompt action, high on Bennett's agenda.[34]

In October 1921 Bennett launched a financial Appeal. He paid tribute to Deans Anson, Howson, and Darby, thanks to whom the bulk of the cathedral was in 'admirable repair'. Now, over the next three years, £20,000 was needed, and he hoped that parishes would contribute generously.[35] He had prepared a lecture on the cathedral, and enlisted volunteers ready to give it in the parishes. The first stage was to culminate at the St Werburgh's Day Festival, in the cathedral, the following 21 June 1922. In line with his thinking on linking Parish and Cathedral, he sent each of the 260 parishes what he described as a 'St Werburgh's Purse'.[36] There would be a 'grand presentation' of these (duly filled!), at the service. Bennett hoped, thereby, to promote a competitive spirit amongst parishes.[37] A 'St Werburgh's Purse', he wrote was only 'a little ornamental bag ... visible symbol ... to add a touch of romance to the prosaic ... a pretty little beggar'. More prosaically, he could also provide copies of the architects' reports, which named 'a larger sum as necessary than I would have dared ask for'.[38]

The experiment of the Parish Purses was not a great success, and their presentation must have been something of an anti-climax. After the St Werburgh Festival Bennett announced that, although '£10,555 had found its way into our Cathedral Restoration Fund since we made our appeal a year ago', only 'about sixty of the two hundred and eighty parishes of the Diocese [had] contributed [donating] altogether £885'. The actual figures present an even more dismal picture of parochial support. The £885 came not only from 66 parishes but also from 23 individual contributors and societies. Mothers' Union branches gave a further £39 15s 0d. Parishes had their own priorities, and Bennett cannot have forgotten that, as a parish priest, he had never evinced much enthusiasm for channelling resources to his diocesan cathedral – hence, perhaps, the exceptional trouble he was now taking to motivate parishes. His 'belief ... that more interest in the centre' would make funds flow in 'for Church purposes of every manner and sort' must have been received with some scepticism at the periphery, and was, as he admitted, 'probably the biassed belief of a Dean'.[39]

Nevertheless, Bennett determined that the St Werburgh Festival and Fair should be an annual event. But he wisely did not repeat the St Werburgh Purses experiment in 1923, seeking instead, contributions in labelled envelopes. Though parishes sent some £250, this did not represent a major contribution. Bennett consulted the Greater Chapter, composed largely of parish priests, on making the cathedral 'more and more the spiritual home of the Diocese and the means of expressing its corporate life'[40] – doubtless the consultation also included reference to the necessary cash nexus. No recommendations were reported to subsequent meetings of the resident Chapter, and as Bennett gives no account in the *Diocesan Gazette* of any decisions, it is safe to assume that the seed fell on stony ground.

In other respects, the 1923 St Werburgh Festival, was a great success. Bennett recruited the Archbishop of York, Cosmo Lang, to preach and Lang was impressed. The whole occasion, he said, had given him 'a new vision of what our Cathedral Churches might be'. There was a procession, with singing, to the now fully functional Refectory, where there was tea on sale, with profits to the Restoration Fund. The Prince of Wales had sent a useful donation of £50, a stimulus to others, not least the local establishment.[41] Meanwhile, Bennett himself continued to make generous personal contributions by dedicating all the profits of his various books, as they appeared, to the Restoration Fund.[42]

By April 1923, the cathedral general account had closed with a credit balance, 'for the first time in living memory', a tribute to the financial management of Bennett. He now revealed, in *Chester Diocesan Gazette*, that he had been warned, before he became dean, about the cathedral's shaky finances.[43] By April, the Restoration Fund had received £12,000, which would pay for all the work done, and also reduce the inherited debt on the Fund from £3,000 to £1,800. Another £8,000 was still needed to meet the target.[44] Bennett wondered if he 'might not cross the Atlantic another day like ... Dean Howson, and once more impress Chester with the generosity of our American cousins'.[45] An invitation did come three years later, but by then not to a mere suppliant for dollars but to the now renowned cathedral reformer. In the meantime, some £18,000 had been received by December 1923 (and largely spent), including the Rigby legacy, 'special gifts', and £2,000 from the cathedral. The Diocese had contributed a third. Receipts from Pilgrims would be ten times the 'miserly' £120 received 'through obnoxious sixpenny fees' in their final year.[46] The Tower was now 'safe and sound'; the conventual buildings in good repair, and in use daily. The wooden floor, planned for the Refectory, would be deferred until it could be paid for from the 'energies of the Nave Choir and other friends, and the fruits of entertaining pilgrims', and an expected £80 from sales of Bennett's book on Coué. £5,000 was still needed to repay the inherited debt, and fund North wall restoration. If the Diocese could give £4,000, Bennett would find the 'odd £1,000' from the cathedral itself.[47] Before 1923, the priority had been the fabric. Now, chairs were repaired, shabby hassocks replaced, a sacristry formed at the East end of the Chapter

House, and electrical installations and the library improved. 'Every year', Bennett wrote, in January 1924, 'the Cathedral finds itself better and better equipped for the service of its big Family [the Diocese]'.[48]

Bennett's own literary labours materially assisted the Restoration Fund. By February his Coué book had already raised some £350, and, in April, he told Bell, the new Dean of Canterbury, that 'it will bring into our Repair Fund, something like £500'. He had recently visited Bennett, who was not above soliciting Bell's help in trying to get *The Times* to notice his second new book, just published, also in aid of the Fund. He sent Bell a couple of copies, one for himself, and the other he asked Bell to send to *The Times*. 'There is also just a touch of sportingness which might induce the Times to take a little more kindly interest in such an unpretentious work, than they would be ordinarily willing to do'.[49] The *Times Literary Supplement* did review it, mentioning that profits would go to the Chester Restoration Fund.[50] Bennett also sent Bell some photographs, for the *The Times*, of the Cathedral repair work, which he thought were 'not without general interest', but these do not seem to have appeared, even though Bennett had offered to pay for the blocks.[51]

The pictures Bennett sent to Bell were probably copies of some of those which he published, in May 1924, in his '£5,000 Appeal' leaflet, This showed, for example, the North Wall repair, captioned 'Just in time and none too soon'; the West End, in 1920, 'windowless and roofless', juxtaposed with the same in 1923 – 'a credit to all concerned'. A photograph of the Interior in 1922, 'full of mess and out of gear', was set alongside the same in 1923, 'hospitality ready for a party of pilgrims'; similarly treated was the North West Corner, in 1912 described as 'mouldy and tottering', and the same area in 1920, now 'safe sound and beautiful'. It was an effective variant on the propaganda technique of double presentation, which extends at least from Cranach in the sixteenth century to Pugin in the nineteenth, and Bennett used it effectively. The leaflet carried a solemn reminder from Professor Lethaby, the cathedral's consultant architect, that – 'The nation's antiquities are a great inheritance entrusted for a short time to our care', balanced by another cheerful exhortation from Bennett worthy of McGonigall:

> One shilling, five or ten or twenty
> If all send something, we'll get plenty.
> So with best wishes, as any toast,
> Here goes ... through the post.[52]

With summer, the pilgrims flocked to Chester in increasing numbers. In June 1924 Bennett reported that the boxes had brought in £1,060, six times the amount produced by the old sixpenny fee, and the parishes had made their modest, but welcome, contribution at the now annual St Werburgh's Day Festival. By July, £1,561 had come in, towards the target of £2,000 which Bennett had set for 1924. 'Perhaps', he ventured in his August 'Notes', 'during the remaining five months some other parishes will think kindly of their Mother Church in Chester and send a modest gift for remaining needful repairs'.[53] Now that the glazing of the cloisters was proceeding satisfactorily, while twelve more lights were on order for new donors,[54] he hoped for a fountain and a pool (with goldfish) in the centre of the cloister garth.

'The worst of a great place like a Cathedral', he said, 'is that when you have got one thing you want another'. A 'place' was now needed for the Royal Air Force, a focus, where it would be represented.[55] It was to be four years before this ambition could be realised. Bennett's hint about the cloister garth produced a response from another donor, Sir A. V. Paton, who came up with £100 to repair the old reservoir in the centre.[56] He followed it up, eight months later, with another donation of £50 to complete the work, as Bennett wanted it, so that the fountain could be playing for the 1925 St Werburgh Festival (for which each parish received an envelope), since the procession of robed parish clergy and others would pass through the cloister after the service, on its way to refreshments in the Refectory.[57] During the summer of 1925 Bennett was in Normandy, with Ida, his son Frank, and sister Edith. He brought back a tiny elm from the Abbey Church of Bec (whence, of course, Anselm had come to Chester), and planted it in the garden in the Cloisters.[58] Eleven years later it was a flourishing young tree.[59] Today, alas, it is no more. Bennett is said also to have planted a Glastonbury Thorn, which he had propagated from the one at Glastonbury.[60]

By 1925, Bennett's reputation already stood high. He was invited to serve on the Cathedrals Commission; he received an invitation to visit America; and his mature thoughts on cathedrals were published. He described *The Nature of a Cathedral*, as another book he had 'ventured to perpetrate'. Profits, as usual would go to the Restoration Fund, to help reach the £1,000, which he hoped his books would eventually bring to the cathedral.[61]

4

Bennett's early years as dean saw the renovation of the cathedral and its surrounds undertaken at a fairly hectic pace, some of the work being of an emergency nature. His remaining years enabled details to be filled in and the further development of a 'welcoming' institution. By 1927, restoration and repair were completed. Bennett considered his appointment of Fyfe to have been amply vindicated: 'None', he declared, 'can overestimate the credit due to him'.[62] Refectory, parlour, undercroft, cloister, tower, and nave, had all been renovated, as envisaged in the 1921 scheme. It had not been realised, then, that the tower would have to be re-roofed, and the north transept roof overhauled, also. Now, by April 1927, the repair of the north transept wall and roof was finished. Fyfe had clearly got on well with Haswell and praised his 'personal initiative, care and resource'.[63] Bennett announced, triumphantly, 'Every atom of the old mediaeval roof that could be conserved has been conserved'.[64] The cloister was now fully glazed, with the exception of one of the 125 lights of the plan, almost all the personal biographies underneath them written by Bennett's son, Francis, who had suggested the gallery of saints, and had composed nearly all the 'many delightfully worded notices of worthies connected with us or in our Cathedral Calendar'.

It was thus, with considerable pride, that Bennett announced that Francis was about to be ordained deacon, in the cathedral, prior to becoming assistant curate at Northwich, within the Diocese. He would be greatly missed in Chester, not least by his father. Looking back over seven years and scanning the cathedral with its 'many items which make it a real home', Bennett felt unable to 'estimate how much is owed to him for ideas which have won their way to men's approval'. Indeed, he averred, 'He's done the work; I've got the credit'.[65]

Bennett, the parish priest writ large, attended to detail which some might have thought beneath the notice of a dean. Proper lighting and acoustics were of prime importance if the building was to be used to best advantage. An article in *The Guardian*, early in 1928, tells us what he was doing at Chester, and why. He had taken 'infinite pains' over lighting. Eye comfort, aesthetic aspects, atmosphere for private prayer, were foremost condiderations. His pulpit was now lit so that the preacher's face was visible to the congregation, but without bright lights to irritate preacher or listeners. He had recently preached, elsewhere, 'towards what might to all intents and purposes have been a motor-car headlight'. At Chester, in 1920, he had replaced all clear electric bulbs in the cathedral with the opalescent variety; a similar change would transform 'not a few churches of our diocese'.[66] Perhaps his defective eye made him especially conscious of glare. Brass candlesticks with electric bulbs were an eyesore, and the illumination of special objects, by bright secreted lights, called for 'the greatest artistic discretion, or the result will be vulgar'.

In the pulpit, Bennett had a clear delivery; but as a delegate to the 1928 Diocesan Conference pointed out later, 'It is not everyone that has the clear diction of the Dean of Chester'.[67] The widow of Alderman David Hewitt responded, and gave loudspeakers, in memory of her husband.[68] Bennett promptly despatched Canon Hughes and a colleague to Worcester Cathedral, to inspect the equipment installed there. They came back with a glowing report, and in November 1929 the Chapter accepted a tender for installation, at a cost of £294.[69] A bronze tablet to Hewitt was inscribed, 'He that hath ears to hear, let him hear'.[70] Six years later, after Mrs Hewitt's death, her daughter provided funds to update the system, as a memorial to her mother. Again, Bennett sought advice, and adopted equipment recommended by York Minster and St George's Chapel, Windsor.[71]

Hughes also told Bennett about some 'quite admirable' seats in the nave of Worcester Cathedral, and Bennett (ever the parish priest, and keen to promote improvements in churches) promptly recommended these to the diocese.[72] He was not yet able to afford new seating in the cathedral – there were other priorities – but he obtained half a dozen of the chairs (with 'folding and tilting seats'), as samples, for display in Chester to parish representatives. If he had been equipping a new church, he told them, he would have bought these, and put out only as many as were required for each service.[73] He did, however, provide one special chair, an episcopal seat. As usual, he drew a response from some generous donor, and the chair was donated, in 1935, in memory of a parish priest.[74]

The overall cost of the north transept repairs and improvements eventually amounted to some £5,000. The Duke of Westminster, with whom Bennett was on good terms, donated £1,500; Mrs Henry Gladstone, a good friend of the Bennetts, gave £200, and the cathedral provided a similar sum. An appeal produced further contributions. Bennett dedicated the North Transept to the memory of the Countess Grosvenor, the Duke's mother, and the Duke promptly gave a further £2,200.[75] In the course of the work on the north transept, the old Norman arch, the oldest part of the cathedral, was opened up (the filling was largely rubble, and not structural stone).[76] There was now open access into the thirteenth century chapel, which Bennett converted into a sacristy.[77]

The open arch also exposed to view the depressing coloured glazing of the sacristy window, which Bennett determined to replace with glass portraying some scene from the life of the founder, St. Anselm, who must have known, and passed through, the Norman arch. In 1935, the opportunity came, when Mrs Coplestone approached Bennett with a view to providing a combined memorial to her husband, the proprietor of the *Chester Chronicle*, and to their son, killed in the war.[78] Frederick Eden and A. K. Nicholson had, between them, designed the windows in the cloisters. Both were well-known, and probably expensive, so Bennett consulted F. C. Eeles, Secretary to the Cathedrals Commission and an authority on church design. He explained his ideas for the design, and asked if Eeles could recommend a young artist 'who would be grateful for an opportunity of putting a window in a Cathedral ... I should ask anyone you are good enough to recommend to me to come to Chester to see the window, with a view to his handling quite freely such ideas as I have in kind for it'. Eeles damped enthusiasm for too much innovation. As Eden and Nicholson were doing work for the cathedral, it would be 'only fair' to give one of them the chance. The work of many of the younger designers had 'got so eccentric' that it was not suitable for Chester Cathedral where 'a more traditional outlook seems to be required'.[79] Bennett backed down and re-employed Nicholson.[80] The window, as executed, embodies Bennett's ideas. Anselm is placed centrally, in Benedictine habit, holding the Norman church; the sidelights show Simon de Whitchurch, and Bishop Bridgeman who commissioned the Jacobean work in St Anselm's Chapel. Below Anselm is Hugh Lupus greeting the Abbot of Bec, in 1092. Above and below are the six coats of arms.[81] The style is traditional.

In 1927 the Cathedral Fund was still overdrawn, but Bennett deferred his final appeal to avoid diverting contributions from the Bishop's Million Shilling (£50,000) Appeal. Paget had launched this primarily in support of candidates for ordination (a topic much discussed at the 1926 Diocesan Conference), but also in aid of church schools and sites for new churches. Bennett was especially concerned at the shortage of ordination candidates, and therefore devoted both the 1926 and 1928 St Werburgh's Day Parish Purses to it.[82] He also visited schools, to talk on Holy Orders as a career. At Birkenhead School, he found the boys 'extraordinarily polite or appreciative, or both, in their applause'.[83] In all this, however, Bennett did not forget cathedral funds, and was soon negotiating a 5 per cent discount for the cathedral from the Million Shilling Fund: a pound to this fund would now earn a shilling for the cathedral.[84]

In August 1929 Bennett floated the idea of an Association of Friends of The Cathedral, in imitation of Canterbury and York which had, themselves, 'flattered Chester by imitating it in sundry directions'. Later, in a lighthearted jingle, Bell remarked on these two highlights of his own decanate, a two-way traffic in ideas between Chester and Canterbury:

> [We] helped all NOBODIES to see
> The Whole Cathedral [sic] without fee.
> We were young, we were wise, and very, very merry
> And founded the Friends of Canterbury.[85]

In 1930, the nucleus of the Chester branch was formed from members of the cathedral's Sunday congregation. Bennett hoped they would emulate Canterbury and York, where the Friends each gave five shillings a year, 'to demonstrate their friendliness'.[86]

He used his personal and other contacts to secure an impressive list of well-wishers. The Prince of Wales became Patron, and sent good wishes; Bishop Paget was to be President, and the Vice-Chairmen were Sir W. Bromley-Davenport (Lord Lieutenant of Cheshire), H. N. Gladstone (Lord Lieutenant of Flint), the Archbishop of Wales (Bennett's former Diocesan, of Hawarden days), and the Bishop of Vermont, USA. In September Bennett announced that he was also approaching Bishop Freeman of Washington (his host during his visit there), and Cuthbert Leicester Warren (Provincial Grand Master of the Masonic Order, of which Bennett was a member). When Freeman returned Bennett's visit, and preached at the St Werburgh Day service, in June, Bennett almost certainly told him about the Friends. The following October Bennett sent a circular about the Friends, with the *Chester Diocesan Gazette*, and advertised the society in America, as a result of which Washington Cathedral's publicity agent sent his dollar, as the first transatlantic member. He also promised to put a notice in *The Cathedral Age*, and to publish in it an article by Bennett on the Friends. Soon, (following the example of York) Bennett had devised a badge for the society (price one shilling), using the figure of the fourteenth-century pilgrim, on the dean's stall, in the choir.[87]

By February 1931, he had recruited 350 members, and was soon out on the road, around the Diocese, with his inevitable lantern lecture, to attract more. His ambition was 1,000 by December, and he hoped for a branch in each parish. By August he was only about half way there, but had his first life member (£20), an American lady. At the beginning of 1932 he reported a total of only 566, who had donated some £600, and continued to give, at this rate, each year. The parish branches did not materialise. Doubtless local church workers and clergy saw the risk of such groups diverting resources from already hard-pressed parishes.[88]

After the war, as we have noted, the parish as a cohesive unit was relatively in decline. Bennett's son was of the opinion that, despite all his father's efforts, the parochial clergy never fully responded to Bennett's various overtures, and were never as fully involved, as he had hoped they would be, in the life of the Mother Church. Local parish teas, bazaars, and other events nearer home, were, for them (as they had been for himself when a parish priest) a higher priority. Often, at special services, the seats that Bennett had reserved for robed clergy, remained only half-filled. Two years later, Bennett was ruefully contemplating published reports of other cathedrals, whose membership of Friends groups ran into thousands, and was glad that Chester's 'very modest size' was not mentioned.[89] Although Bennett continued to push for more members, until he was on the eve of retirement, his best hopes were never fulfilled.[90] The extensive architectural glories of great cathedrals elsewhere had an imaginative, nation-wide appeal, which the very real, but more modest architectural and monumental attractions of Chester, could not hope to match.[91]

Notes

1 Cheshire Record Office [hereafter CRO], Diocesan Archives, 'Chapter Book (1894–1941)' [hereafter Chap. Bk.], 25.11.1907, 30.3.1908.

2 For Scott's involvement with the bells, British Architectural Library [herafter BAL], Scott Papers, GG 86/3, 23.11.1919, 24.11.1919 (correspondence with Frank Simpson, of Chester); 18.7.1919, 21.7.1919 (correspondence with Thompson and Darby).

3 CRO, EDD 3913/3/7; Chap. Bk., 25.11.1919.

4 CRO, Chap. Bk., 23.2.1920.

5 BAL, GG/86, Scott to Thompson, 31.3.1920.

6   BAL, GG 86/4, f.496, 18.8.1920, 19.8.1920. For an earlier disagreement between Bennett and Scott over the Hawarden War Memorial, see Chapter II, section 9, above; and for an almost simultaneous clash in 1920 between the two men over the Chester War Memorial, see J. A. Bruce, 'Giles Gilbert Scott and the Chester War Memorial Project', *Journal of the Chester Archaeological Society*, 73, 1994/1995, 99–114. It is difficult to resist the conclusion that Bennett pursued a personal grudge in his dealings with Scott.
7   BAL, GG 86/4, f.497, 19.8.1920.
8   CRO, Chap. Bk., 27.9.1920. Lethaby had practised extensively, had written widely on the history and methods of architecture, and had recently retired from a Chair at the Royal College of Art.
9   BAL GG 86/1, Bennett to Scott, 28.9.1920.
10   *ibid.*, 29.9.1920, 30.9.1920.
11   *ibid.*, Scott to Bennett, 2.10.1920. Alterations in Scott's draft include, 'I am completely at a loss to understand what [*deleted* I have done] has caused such [*deleted* a sudden change] treatment now.'
12   BAL GG 86/2, Scott to Fyfe, 29.9.1920.
13   *ibid.*, Fyfe to Scott, 25.8.1920.
14   For Fyfe's career and work, *Who's Who in Architecture* (Architectural Press, London, 1926); and obituaries in *RIBA Journal*, Feb. 1945, 116–7; *The Times*, 5.1.1945, 6; *The Builder*, 19.1.1945, 13, 59. For his works in the cathedral, see G.W.O. Addleshaw, 'Architects, designers, sculptors, craftsmen whose work is to be seen in Chester Cathedral', *Architectural History: Journal of the Society of Architectural Historians of Great Britain*, 14, 1971, 82.
15   BAL, GG/86/2, Fyfe to Scott, 25.8.1920.
16   He was to be paid a retaining fee of £100 per annum, and 4½ per cent on all restoration work, up to £10,000 (CRO, Chap. Bk., 206, 21.7.1921). The 4½ per cent was below the Royal Institute of British Architects [RIBA] recommended rate, and at the end of 1922, Fyfe was offered the alternative of a £50 retainer, with 6 per cent on works, and half of his expenses (CRO, Chap. Bk., 220, 24.11.1922). I have found no evidence to indicate which he chose. He probably accepted the new offer, because a year later he was to be offered less attractive terms (see section 3 below). The *RIBA Scale of Professional Charges (1919)* laid down 6 per cent for 'new' works over £2,000, with higher rates, up to 10 per cent, for lesser works, but gave no rate for 'restoration', which might be considered a variety of 'new' work. I have unfortunately been unable to trace any of Fyfe's papers, either in the BAL or at Cambridge.
17   *ibid.*, GG 86/1, Scott to Bennett, 2.10.1920.
18   *ibid.*, GG/86/2, Fyfe to Scott, 20.10.1920; Scott to Fyfe, 21.10.1920.
19   Printed report inserted in CRO, Chap. Bk., 201, 27.9.1920.
20   CRO, Chap. Bk., 202.

THE CATHEDRAL RESTORED 117

21 *ibid.*
22 BAL GG 86/2, Bennett to Scott, 22.10.1920.
23 Report dated 29.10.1920 (CRO, Chap. Bk.).
24 *Chester Diocesan Gazette* [hereafter *CDG*], Jan. 1920, 6. This was only one of the many unsuccessful moves by individuals and different pressure groups to persuade the City's Peace Memorial (later War Memorial) Committee to adopt their own favourite project, on the somewhat unwarranted assumption that the public would subscribe to anything designated as a 'war' (or 'peace') memorial (Chester Record Office, CCF 42, 'Minutes of War Memorial Committee').
25 *CDG*, Mar. 1922, 40.
26 All walls had been attended to, windows overhauled, and, where necessary, reglazed, the roof re-constructed and its inner surfaces painted white. Earth had been removed from the north wall, exposing the buttresses fully, and damp-proofing provided. The floor had been concreted, and would later be laid with pine; a new door gave access to the Cloisters, thus connecting the Refectory and the Parlour (once the coke stores) now appropriately lighted. The old kitchen had been renovated, with a service hatch into the Refectory, from which a new door opened into Abbey Street. Later, when extra heating was required, Bennett characteristically coaxed gifts from local people to foot the £150 bill. For all this, see *CDG*, Oct. 1922, 141; Jan. 1923, 12–13 ('Chester Cathedral Repair Funds – December 1922: Architect's Statement'); Oct. 1923, 236 (*Coué* profits to contribute); July 1924, 182–3; April 1930, 54–5 (a further £500 needed); May 1930 (cost); July 1930, 106–7 (donations). The frequent references illustrate Bennett's persistence and ability to communicate effectively.
27 *CDG*, Dec. 1932, 194.
28 For Rigby's bequest of £6,000, *CDG*, May 1921, 88; for the restoration, Oct. 1922, 142. Haswell of Chester was the main contractor, as he was for most subsequent work. Apart from heating (G. N. Haden and Sons, of Manchester), all other seven contractors listed were Chester firms (*CDG*, Jan. 1923, 12–13 'Repair Funds: Architect's Statement').
29 *CDG*, Jan. 1923, 12–13.
30 *ibid.*, Oct. 1922; Dec. 1922, 142.
31 *ibid.*, Dec. 1922, 177.
32 *ibid.*, 142.
33 CRO, Chap. Bk., 226, 27.11.1923.
34 *ibid.*
35 *CDG*, Oct. 1921, 159.
36 St Werburgh, the daughter of a Mercian king, became a nun at Ely, where she was later probably Abbess. Her uncle, now King of Mercia, gave her charge of certain nunneries in the Midlands. She died c. 700, traditionally on 3 February (her first Feast Day), and was buried at Hanbury (Staffs.). For fear of the Danes, her relics

were translated to a church in Chester in the late ninth or early tenth century; a further translation occured at Chester in 1095, commemorated in her major Feast Day of 21 June. Her shrine (for which see R. V. H. Burne, *The Monks of Chester* (1962), 58–9) became a centre of pilgrimage, famed for miracles of healing, and hence a source of income to the medieval Benedictine Abbey of St Werburgh. Significantly, Bennett used a photograph of the shrine on the cover of his twopenny pamphlet, *Faith to be Healed* (n.d.). In Henry VIII's reign, St Werburgh's shrine was despoiled, the monastic community dissolved, and the Abbey church converted into the cathedral of the new Diocese of Chester and dedicated to Christ the King and the Blessed Virgin Mary. In conceiving the St Werburgh's Purse, Bennett was revisiting the medieval tradition. He was always alert to look for any continuity he could establish between the Benedictine monastery and the modern cathedral. St Werburgh's main emblem in medieval iconography was the goose. (She is supposed to have restored five of these to life: David Hugh Farmer, *The Oxford Dictionary of Saints* (Oxford, 1987), 434; *The Oxford Dictionary of the Christian Church* (Oxford, 1990), 273, 1466). Some of the photographs of Bennett show him wearing the five-goose emblem which had probably been used as the medieval pilgrim's badge.

    37   CRO, Chap. Bk., 28.9.1921, 207; *CDG*, Oct. 1921, 159; 429, Nov. 1921, 179. In August, he said that £25,000 was needed 'quickly' (*CDG*, Aug. 1922, 122).

    38   *CDG*, Dec. 1921, 199.

    39   *ibid.*, July 1922, 102–3; Aug. 1922, 117; Oct. 1922, 142.

    40   *ibid.*, June 1923, 145; July 1923, 145, 171.

    41   *ibid.*, Mar. 1923, 63; July 1923, 171.

    42   *ibid.*, Mar. 1923, 63; June 1923, 145. In March he reported that he hoped for £300 from the sale of his book on Coué (F. S. M. Bennett, *M. Coué and his Gospel of Health* [hereafter *Coué*] (London/Chester, 1922). In characteristic style, he offered a rhymed jingle to advertise it:

> Of the profits of this book, if there should be any
> To our Restoration Fund will go every penny.
> That's the plan,
> So for reading do not lend it,
> But for purchase recommend it,
> If you can!

Despite this perpetration (in the *Chester Diocesan Gazette*), *Coué* sold well, the subject being of topical interest.

    43   *CDG*, Apr. 1923. Cf., in this context, the Chapter's concern at the cost of the long vacancy in the deanery (CRO, Chap. Bk., 5.4.1920).

    44   *CDG*, May 1923, 121.

    45   *ibid.*.

46   *CDG*, December 1923, 289.
47   *ibid.*; Bennett, *Coué*.
48   *CDG*, Jan. 1924, 7.
59   Lambeth Palace Library, Bell Papers, 193, f.25, Bennett to Bell, 14.4.[1924].
50   *Times Literary Supplement*, 8.5.1924, 291–2; F. S. M. Bennett, *A Soul in the Making; or Psycho-synthesis*, (London, 1924).
51   As note 48 above.
52   *CDG*, May 1924, 122.
53   *ibid.*, June 1924, 147; Aug. 1924, 204.
54   *ibid.*, June 1924, 147.
55   *ibid.*, Sept. 1924, 229–30.
56   *ibid.*, Oct. 1924, 252–4.
57   *ibid.*, June 1925, 87–8.
58   *ibid.*, Sept. 1925, 139–40. Bennett enjoyed retailing the story of how he got the plant, amusingly embellished with lurid asides stressing the alleged hazards of discovery and arrest. If he had been seen by a nearby trooper, he would have been arrested for stealing the property of the Republic (he said); but the local press, who by now knew Bennett well, opiniated that he would have assumed 'his most ingratiating smile' and talked the authorities over (*Chester Chronicle* [hereafter *Ches. Chr.*, 6.6.1936, 10c). The real moment, however, is charmingly captured in Edith Bennett's diary, which she illustrated with her sketches. She wrote: 'Friday, 24 July 1925 ... The ch. lay S. of the trees & a tiny bit of Gothic tracery remains in a wall of, I think, a transept. Frank eagerly collected a baby tree for Chester's cloister, & I drew, & we came back, thro' the lovely afternoon to tea' (Somerset County Record Office, Edith Bennett, 'Journal: Normandy with Ida, Frank, Francis. July 1925', 60–1).
59   *Ches. Chr.*, 6.6.1936, 10c.
60   For the Glastonbury Thorn, see Bernard Wall, *Tales of Chester, II* (Market Drayton, 1992). Wall gives no source.
61   *CDG*, Jan. 1925, 3.
62   *ibid.*, Sept. 1927, 134–5..
63   D. T. Fyfe, 'Repairs to North Transept Roof' (dated January 1927), *CDG*, Apr. 1927, 62–3.
64   *ibid.*, Apr. 1927, 54–8.
65   But Bennett was sometimes credited with having written his son's book, *Chester Cathedral* [1925] (*CDG*, Apr. 1927). Within two years Bennett was proudly announcing Francis's marriage, on 30.4.1929, to Bennett's devoted secretary, Margaret Hilda Blain (1902–1973); and the following March he christened in the cathedral his first grandson, Roderick Macaulay (*ob.* 1991) (*CDG*, May 1929, 71; CRO, Diocesan Archives, 'Commonplace Book', 1922–32, 213).
66   *CDG*, Mar. 1928, 33–4.

67 *ibid.*, Nov. 1928, 190.
68 *ibid.*, Nov. 1929, 162.
69 CRO, Chap. Bk., 8 Nov. 1929, 280–1.
70 *CDG*, Jan. 1930, 3.
71 *ibid.*, Feb. 1936, 19.
72 *ibid.*, Nov. 1929, 162.
73 *ibid.*, Jan. 1930, 3; Feb. 1930, 18–9.
74 *ibid.*, June 1935, 86–7. The chair was made by the local wood-carver and craftsman, F. H. Crossley (designer of the 1939 Refectory ceiling), and bore both the diocesan arms and those of the bishop, Geoffrey Fisher, embodying a kingfisher. Fisher, Paget's successor, had been enthroned in September 1932.
75 *CDG*, May 1929, 71; Chap. Bk., 17.5.1929, 275; 12.7.1929, 278. For a biography of the Duke, see George Ridley, *Bend' Or, Duke of Westminster* (London, 1985). The pet-name 'Bendor' was given to him by his grandfather on account of his forelock which reminded the old duke of his horse of that name. Bendor was one of the richest men in England. Some indication of his (and her) lavish life-style is provided by his second wife, whom he divorced, in her *Grace and Favour: The Memoirs of Loelia, Duchess of Westminster* (London, 1962) and the lavishly illustrated H. Vickers, ed., *Cocktails and Laughter. The Albums of Loelia Lindsay (Loelia, Duchess of Westminster)* (London, 1983). Bennett's deference for a relatively paltry donation, verging on the obsequious – especially towards one to whom in his youth he had 'taught his catechism' ('Memoir') – points up the social mentality of an earlier age. Nevertheless, anyone today seeking donations for a good cause must empathise with the dictum of a notorious American criminal who, when asked why he robbed banks, responded with the truism – 'that's where the money is!'.
76 *CDG*, Jan. 1930, 3. For the Report by E. W. Tristram (1880–1952), professor at the Royal College of Art and associate of the South Kensington Museum (Victoria and Albert), see *ibid.*, Mar. 1930, 34–5.
77 Photograph in G. W. O. Addleshaw, *The Pictorial History of Chester Cathedral* (London, 1970), 17. For discussion of a crucifix in the sacristy, see CRO, Chap. Bk., 289, 26.5.1930.
78 *CDG*, Oct. 1935, 154–5. Bennett and Coplestone were old friends, having come to know each other in the days when Bennett was Bishop Jayne's Secretary and Coplestone was the local correspondent of *The Times* (*Ches. Chr.*, 22.10.1921, 8). Coplestone later became editor and proprietor of the *Chester Chronicle*.
79 Archives of The Cathedrals Fabric Commission for England, Bennett to Eeles, 27.9.1935; Eeles to Bennett, 30.9.1935. However, if Bennett really wanted a change, Eeles suggested two designers, Mr P. S. Lee of New Malden, and Miss Ungley of Scarborough. With either of these, he would be 'all right'. Both were 'deserving', and Lee's work was 'specially good'. It would be interesting to know if Bennett did

approach either, but the record is silent.

80   *CDG*, Jan. 1936, 1–3; Addleshaw, 'Architects', 92. This was Nicholson's last work for Chester [*ob*. 1936].

81   *CDG*, Oct. 1935, 154–5; Jan. 1936, 1–3.

82   *ibid.*, Aug. 1927, 118–9.

83   For Birkenhead School, *CDG*, July 1926. The need for ordination candidates was the subject of a mildly humorous piece in the *Diocesan Gazette*. Though unsigned, it bears the stamp of Bennett. In an imaginary dialogue, on a train, in the future 1940, two laymen recall 'some Saint's Day with a queer name', in June 1928, when the dean 'asked each parish to send an offering for the Ordination Candidates Fund. I remember we said there were too many appeals about already and didn't send anything'. At Chester station, the only sign of clerical life is a solitary parson on the platform. They conclude, 'There must be a Diocesan Conference on' (*CDG*, Sept. 1927, 139).

84   *CDG*, Aug. 1929, 118–9.

85   Bell's verses (1948) are quoted in full in R. C. D. Jasper, *George Bell, Bishop of Chicester* (London, 1967), 55.

86   *CDG*, Aug. 1929, 118–9.

87   For the development of The Friends, see *CDG*, Sept. 1930, 120–1; Oct. 1930, 152–3; Nov. 1930, 167; Dec. 1930, 183.

88   For the further development of The Friends, see *CDG*, Feb. 1931, 17; Mar. 1931, 34; May 1931, 70; June 1931, 87; Feb. 1932, 18; May 1933, 78; June 1933, 98.

89   *CDG*, Mar. 1934, 54.

90   *ibid.*, Mar. 1936, 34.

91   Bennett's successor in 1937, Norman Henry Tubbs, was familiar with the Friends, having been a Canon Residentiary and Archdeacon of Chester for three years. He took over as Chairman of the Council of the Friends and continued to encourage the Association, whose aims by now embraced strengthening the spirit of worship in the cathedral, maintaining and improving its fabric and furniture, assisting the library, and helping to develop its music (Frank [F. L. M.] Bennett, *Chester Cathedral*, Chester, n.d. [but a post-1937 reprint, Tubbs being named as Chairman of Council of Friends on the inserted enrolment form, 33]). In the *Victoria County History of Cheshire, III* (Oxford, 1980), B. E. Harris, probably misled by a post-1937 publicity leaflet and presumably unaware of the evidence of the *Diocesan Gazette*, mistakenly credits Tubbs with being the founder of the organisation (*VCH*, 194). The current membership application form follows Harris and gives 1938 as the year of foundation. Following a recent discussion with the Secretary of The Friends, the current *Newsletter* of the Society refers to Bennett as the founder but still gives the date as 1938.

VI

The nature of a cathedral

1

In 1924, the Church Assembly resolved to set up a Commission to report on the constitution, resources, and requirements of Cathedrals, Collegiate Churches, and Capitular Bodies. Cosmo Lang, Archbishop of York was appointed as Chairman. The other initial appointments included the bishops of Oxford, Truro (Frere), and Worcester plus the Dean of Gloucester, and significantly, Bennett.[1] The lay members included Lord Hugh Cecil, Sir Stanford Downing (Secretary of the Ecclesiastical Commission), M. R. James (Provost of Eton), the Organist of Westminster Abbey, Sir Frederick Radcliffe (Chairman of the Liverpool Cathedral Committee), Walter Tapper (President of the Royal Institute of British Architects), Sir Henry Newbolt, and Hamilton Thompson (Professor of Medieval History at Leeds), an authority on cathedral statutes and customs.[2] Bennett was in distinguished company. The Commission established seven sub-commissions, each of which reported on a group of cathedrals. The full report was presented in 1927.[3]

Cathedrals, and their role, were news in the 1920s, interest being in part generated by the establishment of Liverpool Cathedral, as well as by Bennett's work at Chester. Bennett knew that, in 1921, the Church Assembly had set up an Enquiry into cathedrals, whose subsequent Report was to lead to the establishment of the Cathedrals Commission. He chose the moment well for the launch of *The Nature of a Cathedral*. His book – a cheap two-shilling paperback, to ensure wide circulation – was already in print when he received 'the great and unexpected honour' of being asked to serve on the Commission.[4] His old friend and mentor, Walter Howard Frere, now Bishop of Truro, who was much in sympathy with Bennett's ideas, wrote an introduction to Bennett's book. Frere had stayed with Bennett in 1920 and, according to the latter, had 'made both the Cathedral and its new dean much indebted to him for the suggestions ... he then made'.[5] Frere later ensured that Bennett was a member of the sub-commission which he chaired.

The Commission must have been aware of Bennett's recently published work, but *The Times Literary Supplement* drew it further to their attention, hoping that 'his proposals for reform will receive ... the consideration they deserve from the Commission'.[6] The first meeting of the Commission took place on 8 January 1925.[7] The following day, Bennett sent three copies of his book to Bell, the new Dean of Canterbury, asking him to pass one to the Archbishop, which Bell did.[8] Bennett told Bell, 'We had the first meeting of the Commission yesterday and it is setting to its task with all zeal and seriousness'.[9] The Chairman, Lang, was his own Provincial Archbishop, and if a copy went to Canterbury, another almost certainly went to York. Lang had already told Bennett, in June 1923, that Chester had given him 'a new vision of what our Cathedral Churches might be'.[10]

In *The Nature of a Cathedral* Bennett vigorously rehearsed, again, many of the themes of his sermon of June 1920 and of his subsequent paper delivered to the Great Chapter. He stressed the relationship of a bishop to his cathedral church as the central problem, a view shared by Frere.[11] Bennett liked to draw the Aristotelean distinction between the thing 'as it is' and the thing as it 'was to be' – its potentiality.[12] In his own cathedral, the bishop had 'less of right than he has in any other church in his diocese', whereas the original intent and practice was that the cathedral 'should be his great Family House of God ... for the "complete household" of which he is the Father in God'.[13]

The cathedral had been 'the diocese's central spiritual power station', served by a body of clergy, praying for bishop and diocese by saying or singing the daily offices, reading through the Psalter, and offering the Eucharist. Instead, today, Mattins was performed by choristers, with 'a remnant of the clergy'. At Chester, he found 'the whole atmosphere of elaborate singing to a handful of worshippers (or none), 'oppressively unreal'. Often the original purpose was so forgotten that a cathedral had become regarded as 'the special property of a small corporation', charging those 'to whom the cathedral really belonged' sixpence to enter, and shutting them out between services on Sundays.[14] The diocese was the 'true unit' of organisation, saving it from both parochialism, and over-centralisation. In the 1920s there was 'a real quickening of diocesan life': new dioceses were being formed; new cathedrals planned. It was essential to get everything right.[15]

To become '*what-it-was-to-be*' a cathedral needed a complex of buildings – chapter house, refectory, common room (parlour), diocesan offices, consistory court, bishop's house etc. The bishop should live near the cathedral, his chapel, just as a parish priest must live near his church. To ensure harmony, bishop and chapter should meet frequently and informally; they should make their daily communion together. The bishop should have the right to preach whenever he wished. Because, in the past, deans and bishops had not always got on well together, 'the ridiculous plan of making the Bishop his own Dean' had emerged. Each of the jobs 'ought to take a reasonably active man all his time'. Thus was dismissed the solution of E. W. Benson, Bishop of Truro, for linking bishop and cathedral.[16] Management of the cathedral, and oversight of its services was the dean's job. 'If the bishop ought to be frequently in his cathedral', he wrote, 'the dean ought to live in it. It is his life's work'. Bennett had told Bell, on the latter's appointment to Canterbury, that a deanery was 'the greatest opportunity in the world that a man could have'.[17]

2

Bennett considered the staffing of a cathedral with some sprightly but positive opinions and proposals. Statutes governing chapter decision-making should be standardised: some made the dean an autocrat; others limited him. Bennett was silent on his own preferences.[18] The dean works full-time, canons in only three-month stints, though some go beyond their legal requirement; but laggards discourage the enthusiasts. In certain cathedrals the custom is 'no change unless the Chapter is unanimous', with the result, 'amiable futility'. Canonries are not merely to fund leisured scholars, though chapters need scholars. In brief, 'the whole system of three monthly Residentiary Canonries ought to be scrapped'. But at Chester, Bennett added, tactfully, but not entirely accurately, 'things work smoothly and sweetly'.[19]

Two full-time canons only are needed, one as Precentor and Sacristan, the other as Treasurer and Librarian or Chancellor. The Precentor must work closely with the organist – his colleague, not subordinate – an expert musician, versed in music looked at from a religious standpoint: hymns are 'the Britisher's chosen sacrament'. The Precentor supervises ceremonial, 'doctrine in action', and so should be 'a real liturgiologist', understanding and practising 'our English Use', in which cathedrals had not until recently given a proper lead. The Treasurer should also be Chancellor or Librarian. For Bennett, who was developing his cathedral library, 'a real library is alive; it isn't a musty store of unused tomes!'

In addition to their specialist duties, these 'two whole-time canons will find plenty to do once the cathedral is regarded as a great religious opportunity'. Religion interested visitors more than architecture; scope for work with individuals was consequently limitless: confessions, little services, talking religion, praying with people, singing hymns with them, showing them the cathedral, religiously: all things Bennett himself did, daily and energetically. A canon should perform as a 'competent parish priest', be physically fit, and retire if 'incapacitated by age'. He broadcast his own intention to retire at 70 – unlike Darby who died, in office, in his eighties.[20] Minor canons should be young men, serving six years, then moving to a curacy, but the choir school headmaster, if a minor canon, might stay longer.[21]

The savings on stipends of the two redundant three-monthly residentiary canons could be used to supplement the modest pensions of retired clergy who were willing to serve as 'Canon Pensioners'. Their sole duty would be daily attendance at services, thereby helping achieve the ideal of a body of brethren engaged in corporate daily prayer for bishop and diocese, and so restoring the 'what-it-was-to-be' of the cathedral.[22] At present, one archdeacon (as at Chester) often held one of the four canonries. Bennett would give both archdeacons a stall and a voice in Chapter, a proposal obviously aimed at linking Diocese and Cathedral; but the diocese should pay them.

In cathedrals of the Old Foundation, prebendaries (or honorary canons) had certain vague rights. In those of the New Foundation (like Chester) the honorary canons held only an empty title and a stall. The Great Chapter should consist of honorary canons who are present or past rural deans (another link with the diocese, at a lower level) plus the dean, two archdeacons, two whole-time canons, and six to eight pensioner canons. The whole body would constitute a bishop's consultative council, chaired by the bishop himself. Finally, he stressed that for the diocesan clergy the cathedral was the 'Mother Church', where, at services, they should sit, robed, in the choir. (Nevertheless, many of the reserved seats in Chester Cathedral frequently remained unoccupied.).[23]

With an enlarged staff, the older ideal of morning service would be possible, the brethren singing and praying, not being merely sung to; all fit clergy should attend. But one sung service on week-days was enough for boy choristers, whose general education mattered. The principal week-day service should not be Mattins, as at present, but the Eucharist, as intended at the Reformation – a view supported, he claimed, by virtually all returning army chaplains.[24] There would be intercessions for the bishop, for the diocese, and for each parish in turn; and early celebrations of Communion, and 8.00 or 8.30 a.m. Mattins. The innovation of afternoon Choral Evensong met a modern need, and should be retained in old cathedrals and established in new ones.[25] The day would end with Compline, attended, he hoped, by all cathedral staff. But Sunday evening services, which might hamper parish churches, should be avoided. This was the pattern towards which Bennett worked at Chester.

3

The cathedral building and arrangements for visitors are dealt with in some detail and reveal Bennett's grasp of 'religious psychology' and his understanding of ordinary people.[26] Much of it we have encountered already: the meagre revenue from charges contrasted with the largesse of voluntary offerings; cathedrals should be alive, and 'religiously interesting' to both charabanc and Rolls Royce visitors; vergers should be properly paid; volunteers (if necessary, modestly remunerated), were essential; the 'look and feel' of a cathedral, its 'suggestion', mattered.[27] Friendly notices were vital, as was a 'religiously written' Pilgrims' Guide; incense helped quieten crowds; lights (erroneously thought to denote the reserved sacrament) added to 'the religious look and feel', and good lighting generally was 'well worth while'.

One or more clergy should always be present, to welcome visitors, talk religion, and kneel and pray with them. Clergy who cannot do such are of little use. Cassocks are preferred garb, especially for 'gaitered dignitaries', since anyone, including children, will talk easily with 'a man in a cassock'. It is a picture of Bennett himself. As for diocesan clergy, they should conduct little services, and sing hymns, with parties from their parishes – as now happened at Chester.

Refectory, diocesan offices, cosy common room, where clergy can read, write, and smoke their pipes (Bennett was a pipe smoker) and a host of other amenities are all essential, together constituting a 'diocesan Town Hall'. In new dioceses, an old parish church, with restricted surrounds, should never become a permanent cathedral. Planners of new cathedrals must 'think spaciously' and remember 'practical detail'. Bennett concludes by coming back to his 'what-it-was-to-be'. He foresees a 'magnificent ... "what it may be", in the days to come', and offers his 'little book' in this spirit, as a contribution to discussion.[28]

4

The 1924–1927 Commission classified cathedrals as 'Ancient' (that is, governed by a dean and residentiary canons), or 'Modern' (parish church cathedrals), but a detailed questionnaire was circulated to all.[29] Many of the questions relate to matters discussed by Bennett in his *Nature of a Cathedral*, although he was not the only person who had been thinking about such matters. Section XVI, however, does bear his hallmark, though we have no proof of his involvement in its design.[30]

This section enquired when the cathedral was open, (a) on Sundays, and (b) on weekdays; whether fees were charged for admission to (a) any part of the cathedral, and (b) any building in the Precincts; what the revenue from any such fees was; whether a bookstall existed (details required); if fees had been abolished, had boxes for voluntary gifts been substituted; were cheap guide books sold, and, if so, what was the annual profit; had it been necessary to add to the staff of vergers and guides, and could volunteer helpers be obtained, especially in the holiday season; was there any arrangement for parish clergy to bring parties to the cathedral, and could the cathedral provide special services for them, but also a place to entertain them. All these related directly to problems which Bennett had solved in his early days at Chester and on which he had expressed firm views in his *Nature of a Cathedral*.

It is conceivable that Bennett had some influence on the drafting of other parts of the questionnaire. In his book he had addressed most of the subjects covered: the dean and canons, residentiary, honorary, and minor; the bishop and his relations with the cathedral; choristers and their education; services; music; vergers and their remuneration; the library. Sometimes, indeed, one feels that particular questions may have arisen from Bennett's own successes at Chester: for instance, 'If you have cloisters, have these been recently glazed, either in stained glass or otherwise?'; 'If your Chapter has discontinued the system of "guiding" visitors through the Cathedral for a fee, (a) do the guides cease to receive gratuities from visitors; and (b) have you been able to compensate them for this loss?'[31] Initial preparation of a questionnaire is often most conveniently effected by a sub-group, with guidance from the main body.

If this was the Commission's procedure, Bennett would have seemed a logical choice for inclusion in such a sub-group. A number of drafting groups, each with specialist interests, and handling one or more topics, would be another possibility. However, the record is silent, and mere speculation remains.

Bennett could not have expected all his suggestions to have been adopted but 'with the greater part of the Report', he was 'in substantial agreement'.[32] He must have welcomed proposals for strengthening links between cathedral and diocese; to make canons whole-time residents, with 'a period of close residence' (but these did not go as far as he would have wished); to require their attendance at services outside 'close residence'. An age limit of 70 for deans and canons must have pleased him, as must the recommendation that non-residentiary canons should have a constitutional role, and should meet, from time to time, for worship. The Commission endorsed his emphasis on the organist, and recommended increases in stipend. The role of the bishop, vis-á-vis the cathedral, met his criteria too. Certain other proposals in the *Nature of a Cathedral* did not find their way into the main Report, perhaps, indeed, would have been inappropriate in such a document. Bennett, therefore, limited his reservations to broad, major issues. Five other members also entered certain reservations.[33]

The detailed constitution of a chapter and the number and role of canons were issues central to the reorganisation of cathedrals. These were matters on which Bennett felt strongly, but also ones on which cathedrals themselves were divided. In consequence, the Commission proposed to leave the settling of arrangements to a Permanent Commission, to be established by the Church Assembly. This Commission would consult cathedrals and assist in framing revised statutes. The Commission thus avoided the issue. Bennett, along with Walter Frere and Sydney H. Nicholson, the Organist of Westminster Abbey, dissented.[34] The Permanent Commission should merely 'implement the normal routine work after reconstruction', not undertake 'the exceptional work of determining the forms which reconstruction should take'.

Further, the Cathedrals Commission should have examined the total expenditure on cathedrals and measured this against results achieved, before looking to the Ecclesiastical Commissioners for more money, which might be more appropriately spent on raising stipends of poor clergy. Other questions 'which cannot be postponed' had been inadequately dealt with. These included the position of minor canons, their status, tenure, duties, and stipend; the duties and salaries of lay staff; the relation of the Greater Chapter to the

Residentiary Chapter – all these being matters dear to Bennett's heart.

Bennett entered reservations on two other matters which he had discussed in his book. With Nicholson and Frere, he contended that all members of a cathedral body, clerical and lay, should be bound to attend a certain number of services and perform certain duties therein. And failure to comply, or to provide a substitute, would result in reduction of emoluments. With Frere (wise in such matters), he added the proviso that, to implement this desirable reform, the hours of service might have to be altered for the convenience of choir-boys, lay clerks, worshippers, and clergy who were scholars or men of 'action'.[35]

Finally, Bennett underlined his views about parish churches as cathedrals, an important issue in view of the current proposals for new dioceses. The Commission had devoted some time and effort to working out constitutional proposals for such 'cathedrals', on the underlying assumption that the joint arrangement would be permanent. Bennett stood out alone, contending, characteristically, 'that the selection of a parish church for a cathedral should never be regarded as more than a temporary expedient, and that it should never be allowed to postpone plans for securing the best possible site for the building of a cathedral, with surrounding premises, adequate to be the central home of the diocese'.[36]

Detailed work was delegated to seven sub-commissions.[37] Each sub-commission visited a group of cathedrals, held discussions with cathedral clergy, bishops, and officials, then, jointly with deans and chapters, produced reports on individual cathedrals. Bennett was a member of sub-commission III, which reported on Manchester, Southwell, Bury St Edmunds, Norwich, Ely, and Peterborough.[38] Each visit lasted three to four days, the whole programme extending from late June 1925 to early February 1926. Frere was chairman of the sub-commission, and the other members included Henry Edwin Savage, Dean of Lichfield, and Sydney H. Nicholson, who joined with Bennett and Frere in entering a reservation, in the main report, about the terms of the Permanent Commission.[39]

We may detect Bennett's influence in the report of sub-commission III. Three examples may suffice. Southwell Minster was a parish church which had become the cathedral of a diocese formed in 1884, and was earmarked for eventual division.[40] The sub-commission outlined 'a constitution for a parochial cathedral, and for a diocesan chapter associated with it'. Bennett did not formally dissent, but the Report represents a compromise. 'However desirable it might be thought that Southwell should eventually be conformed to the traditional cathedral model [that is, cease to be a parish church], yet it is recognised that such a scheme would be too costly to have a chance of success in present circumstances.'[41]

For St Edmundsbury and Ipswich (formed 1914), with its see in in the parish church of St James, Bury St Edmunds, the sub-commission recommended a constitution on the Southwell lines, although it 'was not entirely satisfied' that St James's 'is or is capable of being made adequate for the central church of the diocese'. Bennett was more positive. St Mary's, Bury St Edmunds, should be the cathedral, and he wished his opinion to be recorded in the Report.[42] However, the bishop was firmly against St Mary's. St James's prevailed, and remains the cathedral today.

The report on Norwich reveals a division in the sub-commission as to the role of the canons in relation to the diocese, though all members agreed that these members of the chapter should not hold parochial benefices.

> But it is much disputed how far the office of a canon could be rightly combined with the tenure of a diocesan office ... which necessitated much absence from the cathedral. Some are mainly anxious lest the cathedral should be sacrificed to the diocese ... Others desire mainly that busy diocesan officials should go forth from the cathedral to the parishes and should themselves have the cathedral as their basis of work and their spiritual home. So there are two views, one discouraging and the other encouraging the combination of a canonry with diocesan office.[43]

The contrast between the 'Benson' and the 'Bennett' perception of the role of the canons, and the relation of cathedral to diocese, could hardly be more clearly stated.

Though Bennett could not carry the day within the sub-commission, the full commission in its final report supported him. The relation between cathedral and diocese should be 'real, close, and continuous', but 'its officers should not become 'mere elements in diocesan organisation'.

> The truest help which the cathedral can give to the diocese is to be a real centre of religious life ... to uphold a high ideal of worship, to offer prayer for the Church and the world, to quicken the religious life of the people, and to confirm their faith by the preaching and teaching given within its walls. But, subject to the fulfilment of this

primary aim, everything should be done to make the cathedral a centre of diocesan life.[44]

In this spirit the Commision deprecated the holding of diocesan offices by canons which made them, at best, only part-time 'residential'. The Commission, however, recommended the inclusion of non-residentiary canons in the chapter, as a link with the diocese.[45]

As to relations between bishop and cathedral, the Commission was less forthright than Bennett had been in his *Nature of a Cathedral*, but agreed that the chapter should decide all matters concerning services, except that the bishop should have definite rights regarding special services which he wished to hold. It stopped short of Bennett's ideal of the cathedral as the bishop's chapel.[46]

5

Chester itself was visited by sub-commission V, from 21 to 23 April 1926. The Chairman was Walter Frere, who knew a good deal already about the changes which Bennett had effected. Other members were Aubrey Lawrence, Chancellor of Worcester Diocese (a nominee of the Ecclesiastical Commission), the Bishop of St Edmundsbury and Ipswich, Professor Hamilton Thompson, and Lord Hugh Cecil.[47] Bennett joined them as *ad hoc* representative of the Chapter.

It comes as no surprise that the sub-commission was able to 'report with enthusiasm' on 'the new developments in which Chester has become a pioneer'. It had become 'the intensive home of the college to a marked degree, and all the more so because the bishop lives in close touch with the dean and chapter'. It was also 'the centre of an influence in the diocese which has grown by leaps and bounds in recent years'. This had been achieved by 'holding a great number of services for diocesan purposes and groups'; by 'encouraging bodies of pilgrims from the diocese and beyond'; and, especially, by 'having the church open and free to all pilgrims and visitors'. High praise was accorded to Chester for ensuring, not merely 'that visitors should ... find the cathedral full of interest, devotional as well as archaeological', but also that they should be 'met and helped by voluntary workers and so led to appreciate all aspects of their visit, the devotional side as well as the rest'. Finally, the refectory, cloisters, and adjoining buildings were singled out for special mention. Bennett's restorations had made these into 'a magnificent centre' for work of the sort which Chester was so effectively doing, and which the sub-commission had so warmly commended. This concluding section of the report constitutes a considered and authoritative judgement, by an experienced and knowledgeable group of clergy and laymen, on Bennett's achievement in his six years at Chester.[48]

6

Bennett was unimpressed by the Church Assembly's initial 'discursive debate' on the Report when it received it in 1927.[49] Legislation, based on the Commission's recommendations was to be considered in July 1928.[50] Early that year he published *On Cathedrals in the Meantime*.[51] This was 'for the Church Assembly', specifically to influence its decisions. Bennett said that after three more years of experience and a stint on the Commission, he had changed his mind on some matters and discovered new problems.[52] Using Chester as a 'specimen cathedral', Bennett described what he would like to see worked out in the diocese, thus discreetly directing his thrust locally as well as nationally.[53] He explained why he had objected to a Permanent Commission. It could be dominated by 'cautious, conservative, consistent' members, in disposition 'priestly' rather than 'prophetic', and so discourage 'burgeoning experiment'. Cathedrals must have freedom to reform themselves, in line with 'present-day needs and aspirations'. Any commission should be 'interim' (that is, of limited term), constituted to help cathedrals emerge, by using their existing resources, from 'the horse-drawn age', and thus 'automobilise' themselves.[54]

No more could be expected from non-voluntary ecclesiastical funds until each cathedral had 'cut the best coat with the cloth it has got'. Ideally, all resources should be pooled, to provide for the personnel which dioceses really needed, and resources of benefices should similarly be pooled, and spread around the parishes. But this notion was 'absurdly premature'. 'The wealth of Barchester cannot yet avail to succour the poverty of Pettyminster'.[55]

Bennett translated the 'coat and cloth' into terms of cash and personnel. In *The Nature of a Cathedral*, he had seen no need for more than two residentiary canons; the Cathedrals Commission had recommended four. But '£600 a year for three months work' was the equivalent of '£2,400 a year'; to pay two at this rate was to pay at a rate which was 'more than sufficient to finance a whole-time Diocesan Bishop'. He would prefer to see money spent on the cathedral's choral foundation rather than on 'an unnecessarily large staff'.[56] He applied his model measure to Chester, an 'average' cathedral, 'normal enough for that which is true of us to be more or less true of a good many other cathedrals'.[57] Chester was over-staffed. One dean, four residentiaries, and three minor canons was excessive; to pay them adequately, the cathedral had not enough money. Instead, he recomended a dean (£1,200 a year – Bennett's current salary), two whole-time canons (£750, or £650 plus house), a senior minor canon (£350, or £400 if master of the choir school), and a junior (£300). From the savings, £120 could augment the organist's stipend; £150 to £180 would provide three extra part-time lay clerks.

The surplus of £1,000 could be divided between the two archdeacons, who received only £250 from the Ecclesiastical Commissioners, thus relieving them of the need to hold a parochial cure, and linking both archdeacons (and thereby the diocese) with the cathedral. The Archdeacon of Chester, living in Chester, would continue as a Chapter member, share in the administrative work, and take part in services. The Archdeacon of Macclesfield would not be on the Executive Chapter, but would have a stall and be a member of the larger Chapter. Perhaps the £500 per archdeacon could be squeezed to £350, thereby freeing money for the cathedral to use in other ways.[58] If the diocese wanted extra clergy to 'jump off from the Cathedral platform for work in the Diocese' (which Bennett regarded as a good scheme) the diocese should pay them.[59]

For Bennnett, financial and administrative reform was merely the means of helping the cathedral to do its real work more effectively. In the context of his financial proposals he reiterated his earlier views: the doubtful value of elaborately sung daily mattins with minimal congregations; a return to the 'natural voice' for large portions of both mattins and evensong, and hence a diminished singing role for minor canons; the central position of the Eucharist; services for special groups; the duty of canons to work with people, take part in the daily offices, and not expect 'uninterrupted leisure for books'; and rural deans as constituent members of the Great Chapter, to link cathedral and diocese.[60]

The proposal for pensioner canons he now withdrew as impracticable, though it had 'borne fruit' in the United States (which he had visited in the autumn of 1926).[61] He regretted that the Commission had not referred to the custom of cathedrals of the Old Foundation, whereby each canon said, daily, a portion of the Psalter, but hoped this 'venerable and laudable custom' would find a place in the statutes of all cathedrals. He welcomed the proposal that, though a bishop should be assured of his proper right in his own cathedral, he ought not to invade the dean's sphere. Nor could the bishop, 'with either propriety or convenience, be the Dean'.

Bennett reiterated his distaste for parish church cathedrals, aired publicly in *The Times* in 1924,[62] and argued in *The Nature of a Cathedral*. He now updated his arguments, in the context of the Commission's report and in the light of his own recent American experience. Cathedral duties and parochial rights would inevitably conflict.[63] Bennett opposed using Church funds to develop, as a cathedral, a parish church lacking space for the buildings necessary to make it a 'diocesan town hall'. Instead, a new diocese should use a parish church as a 'pro-cathedral'.[64] Choose a good site, he urged, build the choir, then erect a temporary nave, after the manner of the Wembley Exhibition buildings – the programme he had recently urged in America, where Washington displayed 'the most magnificent Church venture in the world'.[65] In England, he instanced Truro and Liverpool.

He was to have further opportunities to influence cathedral development. Later in 1928, he presided, as Commissary of the Archbishop of Wales (his old diocesan bishop, A. G. Edwards), at Monmouth Diocesan Conference, in Newport, where the proposed erection of a new cathedral was discussed. The prime test of architecture, Bennett urged, was fitness of the building for its purpose. The cathedral was the bishop's church and unless the bishop lived in the 'family house' the diocese would never achieve what it wanted, a good cathedral. The new cathedral would be the home of the diocese but it need not be large. The objective should be to have, in their midst, an instrument through which the family of the diocese, with the bishop as father, could express its family life.[66]

Another new cathedral, Guildford, the first Anglican cathedral to be built on a new site in the South of England since the Middle Ages, met the Bennett criteria perfectly (though there is no evidence of Bennett's direct involvement). Selection of site was the prime consideration. Critics complained that the location was not on 'the wealthy side' of the town, but, as the bishop pointed out, the diocese needed a 'working cathedral'. There was room for expansion. Land around was leased for five years, with the option of purchase thereafter, providing space for the necessary complex of buildings, including a car park.[67] Consecrated in 1961, Guildford Cathedral represented, symbolically, the 'new Church of England: efficient, sophisticated, progressive'.[68].

Bennett left to last 'the item of Cathedral reform which I regard as the most important of all'.[69] Again, he is reiterating, in the context of the Commission, views he expressed so often before. No cathedral could 'even begin do its proper work' until it had totally abolished entry fees. Yet the Commission had merely hoped 'that all Chapters may at least consider the experiment ... and that the time may come when, through the increase of voluntary offerings, all our Cathedrals will be freely open to the public'. Already, he pointed out, 'the experiment has been tried in Cathedral after Cathedral' and had everywhere been 'an unqualified success'. He went on:

> Had I had the drawing up of this paragraph of the Report, I should have suggested something less *suaviter in modo* and much more *fortiter in re* and said bluntly that no Cathedral could hope for any financial assistance from the Ecclesiastical Commissioners or elsewhere until its Dean and Chapter had sufficient courage and enterprise to follow the example, now set by more than half the great Cathedrals of England, and double or treble their receipts from the golden harvest of a pleased and welcomed public.[70]

7

The Cathedrals Measures of 1931, supplemented later by a 1934 Measure, was passed by the Church Assembly 'to establish and define the functions, powers, and duties of the Cathedral Commissioners, to make provision with regard to the constitutions, the property and revenues, the statutes of the Cathedral Churches and the patronage of the canonries therein, and in certain cases with respect to the election of bishops by the chapters thereof, to enable the Ecclesiastical Commissioners to make grants for the benefit of Cathedral Churches, and for purposes connected therewith'.[71] The Commission was not to be 'permanent', but was to operate for not less than seven and not more than twelve years.[72] Its term was subsequently fixed at ten years.[73]

The Measure matched Bennett's most important criteria. The governing body of most cathedrals would be their 'General Chapter', comprising the whole body of canons, with 'the dean and chapter as at present constituted' becoming the 'administrative chapter'.[74] Cathedral authorities were required to comply with certain requirements regarding tenure of property and the status of minor canons, lay clerks, and other ministers of the cathedral, who must now be engaged on prescribed terms (without the creation of freehold, a past obstacle to reform).[75] A 'permissive' role was prescribed for the Commission, to that extent realising Bennett's hope that the 'prophetic' might prevail. Before framing draft statutes, for example, the Commissioners, were to 'take counsel' with each cathedral's 'consenting body', generally, the Dean and Chapter.[76] With this body, they 'may mutually interchange suggestions', to all of which they were required to give 'due consideration'.[77] Finally, the draft itself was to be approved by the 'consenting body' before it went forward.[78] In its drafting of schemes, the Commission was required to take into consideration the Report of 1927 and 'have regard to the history and customs of each of the cathedral churches'.[79] After final agreement between 'consenting body' and the Commission, the proposed new statutes would 'lie on the table', at the Church Assembly, and if unopposed, would be sealed and in due course become law.[80] Finally, there was provision for appeal to the Privy Council.[81]

Bennett, significantly, expressed no reservations about the Measure and the Commission's terms of reference, having reason to be satisfied with the general outcome. 'Consultation' and 'consent' were safeguards against the imposition of settlements from outside. In theory the safeguards could allow individuals to block change, but the protection of existing rights of tenure, position, and emoluments went far to disarm potential opponents of change. Furthermore, there was no *liberum veto*: 'in any case where a consenting body is divided in opinion, the decision of the majority shall prevail'.[82] Bennett must have regretted that no firm line was taken against the possible permanency of 'parish church' cathedrals, where the complicated structure against which he had inveighed remained and the title 'Provost' were adopted.[83]

As far as Chester itself was concerned, Bennett had good cause to be satisfied. As soon as the Measure became law, he reported, 'we set about drafting new statutes'.[84] These were finally approved in November 1935. As rights of existing holders of offices were protected, it would be some little time before the new arrangements became fully operative. There were to be four canons residentiary, although Bennett had initially considered three to be 'as much as our funds can properly afford'.[85] The recommendations of the Commission and the views of Chester canons probably swayed the decision.

However, as a compromise, it was agreed that two of the canons were to be available for diocesan work, for which their remuneration would be a charge on the diocese. Minor canons disappeared, but there were to be three chaplains choral, six lay clerks, sixteen choristers, and twenty four honorary canons.[86]

Bennett was pleased that the new statutes gave greater flexibility and allowed for the exercise of local discretion. If, for example, it were deemed necessary, for financial reasons, to suspend a canonry, the Greater Chapter, under the bishop, was authorised to act, another welcome example of the new, wider role of the Greater Chapter.[87] The bishop now had the rights in his cathedral which, denied under the Henrician statutes, he had for many years in practice enjoyed, but only by courtesy of the cathedral authorities. 'In some measure', as Bennett reported, the dean was 'dethroned', but this, he hastened to add, was 'with the present Dean's approval'.

The Ecclesiastical Commissioners would take over the cathedral's estates (as laid down in the Measure) but the care already taken of cathedral property and finances, by Bennett's sound and imaginative stewardship, would entitle Chester to generous consideration by the Ecclesiastical Commissioners, in due course.[88] No major changes would occur before Bennett retired in 1937, but he had built for the future. As he pointed out, his successor would have, in place of an 'outdated awkward instrument' (not fully revised since 1544), an 'excellent and up to date one'.[89] This helped to ensure that the cathedral was now indeed the bishop's home, and the 'family house' of the diocese.[90]

The establishment of the honorary canons in a wider and now positive role, as the governing body of the cathedral, gave Bennett special satisfaction. Until now, as he reminded them, they had had no more than an empty title and a stall in the cathedral. The new statutes constituted the honorary and residential canons, collectively, as 'the Corporation of the Cathedral', under the title of 'The Dean and Chapter', with a defined role, including receipt of the *congé d'élire*. Anticipating the new statutes, Bennett summoned a meeting of the Great Chapter, with the bishop in the chair, thus, as he reported, 'making history', but, typically, also seizing the initiative and turning the new 'instrument' to advantage. In no uncertain terms, he told the assembled body – addressing himself especially to the honorary canons – that as the buildings were hereafter vested in them as a corporation, they must share his 'discomfort (not to say distress)' at the £4,000 fabric fund debt which he wanted to liquidate before he retired.[91]

8

Bennett's vision of 'The Nature of a Cathedral' finally triumphed in 1958, when a Commission of the Church Assembly rejected Benson's version, with the decision that cathedrals 'are, indeed, the mother churches of their several dioceses, but that they are churches with their own separate and distinctive ministries'.[92] The Report of the Commission reads, in places, like a roll call of Bennett's ideas: the motor car has made cathedrals places of pilgrimage 'far in excess of anything previously known'; parties should be 'welcomed, shown round, and helped to see the spiritual purpose of a Cathedral; increasingly special services are sought by secular organisations'.[93] The 1958 Commission's proposals for staffing would have met with Bennett's wholehearted approval. Each cathedral should have a minimum establishment of a dean and two residentiary canons, who would be solely concerned with the cathedral's ministry and hence be prohibited from holding any diocesan office. The Church Commissioners, by accepting responsibility for the salaries of the dean and the two canons, endorsed the proposal financially, and the whole arrangement became law in 1964.[94]

Notes

1 Canon J. J. Scott, Sub-Dean of Manchester (a parish church cathedral) was also a member, as was Canon A. G. Robinson, Treasurer of Winchester Cathedral. Later, the Bishop of Ipswich, the Deans of Lichfield and of Windsor, and the Treasurer of Norwich Cathedral were added.

2 A. Hamilton Thompson, *The Cathedral Churches of England* (London, 1925), v and *passim*.

3 *Report of the Cathedrals Commission appointed in pursuance of a resolution of the National Assembly of the Church of England), Parts I and II, Report and Appendices* (London, 1927) [hereafter *Cathedrals Commission*], 5–6.

4 'Author's Preface', dated Martinmas 1924, F. S. M. Bennett, *The Nature of a Cathedral* (London, 1925).

5 *CDG*, June 1934, 78. Neither the Community of the Resurrection nor Truro Diocesan Record Office holds any Frere–Bennett letters. Nor does there appear to be any relevant material at York, where Frere's papers are deposited.

6 *Times Literary Supplement*, 22.1.1925, 51.

7   *Cathedrals Commission*, 5.
8   The third was for the Chief Verger.
9   Lambeth Palace Library, Bell Papers, 193, ff. 251, 9.1.1925 (received 12.1.1925), 252, 12.1.1925.
10 Lang to Bennett, 26.6.1926, following his second visit to Chester (*CDG*, July 1923, 171).
11 Bennett, *Nature of a Cathedral*, xi.
12 He makes a similar distinction for mankind in his *The Resurrection of the Dead* (1929) and *The Resurrection of the Organism* (1930).
13 Bennett, *Nature of a Cathedral*, 4.
14 *ibid.*, 6–7.
15 *ibid.*, 9–10.
16 *ibid.*, 11–14. As stated earlier, Edward White Benson, appointed as the first bishop of the new Diocese of Truro in 1877 (1883 Archbishop of Canterbury) had made himself dean of the Cathedral he founded at Truro and used the cathedral clergy in diocesan roles. This was his solution to resolving the relationship between bishop and cathedral, and to finding a pastoral role for cathedral clergy.
17 Bennett, *Nature of a Cathedral*, 14; Lambeth Palace Library, Bell Papers, 193, f. 23, Bennett to Bell, 18.2.1924.
18 Bennett, *Nature of a Cathedral*, 16.
19 *ibid.*, 16–19.
20 *ibid.*, 18–23.
21 Anachronistic freeholds should be abolished. At Chester, Bennett had been frustrated in attempts to transfer minor canons to more responsible appointments by generous and unassailable extra remuneration from the Barbara Dodd legacy.
22 Bennett, *Nature of a Cathedral*, 23–5.
23 *ibid.*, 25–7. Bennett's son noted the sparse response of parish clergy ('Memoir').
24 Bennett failed to add, however, that before battle, most of these administered the Eucharist to any soldier, irrespective of whether he was 'C. of E.' or otherwise.
25 Bennett, *Nature of a Cathedral*, 32–5; for chaplains and the War, A. Wilkinson, *The Church of England and the First World War* (London, 1978).
26 Bennett was keenly interested in developments in psychology.
27 Cf. F. S. M. Bennett, *M. Coué and his Gospel of Health* (London/Chester, 1923).
28 Bennett, *Nature of a Cathedral*, 45–72. Bennett considered good lighting to be 'well worth while' (*CDG*, Mar. 1928, 33–4).
29 *Cathedrals Commission*, Appendix A.
30 I have been unable to trace any original draft of the questionnaire at either

the Church of England Record Centre or The Cathedrals Fabric Commission for England. The Record Centre holds the cathedrals' replies.

31   *Cathedrals Commission*, Appendix A, X (4), XV (3).
32   Bennett, *Nature of a Cathedral*, 36.
33   ibid., 36–8.
34   ibid., 36–7.
35   ibid., 38.
36   ibid., 38.
37   Bennett stated five. He may have got it wrong, or there may have been a change of plan (*CDG*, Nov. 1925).
38   Bennett was also originally a member of Sub-Commission VII (Wells, Bristol, Truro, Exeter, Salisbury), but because of the 1926 General Strike only Wells and Bristol had been visited (in April 1926) before the autumn, when Bennett was due to depart for his Canadian and USA tour (*Cathedrals Commission*, 306, 312; *CDG*, June 1926).
39   *Cathedrals Commission*, 93-163; for the reservation by Bennett, Frere and Nicholson, 36–7.
40   Formed 1884; divided 1927 into Southwell and Derby.
41   *Cathedrals Commission*, 117.
42   ibid., 122–5.
43   ibid., 131–2.
44   'There is one way of associating the cathedral with the diocese which we do not think satisfactory. It is the attachment of residentiary canonries to purely diocesan offices ... At the present time this may be almost unavoidable in dioceses where financial conditions are specially difficult ... But we think that such arrangements are inconsistent with the ideal that residentiary canons should be whole-time residents, regarding the cathedral as the main centre of their interest and work.'(*ibid*, 19–20).
45   ibid., 20.
46   ibid., 18-19.
47   b. 1869, 5th son of Marquis of Salisbury; Fellow of Hertford College; M.P. for Greenwich, 1895–6; for Oxford, 1910; P.C., 1916.
48   *Cathedrals Commission*, 234–5.
49   *The Times*, 17.11.1927, 11; F. S. M. Bennett, *On Cathedrals in the Meantime* (London, 1928), 1.
50   *CDG*., Apr. 1928.
51   ibid., Feb. 1928.
52   Bennett, *Cathedrals in the Meantime*, 1.
53   *CDG*, Feb. 1928, 19; Bennett, *Cathedrals in the Meantime*, 9 et. seq.

54 Bennett, *Cathedrals in the Meantime*, 6–7.
55 *ibid.*, 7–8.
56 *ibid.*, 9.
57 *ibid.*, 10.
58 *ibid.*, 10-18.
59 *ibid.*, 18.
60 *ibid.*, 18–24.
61 Bennett had visited the USA in October–December 1926; Bennett, *Cathedrals in the Meantime*, 24.
62 *The Times*, 5.8.1924, 6.
63 Bennett, *Cathedrals in the Meantime*, 27–8. Bennett predicted major problems for the Provost (a title he disliked).

> I have tried to imagine myself a Provost, working with the machinery proposed for a Parish Church Cathedral and sitting *ex officio*, first on the Diocesan Chapter, then on the Cathedral Council, and then on the Parish Church Council in turn. The Bishop of Truro suggests that "the special pension for Deans and Canons should begin to be available at the age of 65." Most Deans and Canons will, I think, be all right with a pension at 70; but many a Provost of this sort of Parish Church Cathedral may well deserve and need one at 65 or earlier! (*ibid.*, 28).

64 Cf. Bennett's letter in *The Times*, 5.8.1924, 6.
65 Bennett, *Cathedrals in the Meantime*, 32–4.
66 *The Times*, 7.11.1928, 21.
67 *ibid..*
68 Adrian Hastings, *A History of English Christianity, 1920–1985* (London, 1986), 534.
69 Bennett, *Cathedrals in the Meantime*, 34.
70 *ibid.*, 34–35.
71 Church Assembly, *Cathedrals Measure* (1931), Preamble.
72 *ibid.*, 4 (3).
73 *CDG*, Mar. 1934, 34.
74 *Cathedrals Measure*, 10 (2) (i), (ii).
75 *ibid.*, 10 (xiv); 13 (v).
76 *ibid.*, 3. The 'consenting body' was different for certain other cathedrals; for 'parish church' cathedrals it included representatives of the Parochial Church Council.
77 *Cathedrals Measure*, 2 (2) (ii); 5 (i), (ii), (v).
78 *ibid.*, 5 (v).
79 *ibid.*, 2 (20 (iv).

80   *ibid.*, 5 (viii) (b).
81   *ibid.*, 5.
82   *ibid.*, 3 (2) (i).
83   *ibid.*: *Explanatory Memorandum; Cathedrals Measure*, 11.
84   *CDG*, March 1934, 34.
85   *ibid.*, Aug. 1934.
86   B. H. Harris, ed. *Victoria County History of Cheshire, III* (Oxford, 1980), 194. Bennett's ideal for Chester was the dean plus two full-time canons (Bennett, *Nature of a Cathedral*, 20; *Cathedrals in the Meantime*, 10). He remained opposed to the use of canons, paid by the cathedral, in a largely diocesan role. But in agreeing to the compromise over canonries he must have taken into consideration the fact that the financial burden on the cathedral would be lessened, because the diocese would be paying two canons for the work which they would be undertaking on its behalf.
87   *CDG*, March 1934, 34.
88   *ibid.*, Sept. 1934, 117.
89   *ibid.*, March 1934, 34.
90   *ibid.*, Oct. 1934, 130.
91   *ibid.*, Nov. 1934, 147.
92   Roger Lloyd, *The Church of England, 1900-1965* (London, 1966), 402.
93   *Cathedrals in Modern Life* (Church Assembly, 1961). The 1994 report of the Archbishops' Commission on Cathedrals, *Heritage and Renewal*, reiterates this.
94   In postscript, the 'community' ideal of the new Coventry Cathedral, articulated by its first Provost, can be seen as the translation, into mid and late twentieth century terms, of the Bennett ideal. For Coventry, see H. C. N. Williams, *The Twentieth Century Cathedral* (London, 1964), as quoted in Lloyd, *Church of England*, 569; H. C. N. Williams, *Guide to Coventry Cathedral* (London, 1984).

VII

The new world: 'cathedrals and other things'

1

By 1923, with Chester set on the course he had mapped out, and the 'open cathedral' message spreading, Bennett wondered if he 'might not cross the Atlantic another day like ... Dean Howson, and once more impress Chester with the generosity of our American cousins'.[1] Howson had raised a considerable sum for restoration, and Bennett was doubtless encouraged by the growing interest of American visitors. He wrote 'a very nice letter' for the 1923 summer influx.[2] In July 1925, he accepted an invitation from the Bishop of Washington to visit the United States the following year, to talk about 'cathedrals and other things'[3] – his commitment to the Cathedrals Commission having prevented his going earlier. The invitation was supported by the College of Preachers of Washington Cathedral, which provided post-graduate courses in preaching and was directed by Bishop Rhinelander, first Warden of the College.[4] The visit would not (as the invitation indicated) be 'primarily mercenary', but he hoped to 'bring home some dollars in a bag'.[5]

Although members of the churches of the 'Anglican Communion' made up only about three per cent of the adult population of North America, this represented between two and three million individuals in over a score of dioceses, in numbers not far short of the active (as distinct from the notional Establishment) membership of the 'C. of E.' and its brother churches in the British Isles. In both Canada, and more especially in the United States, there was growing 'Anglican' interest in the development of cathedrals. The first bishop of the American Church had been consecrated in 1784, but for long there were no cathedrals. An 1820 proposal for a cathedral in New York came to nothing. After it had been rebuilt in 1851, it was suggested that St Paul's Church, Buffalo, should become the cathedral church for a bishopric of Buffalo. In England, *The Ecclesiologist* commented that 'the American Church must come to Cathedrals sooner or later, therefore, we say, let it be as soon as possible'. St Paul's, Buffalo, was not what might be wished but it was the best church available; without the *ecclesia cathedralis* episcopacy was mutilated and ineffective. The original Diocese of New York was reviving, and the *Eccclesiologist* suggested one possible church. However, 'were a cathedral to be built *de novo*, as such, with the intention of its being the Cathedral Church of the greatest capital in the new world, we should be still more rejoiced'.

It added that the *Catholic Mirror* of Baltimore had recently given a description of the Roman Catholic cathedral which was being completed at Philadelphia. The *Ecclesiologist* enjoined the American Episcopal Church that 'the size and sumptuousness of this building utter very plainly "Go and do thou likewise" to our communion'. Furthermore, it observed that the *Morning Chronicle*, in noticing the consecration of St Paul's, Buffalo, had asked 'why is it not made the occasion of the restoration of a really ecclesiastical system of episcopacy: Bishop De Lancey assuming the title of Bishop of Buffalo, and planting his throne in this church, after the example of the Bishop of Sydney, Australia?' But in a paper given in 1855 to the New York Ecclesiological Society (founded 1848, after the model of the English society), the Reverend John H. Hopkins jnr. argued that the greatest obstacle to the introduction of a cathedral system was the corruption of the English system of cathedrals.

Nevertheless, during the later nineteenth century and the earlier twentieth, more and more North American bishops designated a church in their diocese as a cathedral and installed their throne therein. By the time of Bennett's visit this movement had gained pace.[6] An American magazine, appropriately entitled *The Cathedral Age*, published by the National Cathedral Association in Washington, was specifically devoted to the topic.[7] It was to carry reports of Bennett's American tour, as well as of his activities at Chester, and Bennett himself later contributed to it. Leading English churchmen were welcomed in the United States, and it is easy to understand why Bennett, with his reputation as an authority on cathedrals, had been invited.[8]

Bennett's hosts planned his three-month tour carefully. He would visit Quebec, Montreal, and Toronto, before crossing into the United States via Buffalo and Niagara, thereafter spending time in New England, then at New York and Philadelphia, before finishing up with a fortnight in Washington. He left Liverpool on 17 September 1926, aboard the White Star vessel 'Regina'.[9] Aboard ship, he was asked to give lectures (predictably, he talked on Coué and Chester Cathedral), and on Sunday he was called upon to deliver the sermon.[10]

Bennett spent ten days in Canada, five of them in Toronto, where quickly he asserted his New World connections. 'In coming to Canada', he announced in a sermon, 'I feel very keenly that in a sense I am only coming home'. He explained – 'My grandfather was, as some of you know, Sir James Buchanan-Macaulay, one of the judges of Upper Canada. My mother was born in Toronto. So was my sister, in what was then Wickham Lodge.[11] It was quite accidental that I was not born here in Toronto myself.'[12] His sermon, and the rest of his visit, were extensively reported in the press, and the leading newspaper featured pictures of him and his son on its front page.[13]

A project for building a cathedral was under way. St Alban's had been planned in the late nineteenth century. It was to be built in Early English style, and would be some 250 feet in length, with a tower 135 feet high, at an estimated cost of $250,000. Because of financial problems, however, only the choir and the chancel had been built, and these were in use in 1926, replacing St James's Church which hitherto had served as a cathedral.[14] Bennett inspected and approved of the extensive site but had other reservations about the project. 'Toronto', he wrote, on his return to England, 'has secured a good site for its Cathedral, but authorities will have to think and think again, if the building is to be at all worthy of a great Church in a great and beautiful City'.[15]

At a luncheon given in his honour at Toronto University, Bennett articulated his vision of New World cathedral architecture:

> I would like to see built in Canada a great Cathedral, imitating in no blind manner the architecture of Europe, but built in a spirit of freedom, and expressing in some way the spaciousness of your country, the vastness of it, the vigor and life and originality of it ... We don't want to set aside all that the generations have learned about the art of beauty in building. But in a new land like this the aim should be to avoid the imitation of ancient models. What you want is freedom in expressing the ideals of the day and country you live in.[16]

It was not, however, the cathedral as a building, but the cathedral as a community house that he had come to Canada to extol, and he presented the ideal with which readers of *The Nature of a Cathedral* would be by now familiar. The cathedral was more than a big church, though that was one part of it. No longer was the parish the 'logical unit', but the diocese; hence the need for the cathedral to be 'the family house, the meeting place of the diocese', and it should include bishop's house, offices, conference hall, common room, library, refectory, hostel. This was 'the new conception of a cathedral' which had 'developed within the last few years'. Chester exemplified, 'more than any other, this ideal of the community church, bearing the same relationship to the diocese as the family house bears to any great family'. This idea of a central complex was 'spreading into other fields', and he characteristically instanced the 'great Masonic order', now so large that it was building such a centre in London 'to express its corporate life'.[17]

Bennett was impressed by the two universities he visited, Montreal and Toronto. Hart House, at the federal Toronto University particularly interested him. Named after a brilliant student, accidentally drowned in Hudson Bay some twenty years before, it provided a well-equipped centre for the whole community of the University.[18] He compared its function to that of a cathedral: 'The true cathedral is to a religious community what this Hart House of yours is to the University of Toronto. It is the family house, the meeting place of the diocese', and 'a splendid embodiment of splendid ideas'.[19] He brought back to Chester a copy of the *Hart House Illustrated Book*, which he placed on display in the Chapter House.[20]. In the event, the University of Toronto prospered[21] – but the cathedral venture languished. Ambitious schemes for completion remained on paper. A fire in 1929 closed the church temporarily, but before it reopened the Synod had decided that it was not to be a cathedral. It became the Church of St Alban the Martyr and St James again became the cathedral.[22]

2

After their ten days in Canada, Bennett and his son crossed into the United States, by steamer over Lake Ontario to Niagara, where they spent a night.[23] At Buffalo Bennett warmed towards the kindly Customs official who helped them to catch the night train to Boston.[24] But there, unfortunately, Bennett ran into trouble with the Customs over the stock of *The Nature of a Cathedral* and others of his writings which he had brought for sale after his lectures – 'profits to the Cathedral Restoration Fund', as he later hastened to assure English reporters.[25] Whatever irritation Bennett may have felt at his rough welcome by the Customs, it did not mar his visit. He preached successfully at Harvard, in the university's Appleton Chapel, conducted men's services, and talked with students and staff.[26] When he preached on the Sunday evening, in St Paul's Cathedral, Boston, Bennett was described by the press as 'one of the most famous preachers in England'.[27]

His sermon was brisk, cheerful, and probably typical. Health and faith, ecumenism, cathedrals were all predictably there. From thankfulness, especially for health – 'the unmistakable trait of the genuine Christian' – he moved to Coué, relating his practice of suggestion as a cure for illness to 'the potency of faith in religion and secular things'. (Doubtless, copies of his *Coué* and *Expecto* were on sale afterwards). On the ecumenical issue, the *Boston Globe* reported him as declaring that

> if he lived in the United States, the question of the reunion of all Christian churches would be a pressing one to him. The first step in that direction ... would be the realisation that all members of different denominations belong equally to the great family of God, because they have been baptised.[28]

Four years later, he was to surprise critics by taking the second step, and giving baptism primacy over episcopacy as the basis for reunion.[29]

Finally, Bennett was of course expected to say something about cathedrals. St Paul's operated an open-door policy, and he was able to praise 'the making of the cathedral church a house of prayer and meditation for all conditions of people at practically every hour of the day', and to make comparisons with Chester, where, he said, 'we, like you here, have an ambition to maintain the most hospitable cathedral in the world'.[30] This was not the mere polite compliment of a visitor. St Paul's policy was rightly attributed to the late Dean Rousmaniere (1858–1926), who had died only a fortnight before Bennett's arrival.[31] A writer in the *Boston Evening Transcript* had compared Bennett with him: 'Like the late Dean Rousmaniere ... Dean Bennett has stood for a liberal policy and opened wide the doors of the cathedral'.[32] St Paul's parish church had become the cathedral in 1912, and Edmund Swett Rousmaniere, rector since 1909, had become dean. An 'open door' policy perhaps came more naturally in such a church, and in a new country, where no age-long tradition of the cathedral as a separate and remote institution existed, and where the very idea of building cathedrals, as such, was only beginning to emerge. Between the work of Bennett and that of Rousmaniere there are undoubtedly parallels, though the two men came from different ecclesiastical traditions and there is no evidence that Rousmaniere had influenced Bennett's thinking.[33]

From Massachusetts, Bennett and his son travelled to other parts of New England. In Providence, Rhode Island, they attended a conference arranged by the diocesan bishop who as yet had no cathedral, but who three years later decided to adopt St John's Church.[34] Bennet described the visit as 'two days of delightful personal contacts and spiritual refreshment for clergy and laity'. The dean and his son were welcomed at a Churchmen's Club dinner, where he spoke of his first impressions of the United States, with what the bishop described as 'kindly satire'. We can guess at his opening remarks. He talked, also, of how the Church could give a lead in expressing the religious aspirations of the Nation. At the subsequent Conference, the bishop reported that the 'reality of God's presence and the realization of a baptized Christian's part in God's purposes were widely set forth not only in the words of the Dean but through his forceful personality'. Bennett supported the current 'Bishops' Crusade', with 'illuminating suggestions gathered from his experience with evangelism in England'.[35]

Bennett made a special trip to New York, where he preached at the British Harvest Festival Service in the famous St Paul's Chapel, Trinity Episcopal parish, on Broadway.[36] The occasion had been well advertised, and an impressive congregation foregathered. The British Consul General and delegations of twenty-one British, Canadian, and American patriotic societies, plus representatives of the Sulgrave Institution and the English Speaking Union, all attended and joined in the procession. Bennett began his sermon by saying that he believed the Harvest Festival to be the oldest form of religious worship in the world. The press, however, and no doubt many others present, were more interested in his social comments. He observed of the United States: 'There is an astounding waste in this country. Things are flung away with profit to no one. This may be my Old World attitude, but on our little island we would not think of approaching the tremendous waste I see here.'

As for post-war Britain – perhaps in an oblique reference to the recent General Strike and the lingering coal dispute – he voiced the current conventional wisdom about the disturbing effect of the 1914–1918 war, but also by implication compared Britain's sacrifice with that of the USA. 'When you hear of difficulties in England you must remember that we gave our boys by the hundreds of thousands. As a result there is a lack of men between the ages of 30 and 40, and that is why we have a dearth of leaders.'[37]

After a brief visit to Concord, New Hampshire,[38] the last three days of October were spent in Burlington, Vermont, following a programme arranged by Bishop Arthur C. A. Hall. Bennett addressed the diocesan clergy on the spiritual life of the priest; gave an address at the university on the life of the world to come, on the lines of *Expecto*; and talked to the Men's Club of St Paul's parish, on 'the nature and value of a Cathedral as a diocesan center and spiritual power house', covering the familiar ground of *The Nature of a Cathedral*, which would doubtless be on sale.[39]

Bishop Hall had known the English Church scene at first hand. He had been a member of the English Society of St John the Evangelist ('The Cowley Fathers'), an Anglo-Catholic order with centres also in the USA. Serving as a curate in America, he had been recalled to England, following his support in 1892 for the consecration of the famous but liberally inclined Phillips Brooks, Bishop of Massachusetts. Hall subsequently left the Society and returned to America, becoming Bishop of Vermont.[40] He found Bennett's account of cathedral reform 'especially interesting' to one who 'personally remembers' incidents connected with St Paul's Cathedral and Westminster Abbey, and who recollected also Christ Church, Oxford, and unregenerate Chester Cathedral. This cathedral was now 'familiar ... to so many of our people on their visits to England'. Nostalgically, he found the visit of 'so cultured and versatile and enthusiastic an ecclesiastic from the old country ... a distinct benefit to the Church in America'.[41]

Moving on to Albany, Bennett preached in All Saints Cathedral.[42] It must have heartened him to be in a church which had been built (in 1884–1904) specifically as a cathedral, in place of a temporary parish church cathedral, after the then bishop had visited England in 1873, to study cathedrals there.[43] Bennett's sermon 'brought out the fact that a Cathedral Church may be made a center from which the Bishop of the Diocese can exercise spiritual leadership in his relations to the clergy and the Diocese', and that this 'would be especially true of a Diocese in which the Cathedral was accessible as a center of devotion and inspiration'.[44] Surprisingly, Bennett is not reported as bestowing laurels for present achievements, which might suggest that Albany Cathedral did not as yet approximate to his ideal; nor did Bishop Nelson in his neutral-sounding and purely factual report in *The Cathedral Age* bestow praise on Bennett.[45]

In contrast, Bennett's visit to Philadelphia (4–11 November) was a great success. The press, noting the marked tone of 'reasoned and achieved good cheer' in all his addresses, hailed him as 'the cheerful Dean'. During the past few years, a number of leading English clergy had visited Philadelphia, but according to the Rector of St James's, Dr John Mockridge, his host and constant companion for the whole eight days, Bennett had made the most significant impact. This was not only the Rector's own judgment but also 'that of many other citizens of Philadelphia who have written or spoken to me'. Mockridge wrote glowingly about Bennett's personal qualities: his great ability to establish instant rapport with an audience; his 'penchant for individual human contacts'; his presentational skills; and his 'common sense, geniality and warmth'. Of the content of Bennett's addresses, he unfortunately says little, though his comment that Bennett was a 'well equipped student of biology and psychology', and 'a sort of specialist in religion', gives a clue to the content of his addresses.[46]

Bennett pursued a hectic programme of talks and sermons.[47] 'With such a schedule', the anonymous writer in *The Living Church* remarked, 'one hardly wonders at the Dean's often expressed feeling that we in America need time to be quiet!'[48] The same writer gave the only detailed account of one of Bennett's talks. This was delivered to the Clerical Brotherhood, some 75 of the city clergy.[49] In a 'quiet and kindly way' he offered 'frank criticism', and, basing his remarks on the great passage on 'the peace of God' in Phillipians 4: 4–7,[50] stressed that times of quiet in the life of the clergy were 'an absolute essential' for effective ministry. His analysis and exposition of his text reflected themes which recur in his writings: the 'sweet reasonableness' (as he phrased 'moderation') needed in dealing patiently with individuals; the security and power springing from faith; the negative effect of worry and anxiety; the need to bring the 'common interests of life' into prayer.[51]

Philadelphia had no cathedral. A Cathedral Project, however, was under way, and Bennett agreed to return to Philadelphia from Washington in order to address an invited group of 'representative citizens' at a publicity and fundraising subscription luncheon. A particular US Senator, another strong supporter of the Project, was to preside.[52] The Project Committee believed that 'The Cathedral, as the home of the unchurched and as a center of diocesan life, is coming to be recognised not as an ecclesiastical luxury, but as a necessity'. They had invited Bennett 'to explain and commend the Cathedral idea'. Some years later, the Senator's sister met Bennett when she was visiting Chester. Subsequently the Senator was so impressed by her reports of 'the amount of service the Chester Cathedral is rendering to the community and ... the spirit in which it is being done', that he sought out a copy of Chester's latest report and copies of relevant literature 'to influence the imagination of visitors' to Washington.[53] Nevertheless, 60 years later Philadelphia Cathedral still remained unbuilt, the eighteenth-century Christ Church, preserved as a national shrine, being considered the Mother Church of the Diocese of Pennsylvania.[54] The funds collected to build a cathedral were used to support a Cathedral Chapter. Only in the 1990s was the cathedral project again carried forward.[55]

After Philadelphia, Bennett spent a week in New York, where Dean Howard C. Robinson had planned his visits. The Cathedral of St John the Divine, a large and impressive church in the style of thirteenth-century French Gothic, was still incomplete in 1926.[56] Although Bennett preached at the cathedral on Sunday morning, he was to make no specific mention of St John the Divine in his subsequent articles in the *Chester Diocesan Gazette* on the American tour.[57] The dean and the bishop arranged for Bennett to show his 'stereopticon pictures' of Chester Cathedral and talk about them, at the important Church Club of New York.[58] Members and friends were invited, 'including ladies'.[59]

3

The climax of the American tour was Washington (20 November–6 December), where the National Cathedral project was actively under way. 'Of all that I saw or heard or felt', Bennett wrote later, 'the one thing – I say it frankly and without reservation – which impressed me most was the cathedral-in-the-making on Mount St Alban'.[60] Bishop Freeman had planned Bennett's engagements to ensure that the important church groups would hear him and be able to discuss problems with him. The emphasis was on the cathedral itself, but Bennett also conducted seminars on religion, took services, and preached. He spoke to the Cathedral Chapter and staff on cathedral administration, 'throwing much light', according to Bishop Rhinelander, 'upon our local problems and making most valuable and practical suggestions'.[61] He addressed the Episcopal clergy of Washington and neighbourhood on 'Modernising Cathedrals'.[62] He pointed to the 'handicaps and past errors' of the English cathedral system, and the difficulties facing attempts to adapt it to American needs, but made 'brilliantly clear' the need for cathedrals as 'necessary and age-long agencies for unifying and intensifying the Church's life'.[63] Following up his campaign, Bennett talked to a key group, the Washington Committee of the National Cathedral Association, and a few days later gave an illustrated lecture on Chester Cathedral at the select Washington Club, where the National

Cathedral Committee had invited special guests to meet him.[64] He repeated the lecture in St Mark's parish hall, the natural centre for the eastern part of Washington.

St Mark's was also the venue for seminars by Bennett on 'Personal Religion, combined with devotion', the series being an innovation which Rhinelander believed 'ought to be permanently useful in the Church'.[65] He conducted a similar exercise in Trinity Diocesan Church, now styled a 'Day of Devotion', for 60 laymen representing 50 Washington parishes, discussing 'practical theology as a preliminary to the work of practical evangelism', making a 'deep [and] lasting' impression on those present.[66] He later held another Day of Devotion for clergy, starting with Communion and concluding with Evensong.[67]

Three of Bennett's several Washington sermons are of special interest. He had the honour of giving the year's Thanksgiving Day address in the Cathedral's Bethlehem Chapel (the only part in use).[68] And on his last Sunday in the capital, he preached at the morning service in St Thomas' Church, on the subject of the future life, on the lines of *Expecto* – copies of which would be on sale afterwards. Finally, in the afternoon he preached at Choral Evensong in the Bethlehem Chapel, speaking, said Philip Rhinelander, with 'most hearty approval and encouraging good will' of the plan and purpose of the developing cathedral.[69] Bennett linked this with a plea to American mothers to 'band together' in the Mothers' Union, in order to preserve the sanctity of marriage, the upbringing of children, and that 'precious possession of civilisation', the home. The Washington National Cathedral would be a means of 'welding together' peoples of different nations in 'peace and amity', just as, in England, the cathedral of the fourteenth century had 'marked the welding together of the Norman-Saxon races'. He bade Godspeed to the edifice, and to the people who had 'overwhelmed' him with kindness. The service was broadcast, and Bennett was heard by an audience estimated at over half a million.[70]

4

Bishop Freeman had called Bennett, unreservedly, 'the greatest authority on Cathedral administration in the Anglican Church'.[71] He must, then, have regarded as worthy of note Bennett's comments on the National Cathedral and his suggestions in relation to to its development.

Before leaving for Britain, on 9 December Bennett wrote his letter of thanks to Freeman from Philadelphia.[72] He believed that, of the 'various suggestions' (unspecified) which he had 'ventured to make, much the most useful ... is the suggestion to erect soon a temporary nave'.

> My own idea [he wrote] would be to erect this at once as a complete building ... with a temporary East end partition which could be removed when the choir and as much of the crossing as you can build in the course of the next 18 months is completed.[73] Such a nave could probably be completed in a few months and you would be able to deal with a couple of thousand people by this next summer.[74] Obviously, a great building designed to last for centuries can only be built slowly, and there would be no temptation to hurry the building of your permanent nave if it was being built round a temporary one which enabled you to meet adequately all immediate needs.[75]

Bennett had already advocated such structures two years before, in a letter to *The Times* on cathedrals in new dioceses. Anyone, he contended, could learn how to do it by inspecting the Wembley Exhibition buildings.[76] He came back to the same idea in his *On Cathedrals in the Meantime* (1928), referring again to the model of the Wembley buildings.[77] The Washington Cathedral authorities do not seem to have adopted the suggestion, however, but to have concentrated their efforts on raising funds to complete the building as designed. It may have been felt that an interim solution could diminish the impetus to achieve a prestigious National Cathedral.[78]

The other suggestion which Bennett considered important enough to reiterate concerned the Mothers' Union. If Ida had not sent the literature, he would have it 'despatched at once', when he got home.[79]

> I do think [he went on] that if the Washington Cathedral saw fit to initiate a society on similar lines it would do a very great thing for the future of this country. The Mothers' Union has "caught on" so vigorously in England and her commomwealth of nations, that such an organization can be sure of success anywhere our Anglo Saxon race has found a home.[80]

The idea did not catch on. By the time of Bennett's visit, there already existed a flourishing organisation known as the 'Women's Auxiliary'. It was 'Auxiliary' to the Board of Missions, which was originally concerned with spreading and developing the Episcopal Church in the expanding west, and later in overseas territories.[81] There is no clear evidence as to why the Mothers' Union did not develop. The fact, however, that the Auxiliary, formed in 1868 to co-ordinate the work previously done by a number of women's societies, was firmly established as the dominating focus of service for Church women long before Bennett visited America must have tended to diminish the attraction of another women's organisation. Furthermore, the goals, and the projects taken in hand by the Auxiliary, very much reflected the aspirations of American women of the period.[82]

5

Bennett did not mention Children's Corners in his letter to Freeman, but the success of his initiative had long been apparent to Americans visiting Chester Cathedral, and the idea had been well received in the United States. In 1928, a scheme to incorporate a Children's Chapel into Washington Cathedral was made possible through a gift of $50,000. A writer in *The Cathedral Age* acknowledged the role of Bennett.

> In England, during the World War designated places in churches and Cathedrals became associated with private devotion and prayer for those in active service. To them unaccompanied children found their way, often clutching ... a flower or two, which they would leave before the altar and slip out after their prayers ... After the Armistice the Dean of the Cathedral did a wonderful thing by devoting first at his church at Hawarden and later in his Cathedral church special places to the sole use of children. He provided a table, some chairs, a prayer desk, pictures and books ... for the care of which the children themselves were held responsible. From that beginning, the idea spread throughout the British Empire. Strange as it may seem, never in any Cathedral had there been built for children a chapel.[83]

Washington made good the deficiency.

Designed as an integral part of the cathedral, the Children's Chapel was conceived as a 'distinct unit' within it. With arches of appropriately small scale, it was built in a late fourteenth-century style, to which an almost fifteenth-century style of fan vaulting adds lightness and grace. It thus contrasts with the massiveness of the adjoining Choir and South Transept aisles. Inspiration for sculpture, lights, and inscriptions was drawn from admonitions, utterances, and incidents relating to children in the Gospel story and Christian history, and also to historical individuals best known for their love and care of children.[84]

The Chapel was dedicated by Bishop Freeman on 15 September 1939, children representative of the whole diocese attending. Freeman is reported as saying that 'only one other cathedral was known to have set apart an entire chapel for the use of children', and the official Guide Book to the Cathedral repeats this. It is tempting to think that he had Chester in mind, but it was a furnished space, not a specially designed area, which Bennett had provided. Freemen was in fact probably referring to Montreal, where Professor Philip J. Turner, FRIBA, of McGill University had converted a portion of the porch of Christ Church Cathedral into a tiny chapel for children. It had been dedicated in April 1939.[85]

Long before being planned as part of a new cathedral, provision of one sort or another for children in churches and cathedrals had proliferated. New York's great cathedral of St John the Divine had a bay set aside; the old Episcopal Church in Vermont had made 'thoughtful provision'. But in 1930, having received from America a Christmas card produced for Children's Corners there, Bennett was prompted to write, with pardonable pride: 'Of these there must now be on the other side of the Atlantic some thousands. The grandmother of them all is the Corner in our own Cathedral, itself just nine years old'.[86]

According to his son, Bennett never proselytised for children's corners. On the other hand, I have found no comments by Bennett on the artistic tastelessness which became a feature of many. In Britain the fashion during the inter-war years for children's corners was a Bennett legacy of dubious value. Regarded as the up-to-date feature to incorporate into a parish church they too often became homes for bad mass-produced sentimental art, sold, together with specially designed furniture, in response to this new market. Bennett's parish-priest son was to observe in his 'Memoir' that few ever served the purpose for which the Chester Cathedral Children's Corner had been designed and which, he believed, it had originally fulfilled. Here and there ideological reaction set in. In 1940 the learned authors of the spoof Puritan survey of Cambridge churches and chapels, *Babylon Bruis'd and Mount Moriah Mended*, found six parish churches with a 'superstition called a Children's Corner', variously littered with trivia (in their view), in one instance including '.i. fause auter, .ij penny candlesticks of brasse, & divers superstitious pictures and Images', all six of which they joyfully 'brake down'. The fashion for merely sentimental children's corners waned somewhat after 1939, as adults were confronted by child evacuees and the grimmer apects of war. Yet it resumed after the war – continuing even after *The Lord of the Flies* appeared in 1954.[87]

The cosy middle-class state of mind which found prettified parish-church children's corners so attractive also found Christopher Robin, the 'Ovaltinies', and the offerings of Margaret Tarrant suitably innocent fare for children. A further instance of this mindset was the comfortable 'domestication' of the Gospel story for childhood consumption, by toning down the realities of the sacrifice celebrated in the Eucharist. Yet Bennett can hardly be blamed for the vulgarization of the children's corner concept. The prototype at Hawarden appears to have been an offshoot of 'Children's Eucharists', not uncommon at the date.[88] The portable altar used was located on weekdays, together with a Christmas crib, in a corner of the church and was the basis for a 'children's corner'. The Children's Corner at Chester Cathedral, as initiated and supervised by Bennett but organized by two devout laywomen (the Misses Giles), does not seem to have been linked to any 'Children's Eucharist' but instead to have had a social purpose, it being intended to draw into the building the unchurched street children who would otherwise never have entered, thus forming a Gospel for the grubby.

To return to America. The planning of Washington Cathedral pre-dated the publication of both of Bennett's books, *The Nature of a Cathedral* and *On Cathedrals in the Meantime*. It is perhaps too much to expect Bennett, writing in the mid–1920s, to have been aware of all cathedral projects world-wide, but his comments indicate some limitations in his researches – limitations equally apparent, it must be said, in the background knowledge of reviewers and commentators on his books. Washington's Children's Chapel was not incorporated into the cathedral's design until 1927–1928, as was announced in the Easter 1928 issue of *The Cathedral Age*.[89] Bennett's influence on the inter-war vogue for Children's Corners is undeniable and could thus have influenced Washington, but the record is silent. In contemporary thinking about children and churches, there may, after all, have been parallel developments on each side of the Atlantic. However, as late as 1930, in his pamphlet *The Resurrection of the Organism*, beneath a photograph of Chester Cathedral's Easter Sepulchre Bennett could not resist adding a note, 'Nearby the Mother of Children's Corners'.[90] A Children's Corner survives in many of today's churches. Abolished in Chester Cathedral, one is now reappearing as a children's chapel.

6

Bennett recorded his impressions of America in two articles in *The Chester Diocesan Gazette*, and his impressions of Washington Cathedral, for the benefit of American readers, in an article in *The Cathedral Age*.[91]

Three inter-related aspects of America struck Bennett: the vastness of the country, the immensity of its problems, and the complexity of its population. With his son he had travelled thousands of miles, rarely spent two nights in the same bed, and yet, 'the little bit of the USA that we covered was about as large compared to the whole as the Isle of Wight is compared to England'. In Britain, people wondered why America had not come into the war earlier, cancelled war debts, or joined the League of Nations. But things did not depend on the half dozen or so eastern states, and the hundreds of thousands of Anglo-Saxon citizens 'who are passionately devoted to England'. The wonder was that 'the States got into the war in time to do any good at all, and of course now they mostly think they won it'. The range of the racial and ethnic mix, and the problems of assimilation and language impressed him greatly. Only the teaching of English 'saves the whole from Babel'. But the essential Englishman of his day is revealed in Bennett's comment, that 'it is the quality, not the numerical quantity of the stock that gives what security there is for an Anglo-Saxon civilization'. Before the visit he was 'a mild supporter of the English Speaking Union ... I have come home an enthusiast'. Finally, the 'stupendous scale' of everything American caught his imagination: buildings, public works, expenditure on education ('they don't care what they spend and nothing is too good for the younger end'), and the size of universities – one with 20,000 students.[92]

In 'More American Notes' Bennett attempted a critical analysis of the state of the American Church. With exceptions in religious art, music, ceremonial, and liturgical understanding, it 'seems years behind England'. He gently chided its theatrical preoccupation with 'coloured stoles, processional and recessional hymns ... with the "recessional" manoeuvred so as to vanish every time in the distance and be closed with an elaborate amen, played on tubular bells by the organ'. In America, the emphasis was on organisation, the Parochial Office sometimes overshadowing the church itself. In choosing bishops (all elected) the laity preferred men smart at raising money, rather than 'Fathers in God'. Yet he found much to admire and praise. The American Church, after the Declaration of Independence, had doggedly surmounted difficulties put in its way by the English archbishops, who refused to consecrate bishops. The organisation of the church, however, had gone ahead, and 'it was not England but Scotland that in the end gave them the Episcopate'.[93] Scotland, Bennett asserted, also gave America 'the treasure of the Scottish Liturgy', which was 'almost ... identical with the form proposed for our own alternative use' (a form much approved by Bennett).[94]

The Church had 'admirable, often noble buildings'; it paid its clergy better than did England; in the missionary field, it contributed generously in men and money. Bennett marked with enthusiastic approval the emphasis on 'colour and beauty, music and orderly ceremonial (not forgetting our sense of smell)', a recognition that it was through 'eye, ear, and nose' that religion made its first appeal, for 'feeling comes first and thinking afterwards ... Suggestion goes deeper and lasts longer than information' – a sentiment Bennett echoed so often in his writings. One suspects that he was seizing the opportunity to present a liturgical recipe to the clergy of Chester Diocese.[95]

Bennett's highest praise was reserved for Washington Cathedral, on Mount St Alban. The building – though Bennett seems unaware of this – had been designed in 1906–1907 by the well-known English gothicist, G. F. Bodley, who was delighted at the opportunity that 'wonderful Gothic art, neglected, dying, nearly dead' had been given. He was assisted by a Cheshire-born architect, Henry Vaughan, who had made his home in Boston.[96] Bennett regarded the cathedral as 'the greatest single Church venture in the world today'. He went on -

> A few years ago I ventured to write a little book on 'The Nature of a Cathedral'. In it I put all that I then saw in connection with our old cathedrals on this side of the Atlantic. At Washington I found almost every idea that I ever had, and a great many more, being splendidly embodied on an altogether majestic scale. I felt curiously at home there – much elated and enlarged.[97]

He had always stressed the importance of site. 'Mount St Alban', he remarked, 'must surely be the the most splendid site in the world for a great Cathedral

Church'. On it was being built everything he had seen as necessary adjuncts to English cathedrals – and more: 'Bishop's House, Library, Synod House, Guest House, College of Preachers, Schools, Gardens, houses for retired clergy and for canons, ample provision for parking cars – nothing seems to have been forgotten'.

Finally, Bennett noted with approval 'a real bit of ancient and modern organisation':

> I mean the provision of a separate Church, close to the Cathedral Church itself for the parish in which it stands. This is just what there should be for the obviating of all sorts of otherwise inevitable difficulties. If ... the ancient plan should be adopted of making the Rector of the adjacent Church a Canon of the Cathedral, Washington ... will have solved ... one of a cathedral's big problems which has never, as far as I know, been solved on any other lines.[98]

This seems to imply that the parish church was conceived as part of the plan for the cathedral. In fact, St Alban's Parish Church was erected in 1857, long before Mount St Alban was dreamed of as a cathedral site.

7

Bennett and his son arrived back in Liverpool on 21 December 1926. Bennett regaled the waiting pressmen with an account of his brush with the American Customs, adding, however, that 'even if he had been the Prince of Wales', he could not have been more royally entertained in the United States.[99] The comment was apposite, for the Prince had visited Chester Cathedral during Bennett's absence.[100] The following day there was a little ceremony in Chester, when a five-seater motor car was presented to Bennett and Ida, by 'a number of the Dean's friends ... in recognition of their services to Chester', and to welcome Bennett home.[101] He was quickly involved, again, with the problems of his own cathedral. One of his ambitions had been to bring back sufficient dollars to pay for the repair of the roof of the North Transept. The Americans had given £750, 'which was very generous', but costs had risen and a total of £2,500 would now be needed to clear the debt. However, 'with a new motor car', he would be delighted to give lectures, 'if there will be a little money in them for the Cathedral'. St Andrew's, West Kirby, was the first to invite him.[102]

In June 1930 Bishop Freeman of Washington came to England for the Lambeth Conference of early July. He stayed with the Bennetts during the week-end of the St Werburgh festival and was able to see the developments in Chester Cathedral for himself. On the Sunday, he preached at the St Werburgh's Day service. Bennett recalled that he had stayed with Freeman for ten days, on Mount St Alban, when he was 'more impressed by Washington Cathedral and the group of men responsible for its building than by anything else I saw during my three months in the States'.[103] When Bennett initiated moves to found a Friends of Chester Cathedral Society, Freeman became one of the distinguished company of Patrons.[104] E. N. Lewis, Washington Cathedral's Publicity Agent, sent a dollar subscription, as the first to join the Friends 'from across the Atlantic', receiving in return his badge and material with which to publicize the Society. A notice, giving full details of how to join and mentioning the Prince of Wales and Bishop Freeman as Vice Presidents, duly appeared in *The Cathedral Age*.[105] Meanwhile, memorabilia of Bennett's visit, on display in the cathedral, remained a continuing source of interest to American visitors, and no doubt encouraged generous contributions.

There is other evidence of continuing links between Washington and Chester. For example, 'a friend of Washington Cathedral', on business in England, visited Chester in January 1930, and sent a postcard of the Cathedral Choir to Mount St Alban, with the following message. 'In the sacristy of Chester Cathedral yesterday, Sunday morning, I saw two copies of "The Cathedral Age", one open to pictures of the gardens; a large photograph of the Cathedral as it will be when finished, and a large brochure "The Story of Washington Cathedral"'. In response, *The Cathedral Age* duly published the picture and the message, adding – 'To our London correspondent and to the genial Dean of Chester who was our guest on Mount St Alban in 1926, cordial greetings'.[106] The controversial new Chester Cathedral vestry was commented on in the Michaelmas 1930 issue of *The Cathedral Age*, and the Midsummer 1931 number carried a finely illustrated article by Bennett, 'Chester Cathedral: a Portrait in Stone'. In this he developed the idea that each style of building was 'an unconscious portrait of its builders', the latest style, of course, as we might expect, being that of Bennett's own addition, the contemporary-style new vestry. His advice, therefore, 'to those who are interested in building cathedrals on the other side of the Atlantic', set in this context, provides a suitable postscript to the comments he had made in Canada and America, five years earlier:

Be not contented to copy the great buildings of previous ages. Such buildings, however large and beautiful they may be, can never be more interesting than a copy of a portrait of an ancestor. If with your present day buildings you want to grip your own generation and its successors, in your native and modern style of architecture you must have the courage to build in stone, or in steel, or in concrete, and to build the very best portraits you can, not of others but of yourselves. There is more, I believe, in this caution than some might think.[107]

Notes

1   *Chester Diocesan Gazette* [hereafter *CDG*], Mar. 1923, 121. Howson, Dean of Chester 1867–1885, visited the USA in 1871 and 1880, and the money he raised went towards the £100,000 restoration of the cathedral completed in 1872 (*Dictionary of National Biography*).

2   *CDG*, Mar. 1923, 121.

3   *ibid.*, July 1925, 107–8. James Edward Freeman: b. 1866; consec. bp., 1923: *Who's Who in America*, 16 (Chicago/London, 1928).

4   *CDG*, Oct. 1926, 148–9; W. W. Manross, *A History of the American Episcopal Church* (New York, 1950), 368.

5   *CDG*, Apr. 1926. For Rhinelander, see *Who Was Who in America 1897–1943* (Chicago, 1943).

6   *The Ecclesiologist*, 88, February 1852, 19–20, 21; Basil F. L. Clarke, *Anglican Cathedrals outside the British Isles* (London, 1958), 137–42. Hopkins advocated the building of a cathedral for New York able to accommodate 8–10,000 worshippers and a choir of 500. There should be a staff of from 12 to 24 clergy, who would act as city missionaries. Around the cathedral should be grouped choristers' schools, seminaries for priests, a hospital, a home for aged clergy, etc. (*ibid.*, 140). Bennett was not the first to think of the cathedral as a 'centre', though his focus was markedly different.

7   The 'National Cathedral' was being built at Mount St Alban, Washington.

8   Following close on Bennett's heels was Winnington-Ingram, Bishop of London.

9   *CDG*, May 1926, 67–8. Bennett was accompanied by his son who had recently graduated from Oriel College, Oxford, and as an intending ordinand must have relished the chance to gain insights into the American Church. He handled administrative arrangements when Bennett was busy, and endeavoured, not very

successfully, to restrain his father's impulse to shower gratuities for small services, which 'cost his son a small fortune' ('Family History'). The pair returned on 10 December 1926. They received Paget's blessing at Evensong on 16 September, which imparted the air of a pilgrimage to the tour. Bennett had feared that 'my American friends [are] ... expecting more than I know myself to be capable of giving them', and had asked *Chester Diocesan Gazette* readers to say for him the Collect for Trinity XX ('...that we, being ready in both mind and soul, may cheerfully accomplish those things that thou wouldst have done ...'): *CDG*, Oct. 1926; CPB, 16 Sept. 1926, 161.

    10   Despite the choppy weather, Bennett had a 'very creditably sized congregation' (*CDG*, Feb. 1927, 23).

    11   Probably Emily Louisa (1858–1937); the other elder sister, Katie Adelaide (1860–1866), was probably also born in Canada.

    12   *Toronto Daily Star*, 4.10.1926, 1.

    13   ibid.

    14   J. Ross Robertson, *Landmarks of Toronto, 4* (Toronto, 1904), 84–6; Clarke, *Anglican Cathedrals*, 61.

    15   *CDG*, Feb. 1927, 23.

    16   *Toronto Daily Star*, 4.10.1926, 1, pt. II.

    17   ibid.

    18   T. A. Reed, *A History of the University of Trinity College 1852–1952* (Toronto, 1952), 252, 261.

    19   *Toronto Daily Star*, 4.10.1926, 1; *CDG*, Feb. 1927, 23.

    20   *CDG*, Feb. 1927, 23.

    21   Robin S. Harris, *A History of Higher Education in Canada, 1863–1960* (Toronto, 1976).

    22   Clarke, *Anglican Cathedrals*, 61.

    23   Bennett found prices exorbitant, and expressed his views forcibly at an excessive charge for peaches in his hotel, 'sold in the street at 10 cents a bushel, but at dinner ... 50 cents for one'. He sums up the exchange of words tellingly: 'What a row!'

    24   *CDG*, Feb. 1927, 23–4.

    25   *The Times*, 22.12.1926. It was all an innocent mistake, which had arisen because of incorrect invoicing by the publishers. However, this availed naught with the US Customs. Bennett was charged double duty, fined $300, and had his stock of books confiscated. He was able to recover them only after signing a bond and depositing $750. Later, an American friend advised Bennett to appeal, but he declined, feeling it would be throwing good money after bad. However, after Bennett got back to England, the friend appealed on Bennett's behalf and won. So, two years later, Bennett got most of his money back, and rejoiced in characteristic style that 'in the famous case of the Dean of Chester v. the USA Government, the Dean of Chester has

come out all right in the end' (*CDG*, Oct. 1928).
  26   *Harvard University Gazette*, XXII, 3, 9.10.1926.
  27   *Boston Morning Globe* and *Boston Evening Globe*, 9.10.1926, 15. The *Boston Evening Transcript*, part 4, 8, commented that 'Like the late Dean Rousmaniere ... Dean Bennett has stood for a liberal policy and opened wide the doors of the Cathedral'. For the cathedral church, see Clarke, *Anglican Cathedrals*, 145, 153 (photograph).
  28   *The Boston Globe*, 11.10.1926, 'Chester, Eng. Dean talks at St Paul's – Would Work to Reunite Christian Churches, If He Lived In U.S.'
  29   F. S. M. Bennett, 'Integration', in H. R. L. Sheppard, ed., *My Hopes and Fears for the Church* (London, 1930), 85–6. In his St Paul's sermon, Bennett commented on the contemporary scene in the United States and Britain, as he saw it: 'You have many men of vision, who see things ahead, and you are putting amazing power and wealth into education. You are great hands at organisation. This is a personal universe and there is need for the right persons to solve its problems'. It would be 50 years before Britain could make up the manpower lost during 1914–1918. 'England', he reminded his audience, 'made an immense sacrifice for the world in the war' (*Boston Globe*, 11.10.1926).
  30   *Boston Globe* (morning), 11.10.1926, 17.
  31   *Providence (Rhode Island) Journal*, 27.9.1926, 1. See also 'Dean Rousmaniere', *The Church Militant*, Oct. 1926.
  32   *The Boston Evening Transcript*, part 4, 9.10.1926, 8.
  33   From a Quaker background, and an initial commercial career, Rousmaniere had entered the Church, after preparing himself for ordination at Harvard and the Episcopal Theological School, Cambridge (Mass.). Like Bennett, before he became dean he had ministered with outstanding success in a range of parishes, where he was 'always the originator and leader'. His aim, as he defined it in 1912, was akin to Bennett's. The new cathedral was to be 'a centre of spiritual influence, the power of which shall be felt throughout the community and beyond'. He rapidly made it a reality. Like Bennett, Rousmaniere stressed the ministry of healing, though we hear no mention of Coué, and the open door and friendly welcome were unquestioned. Unlike Bennett, he was a low churchman, and (in the words of a commentator on Boston churches in 1921) 'not afraid to offer extraneous prayers, or to give out a gospel song ... Nevertheless, the service has a distinctively ritualistic quality and conforms in the main to the canons and rubrics of the Church' (Howard H. Bridgman, 'A little clinic on the status of churchgoing', *The Outlook*, 128 (11), 13.7.1921, 446). Soon, Boston people were flocking to the cathedral church on Sundays and weekdays, 'not chiefly because St Paul's has a ranking superior to that of other churches ... but because Dean Rousmaniere has made it a religious power house ... measured by its constant impact upon the life of the city and of the region' (D. A. Addison, 'The

new Rector of St Paul's', *The Church Militant*, Nov. 1909, 9); *Providence (Rhode Island) Journal*, 27.9.1926, 1–2; 'Dean of Cathedral Passes Away', *The Boston Evening Transcript*, 27.9.1926). See also Bishop of Boston, *The Cathedral* (n.d.); 'The Dean's Message', *The Church Militant*, October 1912, 10. Rousmaniere's bishop shared his vision ('Bishop Lawrence's Address at the Diocesan Service', *The Church Militant*, October 1912, 14–16).

    34   James de Wolf jnr., bishop 1911 (Clarke, *Anglican Cathedrals*, 146).

    35   *The Cathedral Age*, I/8, Christmas 1926, 13.

    36   *Trinity Church Year Book and Register*, 1926, 108. For Bennett's full programme in the USA, *The Cathedral Age*, I/7, Michaelmas 1926, 58.

    37   'Many Societies march to Harvest Festival', *The New York Times*, 18.10.1926.

    38   Bennett received an enthusiastic welcome at the meeting of the Provincial Synod. At a Churchmen's Club banquet he spoke on Cathedrals; St Paul's School entertained him, and he addressed the boys at morning chapel (*The Cathedral Age*, I/8, Christmas 1926, 14).

    39   *ibid.*, 14–15; I/8, 1926, 15.

    40   Manross, *American Episcopal Church*, 310–11.

    41   *ibid.*; W. S. F. Pickering, *Anglo-Catholicism: A Study in Religious Ambiguity* (London, 1989), 74; *The Cathedral Age*, I/8, Christmas 1926, 15.

    42   *ibid.*.

    43   Clarke, *Anglican Cathedrals*, 136 (photograph, 147).

    44   *The Cathedral Age*, I/8, Christmas 1926, 15.

    45   *ibid.*.

    46   *ibid.* 13–4.

    47   The night after Bennett arrived he spoke to a group of some 200 men at St Paul's Church, Overbrook, whom he 'literally enthralled for a full hour, bringing his address to a close against their evidently genuine protest'. His address at a luncheon given in his honour by the English-Speaking Union and the Trans-Atlantic Society was well received by an audience of 'men and women of prominence and distinction in Philadelphia'. The Secretary told Mockridge that, of all their many recent visitors, Bennett held 'a very foremost place'. On Thursday, 11 November, he spoke at a simple, quiet Armistice Day service in St James's Church, where he also gave the sermon on Sunday morning, following it up with another at Evensong, in St Saviour's Church. There was also the expected talk on Chester Cathedral, given at St James's and followed, we may surmise, by the usual sale of his book (*The Cathedral Age*, I/8, Christmas 1926, 13–4; *The Living Church*, 20.11.1926, 92).

    48   *The Living Church*, 20.11.1926, 92.

    49   *The Cathedral Age*, I/8, 1926, 13–4.

    50   'Rejoice in the Lord alway: and again I say Rejoice. Let your moderation

be known unto all men. The Lord is at hand. Be careful for nothing; but in everything by prayer and supplication with thanksgiving let your requests be made known unto God. And the peace of God, which passeth all understanding, shall keep your hearts and minds through Christ Jesus' (A.V.).

51   *The Living Church*, 20.11.1926, 92.

52   The Senator was George Wharton Pepper, a Philadelphia lawyer.

53   Washington National Cathedral Archives, 120.7.4, Pepper to Dean G. C. F. Bratenahl, 11.7.1932; E. N.Lewis to Senator Pepper, 13.7.1932.

54   Clarke, *Anglican Cathedrals*, 166–8.

55   The situation was described in 1992 by the current Bishop of Pennsylvania as follows. 'There were efforts during the early part of this century to establish and construct a cathedral. However, whatever Dean Bennett and Senator Pepper did in 1926 did not produce a cathedral, although it may have raised some money, the proceeds of which may still be invested. It was only in January of this year that, with the broad consent of the Diocese, I designated the Church of the Saviour as the Cathedral of the Diocese. There had long been a Cathedral Chapter, operating mostly in name only, but with some funds to preside over, which had originally been intended to build a cathedral. We are happily moving forward now with a cathedral for this Diocese, although not in the place and on the rather grand scale contemplated in the 1920s' (p.c. Allan L. Bartlett, Bishop of Pennsylvania, 17.9.1992).

56   *The Cathedral Age*, I/7, Michaelmas 1926, 58. Foundation stone, 1892; begun as Romanesque but for structural reasons redesigned as Gothic, 1911 (Clarke, *Anglican Cathedrals*, 153–60, 160–1 photographs); Mervyn Blatch, *Cathedrals* (Poole, 1980), 161–2.

57   The same day (14.11.1926), Bennett preached at Evensong in St James Episcopal Church, Madison Avenue (*The World*, 13.11.1926 – I am indebted to the Executive Secretary of the Church Club of New York, Anne V. Simpson, for providing me with a photocopy of the small announcement, from the Club's archives).

58   The bishop was the Tenth Bishop of New York, 1921–1946 (Clarke, *Anglican Cathedrals*, 156).

59   Washington National Cathedral Archives, 'Washington Cathedral Scrapbook', vol. 20. At The Church Club of New York five meetings wefe held in 1926, four at the Club itself. Of those at the Club, Bennett's was unquestionably the most popular, with an attendance of 160, compared with only 50 at a meeting on the Bishops' Crusade, addressed by the bishops of New York and Washington, and 15 at each of two other meetings. A fifth meeting was cancelled because of a poor response. Bennett was only outdone by the controversial Winnington-Ingram, Bishop of London, who attracted 1,500, but his meeting was not held in the more restricted space of the Club, but in the Great Hall of the Chamber of Commerce (Church Club of New York Archives, 'Report of the Committee on Meetings', 25.4.1927) – I am indebted to the

Executive Secretary for a copy of the Report).
60   *The Cathedral Age*, II/1, Easter 1927, 46–8.
61   Bishop Philip M. Rhinelander, Canon of the Cathedral and Warden of the College of Preachers, who had organised Bennett's tour (*The Cathedral Age*, I/8, Christmas 1926, 16).
62   *ibid..*
63   *ibid..*
64   Washington Cathedral Archives, 'Washington Cathedral Scrapbook', vol. 20.
65   Washington Cathedral Archives, 103.1.1, 'Washington Cathedral: The Bethlehem Chapel: Notices', 21.1.1926; *The Cathedral Age*, I/8, Christmas 1926, 16.
66   Washington Cathedral Archives, 'Washington Cathedral Scrapbook', vol. 20; *The Church Militant*, V/9, 1926, 6.
67   Washington Cathedral Archives, 101.2.10.: 'The Bethlehem Chapel of the Holy Nativity', record of services, entries 670–4, 6 Dec. 1926. Bennett had one relaxed day, when his only engagement was to plant in the bishop's garden a 300 year old yew, brought from Port Royal, Virginia, eighty miles away. Bennett is said to have wielded, 'in true gardener's style', the spade previously used by the Archbishop of Canterbury and the Prince of Wales. He then dedicated the tree (Washington Cathedral Archives, 'Washington Cathedral Scrapbook', vol. 20, notice of ceremony, bearing a photograph of the tree in its original site. Another photograph, reproduced in *The Cathedral Age*, shows the tree in position, with beside it Bennett, Bishop Freeman, and Mrs Bratenahl (the dean's wife, chairman of the Garden Committee). Bennett appears to be addressing the little group (*The Cathedral Age*, I/8, Christmas 1926, 9, 16–7, 57, the address said to be 'delightful'). The press covered most of his various activities and talks and was keenly interested in his comments on American bishops ('should wear hats, gaiters and silk aprons, as do the English'); on the aftermath of war ('in five years time ... England will recover her losses'); on English art treasures in American hands ('return to the British Isles'); and on foreign treasures in England ('return to Greece the famous Elgin marbles, and to Egypt Cleopatra's Needle'): Washington Cathedral Archives, 'Washington Cathedral Scrapbook', vol. 20, press cutting, 'English Dean urges aprons for Bishops'.
68   To be said on the first Thursday in November (*The Book of Common Prayer ... according to the use of the Protestant Episcopal Church in the United States of America* (New York, 1892), 346. The 'annual appointment of the day by the President and the Governors of most of the states is the most notable official recognition of religion in the United States' (P. Dearmer, *The Story of the Prayer Book in the Old and New World throughout the Anglican Church* (Oxford, 1933), 138–9). However, the service is omitted from the 1929 revision of *The Book of Common Prayer*.
69   Washington Cathedral Archives, 103.1.1, 'Washington Cathedral: the

Bethlehem Chapel', 5.12.1926, Order of Service; *The Cathedral Age*, I/8, Christmas 1926, 17.

70   Washington Cathedral Archives, 101.2.10.: 'The Bethlehem Chapel of the Holy Nativity', record of services, entry 669, Second Sunday in Advent, 5.12.1926; 'Washington Cathedral Scrapbook', vol. 20, 'American Mothers should band, Dean of Chester holds'.

71   *The Church Militant*, November 1926, 11.

72   Washington Cathedral Archives, 120.7.4, Bennett to Freeman, 9.12.1926.

73   Amendment from 'projection' to 'partition' in the manuscript.

74   Amendment from 'would' to 'could' in the manuscript.

75   Washington Cathedral Archives, 120.7.4, Bennett to Freeman, 9.12.1926.

76   *The Times*, 5.8.1924, 6.

77   ibid., 33.

78   Margaret D. Lewis, the Washington National Cathedral Assistant Archivist, kindly examined, on my behalf, photographs of the cathedral's exterior, taken at various stages of its erection, and writes: 'at no time is there any indication of a temporary nave ... I have lived in Washington since 1948 and have personally seen the completion of the South Transept as well as the Nave, and the indoor service capacity expanded only as the construction progressed' (p.c., 25.7.1991).

79   Washington Cathedral Archives, 120.7.4, Bennett to Freeman, 9 Dec. 1926.

80   Amended from 'make a' to 'sure of' in the manuscript.

81   The full title was 'Women's Auxiliary to the Board of Missions'. The 'Board' directed the Domestic and Foreign Missionary Society, to which all Episcopal Church members were regarded as belonging (by the 1835 Constitution of the Society).

82   The 'Auxiliary' continues now as 'The Episcopal Church Women'. See Mancross, *History of the American Church*, 236, 343.

83   Agnes Peters, 'A Cathedral Chapel for the Children', *Cathedral Age*, X/1, Easter 1935, 7–13. The chapel was endowed by Robert L. Taylor, a member of the National Committee for the Cathedral, in memory of his six-year old son. Chester's Washington progeny is alive and well today. Margaret D. Lewis, the present Assistant Cathedral Archivist, confirms that the Children's Chapel remains a highlight of the cathedral tour for visitors and continues to be used for baptisms. When her own sons were young, she was among the parents who brought their children to look at the manger scene set up there regularly at Christmas time (p.c., Margaret D. Lewis, 10.9.1992). I am much indebted to Mrs Lewis for considerable help in my investigation of Bennett's American tour.

84   Designed by the cathedral architects, Frohman, Robb and Little, with stained glass designed by Henry Lee Willet of Philadelphia. Description and photographs in *The Cathedral Age*, Easter 1928, 17–20; X/I, 7–13, 1935; *A Guide Book: Washington Cathedral* (10th Edition, Mount St Alban, Washington, 1940), 38, 39

(photograph); *Guide to Washington Cathedral*, 23–5, plates 97, 103. For a plan of the eastern glass, see Richard T. Feller (ed. Nancy S. Montgomery), *Sculpture and Carving at Washington Cathedral* (Washington, n.d.), 68; for the kneelers, Nancy S. Montgomery, *Stitches for God: The Story of Washington Cathedral Needlepoint* (Cathedral Church of Saint Peter and Saint Paul, n.d.), 21–22. In general, see Clarke, *Anglican Cathedrals*, 175.

85 'Dedication of the Children's Chapel', *The Cathedral Age*, Winter 1939–40, 38; Alice Hutchins Drake, 'The New Children's Corner', *The Cathedral Age*, Winter 1939–1940, 19–21. For Christchurch Cathedral, see Clarke, *Anglican Cathedrals*, 59–9, 64.

86 *CDG*, Feb. 1930, 18–9.

87 For mocking dismissal of children's corners, F. Brittain and B. L. Manning, *Babylon Bruis'd and Mount Moriah Mended* (Cambridge, 1940), 6–9, 11, 13, 15. (I am much indebted to Clive W. Cornell of Heffers of Cambridge and to Mrs Brittain for enabling me to see and obtain a copy of this work.) William Golding's novel, *The Lord of the Flies*, is a savage response to the cheerful optimism of R. M. Ballantyne's *The Coral Island* (1857), still popular in the earlier part of the twentieth century, which portrayed boys as finely-spirited, cooperative, and basically noble. 'The Lord of the Flies' is Beelzebub, the potential evil underlying youthful innocence and generating ruthless self-seeking once adult restraints are removed.

88 'Children's Eucharist' was apparently a special service for young communicants or possibly for parents accompanied by non-communicant young children.

89 'Gifts announced for two chapels', *Cathedral Age*, Easter 1928, 17–20.

90 F. S. M. Bennett, *The Resurrection of the Organism* (London, 1930), 2.

91 'Some American Notes', (*CDG*, Feb. 1927, 23–5); 'More American Notes', (*ibid.* Mar. 1927, 38–40); '"Spaciousness of Vision"', *The Cathedral Age*, II/1, Easter 1927, 46–8, subsequently reprinted in *Chester Diocesan Gazette* as 'A Cathedral-in-the-Making' (*CDG*, July 1927, 110–11).

92 'Some American Notes', 23–5.

93 Bennett was over-simplifying. The first USA bishop, Seabury, was consecrated in 1784 in Scotland by non-juring bishops, but the next three were consecrated at Lambeth Palace, and from this combined group the American Episcopate was derived (Manross, *American Episcopal Church*, 196–201).

94 'More American Notes', 39; for the American Liturgy, see C. J. Cuming, *A History of the Anglican Liturgy* (London, 1969), 188–90, 239.

95 'More American Notes', 38–40.

96 Cathedral of SS Peter and Paul; G. F. Bodley (ob. 1907); Henry Vaughan (ob. 1917); design revised by P. H. Frohman after the deaths of Bodley and Vaughan; Bethlehem Chapel finished and in use, 1912 (Clarke, *Anglican Cathedrals*, 170–3). For Vaughan (born Rockferry, Wirral, Cheshire, 1845), see C. L. Slattery, *Certain*

American Faces (New York, 1918); obituary, *The American Architect*, 11.7.1917. Bennett comments that the designers showed 'not only wisdom in not merely imitating the work of our medieval forefathers, but in assimilating their ideas and ideals for free and fresh embodiment ... This is just as it should be with those who are heirs of all the ages' (*CDG*, July 1927, 110). I am again indebted to Margaret D. Lewis for the references to American publications, for information about St Alban's parish church, and for much detailed information about Vaughan.

97   *CDG*, July 1927, 110.
98   'Spaciousness of Vision', 46–8; *CDG*, July 1927, 110–1. For St Alban's Parish Church, see *A Guide Book: Washington Cathedral*, 7th edit., with a photograph (Mount St Alban, Washington, D,C., 1935–1936), 101–2.
99   *The Times*, 22.12.1926, 15.
100   *Chester Chronicle*, 26.10.1926; Cheshire Record Office, Diocesan archives, 'Chapter Book, 1894–1941', 247.
101   *The Times*, 23.12.1926, 13g.
102   *Chester Chronicle*, 22.1.1927.
103   *CDG*, June 1930, 87.
104   *ibid.*, Aug. 1930, 87.
105   *ibid.*, Nov. 1930, 167.
106   *The Cathedral Age*, V/1, 1930, 79.
107   *ibid.*, VI/2, 1931, 5–12.2

VIII

Robust theology, educational philosophy, ecclesiastical politics

1

Bennett laid no claim to original scholarship, but read widely in current works on religion, biology and psychology, and had thought deeply about the issues raised. His writings reflect a conviction that the Christian Gospel and the conclusions of the sciences may be embraced in a single system of thought. His son was later to speak of the 'robust theology of the material world, such as Bennett came to preach'. Another underlying theme of Bennett's thinking was the Aristotelean doctrine that a 'thing' cannot be 'explained' by its origin, but only by its completion, its end, or 'what-it-was-meant-to-be'.[1] This teleological assumption gives his thought a unity, apparent whether he is addressing the resurrection of the dead or the opening of cathedrals.

In wider perspective, however, both Bennett's thought and the favourable public reception his more ambitious writings received may be seen as to some extent a reflection of the *Zeitgeist* in the aftermath of the First World War, in two aspects. First, public shock at realisation of the extent of the casualties included puzzlement about the incidence of mental disorder among those permanently disabled, and particularly about the cases of 'shell shock' where men not physically wounded had suffered breakdown from the stress of trench warfare.[2] This helped to turn elements of the popular as well as the educated mind to consideration of what was then termed the mind-body relationship. Secondly, if life in the trenches had made numbers of men despair of a providential God, numbers at home among those men and women who had lost beloved were driven to explore religious consolation in the form of contemplation of the life-to-come, with some even essaying communication with the dead. Bennett's conceptual writings invoked both aspects.

2

Among the books which Bennett took to America were copies of his recently published *Expecto* (1926), a work significantly subtitled 'An Essay on the Biology of the World to come'.[3] One of his American sermons was based on the ideas in this. *Expecto* is, in effect, the third book in a trilogy whose theme is humankind, its 'what-it-was-meant-to-be', and how it is to reach its proper end. It may be appropriately examined in the context of the earlier works: *M. Coué and his Gospel of Health* (1922), and *A Soul in the Making* (1924).

Coué's technique of auto-suggestion had a considerable vogue in Europe and America in the 1920s. As a chemist Coué had dispensed prescriptions which he knew were in physical terms largely useless yet seemed to cure, and he concluded that faith in the mixture in the bottle was the real element in the cure. 'Suggestion' was the key. He became a psychotherapist and hypnotist devoted to helping the sick. The Coué Institute, with offices in Grosvenor Gardens, London, was directed by an impressive General Committee, which included Julian Huxley, a prominent contemporary scientist.[4] Bennett was almost certainly a member of the Institute, because he was one of the small group who invited Coué to make his first visit to England in 1921. Bennett was an undoubted devotee of 'Coué-ism', and he incorporated it in the mélange of ideas which constituted his 'robust theology'.

In *M. Coué and his Gospel of Health* – a work so popular that it was reprinted twice – Bennett links religion and psychology.[5] Freudians, Jungians, and other psycho-therapists were developing mental healing techniques; correspondingly, Bennett gives details in an Appendix to his book of a visit by Coué to a hospital for shell-shock victims, in order to talk to the doctors and also to treat some of the patients. Coué's success attracted others to attempt similar work. During the inter-war years several faith-healers toured Britain, attracting crowds of sick persons to their meetings. Hymns and general prayers led up to a call for sufferers to come to the platform for a laying-on of hands and directed prayer, after which many felt better. Undoubtedly there was an element of mass hysteria in such gatherings, with a consequent mental effect on those expecting to be healed. But all this seemed to testify to the success of the Coué method with certain types of ailment.

Bennett's *Coué* gives important insight into the dean's thought and pastoral practice. At Bennett's invitation, on 18 November 1921 Coué lectured to

600 people in the cathedral Refectory and then treated, free, some 40 patients. Afterwards, many felt an improvement; for instance, some stammerers talked fluently to Coué.[6] Healing was (and is) also part of the Church's ministry. Bennett claimed no special gift, but regarded sick-visiting as his 'ministerial hobby'. Had he not felt called to the Church, he would have trained as a doctor.[7] As dean, he had continued to visit the sick, praying and anointing.[8] In *Coué* he offers detailed advice to clergy. The Prayer Book assertion that sickness was sent for our own good rests on a misinterpretation of verses in the Epistle to the Hebrews.[9] God's will is health, but man lives in a world where sickness exists; we should co-operate with God in getting rid of it. Prayer should be turned into auto-suggestion 'by getting the patient to say "Thank God I'm going to be better; now I am better" and by sleeping on it'.[10] The Gospel accounts of healing could be reinterpreted in Coué's terms.[11]

Bennett and Coué differed in their psychological explanations of the role of suggestion in healing.[12] But Bennett regarded Coué's doctrines as entirely consistent with Christian teaching; Coué's term 'imagination', approximated to St Paul's 'faith'. To achieve physical health, Coué required the subject to visualise himself as already well; to be holy (the same word, Bennett contended, as 'healthy', but with a wider connotation) St Paul called on the Christian to see himself as 'complete in Christ'. To demonstrate to his readers the effectiveness of suggestion and set it in Christian context, Bennett recommended his readers to 'try M. Coué's own prescription and say to yourself twenty times a month, when you're sleepy: "day by day in every way I get better and better" or if you like, expand it into

> Hour by hour and day by day,
> In all respects and in every way,
> Better I get and better I stay.
> Blessed be God who made me whole,
> Rest and rejoice in him, O my soul,
> And magnify him alway.'[13]

3

The second book in the trilogy, *A Soul in the Making or Psycho-synthesis* – 'a brief compendium of my life's philosophy' – is Bennett's reconciliation of psychology, biology and Christianity.[14] Profits went to the Restoration Fund, and enclosed with each copy was a leaflet, with pictures of Chester Cathedral's restorations and repairs, claimed to be 'a parable in stone of Psychosynthesis'.[15] Bennett was influenced by the writings of a London lecturer in psychology, J. A. Hadfield, especially his *Psychology and Morals: an Analysis of Character* (1923); and Hadfield provided an Introduction to Bennett's 'admirable book'.[16] Hadfield pointed out that emphasis on analysis in psychology had diverted attention from suggestion and 'faith healing', procedures eminently suitable for many 'diseases of the soul' and ones which the clergy were admirably fitted to practise.[17]

The argument of Bennett's book is complex but somewhat loose, and therefore not easy to summarise briefly. He argues from biology that life, by reacting to its total environment, 'makes itself', the 'end' being the production of persons who, however, 'must make themselves'. Of all creatures, only man has reached self-consciousness; to evolve further, he must continue by the same method, to make the 'soul or character' and 'win ... freedom'.[18] The 'sort of self' depends on how it reacts to its total environment, including the spiritual. Psychology reveals the materials out of which the character or self has to be made.[19] Bennett's 'driving forces' in 'the making of persons' are the instincts. Here he follows William McDougall, who stressed the primacy of primitive instincts; socially, these must be directed to appropriate ends by the will.[20] Bennett points out that total repression, especially of the sex instinct, results in disorders which may call for psycho-analysis, yet to apply the sex instinct constructively some repression is required. But total repression disintegrates a person.[21] Instinct must therefore be supplemented by a degree of intelligence.[22] This is in line with McDougall's view that 'all animal and human behaviour is purposive'.[23]

Bennett draws on Hadfield's *Psychology and Morals* in order to group instincts around social objects, the home, school, Church, country, business.[24] However, Bennett says, people inevitably make mistakes, deliberate or accidental, in the building of the self. The world is filled by organisms which have 'turned out of the main stream of life', hence blocking their further evolution. Wrong turns by non-self-conscious organisms are errors, not sins. Self-conscious beings, however, who know 'the better', have chosen 'the worse', and so 'turned out of the main stream of life that flows to perfection and God'. This is sin. Biology and psychology help to explain it, yet neither can help to 'wipe it up'. So this is the role of religion.[25]

Bennett argues that if the end product, the self-conscious individual, is going to be finally eliminated, that is at death, the whole process would be meaningless. Meaning, for Bennett, is thus imported from the Gospel; God's intention was that 'persons' should not be 'scrapped'. The theological implication of Bennett's case is that all individuals qualify for immortality, a conclusion conflicting with his reading of the New Testament. Bennett, therefore, contends (adopting an Edinburgh scientist's term) that man is an 'immortable individual'.[26] Immortality itself 'must be won by psycho-synthesis – by the making of an individual soul'.

He insists that the doctrine of 'inherent immortality' was based on a misinterpretation of the New Testament Greek (in Hebrews x, 39), and offers his own 'legitimate paraphrase'.[27] Christianity is the final stage in the making of immortal out of immortable individuals. We must do it for ourselves; God cannot do it for us.[28] Salvation depends on three factors: (1) the reversal of the principle of no retrogression; (2) the creation of a 'sufficient human self', with whom man can become identified and so re-created; (3) scope for the use (sublimination) of instincts, the driving forces in human life. All this culminates in the person and ministry of Jesus.

But Bennett was aware that the thorny problem of those unaware of the Gospel has to be faced. He resolves it by posing the possibility of reincarnation which he regarded as legitimate speculation since it did not conflict with any article of the Creed.[29]

4

In *Expecto*, the final work in the trilogy – the 'very deliberate thinkings of a lifetime' – Bennett develops ideas hinted at in his previous book.[30] He argues that just as during life in the present world unique 'persons' have developed, it is reasonable to extrapolate, for those who respond to the supernatural, a survival of personal identity, with extended freedom in a fuller life after physical death. But survival is not automatic. For those who do not respond, and do not develop a 'self' with survival value, death is (as in the rest of the animal and vegetable world) indeed the end.[31] Bennett's case rests on two speculative assumptions, neither necessarily unorthodox but certainly not traditional. First, that 'the world to come is the immensity of the universe', *this* universe. And secondly, that life 'here' and in the 'world-to-come' are the same life. 'Earth' and 'Heaven' are obsolete concepts which we have inherited; 'Heaven' is simply the freedom of the universe, to which we may pass on.[32] Bennett does not exclude the possibility of life, even higher life, elsewhere in the universe. The reviewer in the *Times Literary Supplement* believed that many would regard Bennett's speculations as 'fanciful', and A. G. Child correctly foresaw that Bennett's two assumptions would be challenged by 'traditional thinkers'.[33]

Bennett believed that his arguments were buttressed by data from contemporary scientific theory, citing in particular the views of J. Y. Simpson, Professor of Natural Science at Edinburgh, and of the biologist J. Arthur Thomson.[34] As he had done in his earlier books, Bennett sought to harmonise modern scientific thinking with the writings of St Paul and, not least, with the Gospels. He expressed the hope that his speculations would be as soundly framed in biology as they would be in orthodox catholic doctrine.[35] He even ventured into the margins of bio-physics with his view of prayer as a release of personal energy, which thereby releases divine energy from God; claiming, somewhat crudely, that ten people praying released ten times the energy of one person.[36]

The subtitle of *Expecto* indicates the essence of Bennett's thinking on the cosmic scale. The universe is 'biocentric'; hence meaning can be given to it 'only as interpreted in terms of life', its highest product.[37] If, Bennett asserts, the term 'life' in the expression 'life of the world to come' means anything akin to life 'here', then the Biology of this world must have something to tell us about the Biology of the next.[38] Evolution leads to progressive control of environment.[39] Bennett calls to witness his two scientists to demonstrate that progress to greater freedom comes by contact with the spiritual environment.[40] In that environment we grasp 'Purpose', ultimately revealed in Jesus Christ who, in himself, embodied everything 'towards which the whole evolutionary process has been evidently tending' (Simpson).[41]

Man, Bennett believes, would have achieved the same sort of freedom, including the control of his environment (with the ability to change it 'miraculously'), had he not turned from the line of his true evolution by the 'Fall'.[42] Man's intended destiny had been to pass on by continued evolution to a wider spiritual life. This, he goes on to assert, is the significance of the Transfiguration, which he considers to have been 'a revelation of the normal passing-on of a perfect human person'.[43] Jesus's claim that no man could take His life from him, but that He had power to lay it down and then take it up again amounted simply to describing how He could will to return to the state of 'fallen' man (which he was to do, 'for man'); and then, on His resurrection, 'step back to where he was on the Mountain of the Transfiguration'. The 'transfigured' body was merely the body of 'perfect evolution'.[44] Jesus 'deliberately underwent the experience of death'. Man cannot avoid it, and must be born again into the next world as Jesus did not need to be. 'He was at once here or there at will'.[45]

At a more mundane level, Bennett regretted the removal of the feast of the Transfiguration (6 August) from the red-letter days in the Church Calendar.[46] He must have welcomed its restoration in 1928. An unsigned article in *The Times* of 2 August 1930 referring to 'Man and his Exodus' echoes so exactly Bennett's own thinking and turn of phrase that it is difficult to avoid the conclusion that he wrote it, especially as it adjoins a statement by him about Chester Cathedral's new vestry.[47] Furthermore, Bennett had only recently published his *Resurrection of the Dead* (1929), and was about to launch *The Resurrection of the Organism*.[48] In both of these he stressed his interpretation of the Transfiguration. Was he hoping to spark interest in the subject to promote sales of these works and so boost cathedral funds?

5

Effectively a sequel to the trilogy, *The Resurrection of the Dead*, published in 1929, developed ideas Bennett had explored earlier, but embodied the thinking of authors to whom he had not previously referred, especially more recent writers. The train of argument is also more closely sustained, and without the distracting asides of *Expecto*. In the later 1920s, the post-war interest in the question of an after-life, evident in the vogue of spiritualism and manifested also in popular writing and newspaper features, was still powerful. Indeed, the success of *Expecto* is some indication of this continuing interest. Bennett's American congregations had attended closely to his exposition of the *Expecto* arguments, and the book sold well in the United States. In June 1928 the British newspaper, *Daily News*, had published a series of articles under the title 'Where are the Dead?' At the editor's request, Bennett contributed a brief article. He was concerned at the 'frankly materialistic' tone of some of the other contributions, and endeavoured to 'compress the gist' of *Expecto* into the five hundred words he was allowed. He attacked especially the 'amiable outlook of universalism' which a 'leading scientist' had recently called 'the most popular and most demoralizing of all creeds'.[49] The 'leading scientist' was J. Y. Simpson, on whom he had drawn liberally in *Expecto*, and whom he would call in evidence again in his third book.

The *Times Literary Supplement* devoted a review column of ten inches to *The Resurrection of the Dead*.[50] The journal, *Theology*, commended the book.[51] In consequence, when the *Spectator* launched a series on 'Immortality' Bennett was asked again to contribute. His article, slightly expanded, was reprinted in a sixpenny pamphlet, *The Resurrection of the Organism*, which largely follows the lines of his book, to which he gives marginal references throughout.[52]

Bennett rejects the doctrine of 'natural immortality' as both non-Christian and unscientific. The anonymous *Times Literary Supplement* reviewer considered that he was advancing 'a thesis that theologians have condemned as heresy'.[53] Bennett argues, correctly, that the doctrine had come in via Platonism. Moreover, it had been attractive to a persecuted Church, because it offered a possibility of eternal punishment for persecutors. Later, after Constantine took the side of the Church, it served as a goad to nominal Christians, of which there were many. A Papal Bull of 1513 had condemned the assertion that the *intellectivam animam* (the intellectual soul) was not immortal. The Christian hope was the resurrection of the body (1 Corinthians, xv) and this was affirmed in the Apostles Creed. Nor was dualism acceptable to a scientist. A human being was an organism: a human spirit could not be separated from a body. There was no 'central nucleus or self' which could be 'distinguished from the organism as a whole'.[54] Most of the thirty articles in the *Daily News* on 'Where are the Dead' had assumed the natural immortality of a part of the person, a soul. Bennett's aim in *The Resurrection of the Dead* is to put the emphasis back where he believes it should be.

His thinking on this issue (though not widely supported) was by no means original, as is evident from the other authors he mentions. W. E. Gladstone, from whose *Studies subsidiary to Bishop Butler* (1896) Bennett quotes liberally, observed that 'when arguments are offered for the purely natural immortality of the soul, they are rarely, if ever, derived from Scripture'.[55] To support his thesis, Bennett was in effect seizing on the seemingly sceptical conclusions of modern biology and psychology that 'mind', 'self', or 'spirit' could not exist outside the framework of a body. As before, his method is synthetic, working, as it were, not at the interface of science and theology, but selecting and combining elements of both. Nevertheless, Bennett's concise exegesis of the much worked-over Corinthians xv, with which he concludes his book remains impressive today for its creative understanding and imaginative insights. Doubtless it represents some of 'the thinkings of a lifetime'.[56] It is, however, the practical approach of a pastor and teacher, concerned to convey a message that matters to him and his readers or listeners, a concern that often effectively emerges in Bennett's writings. The brief *Resurrection of the Organism* exemplifies this.

The issues discussed by Bennett have not gone away, at least in certain philosophical and theological circles. Bennett's argument for a resurrection 'body' is adopted, for example, by Wolfhart Pannenberg. Man's impulses direct him to conceive of ultimate fulfilment beyond death, but 'until recently the Greek concept of the immortality of the soul has obstructed ... the truth of the Biblical hope of resurrection'. The separation of body and soul is 'no longer tenable ... in the light of contemporary anthropological insights'. An after-life can be thought of only as 'another mode of existence of the *whole* man'.[57] John Hick would adopt a similar position. On the other hand, Maurice Wiles, after examining the arguments of a range of modern theologians, concludes that 'there is much less difference between the two formulations in terms of resurrection of the body and immortality of the soul than is usually claimed'.[58]

In *The Resurrection of the Dead* Bennett claimed that much of the later development of his thought he owed to a recent work, N. P. Williams' *The Ideas of the Fall and of Original Sin* (1927).[59] Yet a consistent strand of thought runs through all of Bennett's theological-philosophical books. For Bennett, God's intention was the continued health and development of man. The insights of St Paul could be re-written in terms of modern biology and psychology. This philosophy also informed Bennett's work as priest and pastor.

Bennett's attempted reconciliation of science and Christianity, supported by the authors he quoted, did not necessarily accord with the views of most in the scientific community. Bennett never attemped to refute these. But the Roman Catholic apologist Ronald Knox deemed such ideas promulgated by influential writers to be of sufficient danger to deserve rebuttal. In his 1932 book, *Broadcast Minds*, he satirically castigated the biologist Julian Huxley, who had argued in his recent book, *Religion without Revelation*, that the existence of a sense of religious experience did not call for the objective existence of a Deity. It was instead merely an aspect of humankind's tendency to personalise, and could be accounted for by other external stimuli, though he did acknowledge the human need for some sort of ritual. Knox regarded Huxley's arguments as an appeal to the unbeliever to pretend to attach a religious value to things which he does already, 'such as listening to concerts or going on Messrs' Cook's tours', and to Christians 'to give up the despairing battle against a world which rejects the notion of God, and join with him in a campaign for the spread of religiosity'. Knox tilted at others, including Bertrand Russell, whose recently published book, *The Conquest of Happiness*, offered a Coué-style secular treatment for ridding oneself of the sense of sin.[60]

It may be conceded that Bennett's 'robust theology' had about it at times an air of optimistic superficiality. It combined populist psychologism, not least in its view that we must 'co-operate with God' to get rid of sickness and thus turn prayer into auto-suggestion, with implied Pelagianism – the heresy that man can take the fundamental steps towards salvation by his own efforts – in the view that 'if any are to inherit eternal life ... they must qualify themselves. God himself cannot do for us what can only be done by us'. Some might indeed also see a relationship between Bennett's 'robust theology' and the complex of twentieth-century religiose and pseudo-scientific cults whose origins and development have now been amusingly and comprehensively explored by Peter Washington in his recent *Madame Blatavsky's Baboon: Theosophy and the Emergence of the Western Guru*. This illuminates some of the West's abiding pre-occupations of the last one hundred and fifty years: the revolt against materialism, the quest for immortality, the argument between science and religion, and the hunger for authority that can momentarily sanctify the charlatan. Housed in Madame Blavatsky's room in the 1880s, the Baboon of the title was a stuffed and bespectacled animal in morning dress, labelled Professor Fiske, after a prominent Darwinian. Following the 1859 publication of *The Origin of Species* a spate of cartoons had featured monkeys; hence Blavatsky's stuffed baboon signified her posture as an anti-Darwinian. More positively, other decoration in her cluttered quarters signalled her taste for 'a generalised Orient', symbolising the living religion and spiritual wisdom still alive in Asia – a perception foreshadowing the presentday attraction, to disenchanted westerners, of Zen and Buddhism. Blavatsky had powerful supporters in her day, and in the 1920s and 1930s continued to be regarded in some quarters as a latterday mystic and saintly heroine.[61]

6

Education, in its widest sense but with a Christian orientation, was an important element in Bennett's ministry.[62] In Chester he had been tutor to Bishop Jayne's sons and later had served as a temporary assistant history master at the King's School. He taught Religious Education in all his parish schools and encouraged Sunday school teachers to adopt the up-to-date methods of the day schools. As dean, Bennett taught confirmation classes.[63] His modernisation and re-stocking of the Chapter Library was aimed at encouraging others to read in subjects he deemed important, notably biology (including evolution), psychology, and religion.[64] He regularly recommended specific books, with his own comments, in the *Chester Diocesan Gazette*.[65] His writings and pronouncements give some insight into what might loosely be called his philosophy of education, which was related to the ideas he had articulated in the works we have examined and is informed by his liturgical views.

In *Mary Jane and Harry John* (1927), Bennett stressed that education started at home, where parents were the 'natural and inevitable head-teachers or unteachers [*sic*]'.[66] He then develops, in simpler form, ideas he had explored in *Coué* and *Soul in the Making*. The 'natural (instinctive, if you like) forces' of the child, which must be harnessed, are clearly related to McDougall's 'instincts'. Bennett asserts that they can all be given religious outlet.[67] Children learn from observing parents' behaviour: prayer, making the sign of the Cross with grace, giving a reverence to an altar or at Jesus' name. The 'wonder and imitate' instinct can be harnessed to encourage imitation of what is not yet fully understood; thus, attendance at a ceremonial Eucharist, a designedly suggestive service, will influence children, who *see* first, *ask* second, and *hear* third.[68]. Young people yearn to excel and then be admired. They learn by heart easily. 'Hear me say a verse of my hymn' is of the same order as any other childish 'See me do this or that'. The acquisitive instinct should be enlisted by providing pictures, figures, books, a palm cross.[69]

In responding to inquisitiveness, parents must aim never to tell a lie. 'Where did baby come from?' is a natural question. The answer may be quite elementary, but must be true. Bennett acquired his own knowledge of sex from 'the boy who cleaned the boots'. If children never ask this sort of question, parents should wonder why children have lost their confidence. Sex is the creative urge, which may be harnessed to artistic or literary activity.[70]

Since play is a natural childish activity children will play at 'church', as naturally as they will play at 'shop'. Religion must have sunshine in it and not be thought of as a dour thing. Childish notions about God should be treated seriously.[71]

Finally, Bennett relates the child's initiation into religion, at Baptism, to the Aristotelean principle which informed all his ideas. 'Nothing is ready made. Everything is made in order to become'. Baptized children are made to grow into inheritors of the Kingdom. They should mark the anniversary of their baptism and remember the three things promised in their name. Bennett taught those who attended his children's services to repeat the promises last thing at night. Such last thoughts, including prayer, he points out, develop during sleep.[72] His psychology is unexceptionable.[73]

Three years later *The Christian Ideal of Health* appeared in a series 'Children and Life' published by the Society for Promoting of Christian Knowledge, and may be regarded as a companion to *Mary Jane and Harry John*. It offered parents further practical advice. Again, the assumptions underlying Bennett's arguments are those which inform his more substantial writings, to which he refers from time to time.[74] The 1930 book owes much to William McDougall's *Character and the Conduct of Life* (1928), McDougall being already recognised as an influential educational thinker.[75] Bennett uses McDougall's observations on the best educational practices – no emphasis on a child's deficiencies; no use of pain and fear; wider human contacts; better hygiene and health – to encourage parents to aim at simplicity, sociability, admiration, and independence. Above all, they must inspire children with faith, defined as knowing the difference between the 'higher' and the 'lower' ways of living, and 'striving for the higher'.[76] Bennett rehearses yet again his views on the Fall, sin, and sickness. The old Prayer Book's 'Visitation of the Sick' still gave the wrong impression of sickness sent for our own good. The care of a chronically sick or handicapped child – more common in the 1920s than today – should be shared happily by younger children and not regarded as an irksome duty.[77] On practical matters of child care and child health, he did not hesitate to give advice and gentle admonition.[78] Thus he recommended care of the ears and the eyes (his personal problem), praising the 'old fashioned bonnet', which protected both organs. (In the street, however, he was more blunt, and would halt any woman he met wheeling a pram with an infant whose eyes were unprotected, in order to utter dire warnings of the long-term risks.) Later, when children were reading, they should sit with their backs to the light. Clear bright glass electric lights should be banned. His opinions on such down-to-earth matters may have had substance but they seemed idiosyncratic and must have irked many, thus giving rise to the view that in his latter days he was somewhat 'eccentric'.[79]

At the end of this, his last book before retirement, Bennett quotes, with great approval, some verses on health written by a Winchester schoolboy, later killed in the war. These had impressed him so much that he had had them printed on card, for use as a Grace in the cathedral Refectory ('Give me a good digestion, Lord ... '). From Chester, the card had gone all over the world, and could be bought in Cape Town, Toronto, Chicago, and New York.[80]

7

In the 1930s, Bennett was becoming increasingly concerned about declining opportunities for the Anglican religious education of school-children. Meeting Government requirements in staffing, accommodation, and equipment was increasingly difficult for Church schools and many had perforce closed, especially senior schools. By 1938, according to Bennett, only some 35% of 'Church' children were in parish schools and so receiving religious education according to the Anglican faith. He hailed the 1936 Education Act as offering new opportunities, and a year after he retired presented his arguments in *This Moment of Opportunity for Religious Education*.[81]

Section 13 of the Act gave parents the right to withdraw children from local authority schools, 'during the period of religious instruction ... to attend religious observation or instruction elsewhere', which had been only possible previously if the Local Authority had adopted the so-called Anson Bye-Law. However, to enable parents to exercise this right, the Church must provide appropriate places and teachers. The incumbent of the parish where the school was situated could best arrange this. Bennett cited an example of the system in action in a Lancashire district.[82] It was also the 'moment of opportunity' for Sunday schools, on which the future of the Church 'may largely depend'. Many were woefully behind the times.[83] It is difficult to assess what effect Bennett's advocacy may have had on attitudes and practices. Chester appointed no Sunday School Organisers, although these had been recommended by Bennett, finance, here as elsewhere, being a limiting factor.[84]

8

Bennett conceived of religious education as a process extending into adulthood. This was an important reason for his membership, from 1900, of the Church of England Men's Society (CEMS). By 1925 he was convinced that the society was losing direction and he addressed an *Open Letter* to the Chairman, Edward Latham Bevan, Bishop of Swansea and Brecon.[85] The 'old CEMS Ford', unlike the smooth running 'omnibuses' and 'charabancs', of other Church organisations, or 'the Rolls Royce [*sic*]' of the Freemasons, needed to be 'shoved'.[86] The CEMS 'Rule of Life' was far too vague.[87] Instead, he wanted a precise objective for members. It should be to sustain themselves and each other in the love of God, and seek the mercy of our Lord.[88] The ideal of the Perfect Man, Jesus, should be set before members, and reinforced, first by a CEMS prayer for daily use (he recommends that of St Richard of Chichester),[89] and second, by study of an appropriate 'Life'.[90] So much for the 'dynamics'. But understanding of the sacraments was essential. The Eucharist was now firmly in place, but Baptism, the 'unifying bond of the Christian Church',[91] had not been fully understood. Bennett would enlist the power of suggestion. On the membership card should be printed the baptismal promises, with the letters 'I.A.O.B.' (I Acknowledge One Baptism).[92] He proposed a ritual Form of Admission, to impress itself on the subconscious.

Bennett was invited to meet two officers of the Society, Bishop Crossley and Canon Savile, to discuss the *Open Letter*. They had already (unbeknown to Bennett) agreed with Bevan on the line they would take.[93] Bennett's brother, George, also took part in the lengthy discussions, after which a consensus was agreed, although this would require endorsement by the Executive. The Rule of Life would stand but a principal aim would now be to help members 'to realise their baptism', by keeping it in 'their habitual thinkings' (probably Bennett's phrase). Bennett reluctantly conceded that as baptismal vows were mentioned at the giving of the badge there should be no new initiation ceremony. Fresh emphasis would be laid on the realisation of the 'three things' needed 'in our day and generation', and St Richard of Chichester's prayer was accepted as the CEMS Collect. Alteration in the badge (probably the addition of 'I.A.O.B'.), though agreed, was later rejected by the Executive. Bennett had not achieved all his objectives but had made an important impact on the CEMS.[94]

The CEMS Conference Committee, doubtless regarding the controversial Bennett as a attraction, invited him to address the 1926 Conference. Whether the Society needed 'shoving' or 'leadership' was hotly argued. Dissension, Bennett said, was generally 'blocking progress' within the Church. Prayer Book revision and attitudes to the current miners' strike must have been in the minds of many delegates. Bennett related the strike (and there were coalmines within Chester diocese) to a central concern of his *Open Letter.* Cosmo Lang, who presided, had urged the miners to accept the temporary reduction in pay demanded by the owners and then work out a solution with them.[95] The *Open Letter* had set social problems in a Christian context: a body of men acknowledging One Baptism 'and relying ... on the Christ in each other' could be a powerful social force.[96] Bennett now suggested controversially that CEMS ally itself with the Industrial Christian Fellowship (ICF), led by the Christian Socialist T. P. R. Kirk. An ICF working party (including eight bishops and eleven Nonconformist leaders) already supported the miners, thereby incurring the displeasure of press, politicians, Archbishop Randall Davidson, Bishop Hensley Henson – and doubtless Lang too. Bennett's intervention can hardly have warmed Lang towards him.[97] But the conference was divided, and hence took no decision to ally with the ICF.[98]

9

Bennett's 'robust theology' reinforced his avowed High Churchmanship, the style already imprinted on him from boyhood by family tradition, by the practice of the family church, and by the affiliations of clerical relatives.[99] 'High Church' constituted a spectrum, extending from Tractarianism at one end to Anglo-Catholicism at the other. Moreover, within Anglo-Catholicism views ranged from stress on the 'Anglo' (Prayer Book Catholicism) to emphasis on the 'Catholic' (Anglo-Papalism), with extremist clergy using the illegal Roman Canon of the Mass. The common ground which all shared with the 'Old High Churchmen' was a 'high' conception of the Church's authority.[100] Bennett, who always described himself as a High Churchman, was a moderate and somewhat idiosyncratic Anglo-Catholic. He did not belong to the English Church Union (ECU), which actively proselytised for Anglo-Catholic practice, nor to any of the more sharply-defined societies such as the Confraternity of the Blessed Sacrament, the Cowley Fathers, or the Holy Cross Society. He adhered to the Book of Common Prayer and did not use ceremonies condemned by the 1906 Royal Commission on Ecclesiastical Discipline.[101]

His 'robust theology of the material world' reinforced and interpreted his religious practices, which he explained in psychological terms. The power of suggestion was at work in the sacraments, while private confession – not prohibited by the Prayer Book – was sound psychology.[102] Incense, whose informal use was permissible, promoted a religious frame of mind by its effect on the sense of smell. This was 'the magic of divine science'.[103] The combined effect of the colour, ritual, and music of ceremonial made a powerful impact. Unreinforced, the bare 'Word' was less memorable, a sound educational principle.

The high tide of Anglo-Catholicism began in the wake of the Armistice of 1918. A sacramental ministry had had considerable appeal in wartime, and Anglo-Catholic priests, already renowned for their devoted work in city slums, now had a heroic record in the trenches. This 'coming of age' of the movement, as it came to be called, was marked by a series of five highly successful Anglo-Catholic conferences between 1920 and 1933.[104] After the 1923 Conference, over a quarter of a million copies of books dealing with Anglo-Catholicism were sold.[105] Bennett attended the great gatherings in the Albert Hall.[106] He also participated in subsequent provincial meetings, but I can find no record of what he said. It is, however, not surprising to learn from Bennett's son that the dean disappointed his audiences by urging practices which he strongly favoured for reasons quite other than those they approved.[107]

10

The part which Bennett played in the controversies over Prayer Book Revision, and his subsequent pronouncements on 'Reunion', constitute significant case-studies of the interaction between his 'robust theology' and his grasp of practical ecclesiastical politics.

The whole story of Revision extends from 1906 to 1928.[108] Consequent on the 1906 Report of the Royal Commission on Ecclesiastical Discipline, the Convocations of Canterbury and York had been instructed to make recommendations on any desirable changes in the law regarding the conduct of worship, having regard to the divergencies in practice reported by the Commission.[109] Fourteen years of debate and discussion ensued, during which the lines were drawn between the opposing wings. As a bishop put it colourfully in 1908, 'partisans ... on one side shrink from a ritualist as they would from a snake ... Those on the other side regard Puritans as "wild boars out of the wood"'.[110] Not until April 1920 were proposals for Revision finally drafted.[111]

Such proposals required parliamentary approval, after these had been endorsed by the newly established Church Assembly, which now included, im addition to the clergy, a House of Laity. It had not been anticipated, however, that the Assembly would intervene in a matter relating to worship, particularly one already approved by the Convocations. Attitudes to Reservation and Holy Communion divided the factions, those who emphasised sacramental aspects wanting the longer, older, less 'Reformed' version of the Communion service in the 1549 Prayer Book, the Protestant wing opposing any change as tending to encourage sacramentalism. A majority of bishops believed, somewhat optimistically, that an enlarged Anglican Canon would help to end the use (secret or otherwise) of the Roman Canon.

Bennett first manifested publicly his interest in Revision in December 1923 when he recommended to those readers of *Chester Diocesan Gazette* who wished to look at matters 'all round', Eeles' *Prayer Book Revision and Christian Reunion*.[112] This examined critically conflicting proposals being offered by the Church Association, the English Church Union, and the Alcuin Club.[113] Bennett's strong recommendation of this book suggests that its approach approximated to his own. Eeles argued for reasoned tolerance all round, in order to reach a settlement – an essential step for those committed to Reunion of all Christian churches since Revision was central to the issue of Reunion.[114] Reunion on the Roman model would involve conceding unwarranted papal claims, but Eeles saw hope in the direction of negotiating with the Orthodox churches, where reservation was accepted but never celebrated, and where Anglican orders were recognised as valid. Meanwhile, Low Churchmen would have to abandon trying to reimpose Protestantism all round, for instance, by trying to enforce outmoded Privy Council legislation; High Churchmen must not expect to enforce all Prayer Book requirements and especially the Ornaments Rubric as interpreted by the Oxford Movement; the 'Roman' section of the Church would have to approach Reunion on the basis of an English rite, with English ceremonial; strict liturgical men of High Church persuasion must concede the continued use by churches which possessed them of 'foreign' or pseudo-Roman ornaments albeit not in their view part of the

English tradition. Finally, Broad Churchmen should realise that liturgies express the mind of Christendom in an area they have seldom explored.[115]

Reservation of the Sacrament was prohibited by the 1662 Prayer Book.[116] In 1911, however, to provide for the sick, the Upper House of Convocation drafted a rubric indicating what they hoped would become allowable, should Prayer Book revision came about. Soon, however, enthusiastic young Anglo-Catholic priests were conducting illegal services of worship and adoration before the reserved host. The massive casualties of the Great War led to pressure for the comfort of such devotions, including intercessions for the fallen. In certain dioceses the pressure became irresistible.

In the Assembly debate, Bennett advocated a *via media*. As 'a parish priest with long experience of large town and country parishes', he argued for reservation to enable clergy to give communion to those whose hours of work prevented their attending the service. But attempts to prevent individuals from saying their prayers in churches where the sacrament was reserved would be unwarrantable interference and it would be futile even to discuss it.[117] The extreme Anglo-Catholic wing wanted more, including authorised services, such as Benediction, which Bennett, discounting the theological pros and cons, declared to be 'not practical politics' and hence also 'futile ... at this time even to discuss'[118] The proposal, as eventually carried, was that 'according to long existing custom in the Catholic Church' the celebrant might reserve so much as may be required 'for communion of the sick *and others who could not be present at the celebration in church* [my emphasis]'. Bennett had won his point, though the margin was narrow, 103 votes for the motion but 98 against.[119] The Council of the Church Association rallied support to defeat the scheme, whose real purpose they regarded as adoration.[120] The calumny heaped on Bennett in the Chester press by Church Association sympathisers indicates the bitterness of the dispute.[121]

The national press portrayed a bitterly divided Church and the public took sides. Bennett, together with others, signed a letter addressed to the newspapers, saying that it would be 'wise and reasonable' to recognise the British principle of *sub judice* and not speak out until the bishops had pronounced. No paper, he later said (not even 'to its shame' the *Church Times*') had published the letter, because talk of a 'divided Church' sold newspapers. Bennett saw 'vigorous life' in the Church, and pointed to the 'thousands' who attended the cathedral. Life would be dull without differences. Agreement in his family included agreement on the right to disagree.[122] In a warm compliment to

Bennett, *The Spectator* drew a sharp contrast between 'the tasteless controversies which unhappily represent to the public the current domestic life of the English Church', and the 'gradual transformation of our Cathedrals to something approaching the purpose for which they were made'. The writer pointed to 'the rapidity with which his [Bennett's] main principles are being adopted and adapted to the particular conditions of each Cathedral-Church', and concluded that 'the abolition of the locked choir, compulsory tour, and facetious verger, with the resulting transformation of the sightseer into the pilgrim; these things are now becoming so general that the visitor feels a genuine grievance when he finds the bad old methods still unreformed'.[123]

On 7 February 1927, the archbishops presented the bishops' draft of a revised Prayer Book to the Convocations, so that the Lower Houses could comment when they met on 22 February.[124] In a letter to *The Times* of 17 February, Bennett hailed the proposals as an answer to daily prayer in Assembly, Convocations, Chester Cathedral and 'no doubt ... elsewhere ... all these many weeks'. Parallels existed in the early Church. The Church should, like other associations of Englishmen, now loyally follow its leaders.[125] Bennett was active in the League of Loyalty and Order whose avowed purpose was to back the bishops' proposals.[126] In March, both Convocations duly endorsed a revised Prayer Book, including a variation in the Order of Communion and allowing some liberty regarding reservation.[127] The Church Assembly, meeting in a blaze of publicity and bombarded by rival pamphlets, finally endorsed the Revised Prayer Book in July, with three quarters of members in favour, despite influential lay and clerical opposition from within.[128] According to a scribbled jotting in Lambeth Palace archives, a few days after the Assembly decision had been taken Bennett voiced his views, forthrightly, at a meeting of deans. Further opposition now was not 'playing the game', not to say disloyal. Deans, the 'only body [containing?] no ... opponent', were in charge of liturgy in their own cathedrals and so were in a sense detached; nevertheless, being in this peculiar position they should give an example for parish church councils to see.[129]

It had been anticipated that Parliament would endorse a doctrinal measure approved by Assembly and Convocations. The Lords approved the Revised Book but the Commons rejected it (voting 238 to 205).[130] Bennett claimed (not entirely justifiably) that never before had it been thought appropriate for Parliament to decide the doctrine of the Church of England. Failing ultimate accommodation, he paraded the last resort, freedom by Disestablishment. Paget supported him.[131] The bishops now agreed that as the Convocations had approved the Revised Book, they would permit its use, as an Alternative to, but not replacement of, the 1662 Book. It could be used 'during the present emergency, and until further order be taken'. Under these terms the Book was published.[132] Bennett used it.[133]

In the aftermath of the Prayer Book controversy and as a prelude to the Lambeth Conference of 1930, Dick Sheppard, now Dean of Canterbury, edited a collection entitled *My Hopes and Fears for the Church*.[134] Bennett was among those who agreed to contribute.[135] In an article entitled 'Integration' he expounded his ecumenical vision in the familiar terms of 'robust theology' and assumptions about science and religion which we have repeatedly encountered. Focused on an issue of concern to most Christians, 'Integration' provides a synthesis of his mature thought.

The 1920 Conference had recognised Baptism as conferring membership of the Universal Church.[136] But because of internal divisions it had hedged with restrictions any exchange of pulpits and intercommunion; no concessions had been made on episcopacy, and there had consequently been no progress towards unity.[137] Bennett regarded 'Integration' as a more correct term than 'Reunion', because the latter implied that the various denominations had once been united whereas in fact these 'new churches' had emerged as a result of toleration in modern times. The baptised, he said, were the Creed's 'Communion of Saints' and constituted 'one body', in St Paul's words, 'whether Jews or Greeks, whether bond or free'. 'Today', (he argued) we should say 'whether Roman Catholics or Presbyterians, whether Anglicans or Congregationalists, or Wesleyans, whether we tolerate the bondage of establishment [*sic*] or enjoy the liberty of the Free Churches'. Baptism was thus 'the only possible basis for any reunion (or integration) of Christendom'.[138] Significantly, Bennett stressed the symbolism of Baptism, which he managed to relate to that of Masonry, an institution which 'grows and fruits round a core of symbolism'.

Integration was a biological term relating to organisms, organised bodies with interdependent parts, each with a specialised function but working together for the good of the whole. Had St Paul been writing in 1930, he would have referred to the Church, not as the 'Body of Christ', but as 'the Organism of Christ'. St Paul was thinking biologically when he wrote, "The body is not one member but many ... "'.[139] Episcopacy as a pre-condition for 'reunion' Bennett thus regarded as a deterrent. That some Churches had bishops was merely 'a historic fact'. Exchange of pulpits appeared different when viewed in terms of integration, since this implied learning more about each other's specialised functions. Reunion would instead merely brush over differences and 'preach smooth nothings'.[140]

To illustrate the situation in the Church throughout the world, he cited the Church of England, whose three distinct and legitimate schools of thought, were *'all .., essential to the richness of our life'* [my emphasis]. Consequently, 'We need integration'. Over the New Prayer Book, the 'two extremities' combined to defeat the purpose of 'the whole body', ultimately by enlisting external forces. They thus acted as tubercular growths do in a human body, preventing the Church from functioning as 'an integrated organism', a process signalling the road to death. 'Thinking biologically', he had favoured alternative Canons in the Revised Prayer Book, thereby effecting 'unity in diversity'. However, he concluded, 'the political complex of uniformity dies hard. Otherwise we should all combine to get the Act of Uniformity removed from the Statute Book before it completes its mortifying work'.[141] If this meant Disestablishment, 'so much the better'. And, Bennett added defiantly, 'No one in their senses wants Establishment back in Wales to-day'.[142]

Bennett's case did not commend itself to all shades of opinion within the Anglican Church. One commentator pointed to the 'glaring opposition' between Bennett's plea for integration and two other articles in the volume, labelled 'Anglo-Catholic Views'.[143] Bennett's local newspaper commented that it would be interesting to see what those who favoured episcopacy as 'the core of the Church' had to say.[144] In fact, Bennett had been emphasizing a key passage in the preamble to the Lambeth Conference Appeal of 1920 which had been largely ignored: 'We acknowledge all those who believe in our Lord Jesus Christ, and have been baptized into the name of the Holy Trinity, as sharing with us membership in the universal Church of Christ which is His body'.[145] In the face of entrenched attitudes, perhaps even vested interests, Bennett's advocacy availed little. He must have been disappointed, though perhaps not surprised, that the 1930 Lambeth Conference failed to move this matter forward.[146] But today, at the ending of the twentieth century, Bennett would have recognised many features of 'Integration' in the Church, not least in the ministry of the cathedrals.

Notes

1   F. S. M. Bennett, *A Soul in the Making or Psycho-synthesis* (London, 1924), 46.

2   Present-day interest in war neuroses, 'cowardice' as well as 'shell-shock', has produced a fairly considerable critical literature (e.g., Hugh Cecil and Peter H. Liddle, eds., *Facing Armageddon: The First World War Experienced*, London, 1996), which in turn has generated a spasm of popular treatment on television. However, none of the recent writing appears to address itself directly to the point made in the text.

3   F. S. M. Bennett, *Expecto: An Essay on the Biology of the World to Come* (Chester/London, 1926). 'Expecto' is taken from the Latin version of the Nicene Creed: *Et expecto resurrectionem mortuorum, et vitam venturi saeculi* 'And I look for the Resurrection of the dead, And the Life of the world to come' (*The Book of Common Prayer*, [1662]).

4   The Institute's aims were, 'the promulgation of M. Coué's principles of Applied Psychology as taught at Nancy, and to extend these principles for the Cure of Disease, Maintenance of Health ... training of character, more especially with regard to children ... development of Backward Children, and Redeeming of Young Delinquents' (advertisement in F. S. M. Bennett, *M. Coué and his Gospel of Health* (Chester/London, 1922), 88). 'Coué-ism' had echoes of the thinking of Mary Baker Eddy (1821–1910), the American founder of the Christian Science Church, which proclaims the illusory nature of disease (see note 11 below); and it may in turn have influenced a later American 'guru', Norman Vincent Peale (b. 1898), a popular Reformed pastor (ordained 1922), writer, and public lecturer, who established next door to his church a psychiatric clinic (The American Foundation of Religion and Psychiatry). The titles of Peale's much later books (*The Power of Positive Thinking* (1952), *The Tough-Minded Optimist* (1962) indicate his lines of thought. It is conceivable that Bennett's enthusiasm for the brave New World owed something to his recognition of this American taste for mind-body sermonising.

5   The Preface to *M. Coué and his Gospel of Health* was by William Brown, M.D., D.Sc., Wilde Reader in Mental Philosophy, Oxford.

6   Bennett, *Coué*, 8–9, 5; *Cheshire Diocesan Gazette* [hereafter *CDG*], Oct. 1922, 142. In 1921, in a lecture delivered at the Royal Hospital Chelsea. D. Monier Williams had argued that the influence of auto-suggestion. was only beginning to be understood. He would have liked to see the term 'incurable' disappear (*Cheshire Chronicle* [hereafter *Ches. Chr.*], 22.12.1921, 2).

7   'Few priests can have visited more sick people than I have – unless they be chaplains of hospitals or infirmaries – during the last five and twenty years' (Bennett,

Coué, 12).
    8   *CDG*, Dec. 1921, 199.
    9   *Book of Common Prayer* [1662], 'The Visitation of the Sick'.
   10   Bennett, *Coué*, 79–80.
   11   *ibid.*, 40–3, 9. Bennett discerned kinship between 'the methods and (if you like) credulities of the medieval minister of healing at our St Werburgh's and other shrines' and the techniques of the modern psychotherapist. Further, he hinted at some parallels with the methods of Christian Science, which filled the gap when the Church forgot or neglected its duty and thus genuinely restored many people (F. S. M. Bennett, *Faith to be Healed* (Chester, n.d. [a pamphlet of 12 pages, price twopence, copy kindly lent me by Guy Bennett]).

   12   Coué believed that when 'will' (holding to the objective situation) and 'imagination' conflicted, imagination always won; he told patients they were cured, and they were. Bennett saw the direction of a person by unfettered or perversely directed suggestion as potentially disastrous, not least for morals and religion. Hence, the role of 'will' (merely the whole person) was to direct imagination aright; 'when my will – my purposive self – brings my 'thinks' [a clumsy term Bennett was fond of] into line, I attain my maximum effectiveness'. Therefore suggestion had a role in morals and religion (Bennett, *Coué*, 28–9, 32, 40–1). (In this context, the concepts 'imagining' and 'thinking' could probably be better described as 'deciding that', though Coué does not make this point.) One reviewer considered Bennett's definition of 'will' and its relation to the 'imagination' to be 'the most important contribution to the subject in the Dean's book' (A. G. C. [= A. G. Child – see *Crockford*, 1963–4, 212, and note 33 below] in *CDG*, Jan 1923, 14–15). A late manifestation of Coué-ism was Aldous Huxley's 1940s abandonment of spectacles after being treated on Coué principles (Aldous Huxley, *The Art of Seeing* (London, 1943); Sybille Bedford, *Aldous Huxley: a Biography*, (2 vols., London, 1973–1974), I, 43, 373–5; II, 2, 29–30, 33, 35–6, 38, 78, 226).

   13   Bennett, *Coué*, 10, 18.
   14   Bennett, *Soul in the Making*, reviewed in *Times Literary Supplement* [hereafter *TLS*], 8.5.1924, 291–2. Bennett's booklist contains works on psychology, biology and religion, with almost equal numbers on each topic.

   15   These were probably copies of pictures which Bennett had asked Bell to persuade *The Times* to print. He had also sent Bell a copy of his new book for transmission to *The Times*, with a request that it be noticed, and Bell may have written the brief review (Lambeth Palace Library, Bell Papers, 1920–29, Bennett to Bell, 193, f. 25, 14.4.1924). *Ches. Chr.*, 3.5.1924; *TLS*, 8.5.1924; Bennett, *Soul in the Making*, 115–6).

   16   J. A. Hadfield, *Psychology and Morals: An Analysis of Character* (London, 1923). See esp. 146–7, 150–1. Hadley was a Harley Street practitioner and a lecturer

in psychology at King's College, University of London.

17   Bennett, *Soul in the Making*, 3–6.
18   *ibid.*, 46, 48, 50
19   *ibid.*, 46, 47, 60.
20   Bennett, *Soul in the Making*, 55–6; William McDougall, *An Outline of Psychology* (London, 1923). McDougall had coined the neologism 'hormic' to describe his approach: William McDougall, *An Introduction to Social Psychology* (London 1908).
21   Bennett, *Soul in the Making*, 55; on the repression of anger, cf. Hadfield, *Psychology and Morals*, 146–7.
22   Bennett, *Soul in the Making*, 59.
23   McDougall, *Outline of Psychology*, 72; Bennett, *Soul in the Making*, 59.
24   On instincts, Hadfield largely followed McDougall (Hadfield, *Psychology and Morals*, 12–17; Bennett, *Soul in the Making*, 60–1).
25   Bennett, *Soul in the Making*, 61–2.
26   The term was that of James Y. Simpson (1873–1934), Professor of Natural Science, New College, Edinburgh, in his *Man and the Attainment of Immortality* (London, 3rd. edit., 1923), described by Bennett as a 'really great and courageous book' (Bennett, *Soul in the Making*, 110). See Simpson, *Man and Immortality*, 224–62; Chapter XI 'Evolution as the Winning of Freedom'; Chapter XIII 'The Scriptural doctrine of Immortality'. In relation to Bennett's resolve to 'reconcile' theology and 'science', it is notable that his colleague, the Archdeacon of Chester, Paige Cox, had much earlier borrowed the prescriptive term, 'scientific', for the title of a published work, *The Scientific Study of Theology* (London, 1893), although this book has little in common with Bennett's writings.
27   The text reads, in translation, 'But we are not of them who draw back into perdition; but of them that believe to the saving of the soul'.(Authorized Version). For 'saving' the Revised Version gives an alternative, 'gaining'. Bennett offers: 'But we are not of those who furl the sails of life's adventure, seeking an effortless equilibrium which means destruction; but we are of those who have faith – the dynamic faculty for realising ideals – for the making of our souls with survival value' (Bennett, *Soul in the Making*, 111–2).
28   Bennett, *Soul in the Making*, 110.
29   *ibid.*, 114.
30   *ibid.*, 169.
31   Curiously, although Bennett embarks on a discussion of baptism and infancy, he does not relate this to any potential 'survival value' of the baptised infant who dies shortly after birth – as three of his own children had done.
32   Bennett, *Expecto*, 11–13, 110, 159 ff.
33   Child was at Keble with Bennett; in 1926, Vicar of St John's, Chester,

Honorary Canon 1919, Honorary Canon Emeritus, 1936 (*Crockford*, 1962–4, 212).
34   For Simpson, see note 26 above.
35   *CDG*, Apr. 1926.
36   Bennett, *Expecto*, 23–26; *orare est laborare*, therefore a sick person is less able to pray.
37   *ibid.*, 43
38   *ibid.*
39   Bennett, *Expecto*, 51–2
40   *ibid.*, 43, 51, 52–3.
41   *ibid.*, 63–4; Simpson, *Man and Immortality*, 259, quoted in *Expecto*, 101.
42   Bennett, *Expecto*, 102–3.
43   Mark, ix: 2.
44   Bennett, *Expecto*, 104–6
45   *ibid.*, 157
46   *ibid.*, 105.
47   *The Times*, 2.8.1930, 13.
48   *CDG*, Nov. 1930, 167.
49   *ibid.*, July 1928, 104.
50   *TLS*, 9.1.1930, 20.
51   R. D. Mackenzie, in *Theology*, 20, 17, Mar. 1930, 177–8.
52   F. S. M. Bennett, *The Resurrection of the Organism* (London, 1930), 5.
53   *TLS*, 9.1.1930, 20.
54   L. S. Thornton, *The Incarnate Lord* (London, 1928), 48–50, quoted in F. S. M. Bennett, *The Resurrection of the Dead* (Chester/London, 1929), 44.
55   W. E. Gladstone, *Studies subsidiary to Bishop Butler* (London, 1896), quoted in Bennett, *Resurrection of the Dead*, 6.
56   Bennett, *Resurrection of the Dead*, 206–13. 'The thinkings of a lifetime' is from *Expecto*, 169.
57   W. Pannenberg, *Jesus – God and Man* (translated, London, 1976), 86–7. A later book by a physicist reviewed and commended by Pannenberg, Frank J. Tipler, *The Physics of Immortality* (London, 1994), 240–68, argues a case for resurrection and immortality from the theses of modern physics.
58   J. Hick, *Death and Eternal Life* (paperback edition, Glasgow, 1979), 278–96; M. Wiles, *The Remaking of Christian Doctrine* (London, 1974), 125–46.
59   Bennett, *Resurrection of the Dead*, 71, 78, 80, 82, 85, 106, 112. N.P. Williams' 1924 Bampton Lectures were published as *The Ideas of the Fall and of Original Sin* (London, 1927). In his lecture on '"Original Sin" reinterpreted', Williams pointed to 'the inconsistency of Augustinianism with a genuine belief in the goodness and justice of God, and the moral accountability of man' (483); original sin is 'orientation away from God and in the direction of ruthless self-determination' (527). Norman

Powell Williams, a Fellow of Exeter College, Oxford, and eventually Professor of Divinity at Oxford, was a founding member of the Anglo-Catholic Society of SS. Peter and Paul and Secretary of the ECU.

60   For Knox's criticism of Huxley and Russell, see Ronald Knox, *Broadcast Minds* (London, 1932), 66–120; for Knox himself, F. L. Cross, ed., *The Oxford Dictionary of the Christian Church* (Oxford, 2nd edit., 1974), 786–7. Russell had also contributed to the *Daily News* series of articles on 'Where are the Dead?' Bennett commented on Huxley's views in *Resurrection of the Dead*, 46–8.

61   Peter Washington, *Madame Blatavsky's Baboon: Theosophy and the Emergence of the Western Guru* (London, 1993), 4, 44–45. Washington aims to 'bring into some kind of focus what remains of our deepest human needs, if not the deepest of all: the need to explain'.

62   In Canada and the United States he had been specially interested in universities, and had expressed admiration for the generous funding of education in the United States.

63   *CDG*, May 1929, 36.

64   ibid., Mar. 1921; Oct. 1922; Apr. 1923.

65   ibid., Apr. 1921; Feb. 1922; May 1923; Dec. 1923; Dec. 1925; June 1928; Oct. 1929; Sept. 1933.

66   F. S. M. Bennett, *Mary Jane and Harry John or Home the Premier School* (Oxford, 1927), 7. For a review, see *TLS*, 23.6.1927, 443.

67   *Mary Jane and Harry John*, 8–9.

68   ibid., 9–12.

69   ibid., 12–15.

70   ibid., 15–18; Bennett, *Soul in the Making*, 91–7.

71   Bennett, *Mary Jane and Harry John*, 18–9. An elderly man who attended Bennett's children's services recalled for me how Bennett spoke to him with respect, inculcating in him a lasting love of Chester Cathedral. A Chester lady, now a guide at the cathedral, writes in similar terms (D. C. Kelly (ed)., *Chester Cathedral 1992: Close Encounters in the First Person* (Lincoln, 1991), 4).

72   Bennett offers sets of morning and evening prayers, all suggested by a child of ten (his son had been that age in 1912, so perhaps the anonymous child was one of his later Sunday School pupils), 'whose religion was very real to him'. The evening prayers ended with a simplified version of St Richard of Chichester's prayer, which he later persuaded the CEMS to adopt in full. The children's version reads: 'Day by day, / Dear Lord, of Thee three things I pray – / To see Thee more clearly, / To love Thee more dearly, / To follow Thee more nearly / Day by day'. He considered this prayer an equivalent of Coué's 'Day by day, in every way, I get better and better' (Bennett, *Mary Jane and Harry John*, 32, 36; F. S. M. Bennett, *An Open Letter to the Chairman and Council of the CEMS* (Chester/London, 1925), 8).

73   *CDG*, Dec. 1929, 162. The little book had a wide appeal. In 1929, Bennett gladly agreed to allow the making of a Japanese translation (*CDG*, Dec. 1929, 178). The fact that in 1924 the Anglican-inspired Holy Catholic Church of Japan (Nippon Sei Ko Kai, founded 1887) had become 'an autocephalous entity', and that new sees had been created at Tokyo and Osaka under native bishops, may have prompted the move (*Crockford Prefaces: The Editor Looks Back* (Oxford, 1947), 25). However, neither the British Lbrary nor the Bodleian Library can trace a translation of Bennett's book, and the National Diet Library of Japan, Tokyo, is unaware of one. If a translation had actually appeared Bennett would certainly have mentioned it in the *Diocesan Gazette*, and as he did not it would seem that no translation was published.

74   F. S. M. Bennett, *The Christian Ideal of Health* (London, 1930).

75   William McDougall, *Character and the Conduct of Life*, London, 1928. Bennett recommended the book to readers of the *Diocesan Gazette* for its 'learned and lucid commonsense' (*CDG*, June 1928, 87).

76   McDougall, *Character and Conduct*. chap. xiv; Bennet, *Christian Ideal of Health*, 6–9. Bennett relates faith to Westcott's description of it as the means whereby 'we penetrate the future', and also to Coué's thinking and practice (7–8).

77   Bennett, *Christian Ideal*, 15–17.

78   Much of the advice was sensible enough, if somewhat commonplace and perhaps a shade patronising. Health should be the parents' prime concern, and desire for children to excel at school should never override it. Increasing maturity, as he had himself found as a boy, led to sudden progress (Bennett, *Christian Ideal*, 21). When children are well, Bennett advises, do not coddle them; when ill, be careful. Never discuss their health when they are present. Tiny children take in more than adults suppose. Baneful suggestions are anathema. Bennett cites McDougall, who, as a boy, was discouraged when told he lacked the 'brains' to become an engineer (*ibid.*, 22–3; McDougall, *Character and Conduct*, 190). Children's love of rhythm and pattern in life should be harnessed. Suggestion, not punishment, should be employed to cure bad habits such as nail-biting. Suggestions made before sleep were most effective.

79   Bernard Wall, *Tales of Chester II, Cathedral Cameos* (Market Drayton, 1992).

80   This has echoes of Bennett's 'robust theology'. Since he endorsed it as 'the best attitude to health and other things for every one of us, young and old', it deserves to be quoted in full:

> Give me a good digestion, Lord,
> And also something to digest:
> But when and how that something comes
> I leave to Thee, who knowest best
> Give me a healthy body, Lord;
> Give me the sense to keep it so;

> Also a heart that is not bored,
> Whatever work I have to do.
>> Give me a healthy mind, Good Lord,
> That finds the good that dodges sight
> And, seeing sin, is not appalled,
> But seeks a way to put it right.
>> Give me a point of view, Good Lord,
> Let me know what it is, and why.
> Don't let me worry overmuch
> About the thing that's known as "I".
>> Give me a sense of humour, Lord,
> Give me the power to see a joke,
> To get some happiness from life
> And pass it on to other folk.
>
> (Bennett, *Christian Ideal*, 27–8).

I recently found these verses on a printed card displayed in Staunton Park, Herefordshire, and attributed to T. H. Webb.

81   F. S. M. Bennett, *This Moment of Opportunity for Religious Education* (London, 1938), iii-vi. Viscount Sankey's Foreword summarised and emphasised Bennett's arguments. As Sankey was Chairman of the Standing Committee of the National Society, his endorsement gave added weight to *Moment of Opportunity*.

82   Bennett, *Moment of Opportunity*, 22–30; 37–9.

83   *ibid.*, 15. They should emulate the day-schools, where sound teaching and good equipment were the keys to success. Dioceses could profitably appoint Sunday School Organisers, and bishops could insist that ordinands had some teacher-training; theological college courses should include teaching techniques. Local vicars should insist that Sunday school teachers attended preparation classes, and should enlist practising day-school teachers to conduct these (*ibid.*, 15–22).

84   Parochial practice regarding Sunday Schools was, in any case, changing where there were younger clergy. The application of clause 13 of the 1936 Education Act varied considerably from area to area, then war and the evacuation of children in 1939 disrupted arrangements. The 1944 Education Act preserved the dual system and continued the 'withdrawal' provision of the 1936 Act, but in general parents and clergy made little use of it.

85   Bennett, *Open Letter*, 3; *CDG*, Feb. 1921, 420; July 1924, 183.

86   Bennett, *Open Letter*, 3–4.

87   *ibid.*, 4–6.

88   *ibid.*, 7; General Epistle of Jude, 21.

89   For childrens' version, note 72 above.

90 J. Paterson Smith, *A People's Life of Christ* (London, 1921), was his preference, and he urged the Society to sponsor a cheap edition (Bennett, *Open Letter*, 9–10). This was eventually produced (*All in One*, Apr. 1926, 33–4).

91 Cf. F. S. M. Bennett, 'Integration', in H. R. L. Shepherd, ed., *My Hopes and Fears for the Church* (London, 1930), 83–95.

92 Bennett, *Open Letter*, 10–15. I.A.O. B. = 'I acknowledge One Baptism', from the Prayer Book translation of the Nicene Creed (also the source of the title *Expecto*).

93 Lambeth Palace Library, MS 3377, f. 245, Church of England Men's Society Minutes, 7.10.1925. For other background, MS 3377, f. 250, CEMS Minutes, 4.11.1925; *All in One*, Apr. 1926, 34.

94 Lambeth Palace Library, MS 3377, CEMS Minutes, f. 255, 2.12.1925; f. 267, 3.2.1925; f. 271, 3.3.1926; f. 291, 6.10.1926; *All in One*, April 1926, 33–4.

95 *The Times*, 10.6.1926.

96 Bennett, *Open Letter*, 28–9.

97 E. R. Norman, *Church and Society in England, 1770–1879* (Oxford, 1976), 314, 338–41. Adrian Hastings, *A History of English Christianity, 1920–1985* (London, 1986), 175, 178–9, 186, 190.

98 Paige Cox, in a letter dated 30.6.1926 to an unnamed Canon of Peterborough aligned himself against ICF and miners. 'It is a question now', he wrote, 'if it is worthwhile to get up a Manifesto. The Bishops who sided with the miners have been out argued and practically silenced by other Bishops and clergy who have written to *The Times*, and it is pretty well known that they are not representative. I see that Mr Kirk of the ICF [Canon T. P. Kirk, Director of the ICF], had a letter in *The Times* on Saturday, but it is hardly worth noticing, as he is quite discredited. If, however, the ICF should make any serious move again with the backing of Bishops it would be imperative that a protest should be made.' (Peterborough Cathedral Archives). The fact that Paige Cox does not criticise Bennett for his proposal to support the ICF suggests that he sensed no socialist leanings in his dean, of whom he is otherwise critical in his letter. I am grateful to Canon Higham, Canon Chancellor of Peterborough, for bringing the letter to my attention. See also Hastings, *English Christianity*, 186–92.

99 Bennett's son believed that his father had learnt the love of ceremonial, which he would later introduce in the cathedral, from his two Hawarden curates, Philip Speight and Robert Dearnley, who both came to him from The Community of the Resurrection at Mirfield (F. L. M. Bennett, 'Memoir'). But Bennett was no stranger to ceremonial before he arrived at Hawarden, though – always a ready learner – he may well have acquired knowledge of advanced ceremonial there.

100 W. S. F. Pickering, *Anglo-Catholicism* (London/New York, 1989); Cross, *Oxford Dictionary of the Christian Church*, 58, 467, 965–6, 1019–20, 1388. On Ritualism and its impact, see G. I. T. Machin, *Politics and the Churches in Great*

Britain, 1869 to 1921 (Oxford, 1987), esp. 234–55. For a reassessment of the antecedents of the Oxford Movement, and its relationship to Old High Churchmanship, see Peter B. Nockles, *The Oxford Movement in Context: Anglican High Churchmanship, 1760–1857* (Cambridge, 1994).

101 The condemned ceremonies were prayers for souls in Purgatory; veneration of images; Mariolatry; use of the Canon of the Mass. Reservation was included, but the Prayer Book allowed it for administration to the sick. Bennett thus reserved it, but not for services of adoration.

102 During Holy Week, 1923, Bennett, Canon Eck, and Minor Canon Gravell heard altogether 150 confessions. Bennett announced that they 'obviously met a widespread need', and so made it known that he and his colleagues were 'at all times gladly willing to see those who wish to come to us at the Cathedral for their souls' health' (*CDG*, May 1923, 121). He arranged for the publication of an English edition of a little book by Mary Felkin (originally published in New Zealand), which gives specific advice on the making of confessions. Bennett provided a commendatory preface (E. Mary Felkin, *The Cup of the Lord* (Chester/Oxford, 1925). At Hawarden he wrote two leaflets on the subject (F. S. M. Bennett, *Helps to Self Examination,* and *How to make a Confession* (*Hawarden Parish Magazine*, March 1915)). Mary Felkin had, 'years ago', taught Bennett 'the practice of meditation, being herself then a mistress of that difficult but spiritually remunerative art'. This is the only direct reference to his practising meditation which I have found in his published writings ('Preface', *The Cup of the Lord*).

103 Bennett, *Expecto*, 139; Bennett, *Nature of a Cathedral*, 57.

104 Pickering, *Anglo-Catholicism*, 29. 48–64, 96–8.

105 Conference Report (copy at British Library, 4110 a 4); *The Times*, 13.9.1923. The controversial and charismatic Frank Weston, who had inspired the 1920 Lambeth Conference appeal for Christian unity, presided at the 1923 Conference.

106 British Library, 4110 a 4; Bennett was not a principal speaker, and reports make no mention of any discussion in which he might have participated. An Anglo-Catholic Priests Conferences followed. Eleven hundred registered for the first, in 1921, but Bennett was not among them (*The First Anglo-Catholic Priests' Convention* (copy at British Library, 4107 g 11), 'Names and Addresses of the Members'; *Report of the First Anglo-Catholic Priests' Convention* (Society of SS Peter and Paul, 1921). Chester's turn came in May 1923 (*The Times*, 5.2.1923, 3). Paget was attending a bishops' meeting in London (*CDG*, May 1923, 120), but Bennett was present throughout the three-day event. Canon Leary of Birmingham, the Reverend H. P. Leary of Kilburn, and Father Bold, S.S.J.E. (the 'Cowley Fathers') led, respectively, discussions dealing with the Priest in relation to his parish, to his Church, and to his own life (*The Times*, 5.2.1923, 3). Bennett later praised the event, but described it merely as 'the Priests' Convention', omitting the possibly divisive 'Anglo-Catholic'. He rejoiced

to see the old conventual buildings used and hoped that the convention would lead to retreats for clergy and laity at Chester, an ambition realised when he was able, two years later, to establish the Hostel in Abbey Square (*CDG*, June 1923, 145–6).

107   'Memoir'.

108   For Revision, see G. K. A. Bell, *Randall Davidson, Archbishop of Canterbury* (Oxford, single vol. edit., 1952), 1325–60.

109   The two ancient provinces in the Anglican Church (each consisting of a number of dioceses) are Canterbury and York. Each province has its own Convocation, a gathering representing the clergy of the province. Though these are exclusively clerical assemblies, in 1885 a 'House of Laity' was associated with each. The Upper House of Convocation consists of the diocesan bishops and is presided over by the archbishop; the Lower House consists of clergy elected as 'proctors' to represent the dioceses, together with *ex officio* members, and it chooses its own presiding officer (the prolocutor). The two convocations may sit in joint session. Originally a convocation had the right (or duty) of approving grants to the sovereign from the clergy (i.e., voting taxes), in the same way as Parliament taxed the laity, but in 1664 this right was surrendered. In 1920, the Church Assembly – two houses of clergy and a house of laity – was established, whose most important role was to prepare ecclesiastical measures for transmission to Parliament. (In 1969, practically all the functions of Convocation, including the power to legislate for the church by 'Canon', were taken over by the General Synod, which superceded the Church Assembly.)

The 1662 Book of Common Prayer was annexed to the 1662 Act of Uniformity (which enforced use of the book), but was not discussed or debated in Parliament, it having been earlier approved by the (joint) Convocation. Earlier versions, each with a different doctrinal emphasis, had been enforced by similar Acts (1549, 1552, 1559), given that the sovereign was now recognised as Supreme Head (Governor) of the Church. It followed that any revised Book of Common Prayer could not be enforced without parlaamentary approval. This was the situation in 1926. (For more extensive discussion, see 'Convocations of Canterbury', 'Synodical Government', 'Uniformity, Act of', in Cross, *Oxford Dictionary of the Christian Church*).

110   Bishop John Wordsworth, quoted in Bell, *Randall Davidson*, 652–3.

111   *ibid.*, 1326–7.

112   Francis Carolus Eeles, *Prayer Book Revision and Christian Reunion* (Cambridge, 1923); *CDG*, Dec. 1923, 289. Eeles was an authority on liturgy and ornaments.

113   Bell, *Randall Davidson*, 1329.

114   Eeles, *Prayer Book Revision*, 10.

115   On Reunion, see Bell, *Randall Davidson*, 229–37, 1039, 1104 ff; Hastings, *English Christianity*, 86–99, 208–20. At Hawarden, Bennett had propounded a view about Reunion in the direction of one between the Church of England and the Orthodox

churches, a view similar to that of Eeles (*Ches. Chr.*, 16.1.1915, 6; *Hawarden Parish Magazine*, Jan. 1915). As for Ritualism, in Oxford by 1878 the extension of ritual practices and ceremony was offering Anglicans much that had previously been largely the province of Rome and thus halting conversions to Roman Catholicism. W. E. Gladstone had percipiently noted another aspect: 'the new wealth flooding England was often allied with ritual, and that new churches, vestments, altar frontals and the like were evidence of a kind of conspicuous consumption of goods showing off the donors' wealth in a fashion so socially acceptable that it nearly sanctified ostentation' (Robert Bernard Martin, *Gerard Manley Hopkins: A Very Private Life* (1991), 290–1).

116 Reservation is the retention of some of the elements of bread and wine, after consecration and distribution to communicants at the Eucharist. Prior to the Reformation, Reservation had been a normal practice in England, as in the rest of Christendom, mainly in order to bring the Eucharist to the sick in their own homes, without the lengthy process of consecrating at the bedside. Much of the Reformation theological debate focused on the significance of the consecrated elements. Reformers opposed Reservation as conducive to adoration of these, and hence as exalting the priest's mystical and paramount role in the Eucharist, at the expense of the communal and expressive participation of the laity, the latter signifying the doctrine of the Priesthood of All Believers. The 1549 Prayer Book had however permitted Reservation to allow the priest to administer communion speedily to the sick or dying in their homes. Today, Reservation is common practice in many Anglican churches, ostensibly for this reason.

117 *CDG*, Aug. 1924, 50–51.
118 *ibid.*
119 *The Times*, 2.7.1924, 11.
120 *ibid.*, 21.7.1924, 14, d.
121 *CDG*, Aug. 1924, 50–51. The local press also included totally untrue allegations that Bennett had spoken of a 'High Mass' in Chester Cathedral.
122 Bennett responding to a toast to 'The Church', at Chester Cathedral Old Choristers' Dinner (newspaper cutting, unattributed, pasted in Cheshire Record Office, Diocesan Archives, 'Commonplace Book', 14.11.1925, 129.
123 Quoted in Bennett, *On Cathedrals in the Meantime*, 35–6.
124 Bell, *Randall Davidson*, 1334–5.
125 At a meeting of Chester Diocesan Synod, the Archdeacon of Macclesfield pointed out that all opponents were not extremists, and 'neither was all the prayer on one side. Minorities were not always wrong' (*CDG*, June 1927, 86–7.); *The Times*, 17.2.1927, 15.
126 *CDG*, April 1927, 70–1.
127 Davidson did not 'greatly long' for any changes, or regard them as 'of supreme deep-down importance'. As to Reservation, 'in the present unsettled conditions

in London and some other places' the only chance of peace lay in allowing 'some degree of Reservation-liberty' and guarding it against abuses (Bell, *Randall Davidson*, 1335).

128   Bishops, 34–4; clergy, 253–37; laity, 230–92; majority, 384 (Bell, *Randall Davidson*, 1340).

129   Scribbled MS note, 'Deans Meeting July 12 1927', in Bell's handwriting, probably his note of the meeting, on the reverse of a carbon copy of a typed letter, dated 8.6.27, addressed to the Dean of Windsor (Lambeth Palace Library, Bell Papers, 1920–1929, f. 279).

130   Bell, *Randall Davidson*, 1346; see also 1340–6.

131   *CDG*, Feb. 1928, 19; Mar. 1928, 35–7. The ancient and irrational fear of Rome was at the root of the Protestant opposition in Parliament. Davidson should have given a firm and decisive lead, and voiced publicly to opponents of Revision the questions he committed to his own private Memorandum, as follows. 'Will you support the inclusion within the church of deeply devout men who are by temperament or training or belief irrevocably tied to a view of the Holy Communion which seems to you quite erroneous? You say nothing will induce you to do so. Are you sure that you are thus acting in accordance with the Holy Spirit, or that your actions will be justified when the history of this century is completed?' This, coupled with unequivocal assurances that he would discipline deviating clergy (that is, those who conducted services of Adoration before the Reserved Elements, on the Roman model), might have led to a somewhat different outcome (Bell, *Randall Davidson*, 1354–8) A second bill, later in 1928, was rejected by a slightly larger Commons majority (266–220).

132   *The Book of Common Prayer with the Additions and Deviations proposed in 1928* (Oxford, 1928); for an account, see Bell, *Randall Davidson*, 1358–60.

133   Full justice was not finally done to the 1928 proposals until 1965, when the Prayer Book (Alternative and Other Services) Measure made it possible to give full parliamentary authority to the Revised Book. This, however, was soon to be overtaken by other optional alternative services, including, after 1973, versions using allegedly 'contemporary' language. The ultimate outcome was the *Alternative Service Book*, which to the regret of many has often led to the quiet banishment of the *Book of Common Prayer* (Hastings, *English Christianity*, 665).

134   'Dick' Sheppard (Dean, 1929–31), succeeded George Bell, who became Bishop of Chichester.

135   Bennett, 'Integration', 83–95.

136   'The Lambeth Appeal of 1920', in R. P. Flindall (ed.) *The Church of England 1815–1948: A Documentary History* (London, 1972), 360.

137   'Appeal, VII, VIII' (Flindall, *Church of England*, 362). The verdict of Bell, who was Assistant Secretary to the Conference, that there had been struck 'a great blow for the Reunion of Christendom' was over-optimistic (Bell, *Randall*

Davidson, 1008, 1014; D. L. Edwards, *Leaders of the Church of England* (Oxford, 1971), 315).
    138   Bennett, 'Integration', 86.
    139   *ibid.*, 87–8.
    140   *ibid.*, 90–1. Note Bennett's regular meetings and friendly relations with Nonconformist clergy at Hawarden, and his establishment in 1920 of the Societas Fratorum at Chester. The first meeting, at his suggestion, had discussed the 1920 Lambeth resolutions on Reunion, and the second, the nature of episcopacy, which Bennett had described as 'a big crux of the whole problem' (*CDG*, Oct. 1920, 147–8; Dec. 1920, 84). In 1946, Geoffrey Fisher (by then Archbishop of Canterbury) suggested, in a Cambridge University sermon, that the Free Churches might, without surrendering their identity, 'take episcopacy into their system' and thus prepare the way for intercommunion in England (Cross, *Dictionary of the Christian Church*, 1181).
    141   Bennett, 'Integration', 91–92.
    142   *ibid.*, 93. With integration in view, Bennett hoped that even 'that most Christian body, the Society of Friends', might 'look at baptism again' (95).
    143   A. J. Humphreys, 'Hopes and Fears', *CDG*, June 1930, 6; 'Anglo-Catholic Views' in Sheppard, *Hopes and Fears*, 175–206. The articles were by Maurice Child (Secretary to the Anglo-Catholic Conference), and Kenneth Ingram (editor of *The Green Quarterly*).
    144   'The Dean's latest Pronouncements', *Ches. Chr.*, 12.4.1930. This remarked that 'the Dean's friends will in many cases be surprised' to read his pronouncement that while episcopacy could not claim scriptural authority for recognition as fundamental to Christian society, Baptism could; and equally his assertion that 'baptism stands for unity'. But *The Times Literary Supplement* commended Bennett's 'considerable daring and common sense' (*TLS*, 1930, 418).
    145   Flindall, *Church of England*, 360.
    146   'Reunion', Cross, *Oxford Dictionary of the Christian Church*, 1180–1.

IX

Harmony and discord: a dean and his two communities

The volume in *The Victoria History of the County of Chester* dealing with ecclesiastical aspects sees 'relations between the cathedral and the community' as 'the particular interest of Darby's successor as Dean'. The writer instances Bennett's opening up of the cathedral, the appropriation of chapels to particular groups, the drawing of the whole diocese into the work of the cathedral, the restoration fund, and the encouragement of greater use of its library – all aspects of Bennett's work which we have looked at in other contexts.[1] It is in fact arguable whether 'the community' was his 'particular interest'. Nevertheless, his community involvement ran rather deeper and was more extensive than suggested. From his earliest days in Chester Bennett realised that to many in the local community the cathedral was a place apart which they had never visited, and did not contemplate visiting. This perception he at once set about altering. Soon he was cultivating members of the city establishment, starting with the few who, like H. F. Brown, a City Alderman and the proprietor of the leading multiple store, did have previous cathedral connections.

Despite his sincere desire to bring Cathedral and Community together – or possibly because of this – over specific issues tensions and disagreements between the dean and the community from time to time occurred. Perhaps not surprisingly, Bennett's relations with his more immediate community, the cathedral clergy, included elements of the same. While he possessed considerable public-relations skills, Bennett could, on occasion, be irritating to others. His own accounts suggest that he was rather too keen to demonstrate, as a last word, that he was right after all. Often in fact right, he could exult in self-satisfaction. Two specific incidents illustrate tensions with the city community and Bennett's determination to have his own way.

On arrival as dean, Bennett joined the City War Memorial Committee, replacing Canon Paige Cox, Archdeacon of Chester.[2] By this time a range of 'practical' memorial projects had been considered and rejected. Bennett suggested another project: the much-needed re-hanging of the cathedral bells. He dressed this up as a means of linking City and Cathedral, by proposing that the bells be rung on Armistice Day, and on other occasions at the request of the Mayor.[3] However, a public meeting had already voted for a memorial cross, and Paige Cox had agreed this might be erected on the cathedral green, the only remaining central site (the other two possible sites having been refused by the City Council and King's School respectively).[4] Given the site, the dean's approval of the design of the cross was essential. The Committee had commissioned Giles Gilbert Scott to design a cross for erection on the cathedral green and had endorsed his impressive design, but Bennett turned it down. Perhaps he felt that the monument would dominate the cathedral;[5] but perhaps, less highmindedly, he also recalled Scott's derisive rejection of his own proposed model for the Hawarden memorial and was determined to have something to his own taste at Chester.[6] His views on the new brief to Scott were inevitably influential. Scott was now asked to design either a 'cross-on-steps' style memorial, or one based on an Eleanor cross. Bennett approved the 'slim' Eleanor Cross (probably based on Geddington) which Scott offered, but the Committee claimed that it did not comply with their brief and rejected it.[7]

In this impasse, it was agreed to mount a competition for a design. Bennett's new architect, Fyfe, acting as assessor, represented Bennett's views to the Committee and selected the short list. The winning design was by Thomas Rayson, an Oxford architect.[8] He collaborated with F. H. Crossley, who, being a local man and well aware of the events leading up to the competition, had been in a position to advise Rayson (and the carver, Alec Miller) as to what was most likely to meet with the approval of the Committee, and, more importantly, the approval of Bennett, who subsequently composed the inscription to go around the hexagonal pedestal. Significantly, the winning design was a 'cross-on-steps', reminiscent of a churchyard cross (as had been Bennett's proposal for Hawarden), and it included symbolic carvings of saints, an echo of Bennett's cloister scheme.[9] Bennett perceived it not only as a memorial but also as an architectural enhancement of the cathedral, 'exactly the right thing in the right place'.[10] The entry in the Chapter's Commonplace Book claims: 'It is generally recognised that the memorial is one of the most beautiful in the country'.[11] The words are probably Bennett's as they echo closely those he had used in 1919 about his own suggested model for Hawarden.[12] The local press considered it 'a beautiful work of art'; Bishop Paget lavished praise on it for blending so well with its cathedral setting.[13]

The City's annual combined civic, military, and religious celebration of Armistice Day, with its emotionally-charged Silence, was organised by the joint Armistice Day Consultative Committee, of which Bennett was a member. Until 1928, the service was held at the war memorial. In 1928 Bennett and the Mayor agreed to mark Armistice Day and Mayor's Sunday with a combined service in the cathedral, where a new stand for the civic mace and sword, symbolically linking city and cathedral, would be inaugurated. This had been presented in memory of a former Mayor, Colonel John Sheriff-Roberts, who had lost three sons in the war. After the service and the inauguration, wreaths were laid on the war memorial. But the dean and mayor had misjudged the public mood. There was comment in the press about the disappointment of the 'thousands' who had massed and been unable to get into the cathedral. Instead they wanted to 'join in a simple service', out of doors, at the memorial, for 'the most important two minutes of the day, of the week, of the year'.[14]

The following year, 1929, the joint committee arranged for the service to take place again in the cathedral, allegedly because of the likely wet weather. Dissatisfaction with both Bennett and the City authorities exploded in a spate of letters to the press, many from ex-servicemen and parents of the fallen. Bennett was, by implication, a special target. Some writers suspected that the weather was merely an excuse; many complained that the Armistice Day ceremony was being transformed into 'an ecclesiastical function'.[15] If the 'Cathedral authorities' – that is, Bennett – wanted to make a religious service of it, let the military hold a drum-head service at the Castle;[16] this was 'a soldier's day' and the service should be held in the Town Hall Square.[17] As for the Mayor and his entourage, if 'the King and Prince [of Wales]' could stand bareheaded at the Cenotaph, so too could the dignitaries of Chester.[18] The war memorial itself had been appropriated by the cathedral: placing it on the green was 'the most unfortunate mistake the city authorities ever made ... Many citizens and ex-service men cannot conscientiously regard it as theirs in any way'.[19] Some of the letter writers pressed for the removal of the railings, and one enclosed a sketch showing a proposed open paved area around the memorial.[20]

After the 1929 debacle, the joint committee decided to hold the 1930 Armistice Day service in the spacious Town Hall Square (where, incidentally, had the City authorities been more accommodating a memorial could have been erected much earlier). Bennett conducted a simple service, after which there was a military march-past and the Mayor and others laid wreaths on the memorial. This pattern continued until 1938; in 1939 there was only a simple wreath-laying.[21] After 1929 Bennett had been anxious to repair the rift with the community. The Town Hall Square, he conceded, was much better than the confined cathedral green, but to meet all needs he provided for an evening service within the cathedral.[22]

2

Another occasion for tension arose over the building in 1930 of a new canons' vestry, needed after the opening of the Norman arch into the sacristry, the former vestry. Instructed to prepare a design, Fyfe planned a modern style building in brick, to be formed against the north wall of the chancel, without any pretence of its being a pastiche of its surrounds.[23] Soon there were murmurings in the city against the setting against a medieval cathedral wall of a non-traditional, brick-built structure. The editor of the *Chester Chronicle* voiced the concern of well-meaning citizens: 'We hope the Dean will give the project as originally designed second thoughts, which are proverbially best'.[24] Bennett sought to dampen criticism by hinting that plans might after all be modified because of the cost. As this made little impact, at Bennett's behest Fyfe made a professional response in the *Diocesan Gazette*, arguing cogently that the site selected was the only possible one.[25] The plans were not modified.

Opposition hardened. The City Council and the Chester and North Wales Archaeological Society sent resolutions to Bennett.[26] On 31 July 1930, at a formal session of the Chapter, Bennett received a civic deputation which described the new building as 'unsightly'.[27] Bennett replied that it was not intended to be an imitation of the cathedral work and therefore 'the highest Authorities possible [no details given] had been consulted'. He then 'went very carefully into the whole story', asking why, if there was 'so much misunderstanding' no information of this had come earlier to the Chapter. It seemed unreasonable to alter things at this late stage, especially in view of the expense involved. The minute concludes, tersely, 'The deputation viewed the New Vestry and thanked the Chapter for receiving them'.[28] The next day, under the headline 'Dean's agreement to seek new advice', *The Times* reported the meeting more fully, and we catch the authentic flavour of Bennett's somewhat testy response to the deputation. He had said that a body which had spent a quarter of a million pounds on improving the cathedral deserved the confidence of the citizens 'and the world in general'. The vestry could not be 'pulled down' at the moment, but he was prepared to await the opinions of 'artists and architects of eminence' and after two years might reconsider the matter. Fyfe had already described the new vestry as a 'chance for Chester to show that a modern-style building could be placed against the wall of a building like the Cathedral'.[29]

The following day, the professional journal, *The Architect and Building News*, joined the attack, under the headline, 'An amazing and stealthy addition to Chester Cathedral'. It added photographs of 'The "red brick shanty on the green", Chester's new vestry in the making', plus a plan showing the location of the offending addition. The piece, written (on internal evidence) prior to the mayoral deputation is unsigned, but its content suggests that it was written either by a Chester person, or more probably (in view of occasional inaccuracies), inspired by Chester sources. 'Vestries and sacristries', it claimed, were 'becoming fashionable'. Chester was 'the latest victim of this urge to be *dans le mouvement*'. Years ago, citizens of Chester 'on their own initiative' demolished houses to clear the prospect of 'their' [*sic*] cathedral. Not surprisingly, 'a storm of indignation' had been raised at this 'squat red brick structure ... unpleasant and obtrusive'. The Dean and Chapter were 'at least guilty of discourtesy towards the people of Chester, who might well have expected to be informed, if not consulted, about so important an addition to a building round which their affections have been entwined for centuries'. Moreover, 'innovations to a famous English Cathedral' were a national concern, not a matter for 'the whims of a Dean and Chapter'. The 'ill-advised action' was 'calculated to provoke not only the citizens of Chester but to scandalize all who regard our cathedrals as a national heritage, secure from the tampering of self-appointed priest-builders'.[30]

Following the meeting with the City deputation, *The Times* published 'The Chester Vestry: Statement by the Dean'. Critics, Bennett argued, had neither seen nor asked to see the plans. He and the Chapter had entrusted Fyfe with designing a modern building adjacent to an ancient one, and in their judgment he 'had achieved very great success'. The building was too far advanced to stop now, but if eventually 'educated opinion' [*sic*] proved to be opposed it could be moved. However, the vestry was 'absolutely necessary', was in the only possible place, and would enhance, not mar, the view of the Chapter House.[31] Bennett sought 'further expert opinion',[32] and the opinions of 'artists and architects of eminence'.[33]

He was referring to The Society for the Protection of Ancient Buildings, whose Committee on 21 August considered 'the case of the new vestry of Chester Cathedral'. Fyfe conveyed his views and was invited to attend; he may have done so.[34] Bennett contended that when the building was finished and had 'mellowed', people would marvel at all the 'pother'. Meanwhile, the 'public will believe that we are as concerned as anybody else (perhaps more so) to preserve the beauty of the cathedral and its surroundings'.[35] The Committee found that the vestry accorded with the principle that additions to ancient buildings should show 'decent respect' for neighbouring old work and yet should not consciously imitate its style. They gave 'cautious but decisive support to the Dean and Chapter and their Architect, Mr Theodore Fyfe'.[36] This ended the matter, but Bennett had the last word.

The following summer he called in the New World to redress the balance of the Old. As noted in Chapter VII above, in an article published in the United States he argued that the styles of all parts of the cathedral fabric could be read as symbolic portraits of those who had commissioned them. He told future American visitors that, after viewing the medieval splendours of the cathedral, if they looked for it carefully they would see

> a modest little building – a vestry erected in 1930 and frankly in the style of today. Its lines and colour are designed to work in well with its surroundings; but it tells its own tale as clearly as do the Chapter House or Nave. Perhaps it is no bad portrait of the Dean – a modest man and retiring with an eye to the usefulness of the buildings and with profound respect for the work of his predecessors, but by nature a trifle original in mind and methods. In venturing to put up a small building in the style of his own day and not an 'imitation Gothic edifice' he has shown the true medieval spirit.[37]

It was a characteristic riposte from the man who had urged the expansive New World to be adventurous in its ecclesiastical building, but it also reflects a smug satisfaction at triumph over critics. The vestry fulfils its purpose today and attracts no special notice. The fabric has weathered and mellowed and the building blends easily with its background. Time has fully vindicated Bennett's judgment.[38]

3

Another of Bennett's changes excited no comment. In the 1920s private cars were proliferating and as few Chester inner city houses had garages local people parked in Abbey Square, through the old gateway. Tourists used the Square too and summer traffic became heavy. In 1929, Bennett, wedded to his 'no fees' policies, put an 'honesty box' at the entrance, with a notice seeking 'Gifts ... in lieu of fees for garage', the money to go towards repairs to the 'fine old gateway'. Cathedral staff were exempt.[39] In three months less than ten pounds came in. Bennett calculated that, at a shilling per car as was charged elsewhere, he would have collected ten pounds in a week. Since collections remained unimpressive,[40] in 1931 he breached his 'no fees' principle and imposed a set charge.[41] Four years later he introduced modern methods: realistic charges, surcharges for overstaying, double charges at key times, and season tickets. Those attending services or meetings parked free. By September 1935 he was able to pay for the restoration of the Abbey Gate.[42] Today, entry is free but mainly restricted to Abbey Square residents, their visitors, and cathedral staff.

A further minor episode points to an impressive – or depressing – feature of today's Chester. When local caterers created a minor irritation by complaining that the new refectory was poaching their customers, Bennett responded sharply. For each who has tea in the cathedral, he told them, 'we attract to Chester by our pleasant ways at the Cathedral fifty who get tea in the town'. Expressions of gratitude, not grumbles, were in order.[43] He was on sure ground. The bulk of shopkeepers now saw the cathedral as a tourist attraction, bringing trade to their various businesses.

4

Bennett associated himself with the city through membership of various societies. His interest in history was manifested in 1922, when he established a branch of the Historical Association, a national body.[44] Bennett was elected President of the local branch, a post he continued to fill until his retirement.[45] Regular meetings took place in the Chapter House until 1936 and thereafter in the refurbished Parlour.[46] Bennett was an active president, chairing at every meeting, and the branch paid him handsome tributes on his retirement in 1937.[47]

When in 1937 the Chester Historical Pageant was organised, Bennett served on the Executive and Finance Committee and the Lecture Committee.[48]

In 1922 Bennett accepted an invition to join the newly formed Rotary Club. Bennett and the President, Frederick Coplestone, were old friends, in a mutually fruitful professional link dating from the days when one was Bishop Jayne's secretary and the other *The Times* local correspondent. The Rotary ideal of service to the community appealed to Bennett and he valued the friendship which a group of like-minded men engendered; he also had opportunities for informal contacts with influential individuals.[49]

At Hawarden, Bennett had been a member of a Freemasons' Lodge and his fellow Freemasons had greeted him on his arrival at Chester as dean.[50] He now transferred to the Cestrian Lodge, later serving as 'Provincial Grand Chaplain'; in 1922, he is listed as 'Grand Chaplain of England', receiving his regalia in the cathedral Refectory.[51] Today, few clerics join Masonic lodges but the practice was not unusual in Bennett's day; unlike the continental variety English masonry was not avowedly deist. The organisation gave Bennett early privileged access to the city establishment.[52] As we have seen, the ritual and symbolism appealed to him.[53] In 1925 Bennett provided a special cathedral service for the bicentenary of the Cheshire Province of Freemasons. His sermon illustrated his perception of Masonic ideals by reference to his beloved cathedral, urging his congregation to 'let this old house talk to you of our great principles of masonic life'. The Norman door, 'built with many masonic symbols – squares and circles', was massive and stern, symbolising the law, order, and stability which (he claimed) the Normans had established. The greatest contribution the Masonic Order could make to society was to promote these ideals, through men of 'honour and loyalty'. The collection was devoted to providing a four-light window for the cloisters, which Bennett hoped to dedicate with 'masonic ceremonial'; the Masonic Province donated £100 to the Restoration Fund.[54] In 1930 Bennett founded St Anselm Lodge for men associated with the cathedral and became its first Worshipful Master (that is, chairman). The Chapter presented a bible.[55] Current Masonic sources will not divulge the names of its past members, and so we can only speculate as to whether the future Archbishop of Canterbury, Geoffrey Fisher, Bishop of Chester 1932–1939 – 'probably the last senior ecclesiastic to be a Freemason' – was a member.[56]

Bennett supported several good causes that were specifically socially oriented. As bishop's secretary he had followed Jayne in promoting the temperance movement and reform of the licensing laws.[57] As noted earlier, when Jayne founded the People's Refreshment House Association, to provide public houses where food and non-alcoholic drinks were available, Bennett placed the Sparkford Inn and Posting House at its disposal.[58] As dean, Bennett backed the Church of England Temperance Society and served on the Diocesan committee.[59] While temperance seems outdated in the recent 'permissive' decades, it is arguable that in Bennett's period the campaign to reduce heavy drinking did – occasionally and in some quarters – serve a useful purpose.

More in keeping with present day 'responsible' attitudes, when the League of Nations Union was formed Bennett supported it enthusiastically. Branches proliferated and by 1926 there were nine in Cheshire. Bennett became Chairman of the Cheshire District Council and used the *Diocesan Gazette* to encourage readers to join.[60] He regarded the League as the 'only safeguard of civilisation' and 'applied Christianity'.[61] Bennett's other good causes included the Council for the Preservation of Rural England, which he advertised through the *Diocesan Gazette*. Again, when a Chester and District Council was formed he became chairman.[62]

Bennett sat on various other local committees, including the Archaeological Society Council (as vice-president); the Board of Guardians (attending when he could); and, as chairman, the Police Court Mission Committee. The Mission – an offshoot of the Temperance Society and parent of the later Probation Service – had committees of volunteers who reviewed cases of young offenders, and Bennett approached this activity as a pastor, not as a judge, condemning as immoral 'punishment which does the punished no good'. In 1935 he displayed his social concern by extending the cathedral 'community' and 'adopting' the large Merseyside parish of Ellesmere Port, where the cathedral owned property but whose large working-class population was severely affected by the depression.[63]

At least one public office, however, Bennett filled only half-heartedly. Elected as a Governor of The Queen's School, a prestigious girls' high school, in May 1922 and serving until 1931, he did not attend a single meeting until March 1924 and thereafter was present only sporadically, often forgetting to send apologies, and even missing the June 1925 meeting called to appoint a new headmistress. Given his professed interest in education, this seems surprising. Attendance, however, was frequently thin, and Bennett was not the only offender. Most of the business was routine and Bennett was impatient of boring meetings.[64] At the cathedral he had an escape technique. By prearrangement, a trusted verger would drop a chair noisily outside the door, and a worried-looking dean would hasten out to investigate, and then disappear. This option was not available at Queen's.

Another educational institution did interest him. The 1932 rationalisation programme of the Council of Church Training Colleges proposed the closure of Chester College, an Anglican foundation of the mid-nineteenth century, provoking strong community opposition in the city and beyond. Bennett put down a resolution for the Church Assembly, where the final decision would be taken.[65] Unfortunately, an attack of influenza prevented his attending.[66] He subsequently reported in the *Diocesan Gazette* that his brother, George, had carried his resolution, 'assisted' by the new Bishop of Chester, Geoffrey Fisher.[67] This was misleading. It was Fisher, with a brilliant speech 'compounded of facts, adroit argument, and wit', who actually carried the day.[68] Chester (with two other Anglican colleges) was saved.[69]

In community relations, as in so much else, the Bennett years were a watershed, partly shaped by the changing attitudes and concerns of post-war England but also formed by the conscious effort of Bennett himself. Cathedral and community came more closely together. Tensions did not, in the long run, permanently sour relations. Bennett could compromise, but was adamant on matters of principle, and jubilant – perhaps irritatingly so – when proved right. As chairman or leading member of so many causes Bennett made the new and friendly cathedral a focus of city activity. To many of all classes he was pastor and friend – informally clad in black cassock, moving about the cathedral, ready to talk to anyone. One can only marvel that he found time and energy to attend to so many extra-mural activities.

5

It will not surprise historians to learn that Bennett and his cathedral colleagues were not always of one mind, at least one of them, from Bennett's viewpoint, being 'difficult'. When Bennett's appointment as dean was announced in March 1920, the Chapter's scribe recorded optimistically in the Cathedral Commonplace Book that members of the Chapter were 'all so thankful for the appointment'. Knowing Bennett's reputation, they must have been aware that changes would be in the offing. Equally, Bennett must have known that he might well face opposition to his intended reforms, although as dean of a cathedral of the New Foundation he would have considerable power.

In general, relations between Chapter and Dean turned out to be good, Bennett's subtle diplomacy usually carrying the day. He found an invaluable ally in the charming Alexander Nairne, scholarly theologian and Fellow of Jesus College, Cambridge (later to be Regius Professor of Divinity), who always kept his three month term as canon in residence during the University long vacation and was thus at Chester in June 1920.[70] Just over a year later, however, Nairne was appointed to a canonry at Windsor, and so his second term of residence, in 1921, was his last. Nairne's successor was Herbert Vincent Shortgrave Eck, who had graduated at Keble in 1886 and must therefore have still been there during Bennett's first year. Bennett and he had an easy rapport until Eck left Chester in 1926.[71] Eck was a colourful character, quite different from Nairne, and from Bennett too, though he and the dean shared some common ground in aspects of churchmanship. He was a member of the English Church Union (which Bennett was not), and, some twenty years before, when he was in Bethnal Green, the Church Association had listed him as one of those who were 'helping the Romeward movement', by adopting the eastward position when celebrating, ceremonially mixing wine and water, and burning candles in daylight.[72] At Chester, Eck proposed in 1926 that the sacrificial vestments, chasuble, dalmatic, and tunicle, be adopted for Choral Eucharist, but the proposal was not accepted. Bennett may have felt that such change was too controversial. It went beyond his practice of simply wearing a cope, and is unlikely to have been favoured by Paige Cox.[73]

William Lang Paige Cox, Archdeacon of Chester, former Vicar of Hoylake and Canon of Chester since 1917, was less enthusiastic about Bennett's reforms. He continued in office, dutifully keeping his three-month residence, until his death in 1934. In his earlier days Paige Cox had been considered a High Churchman, but later 'it was said that he was a "Modernist", which in those days meant to a good many people, a disbelief in the scriptures'.[74] Bennett's son, as an observer of the ecclesiastical scene in Chester, categorised Paige Cox as 'a typical appointment of Bishop Jayne's last days'.[75] As Jayne himself had veered from High Churchman to Low Churchman, Paige Cox perhaps suited him.[76] The Archdeacon had some claims to scholarship, having written on the miracles, the nature of the Church, and, in the aftermath of war, on peace problems in the light of Christian ethics.[77] He was a man of strong convictions and by now somewhat settled views, yet 'anxious to refrain from criticism unless it had to be spoken'.[78] The record shows only when it was spoken in Chapter, but there were almost certainly other unrecorded occasions when, despite Paige Cox's natural courtesy, it was spoken firmly in private also.

Bennett's son, with the advantage of a view from inside the deanery, was aware of this, and noted the contrast between the attitude of Nairne and that of Paige Cox to his father's reforms.[79] When Bennett started the sale to pilgrims of picture post-cards and literature within the cathedral, Paige Cox made difficulties. He wanted 'a careful watch' kept on the amount of literature 'exposed in or near the chapels', in case 'over duplication took place again'. It required patience on Bennett's part to meet such obstacles put in the way of his changes.[80]

Nor was Paige Cox happy about the nave altar which Bennett had set up.[81] He viewed the new and increasing influx of visitors – to Bennett, pilgrims – with some reservation. Someone 'tactful but firm' should be on duty to ensure that services were not disturbed. Bennett dutifully detailed a Bedesman. When Bennett established the new sacristry, he placed a crucifix in it. Paige Cox was opposed to this – as Darby had been opposed to the crucifix on the proposed Egerton Cross. The Chapter divided and on a majority vote Bennett's action was approved. The crucifix remained but Paige Cox required his vote against the proposal to be recorded in the minutes.[82] When Bennett proposed the appointment of S. J. Marston, a well qualified and experienced parish priest, to the living of West Kirby, the appointment went through Chapter with 'the Archdeacon withholding his consent'.[83] Again, he disagreed with Bennett on the appointment of a minor canon as Sacrist and Precentor (a job eminently suited to one of the minor canons, appointed for their musical skills and knowledge), rather than a canon as previously, but Bennett got his way. Paige Cox also voiced his 'regret' that the Chapter had not had an opportunity to discuss Bennett's initiation of the cathedral's cooperation in the Bishop's Million Shilling Jubilee Fund, but had to agree with Bennett on the difficulty of calling the Chapter together during the holidays.[84] When Bennett, adopting his favourite technique, 'threw out the suggestion' that they might now terminate said Sunday Eucharist (done once a month, without music and vestments) 'so as to make our use always the same on Sundays', that is, choral celebration at 11.30 a.m,, Paige Cox dissented. And Bennett quietly dropped the matter for the time being.[85]

Paige Cox's views emerge more forcibly in a letter to a fellow canon at

Peterborough. Despite the 'good support from the trippers', offerings in 1926 were down on 1925. The Dean of Winchester had 'told a friend of ours' that Bennett 'was in the habit of begging from Americans whom he took round', adding, somewhat illogically, 'but that sort of thing is not normal'. He went on,

> There are pros and cons about the system of freeing the Cathedral ... [It] is in a disturbed and noisy state while the services are going on. I cannot worship in it with any comfort. To me it is a show-place rather than a place of worship. The system won't work properly unless the Cathedral is well policed. We ought to close the doors before the services and station men about to prevent people from sight-seeing ... The Chapter are in favour of this but the Dean likes to make the place a liberty hall. Hence we are getting a bad name. I am told they are being strict at Canterbury. I should hesitate to recommend the system if it is not possible to have a strong police.[86]

That Paige Cox based his objections on principles which he firmly held is not to be disputed. But Bennett based his changes on principles which he held with equal conviction. There is no evidence in Chapter minutes of formal opposition from any canon other than Paige Cox. Nor is it clear with whom 'we are getting a bad name', and no other criticisms akin to those of Paige Cox have emerged in the records studied. He yearned for the cathedral as it had been; Bennett sought to make it 'what-it-was-to-be'.

In 1920, the Vice-Dean was A. J. Blencowe, who had been a Canon of Chester since 1886 and had just retired from a thirty-one year incumbency as Rector of West Kirby.[87] His name does not figure in Chapter minutes in connection with anything contentious and he seems to have been content to go along with Bennett's changes. He is likely to have been in sympathy with Bennett's High Churchmanship, having already incurred the disapproval of the Church Association as an Anglo-Catholic.[88] His 1926 gift to the cathedral restoration fund of what Bennett obliquely described as 'a Bank of England note of noble value', to mark the Blencowes' Golden Wedding and the canon's 40th anniversary of his installation, might be taken as a token of approval of the dean's reforms. Bennett spent the money on a figure of St Christopher for the corner of the nave and south transept, noting that this would record probably the longest term of service of any Chapter member in four hundred years.[89] When Blencowe retired in 1927, Paige Cox – 'the Patriarch amongst us', as he was to be later described – succeeded as Vice-Dean.[90] Blencowe's successor in the canonry was John Francis Lovel Southam, who continued to serve for the remainder of Bennett's ten years. Appointed by Bishop Paget, he also seems to have been in sympathy with Bennett's way of thinking. The dean wanted to replace the traditional, and poorly attended, sung matins with a said service. Bennett circulated a memorandum on the subject, asking each Chapter member to give his views. Two (Hughes and Newbold) followed Paige Cox's lead and voted against the change; Southam supported Bennett.[91]

At Chester the minor canons were in a privileged position. Like other holders of cathedral offices they had freehold rights. Additionally, thanks to a skilfully invested bequest, they were largely financially independent of the Dean and Chapter. They did of course serve individually in a variety of tasks and did participate, as required to do, in services. Among their number was one who deserves special note. Aubrey Baxter, a former Choral Scholar of King's College, Cambridge, whom Bennett knew well from Christ Church days, a man of considerable ability and efficiency also acted as Librarian. Bennett wanted Baxter to move into employment more consistent with his undoubted talents, but Baxter would not be persuaded, nor could he be compelled, to accept pressing offers of incumbencies. He confessed privately to being 'allergic to deans'.[92] Baxter lived happily to a great age, retiring eventually with an honorary canonry.

Finally, after the death of Paige Cox in 1934, Norman Henry Tubbs came to replace him as Canon and Archdeacon.[93] The decision to appoint Tubbs, to which both Fisher and Bennett were party, may have been made with an eye to his possibly succeeding Bennett. Whether this was the intention or not, it was Tubbs who did become dean when Bennett retired, three years later.[94]

6

In *The Nature of a Cathedral* Bennett had set out his views on the relationship which he believed should exist between bishop and dean, and the role a cathedral should play in the life and work of a bishop. His own bishop fitted the ideal scenario. Henry Luke Paget had come to Chester in 1919, aged sixty-eight. Bennett, who had been a chaplain to Jayne, was delighted when Paget invited him to continue to serve in this post, and he 'came back to Hawarden from the [bishop's consecration] service, made happy ... by Bishop Paget's friendliness'.[95] This was the prelude to a firm and fruitful alliance. Paget had already had some fourteen years' experience as a suffragan bishop, in Norwich and London dioceses. Whereas his predecessor at Chester had veered from the High Church to the Protestant wing,[96] Paget, like Bennett, was a High Churchman, and as such had attracted the attention of the Protestant Church Association in its 1890s survey, when he was incumbent of St Pancras.[97]

His relations with Bennett could not have been more different from those which had obtained between Jayne and Darby, Bennett's predecessor. Bishop and dean had not been on speaking terms after the period during which they engaged in litigation over their respective rights, Jayne winning in the Court of Appeal but finally losing in the Lords.[98] Thereafter Jayne had come to the cathedral as seldom as he could, preferring the church near his palace, St John's (which had served as the cathedral prior to 1540, Chester being then part of the Diocese of Lichfield and the present cathedral a Benedictine house). When the bishop was obliged to visit the cathedral, the dean had almost invariably an appointment elsewhere.[99] Bennett may have had Jayne (and perhaps Darby) in mind when he wrote, 'Not seldom some other Church, near which he [any bishop] lives, sees more of him than does his Cathedral'.[100] He had gone on to argue that 'the bishop should live near to his cathedral. For many a long year bishops have not taken their cathedrals seriously or there would not be so many awkward situations either now irremediable, or still to be remedied'.[101]

In 1921, when 9 Abbey Square became vacant, Bennett acquired it as a new deanery, and he converted the old deanery into the Bishop's House, the former Palace ('Deeside') being taken over by the YMCA.[102] Dean and bishop were now close neighbours and the bishop lived next door to his cathedral. His widow later described the happy partnership. 'Chester in 1921 was on the edge of a big experiment, long overdue in the history of the Church. While Paget ... was perambulating the diocese and country at the circumference, Frank Macaulay Bennett ... was using his rapid gifts of imagination to recreate the centre.'[103]

A development in the same direction followed. In 1925 Bennett converted 12 Abbey Square, until then occupied by a firm of accountants, into a Diocesan Centre, and the following year established a Bishop's Hostel in another newly vacant house, securing sponsors to fund the work. The hostel was to provide accommodation for visiting diocesan clergy. As Bennett said, if the hostel had existed when he was at Portwood, and if the cathedral had 'had its present-day free and open welcome', he would have enjoyed a visit to Chester.[104] Under the management of Canon Eck and Sister Margaret Blanche the Hostel proved to be a great success. Sister Margaret had previously worked in the Refectory, and Eck, appointed to a canonry in 1921, had had relevant experience as Warden of East London Deaconesses Community and as Vice-Principal of Ely Theological College. Ordinands kept their retreats and held reunions in the Hostel; conference members and visitors used it; Paget was in and out of it regularly. In its chapel the bishop would occasionally hold private confirmations. Soon around a thousand people were using the hostel in the course of a year.[105] Above the door, on Bennett's instructions, were painted the diocesan arms, and the inscription, *Pax huic Domui / Sit Pax introeventi / Sit Pax in hac habitanti / Sit et exeunti pax*. It stood, Bennett said, for what they were trying to do in the Great Family House of God. The whole cathedral and its environs – Bishop's Hostel, Diocesan Centre, Refectory, Parlour, Chapter House – exemplified an important aspect of the vision to be proclaimed in *The Nature of a Cathedral*.[106]

As there was no private chapel in Bishop's House, the cathedral became the focus for Paget's devotions. He was regularly there in the early morning and would 'put the Cathedral to bed' with Compline, at nine in the evening. It 'summed up and expressed everything that the Bishop held dear'.[107] Bennett's son, in later years, remembered how St Anselm's Chapel drew a small company from the precincts and further afield to say Compline together. It was 'a community without limits and rules'. For his father, who 'loved his elevenses', the Refectory kitchen and St Anselm's were like body and soul, two facets of his life. This was the community which Paget had joined. On Thursdays he celebrated communion in St George's Chapel.[108] Work took him away from Chester but when at home, 'the Saint's Day Eucharist drew him from his study like a temptation'.

Paget was a man of prayer and private devotion, but he too mingled happily with the crowds which frequented the cathedral and was fully identified with the 'vigorous new life' there.[109] He wondered what people would have thought of it when he was a boy. His comments on 'the immense crowds, the quietude and reverence, the arrangements made for short services, and for guiding people round and for singing hymns', contrast with Paige Cox's perception of the scene.[110] Paget praised Bennett's 'brilliant imagination, his clear head, his immensely kind heart'. It was he who had 'wonderfully linked up the Cathedral with that of the diocese'; had 'guarded so carefully the dignity of the Bishop's office'; and had been 'gentle and considerate at every turn'.[111]

However, despite the common ground they shared, their styles were markedly different, Paget bursting into superlatives, Bennett exercising restraint. They may have jarred on each other at times but they never came into conflict, no doubt because Bennett was determined to respect and preserve the dignity of the bishop's office. His son, however, who 'shared the intimacies of Bennett's home' noted 'what a deal of thought, self-effacement ... [and] self-discipline' his father had had to put into the relationship.[112] Though Paget used superlatives about Bennett, we have no access to perceptions of the relationship from inside his home, merely his widow's published eulogy of Bennett. Nevertheless, the bishop thought sufficiently highly of his dean to put him forward in 1930 for the award of the Lambeth D.D., citing as his great achievement that he had 'really *led the way* in the full use and enlitenment [*sic*] of our Cathedrals', and adding 'that *many* would be glad if you were able to honour him'.[113] Archbishop Cosmo Lang rejected the request.[114]

Paget retired in 1932, at the age of eighty, and died the same year. His successor was Geoffrey Fisher (1887–1972), previously headmaster of Repton (1914–1932), where he had established a considerable reputation. Consecrated in York, he was enthroned in Chester on 29 September. Bennett organised a special train, which made its way from Chester to York by a roundabout route – as was possible in those days – picking up people from all parts of the diocese on the way. It doubtless recalled his famous Christ Church and Hawarden Church Sunday School outings. But this was something more. Bennett also saw the undertaking as an expression of his office, for he still had a sense of the dean as leader of the bishop's *familia*. It was his duty to ensure that his new bishop was 'worthily welcomed, before God by his people', not only at his enthronement in the cathedral but also at this preliminary stage.[115] On the train, Fisher mixed happily with members of the diocesan party. One old layman assured him that he would be 'all right', for they 'would see him through'. With his outstanding ability to mix with people of all sorts, Fisher was a man after Bennett's stamp.[116] A son of the parsonage, he was popular with the diocesan clergy, whom he managed effectively.[117] Fisher, however, had never worked in a parish, and so Bennett was an ideal partner. As in Paget's day, Bennett was in and out of Bishop's House, often, as Fisher may have discovered, not mentioning his real purpose until he was about to leave.[118]

Fisher recognised Bennett's great gifts and valued the partnership, though, as a central churchman, he did not see eye-to-eye with Bennett, or Anglo-Catholics generally, on every aspect of churchmanship. Indeed, Fisher had found 'a weak spot in Paget's mind', often found in 'quite reasonable Anglo-Catholics. They cannot believe that the conservative evangelicals do any good'. There were a few very high, and a few very low churches in the diocese, but Fisher got on well with them all and never interfered or marginalised them. Bennett certainly did not belong in the 'very high' category, and his attitude to the extreme wings was akin to Fisher's. During their five-year partnership they backed one another heartily.[119] That they were both Freemasons may have contributed to their mutual rapport.

Fisher met Bennett at 'the culmination of his achievement' and later penned the following tribute.

> Dean Bennett was a great man. It was he who freed the Cathedral. When he came to Chester he threw it open to all. He was always there, he lived in it and would go round with people, talking to them, and now and again he'd assemble them round the pulpit to give them a short address on the Cathedral, and then say some prayers for them. He was rapidly turning the Cathedral into a lovely house of God. Attached to it was the Refectory, and there meals were provided and all sorts of meetings held.[120]

Fisher wanted Bennett's achievements recognised, before his retirement, by the award of the Lambeth doctorate. Unless Paget had mentioned it, he would not have known of Lang's refusal of the award in 1930. In October 1936 he asked Lang if he would think it 'suitable' to offer Bennett the degree, mentioning that he would be retiring the following autumn, and submitting his name 'in recognition not of any work of scholarship but of a general service rendered to the Church'. The dean had been 'largely responsible' for 'the new spirit' which had been introduced into cathedral life all over the country. At Chester, 'abolishing entrance fees, making the Cathedral a spiritual centre for the Diocese and so on, was largely pioneer work', and 'it might not be out of place to recognise what he has done in this way on his retirement'.[121] It was two months before Lang replied, in contrast to his speedy rejection of Paget's recommendation. He had 'not yet been able to give very careful consideration to this proposal', but 'ought to do so now'. It presented 'considerable difficulties', but he would be grateful if Fisher would telephone to let him know when Bennett's resignation was likely to take effect.[122]

Eventually, in May 1937, Lang wrote to Bennett, offering him the D.D., 'to mark my sense of the very good service you have rendered to the Church of England and to Religion generally in the efforts you have made so successfully to revive the life and spirit of Cathedral Churches'. He told him also that 'the greater part or probably the whole, of the Fees which are considerable – none of which reach me', would be 'defrayed by some of your friends'.[123] Bennett accepted by return, and later thanked publicly 'all the kind donors to the noble contribution which I received towards the fee of £71 for my honorary D.D. degree'. But for this gift he 'would not have felt justified in accepting so expensive an honour. The only thing I know about the fee is that none of it goes to the Archbishop'.[124] The 'D.D.' appears after Bennett's name on the title page of his last published work, *This Moment of Opportunity for Religious Education* (1938).

Notes

1   B. H. Harris, (ed.), *Victoria County History of Cheshire, III* [hereafter *VCH*] (London, 1980), 194.

2   For the whole war memorial project, Alex Bruce, 'Oxford War Memorial: Thomas Rayson and the Chester Connection', *Oxoniensia*, 56, 1991, 155–67; 'A City War Memorial: the Chester Experience', *Cheshire History*, Autumn, 1992, 21–6; 'War Memorials', *The Historian*, Autumn 1990, 17–20; 'Giles Gilbert Scott and the Chester War Memorial Project', *Journal of the Chester Archaeological Society*, 73, 1994/1995. 99–114.

3   The estimated cost was about £3,500. Because the tower was unsafe, the bells had been silent on Peace Day, 1919, though parish church bells had sounded out (Chester Record Office, CCF 42, 'Minutes of War Memorial Committee', 20.10.1920; F. W. Longbottom, *Chester during the Great War* (Chester, 1921), 28).

4   Chester Record Office, 'City and Council of Chester, Minutes and Proceedings of Council and Committees: Improvements Committee', 9.2.1919; 'The King's School, Chester, Minutes of Governors Meetings', 5.12.1919.

5   When serving on the Committee Paige Cox had proposed, with Chapter backing, the adoption of a cross designed by Scott as a memorial to the 13 war-dead of the Egerton family, who, however, had opted for a memorial window instead. The argument about 'dominating the Cathedral' could equally well have been applied to the Egerton Cross.

6   *Hawarden Parish Magazine*, quoted in *Chester Observer*, 7.6.1919;

Bennett had 'the memory of a not unnatural disdain with which Scott in designing a war memorial for Hawarden had rejected the idea that he should copy a churchyard cross in Bennett's well-loved Somerset' ('Memoir', 45). See Chapter II, section 9, above.

7   Despite extensive searches I can find no copies of the designs.
8   *The Builder*, 21.1.1921.
9   The saints are St Werburgh (Cathedral and City); St George (the Cavalry); St Maurice (the Infantry); St Alban (proto-martyr of England); St David (Wales); St Michael (vanquisher of Satan).
10   *Chester Diocesan Gazette* [hereafter *CDG*], June 1922, 85.
11   Cheshire Record Office [hereafter CRO], Diocesan Archives, 'Commonplace Book' [hereafter CPB], 24.5.1922.
12   Bennett, in *HPM*, quoted in *Chester Observer*, 7.6.1919.
13   *CDG*, June 1922, 84–5; *Chester Chronicle* [hereafter *Ches. Chr.*], 10.6.1922.
14   *Ches. Chr.*, 17.11.1928.
15   *ibid..*, 16.11.1929, letter from Percy Davies. For the views of the Labour government (1928–1931) on Armistice Day commemoration, see A. Gregory, *The Silence of Memory* (Oxford/Providence, 1994), 121, 125–6.
16   'Reg, no. 165318'.
17   'Gunner'.
18   'R. L.'.
19   'ex R. E.'.
20   In face of this outburst, the Committee recommended that the railings be removed, to allow crowds on both road and green to gather around the memorial. Bennett supported the idea and the Chapter agreed that they 'should be removed for a time, as an experiment'. However, the City Council demurred, as this would be 'disadvantageous' (probably in cost to the city) and the railings remained (*Ches. Chr.*, 15.11.1930; CRO, Diocesan Archives, 'Chapter Book, 1894–1941' [hereafter Chap. Bk.], 286, 10.1.1930; Chester City, *Minutes of Council and Committees*).
21   Bruce, 'A City War Memorial', 25. Since 1945 a cathedral service and wreath-laying have been combined, without complaint.
22   *CDG*, Dec. 1930, 183. However, Bennett was unable to take part in either service, because he was in the Westminster Nursing Home recovering after an emergency operation for appendicitis carried out the week before Armistice Day. It is some indication of his national standing by this time that his name was listed twice in the 'Invalids' column of the *The Times*, alongside the names of peers and other notables (*The Times*, 3.11.1930, 14; 12.11.1930, 14).
23   *Ches. Chr.*, 12.4.1930.
24   *ibid.*

25   He explained that he was using the red sandstone of the cathedral, in combination with a warm brownish-grey brick, and provided various technical details (*CDG*, June 1930, 87–8).

26   The Council asked the Dean and Chapter to consider whether it was desirable to proceed, and expressed doubt as to whether a building 'in these materials' should go in 'this position', indeed whether *any* building should go on this site. The Archaeological Society pointed to the 'diverse views' regarding materials and position and asked the Dean and Chapter to obtain 'expert opinion' before proceeding further (*The Times*, 28.7.1930, 15).

27   CRO, Chap. Bk., 291–2, 31.7.1930.

28   *ibid*.

29   *The Times*, 1.8.1930, 17. Fyfe was by now Director of the School of Architecture, Cambridge.

30   The bricks showed up 'stridently' against the cathedral. The building was 'just high enough to spoil the lines of the fine 13th century lancet windows', and was so obtrusive, 'although only three-parts finished', that a 'shocked Chester rector' had already called it 'a festering boil of brick' [an anticipation of current royal architectural criticism?] (*The Architect and Building News*, 1.8.1930, 140–1). There were five rectors in Chester but the 'shocked rector' cannot be identified.

31   *The Times*, 2.8.1930 13. On the same page appeared an article by a Correspondent, 'The Transfiguration: Man and his Exodus', whose content and style strongly suggest that it was written by Bennett.

32   *ibid.*, 28.7.1930.

33   *ibid.*, 1.8.1930.

34   Archives of the Cathedrals Fabric Commission for England, Powys to F. C. Eeles, Victoria and Albert Museum, 15.8.1930; Fyfe to Powys, 12.8.1930. A 'Mr Wood' had written letters of complaint to both the Society and to Fyfe. There is no evidence to identify him. The Chester Directories of 1929–1932 list four men called 'Mr Wood' but the letter writer may not have lived in Chester. The Society replied (no copy-letter in file).

35   *CDG*, Sept. 1930, 137.

36   Report of letter from Powys, the Secretary, *CDG*, Oct. 1930, 153.

37   The Dean of Chester, 'Chester Cathedral': A Portrait Gallery in Stone', *The Cathedral Age*, VI/2, 1931, 5 ('each style is an unconscious portrait of its builders ... So let me walk round our Cathedral with you and show you your ancestors'), 11.

38   The affair had an interesting parallel some 40 years later. Dean Addleshaw (1963–1977) built a new, detached bell-tower, in a modern style, but in materials which made no pretence of blending with the cathedral. The work promptly attracted critical comment, which even now has not entirely abated. Meanwhile, the current project to repave the uneven stone floor of the cathedral and provide under-floor heating has

again summoned the antiquarian lobby to arms.
39   *CDG*, Sept. 1929, 136.
40   *ibid.*, Mar. 1930, 34–5.
41   *ibid.*, Dec. 1931, 177.
42   *ibid.*, Sept. 1935, 138.
43   *ibid.*, Aug. 1923, 192.
44   When Bennett was Jayne's secretary, he had taught history, part-time, at the King's School; 25 years later, as dean, he confided that he 'didn't understand very much about it ... but fortunately a little more than the boys' (*Ches. Chr.*, 24.7.1920).
45   C. K. Webster, Castlereagh's biographer, later gave the inaugural lecture, on 6 October, appropriately enough, in the context of the recent Versailles settlement, on 'The Practical Value of Modern History'. Later, leading academics lectured; papers were given on methods of teaching history and teachers joined in the discussions; local history was represented, and Bennett spoke on his American visit. In January 1931 the Historical Association recognised the success of the branch by holding its Annual General Meeting in Chester ('Cheshire' and 'Chester', *Branch Reports* (Historical Association, 1922–1937).
46   *Branch Reports*; *CDG*, Oct. 1922, 141.
47   When the branch had been founded in 1922 Bennett had said that though it was extraordinarily easy to start anything in Chester, the problem was to keep it going. He succeeded, and the Chester branch flourished. Within two years membership stood at 90, and though it fluctuated, by 1937, when Bennett retired, it stood at 65 (*Branch Reports*). At Bennett's final meeting, his son lectured appropriately on 'What is a Cathedral?'. Tributes were paid to Bennett and the secretary reported, 'The branch has suffered a great loss in the retirement of the Dean of Chester ... his most regular attendance at the meetings has been a source of delight to the speakers and audience alike. All the members owe him a very real debt of gratitude' (*Branch Reports*, 1937, 33).
48   *Chester Historical Pageant, July 5-10 1937: Book of Words* (Chester, 1937).
49   *Ches. Chr.*, 11.6.1921, 22.10.1921; cathedral memorial window for Coplestone (*ibid.* 6.6.1936). Coplestone (b. 1850), editor of the *Chester Chronicle* and Chairman of Chronicle Associated Newspapers, was also proprietor of Carnarvon Herald and Associated Newspapers. A J.P., he had been appointed C.B.E. (*Who was Who*, 1928–1941).
50   CRO, CPB, 3.6.1920.
51   S. L. Coulthard, *The Cestrian Lodge, No, 425, Chester, Province of Chester* (? privately published, Chester, 1935), 8, 85, 96, 148; see also Bennett's obituary in *Chester Observer*, 22.11.1947.
52   Coulthard, *The Cestrian Lodge*, 107–52, lists among the members in

Bennett's day several mayors of Chester, a Town Clerk, the Chief Constable, several other clergy, and a number of lawyers, architects and businessmen.

53   Discussing symbolism in baptism, he used Freemasonry to illustrate a point which had general liturgical reference in the context of his own tolerant Anglo-Catholicism: 'the Brotherhood' flourished around 'a core of symbolism ... One may see more, and another less, in a particular symbol. Neither need quarrel with the other about how much' (F. S. M. Bennett, 'Integration', in H. R. L. Sheppard (ed.), *My Hopes and Fears for the Church* (London, 1930), 86).

54   *CDG*, Dec. 1925, 188–9; CPB, 23.10.1925. The collection totalled £61. 19s. 11d. I have found no subsequent reference to the dedication. Bennett does not specify to whom or to what Freemasons should be loyal, the Order, fellow-masons, or the ideals he mentions.

55   CRO, Chap. Bk., 288, 12.4.1930.

56   Adrian Hastings, *A History of English Christianity, 1920-1985* (London, 1986), 664.

57   From the time of his appointment to Chester, Jayne regularly contributed to the correspondence columns of *The Times* on the subject.

58   'Family History'.

59   *CDG*, Jan. 1929, 3–4.

60   Following the Treaty of Locarno, a now democratic Germany joined the League and hopes of lasting peace ran high. Led by Bennett, the Cheshire LNU sent resolutions to the Government welcoming the admission of Germany, but urging use of the veto against increasing the number of permanent members of the Council and thereby imperilling the League (*CDG*, June 1926, 73–4).

61   Bennett hoped that the 'secret conclaves' preceding Germany's admission would mark the end of secret diplomacy, then popularly believed to be a root cause of the war. His *vade mecum* was P. J. Noel Baker's *The League of Nations at Work* (London, 1926), and he drew inspiration from Edith Picton-Timbervill's *Christ and International Life* (London, n.d.) (*CDG*, June 1926, 73–4; Dec. 1928, 195–6). Noel Baker, who was Professor of International Relations in London University, aimed 'to give a plain sketch of the League at work for people, young or less young, who have not given much thought to international affairs or who have not followed closely what has been happening in Geneva in the last few years' (Noel Baker, *The League of Nations*, vii). The purpose of Picton-Timbervill's book (for which she secured an 'Introduction' from Lord Robert Cecil) was to demonstrate that 'our national policy, both internal and external, must be Christianized' and that 'Christian morality must in its essence be the guide to our national conduct'. She dismissed as 'narrow', 'dogmatic' and 'ignorant' a sincerely held view she had encountered that Christianity was 'an "arid" occupation' and that people now 'did not look to the past for guidance on modern problems' (Picton-Timbervill, *Christ and International Life*, 'Author's

Foreword', vii, ix). Bennett does not, however, mention the Archdeacon's book, W. L. Paige Cox, *Christian Ethics and Peace Problems* (London, 1919), which he must almost certainly have known about, if not read. Paige Cox's emphasis was different from that of the two writers recommended by Bennett, and probably nothing personal need be imputed to Bennett in not referring to the book. Paige Cox argued that war is executing the divine will, as 'an inevitable expedient in certain circumstances in the putting down of wrong doing'; God carries out His purposes by force as well as persuasion (19–20). Paige Cox explained the different meanings of the two Greek words 'philia' and 'agape', both translated as 'love'. Loving one's enemies is 'agape'. We are all children of God, and are thus enjoined to 'love' our enemies but are not asked to be blind to their faults, and must bear in mind God's own sacrifice in the loving task of redeeming mankind by the sacrifice of his son (39–40). It might be claimed that Paige Cox's argument about 'putting down of wrong doing' smacked of special pleading in relation to the war he wrote about, yet was prophetically not inappropriate in relation to the war he did not live to see.

62   Bennett's son, by then ordained, became secretary (*CDG*, Aug. 1929, 118–9).

63   *CDG*, Sept. 1935, 138.

64   CRO, Chap. Bk., 212, 8 May 1922; Chester Record Office, 'Governors of The Queen's School, Minute Book, 1900–1927', 316–7, 8.7.1922; 335, 24.3.1924; 357, 25.3.1924; 'Governors of The Queen's School, Minute Book, 1928–1958', 2–65.

65   L. Bradbury, *Chester College and the Training of Teachers, 1839–1975* (Chester College, 1975), 201–3. The Church Assembly was to meet in February 1933, and it discussed the Teacher Training Colleges under threat (including Chester) on 9.2.1933.

66   *The Times*, 31.1.1933, 10, reported that Bennett was a little better, but still weak.

67   *CDG*, Mar. 1933, 38.

68   Bennett must have recovered sufficiently to write the account for the March issue of the *Diocesan Gazette*, and thus well enough to read press reports of the Assembly debate which make no mention of George Bennett, from whom he might well have expected a first-hand account (*Ches. Chr.*, 11.2.1933, 18.2.1933). In any case, Bennett made neither a correction nor any further mention of the matter in the *Diocesan Gazette*. See W. Purcell, *Fisher of Lambeth* (London, 1969), and 'The Crisis of 1933' in Bradbury, *Chester College*, 198–206.

69   *Ches. Chr.*, 18.2.1933, 12. This was Fisher's debut in the Church Assembly but his experience at Repton in addressing the School and exhorting his staff doubtless stood him in good stead. The *Chester Chronicle* reported that Fisher found the debate 'thoroughly congenial'.

70   CRO, CPB, 23.3.1920; Chap. Bk., 189, 15.11.1919; Nairne was, at times,

'slightly mystified' at what Bennett was setting out to do (Bennett, 'Memoir').

71   Eck developed a flourishing Boys' Club, and made other significant contributions to the corporate life of the cathedral. Along with Hewlett Johnson (later the 'Red Dean' of Canterbury) and two others he joined Bennett on the editorial committee of the *Chester Diocesan Gazette*, which now appeared in a 'new dress' (*CDG*, Jan. 1923). In 1926 Eck returned as parish priest to Ardeley, in Bedfordshire, from where he had come.

72   Church Association, *The Disruption of the Church of England by More than 9000 Clergymen who are Helping the Romeward Movement in the National Church* (London, 1900). Bennett's son recalled that Eck had a 'distinctive devoutness' about him, and was 'something of a Jacobite', with pictures of Charles I, Laud, and Strafford hanging in the hall of his Abbey Square house. Pompous, however, he certainly was not, and like Bennett he had no sense of his own importance. On his arrival, someone had asked how they should address him. 'Call me plain Mr', he replied, and so 'Mister' he became, and remained to everyone who knew him, including Bennett. ('Memoir').

73   CRO, Minutes of Fortnightly Informal Meeting of Chapter, 22.1.1926. The three existing copes remained in use.

74   *CDG*, May 1934, 66–8.

75   'Memoir'.

76   Significantly, Paige Cox's name does not appear in the list of those who were anathema to the Protestant Church Association, which was always quick to spot any hint of High Church practice (Church Association, *Disruption of the Church of England*).

77   W. L. Paige Cox, *Aids to Christian Belief in the Miracles and Divinity of Christ* (London, 1905); *The Church of England as Catholic and Reformed* (London, 1910); *Christian Ethics and Peace Problems* (London, 1919).

78   *CDG*, May 1934, 66–8.

79   'Memoir'.

80   CRO, 'Minutes of Fortnightly Informal Meeting of the Chapter', 22.1.1926, 18.

81   CRO, Chap. Bk., 26, 10.11.1927.

82   *ibid.*, 281, 8.11.1929; 289, 26.5.1930. On the appointment of a minor canon as Sacrist and Precentor, Bennett (who wanted to employ minor canons more profitably) disposed of the objection by pointing out that the Statutes allowed the appointment of a minor canon, and any objection should be raised on the issue of the Statutes and not on a specific case (*ibid.*, 13.10.1932, 327).

83   Marston's appointment involved Bennett in a scrape. He announced it in *The Times* and then wrote to the West Kirby Parochial Church Council, only to have it politely pointed out that he had ignored a provision of the 1931 regulating act, by not

consulting the PCC before a final decision. He apologised, pleading forgetfulness, sent two members of the Chapter to discuss with the PCC – and the Chapter's publicly-announced candidate was, inevitably, accepted. I owe knowledge of this episode, recorded in the West Kirby PCC Minutes (now in CRO), to Professor Paul Hair.

84   'Fortnightly Informal Meeting', 17.10.1927.
85   *ibid.*, 10.11.1927.
86   Peterborough Cathedral Archives, letter from Paige Cox to an un-named canon ('My dear Canon'), dated 30.8.1926. Paige Cox dealt with two topics: bishops' support for the miners (see Chapter VIII, note 98, above), and Chester's 'system of freeing the Cathedral'. He was probably responding to a letter from the Peterborough canon. There is no record of requests for closing of doors in Chapter minutes. The hearsay nature of comments from Winchester ('told a friend of ours') and Canterbury ('I am told') may be noted. I am indebted to Canon Higham of Peterborough for directing me to this letter. See also Chapter I, note 39.
87   St John's, Oxon., B.A. 1870, M.A. 1874; deacon 1874, priest 1875; curate, Applethwaite, 1874–1876; vicar, Witton, 1876–1886; vicar, Christ Church, Chester, 1887–1889; rector, West Kirby, 1889–1920; honorary canon, Chester, 1885–1886, canon, 1886.
88   Church Association, *Disruption of the Church of England*, 14.
89   *CDG*, Oct. 1926, 148–9.
90   *ibid.*, May 1934, 1926, 66–8.
91   CRO, Chap. Bk., 256, 10.11.1927.
92   Bennett, 'Memoir'. I owe 'allergic to deans' to Baxter's daughter, Miss C. M. Baxter. Baxter had known not only Bennett, but also Darby, Bennett's predecessor, and Tubbs, his successor.
93   CRO, Chap. Bk., 331, 14.3.1934, 21.7.1934. Another canon (Michael Robert Newbolt) had already been appointed by the Chapter as Vice-Dean immediately following Paige Cox's death.
94   The deanery was a Crown appointment (CRO, Chap. Bk., 368, 24.3.1937). The Prime Minister of the day responsible for the filling the vacancy was Neville Chamberlain, but there is no evidence available to show whose advice he sought. Tubbs, all of whose previous ministry, apart from a brief curacy in Whitechapel, had been in the East, had been Bishop of Rangoon (1928–1937), and Fisher appointed him, additionally, as Assistant Bishop in Chester Diocese. He retired from Chester in 1953.
95   'Memoir'.
96   He was recorded as adopting the eastward position and burning candles in daylight, procedures commonly complained about by the protestant Church Association, but both increasingly common in the post-war high tide of Anglo-Catholicism (Church Association, *Disruption of the Church of England*, 195).

97 Cf. Jayne's support of a manifesto against Convocation's suggestions regarding reservation, vestments, and Prayer Book amendments (*Ches. Chr.*, 2.11.1918, letter from W.H. Goodman).

98 *Ches. Chr.*, 1.1.1921.

99 'Memoir'.

100 Bennett, *Nature of a Cathedral*, 13.

101 *ibid.*, 14.

102 *CDG*, June 1921, 92–3.

103 Elma K. Paget, *Henry Luke Paget* (London, 1939).

104 *CDG*, Mar. 1925, 35; Feb. 1926. The house ('The Residence') had been occupied by the Canon in Residence; as all the canons now had their own houses in Chester, The Residence was redundant.

105 Paget, *Paget*, 233.

106 *CDG*, Mar. 1925, 35; Feb. 1926. When Bennett arrived in 1920 he had found this inscription over the door of the deanery (Bishop's House from 1921). Howson, Bennett's predecessor at Christ Church, had also had it painted over the door of his vicarage, Egerton House, Northgate.

107 Paget, *Paget*, 230–1.

108 'Memoir'.

109 Paget, *Paget*, 230–3.

110 Quoted in *ibid.*, 231.

111 Quoted in *ibid.*, 239.

112 'Memoir'.

113 Lambeth Palace Library, Lang Papers, 101, f. 121.

114 Lang, in his reply to Paget, justified his decision by saying that there were many able men who had not received the degree, and to 'single out your good Dean' would only increase the number of applications. He recognised 'the special place he has had in the fuller use of our cathedral[s]', and 'the stimulus and interest of some [*sic*] of his literary work', adding, somewhat patronisingly, 'though I do not think that even he would claim to be a theologian of much learning' (Lambeth Palace Library, Lang Papers, 101, f. 121, 18.1.1930; f. 122, 21.1.1930. Lang refers to Paget's letter of the '10th', although it is clearly dated the '18th'.). Bennett would almost certainly be unaware of the correspondence with Lambeth Palace.

115 'Memoir'; enthronement, *CDG*, Oct. 1932, 161–2.

116 Fisher was observed 'happily swinging his legs from schoolroom desks' at post-induction teas ('Memoir'). Burne, Archdeacon of Chester, recalled how difficult it was to tear him away from these gatherings (Purcell, *Fisher*, 69–70).

117 *ibid.*, 69.

118 'Memoir'.

119 Purcell, *Fisher*, 67, 77.

120   Quoted, *ibid.*, 76–7.
121   Lambeth Palace Library, Lang Register, f. 282, 2.10.1936, Fisher to Lang.
122   *ibid.*, f. 284, 8.12.1936, Lang to Fisher. Lang subsequently told Fisher – perhaps not until the following spring – that he would accede to the request, because Fisher wrote on 7.5.1937: 'You asked me the other day what time would be most suitable to offer the Dean a Lambeth D.D. It would, I think, be a good thing if your intention could be made public before June 26th which is the day of the Diocesan Festival, at which the Dean is preaching, and for another reason I should wish that it might be made public before the end of this month. I shall hope to raise the greater part or even all of the money required to meet the cost of the degree from friends of the Dean, but I should like to be able to begin on it fairly soon, and at any rate not later than the beginning of June' (Lang Register, f. 285, 7.5.1937, Fisher to Lang).
123   *ibid.*, f. 286, 8.5.1937, Lang to Bennett; f. 287, Lang to Fisher.
124   *ibid.*, f. 288, Bennett to Lang; *The Times*, 26.8.1937, 15. Bennett's son, who would not have known that Lang had turned down Paget's recommendation but was certainly aware of the less than warm relations which prevailed between Bennett and the archbishop, hazarded the opinion that Lang granted the degree 'perhaps with some reluctance' ('Memoir').

X
Private lives, last lap, and journey home

1

The memoir of Bennett written by his son towards the end of his own life contributes a private dimension to our view of the dean, especially throwing light on his relations with his wife, Ida, and with their children. It also tells us something of the son's attitude towards his father, for whom he felt an 'intimate affection' combined with 'a touch of awe'. He quoted this later, in his own sermons, to 'illustrate the fatherhood of God toward whom we feel ... both fear and love'. The association in his mind of dean-father and Father-Deity is significant.[1]

As we have seen, Ida and Frank came from different backgrounds. Their son writes of 'a long and loyal partnership' but recalls 'the inevitable misunderstandings incidental to such different upbringings ... of most of which the other was unaware', concluding, with a touch of filial devotion, that 'love triumphed' over misunderstandings.[2] After 25 years of married life, Bennett himself remarked that he and his wife had been 'happy together' but had not always agreed, characteristically adding that it would have been a 'dull performance' if they had. They agreed on one thing only, 'to differ'.[3]

From the beginning Ida was never at ease when visiting Sparkford, where the household routine was more relaxed and less predictable than at Ardern.[4] The Bennetts, glossing over the fact that their own family's now depleted wealth had originated in 'trade', quietly regarded themselves as 'more aristocratic' than the wealthier Liveseys.[5] Most of the Bennetts were somewhat puzzled by Ida. She sought, by little acts of generosity, to win a response which it was not in the nature of her undemonstrative in-laws to give. Frank never grasped that she would have liked holidays away from his family. Even on the journey home from their honeymoon-holiday, typically in Frank's native Devon, Ida had a visit to the formidable Macaulay aunts inflicted on her. While Frank enjoyed his pipe, she was conducted on a tour of the house, not only to be inspected closely by the aunts but also to be introduced, via their array of portraits, to departed Macaulays. The next day the tour was repeated and Ida was invited to give names to the faces on the wall. She miserably failed this initiation test. The breach was complete when she inadvertently sent back a replica of the aunts' Christmas card the following year.[6]

The Liveseys had been unenthusiastic about Ida's marriage to a local parish priest with seemingly few prospects. Soon after the wedding Clegg Livesey died, and for a short time Frank and Ida lived with Ida's mother, a 'jealous and selfish woman'.[7] Strains on the newly-married couple were intensified by Mrs Livesey's enforcement of a rigid domestic routine. Ida, already distressed at her father's death, was miserable and began to develop into the chronic worrier she soon became. In desperation, Frank insisted that they leave for the Portwood Vicarage before her health broke down. At Portwood, Livesey money made for more comfortable living all round.[8] But Ida became acutely conscious of the omnipresent Bennett sisters, and was ill-at-ease in replacing Emily as mistress of Frank's household. Presiding at meetings of the Mothers' Union, Women's Help Society, sewing parties, and the like, was an agony at first, but Ida had a sense of the duty she had undertaken in a clerical marriage and seems to have disciplined herself. To the Bennetts such manorial responsibilities came naturally.

Experience in three parishes, however, equipped Ida well for her ultimate role at Chester where one old lady recalls her as 'a very kind lady' (although another recollects only her large hat). She developed a close friendship with the wife of Minor Canon Baxter (he who was 'allergic to deans', conceivably reflecting his wife's justified or unjustified sympathy for Ida). Deafness, however, was an increasing problem, and Ida's indispensable silver and ivory ear-trumpet is remembered by those who latterly met her. Ida and Frank differed markedly in temperament. Ida, a serious-minded and somewhat humourless person, was an easy butt for Frank's April-fooleries, which may be seen as mildly, if unconsciously, cruel – fun perhaps at Sparkford and Sherborne but alien to her way of life.[9]

In 1902 the Bennetts' first son, Frank Livesey Macaulay Bennett, was born. Three other sons followed: Michael Livesey (1904), Leonard (1907), and Peter (1909). All three died, shortly after birth, of haemolytic disease, a condition of the blood not then understood by medical science.[10] Apart from contributing to the over-protective care which Ida bestowed on her surviving son, these tragedies must have deeply afflicted both parents, who endeavoured to come to terms with the deaths by providing commemorative eastern lights in Sparkford Parish Church. Ignorance of the cause of the deaths could well have occasioned some sense of guilt in both parents, who after the third death almost certainly determined to entertain no possibility of further pregnancies. Though contraception was already practised in middle-class society in 1909, it would not necessarily have been acceptable to Frank or Ida, either on grounds of efficacy or of religious scruple. This opens cautious speculation regarding conjugal abstinence, with consequent strain on the marriage relationship. The singular energy which Bennett devoted to his work at Hawarden, and later at Chester, could have been, in part, a sublimatory diversion of sexual drive. The challenge of Hawarden in 1910, with a move away from two parishes marked by tragedy, might thus have been especially welcome. Bennett's public statements give no hint of such and reveal no private thoughts.

At Hawarden and at the deanery Ida suffered badly from asthma. On many Hawarden occasions Dr Blackwell-Roberts was called to attend her, often at night. Bennett tried his Coué technique, suggesting that the sufferer was 'getting "better and better"', but to no avail.[11] At Chester, a doctor attributed the asthma to the presence of Cocklebun, the parrot, and so Bennett gave it away.[12] But Ida's ailment persisted. Poor health and worry dogged her, while Bennett was daily and hourly immersed in the cathedral or busy elsewhere. It was suggested that perhaps Abbey Square did not suit her and so the Bennetts moved to 59 Liverpool Road, Bennett establishing a study and office at 3 Abbey Street, adjoining the cathedral, where he hoped still to spend 'most of my time' – and did. Ida must have seen even less of him, and despite Bennett's initial hope that the move seemed to 'solve the problem' her asthma got no better.[13] It is significant that, in retirement at Taunton, it disappeared completely, though her deafness got worse. However, she now seemed glad to have Bennett continually near to her. 'My "old lady" spoils me', he confided, 'but seems happy in the doing of it'.[14]

Bennett's grandson, Guy, perceived his own mother, Margaret Hilda [née Blain], who had been the dean's secretary-cum-chauffeur for six and a half years, as being cast more in the mould of Bennett than was his father, Frank Livesey. The secretary adored her boss. A brief 'Post Script' to the 'Memoir' by her husband is her personal tribute to her father-in-law.[15] The writing is lighter and more personal than that of the 'Memoir' itself. She admired the dean's imperturbability and his amused disregard for rank and titles. All his young friends, and many of his older ones, never called him anything else but 'Very Rev'. He enjoyed this hugely. Hilda Blain could never resist the 'beaming smile' with which he confidently left her to sort out problems not of her making. In Bennett she sensed a 'deep love and sympathy and understanding for ordinary people'. She recounts how an old lady remembered Bennett's talk with her years before in the cathedral. Deeply worried, she had taken her troubles to the dean and he 'transformed my life'.[16] Margaret Hilda Blain learnt much from Frank Bennett, but 'of all the things without number that I personally owe to him', she wrote, 'I put first that he showed me something that I think and hope I shall never lose – the *attractiveness* of Jesus'.[17] In marrying Frank Livesey Macaulay Bennett she was remaining close to the dean – even unconsciously, in a sense, marrying him by proxy. She transmitted to her own son, Guy, the love of God-in-Jesus which she had acquired from Bennett; his serious-minded father gave him theology.

As for Bennett the man, the phrase the 'attractiveness of Jesus', like references to His 'manliness', and such Bennett soubriquets as 'the Cheery Dean', may be read as an expression of a hearty public school Anglicanism. This early moulding enabled Bennett to overcome deep personal difficulties and develop a life style dynamic yet humanized by an approachable informality, to the manifest and lasting benefit of his church and the faithful – even if the heartiness was not always to the taste of some of those within his shadow who had suffered the trauma of the trenches or been bereaved by the war. But the cheerful informality told. A young girl visited the cathedral and encountered Bennett. Sixty years later, Dr Cornish recalls – 'I enquired what he was doing, and he said he was ringing the five o'clock service bell, and if I liked I could do it for him. So I did.'[18]

2

Bennett's vigour and determination seemed undiminished as he approached retirement. Towards the end of 1934, with his major work accomplished, new statutes for Chester approved, pressing restoration and repair completed, and the cathedral with all its ancillary features in full use, Bennett turned again to finance. Anxious, he said, as he approached his 'three score and ten', to leave the cathedral free of debt, he launched his 'Last Lap' Appeal, disarming criticism with a Sherborne 'Please sir, I won't do it again'. He reminded the Great Chapter, and especially the honorary canons, that as the buildings were now vested in that body, its members must 'share his discomfort (not to say distress) at £4,000 fabric debt which eats up in interest all that Friends produce'. Half of this debt, of course, he had inherited in 1920.[19] He contrasted 1934 with 1922. On one day in November 1934 sixty Diocesan Lay Readers had met at the cathedral, afterwards attending Evensong and taking tea in the parlour; 260 'Girl Guiders' had held their conference in the Refectory, followed by tea in the Undercroft; the Sunday School Board had convened in Abbey Chambers and later had tea in the Hostel – all impossible 'a dozen years ago'. In 1922, the Hostel had been a Canon's residence; Abbey Chambers a solicitor's office; the Refectory semi-roofless; the Chapter House full of book-cases and locked; the kitchen non-existent. He impressed on users of the cathedral's facilities what value they got for their money. By May, his legendary persuasiveness had reduced the debt to a mere £500.

He now targeted diocesan groups who used the cathedral and parishes situated outside Chester, having 'combed the city by other methods'. Nevertheless, his own old local parish of Christ Church sent a guinea, and The Queen's School £12.2s.0d. Finally, at the end of 1935, with the debt at less than £400, he invited laggard parishes to enjoy 'the pleasure of sharing in this great achievement to secure a place on the list of our Friends before 1935 closes'.[20] As the list would be published, few on this occasion could resist, and in January 1936 he proudly announced that 'for the first time for many a long year, the Cathedral will start a New Year free from debt'. Since 1920, between £40,000 and £50,000 had been spent on putting the building into an excellent state of repair.[21] Now, some £700 to £1,000 should be put annually into a reserve fund, for continued upkeep.[22] The 'Last Lap' Appeal had ended with eighteen months to spare.

3

A special committee, headed by the bishop, the Lord Lieutenant, and Lord Stanford raised subscriptions from Bennett's many friends to commission a portrait of the dean by Gerald Kelly, R.A. The presentation, in the Autumn of 1936, was, as the local press observed, 'appropriately held in the Refectory, a building very intimately connected with the Dean's work in Chester'.[23] Sir William Bromley-Davenport, the Lord Lieutenant, who made the presentation, spoke of Dean Darby as 'great', but said that 'a far greater work was undertaken and achieved by his successor, Dean Bennett'. He recalled

Bennett's genius for fund-raising. This, and a reference to the abolition of entrance-fees, drew great applause. There were, he said, 'probably few of them who had not had some experience of his irresistible, persuasive methods, when funds were required for any good cause ... If they wanted a monument to him let them look around'. The echo of Wren's epitaph was not inappropriate. In future years, he concluded, 'people would ask about the subject of the picture, and someone would say, "It is the good Dean Bennett, who did so much for the Cathedral", and they would add, "He has a nice face, he must have been a good fellow."'. Bennett received the picture, but asked the Vice-Dean and the Chapter to honour him by accepting it for the cathedral. The press reported that it would hang in the Parlour.[24]

It is some indication of the significance which was attached to Bennett's achievement by his contemporaries that, on 30 August 1937, shortly after the award of his Lambeth doctorate,[25] and while he was still in office, *The Times* drew public attention to his imminent retirement, 'a few days hence'.[26] In a retrospect of Bennett's 17 years in Chester, the writer recalled that the dean had found the cathedral a museum and had left it 'the family house of the Diocese'. Further, that as a result of his vision there had taken place, in the world beyond Chester, 'something like a revolution in the conduct of English Cathedrals and the conception of their place in the life of the people'. Bennett's trust in the public, exemplified in his determination to 'lock up nothing except the safe' and to 'exclude every forbidding notice', had been amply repaid.[27] 'Great sums' had been spent on repairs but the foundation was richer than it had been when Bennett took over. Absence of damage, and the honest payment for handbooks taken from open display 'by the hundred thousand', were testimony to his success with a public whose behaviour had been 'as reverent as it had been appreciative'. Bennett had seen that to make the cathedral as he wished it to be, he had to make it interesting to all classes and ages, religiously, as well as architecturally, historically, and aesthetically. His pioneering Children's Corners, allocation of chapels to different bodies, and involvement of the whole Diocese, especially the parish clergy, were singled out for specific mention and related to his *Nature of a Cathedral*, which the writer analysed, concluding:

> To the author of the book a cathedral meant more than a cathedral church. It meant, in its perfect state, the whole congeries of buildings from the Bishop's house to the lending library and to the refectory ...

where the modern pilgrims could have meals. Such has Chester Cathedral become under the Dean who is now retiring. Every cathedral has its own characteristics and most have their own ways, but the past seventeen years at Chester have made a uniquely interesting contribution to the history of English Cathedral life.[28]

4

In the autumn of 1937 Bennett retired to his beloved Somerset, where he and Ida lived at Orchard House, Taunton, in the Wilton parish of his bachelor brother George, whose ministry had over the years been so closely associated with his own.[29] In retirement he kept a low profile, content to assist in the parish, to preach occasionally in other churches around Taunton, and to give time, at last, to Ida.[30] The year after he retired he published *This Moment of Opportunity for Religious Education*, but after this wrote no more. Nor did he continue to contribute to the correspondence columns of *The Times*. In November 1937, the Chapter recorded its 'deep gratitude for the seventeen years of his wise and sympathetic leadership of the Cathedral Body, its high appreciation of his conspicuous achievement in the development of the life and activities of the Cathedral'. It expressed its 'earnest hope that he will still find many opportunities of rendering service to the Church to whose advancement he has contributed so notably in the past'.[31] Over the next decade, Bennett, who had always been a parish priest at heart, was to find these opportunities for completing his ministry in a family milieu and in familiar country, assisting in the work he loved best. His son Frank, with his wife, Bennett's former secretary, and young sons, Roderick and Guy, visited him from time to time and kept him in touch with affairs in the Chester Diocese, where Frank was Vicar of Helsby, then of Neston. From 1939 Frank served as an army chaplain, and Bennett must have been interested in his son's trenchant post-war critique of the Church's current problems, *Laodicea in the Twentieth Century* (1946), an expanded version of a widely praised article he had earlier published in *Theology*. As the author's name was given as 'Frank Bennett', some seem to have attributed the book to the aged dean.[32]

A letter written by Bennett, dated 29 December 1943, to his Hawarden Churchwarden, W. Bell Jones (and perhaps a reply to a Christmas letter), gives some insight into Bennett's latter days.[33] Ida's asthma had 'completely gone' but she was 'dreadfully deaf and finds it a very trying disability'. Though he and Ida were 'both very well', he claimed to be 'a bit senilely decrepit', but managed to 'get about and enjoy my home and books'. They now had 'Miss Olive Meredith (once my secretary) as our Nurse-Housekeeper and she is a tower of kind strength'. He hoped Bell Jones would complete his book on Hawarden, 'for most interesting it will be and no one but "the King of Hawarden" could write it'.[34] By 1947 Bennett was growing frail and in the autumn became ill.[35] He died at The Orchard, on 14 November 1947. His funeral took place three days later, at Sparkford, where he was laid in the family plot.[36] After her husband's death, Ida moved to a private nursing home in Chester, where she still had friends. She died four years later, on 27 May 1951, and was buried beside Frank, at Sparkford. On the day of Frank's funeral, a memorial service, in the form of a Solemn Eucharist, was held in the choir of Chester Cathedral, the celebrant being the dean, Bishop Tubbs, who was assisted by two of the canons. The living Bennett is recalled by the thanks offered, in the memorial prayer, for his many qualities, not least his wit, humour, infectious happiness, love of children, friendliness to 'all sorts and conditions of men', and his 'joy in the unseen world of saints and angels'.[37] Elma Paget's concise and perceptive obituary, too, must have awakened for many their own memories of the great dean:

> The cathedrals, and indeed the whole Church of England, owe immeasurably to Frank Selwyn Macaulay Bennett, formerly Dean of Chester. It was his determination to set Chester Cathedral open without 'fence or fee' that awakened the conscience of all church dignitaries to the fact that the House of God belongs to all as a place of worship. His genius, for he had a real touch of genius, was wayward and challenging, and the element of the boy never wholly left him. He liked to shock convention into life; he loved hospitality in every form. Restoration work was carried on keenly throughout his whole term of office; side chapels sprang into real use, the big refectory was restored and set open as a centre of rest and refreshment for the many groups that found their way to the cathedral, while a band of more than 40 voluntary helpers made pilgrims welcome. Holiday crowds from the great industrial centres would gather round the tall attractive figure who loved to be among them and who rarely left his

cathedral. On Bank holidays he would ring a bell from the pulpit calling sightseers together that they might enter into the joy of the Sanctuary, to hear its history and join in a prayer or hymn.[38]

Notes

1   He was 'deeply shocked' when another boy, at Hawarden, threw a snowball at his father. Years later, responding, with trepidation, to a summons to his father's study, to explain a report from school that he had been punished for smoking, he was first ashamed, then taken aback to hear, 'Frank, I am ashamed of you' – sad look and long pause by Bennett – then, 'I never thought that any son of mine would be be such an ass as to be caught' ('Memoir', 35–6). Frank Livesey was closer to his mother, who had lavished great care on this only surviving son. Guy Bennett, Frank Livesey's own son, has recounted to me his boyhood perceptions of his grandparents, which, combined with other small pieces of evidence, assist in establishing a picture of Ida and Frank and their relationship.

2   'Memoir'.

3   Cheshire Record Office [herafter CRO], Diocesan Archive, 'Commonplace Book', 14.11.1925, unidentified newspaper cutting reporting speech at Chester Choristers' Dinner. Bennett is speaking in the context of the differences in the Church Assembly over Prayer Book Revision and quotes the different political preferences, in a parliamentary election, of himself (Liberal), Ida (Conservative), and their son (Labour).

4   When staying with the Bennett family on holiday, Ida walked in fear of committing some *faux-pas*. When she wanted a clean towel, she hesitated to emulate the Bennetts by taking one from the linen cupboard. At Ardern its disappearance would have occasioned concern and so she went into Yeovil to buy one ('Memoir'). Sparkford Hall had been leased after the death of Bennett's father in 1897, since Frank and George were established elsewhere, with the sisters. In Ida's day the Bennett family gathered at the large rectory, where Emily Louisa, the eldest Bennett sister lived. In 1900, she had married Trevor Griffith, Bennett's former curate at Portwood and now Rector of Sparkford. But the Sparkford Hall atmosphere persisted at the rectory.

5   'Memoir', 18.

6   The 'Family History' when dealing with Dean Bennett is largely derived from the 'Memoir'. The 'Macaulay aunts' episode is not included in the 'Memoir'. Roderick Bennett must have been told of it by parent or grandparent.

7   'Family History'. The 'jealous and selfish' judgment is not included in the

'Memoir'.

8   A cook, Martha Crofts, arrived from Puddington, in Cheshire, followed later by relatives as maids, most of whom migrated with Frank and Ida to their later parishes and finally to the deanery. Ida seems to have treated her young maids generously ('Memoir').

9   Guy Bennett remembers that, during visits to his grandparents in their retirement, Frank would play with him and his brother, while Ida showed little rapport and fussed about while undertaking minor domestic tasks.

10   I deduce the nature of the disease from Guy Bennett's remark to me that the deaths occurred because of incompatible blood groups. The condition arises from the mother's having rhesus negative blood. Today, doctors check parents' blood groups and save the affected infant by blood transfusion soon after birth.

11   Information from the twin daughters (now aged around 90) of Dr Blackwell-Roberts, via Miss Constance Baxter.

12   'Memoir'.

13   *Chester Diocesan Gazette* [hereafter *CDG*], Oct. 1928, 156; Dec. 1928, 195–6; Jan. 1929, 3.

14   Flintshire Record Office, Hawarden, D/BJ/466), letter of 29.12.1943, Bennett (Orchard House, Taunton) to W. Bell Jones. The climate and doubtless cleaner air perhaps helped Ida, but she must still have had Bennett's pipe smoke to cope with.

15   'Memoir' and conversations with Guy Bennett. 'My husband having had a stroke and being unable to finish this memoir, I have been asked to try and round it off as best I can' (Margaret Hilda Bennett, Post Script to 'Memoir').

16   The old lady's son was 'a canon of one of the south country cathedrals' and she spent the time in the cathedral while waiting for her train (Blain, 'Post Script); Guy Bennett identified the distant canon for me as Roger Lloyd, who was appointed a Canon of Winchester in 1937 (*Crockford*). The incident (no names given) is mentioned in the section on Bennett in Roger Lloyd, *The Church of England 1900-1965* (London, 1966), 399.

17   The 'attractiveness of Jesus' has resonances of Bennett's devotion to the Prayer of St Richard of Chichester, versions of which he had commended to young people and persuaded the CEMS to adopt, together with a life of Jesus.

18   Dr M.W. Cornish of Didcot in a letter to A.B..

19   *CDG*, Nov. 1934, 147. CRO, 'Minutes of Fortnightly Informal Meeting of Chapter', 10.11.1927; *CDG*, Dec. 1934; Feb. 1935, 18; Mar. 1935, 35–6; Aug. 1935, 122–3.

20   *ibid.*, Aug. 1935, 122–3, Dec. 1935, 186.

21   *ibid.*, Jan. 1936, 1–3.

22   *ibid.*, Apr. 1936, 54.

23   See *Chester Chronicle* [hereafter *Ches. Chr.*], 24.10.1936, 10. With the

principal guests on the platform was 'Master Bennett' from Helsby, presumably Bennett's elder grandson, Roderick, who would then be six years of age. His father was at the time Vicar of Helsby.

24   *CDG*, Dec. 1935, 186. *Ches. Chr.*, 24.10.1936. Bennett's grandson, Guy Bennett, has another version of Kelly's portrait of the dean, perhaps inherited from him.

25   *The Times*, 26.8.1937, 15.

26   *ibid.*, 30.8.1937.

27   The scarcity of reports of such robberies in the Chester press may only indicate that few were detected. Magistrates dealt sympathetically with a 24-year old unemployed man (*Ches. Chr.*, 2.5.1936, 10; 9.1.1936, 10), but severely with a 15-year old girl (*ibid.*, 26.9.1936, 5). However, Paige Cox claimed that 'money boxes are rifled pretty often' (Peterborough Cathedral Archives, letter of Paige Cox to a canon of Peterborough, 30.8.1926).

28   *The Times*, 30.8.1937.

29   Orchard House is at the corner of Middleway and Fons George, and is now on a busy road. It is still occupied, and is near to the house occupied by George Bennett where the dean's son and his family stayed when visiting. Edith, who was unmarried and had kept house for George in the past, probably continued to do so.

30   There are few references in the local Somerset press to Bennett but such as there are indicate typical activities. In January 1939, for example, at the annual parochial meeting of Wilton Parish, 'Thanks were expressed ... on behalf of the parish, to Dean Bennett ... for assisting with the services on different occasions' (*Somerset County Gazette*, 28.1.1939, 6). When the National Day of Prayer was observed in all Taunton and district churches in October 1939 and the Bishop of Bath and Wells visited St John's Church, Taunton, Bennett preached the sermon at Evensong (*ibid.*, 7.10,1939).

31   CRO, Diocesan Archives, 'Chapter Book, 1894–1941', 375, 17.11.1937.

32   Frank Bennett, *Laodicea in the Twentieth Century or The Church of England in the England of Today* (London, 1946), based on 'Our Struggle', *Theology*, July 1944.

33   Flintshire Record Office, D/BJ/466.

34   Bell Jones's unpublished typescript, 'History of Hawarden Parish' is in Flintshire Record Office, Hawarden. The 20 lines devoted to Bennett give no information not available more fully elsewhere. Bennett told Bell that he had been 'looking through again the book of Wells photographs you gave me – and very good they are, like the days whereof they are a reminder ... I often go [to] sleep going over the old motor drives in retrospect – how pleasant they were! ... I doubt if I shall ever get up to Chester and Hawarden again ... I expect the lime avenue across the new Churchyard is now quite large – I wonder if it's getting too big for its place! We both hope that 1944 has much good in store for you – a very great help to us you were' (Flintshire Record

Office, D/BJ/466).

35 Twenty-five years later, the Reverend T. C. Teape-Fugarde recalled that in late 1947 he was due to officiate in Chester at the funeral of a friend. At the last moment, the head verger of the cathedral, who had been a great friend and ally of Bennett, brought out the former dean's festal cope, saying, 'Wear it for his sake; he is very ill. I think he is dying'. Teape-Fugard said, 'I am proud that for a little while I wore his mantle' (*Ches. Chr.*, 5.5.1972).

36 *Somerset County Advertiser*, 29.11.1947. At probate (Bodmin Probate Registry), Bennett's estate, including presumably his house, was valued at £7,500 – perhaps £100,00 in presentday money – a modest sum. But he may have earlier passed to his son part of his resources.

37 *Cheshire Observer*, 22.11.1947.

38 *The Times*, 21.11.1947.

Epilogue
Today

1

In 1989, Owen Conway, Rural Dean of Headingley and a member of the Cathedrals Advisory Commission for England, followed in the footsteps of Bennett and devoted a 6-month period of sabbatical leave to visiting every Anglican cathedral in England. Conway made his preparations carefully, first paying incognito informal visits before his leave began, and following these up with pre-arranged visits, backed by a questionnaire which he had circulated to all the cathedrals. His carefully prepared 44-page report is a valuable survey of the life and work of 43 English cathedrals a few years ago. Even more recently, in 1994, the Archbishops Commission on Cathedrals published its report, *Heritage and Renewal* (the Howe Report).[1] This contains a useful section on the historical background to cathedrals, but its approach to other issues differs in emphasis and purpose from that of Conway, whose report is more directly relevant to a study of Bennett. How far does what Conway found indicate that Bennett's views are still acted on, or at the very least accepted as still relevant or felt to provide an ideal aim?

Conway had not heard of Bennett when he started his journey, but quite early in his travels the Dean of Carlisle lent him a copy of *The Nature of a Cathedral*, which gave a focus to his pilgrimage. 'Having read and re-read this excellent book [Conway writes], and having taken into account the immense changes in both Church and social attitudes and practices, much of my own pilgrimage was seeing how in today's world our Cathedrals were living up to the pattern and vision recommended by Dean Bennett.'[2] Conway devotes the opening chapter of his report to the book and refers throughout, in the context of his own pilgrimage, to Bennett's 'thoughts and vision'. He told me that, time and time again, the name of Frank Bennett cropped up, quite unprompted, in the remarks of the cathedral officers he interviewed.

He points to the extensive tourism of today, which brings cathedrals to the forefront of the Church's mission, reaching millions who would never enter a parish church except for a wedding, baptism or funeral. Thus, 'in the world's eyes', cathedrals are 'something of a success story'. Conway, however, seeks to know 'what people find and experience once they have gone to a Cathedral'. Is it, he asks, 'clearly and uncompromisingly, "the seat of the Bishop and a place of worship"?' Are its resources (buildings, furnishings, personnel) being used to make it 'a genuine centre for the Church's mission?' 'Such', he explains, 'is the subject of my sabbatical pilgrimage'.

Bennett had emphasised that the cathedral was the bishop's spiritual home, where he should be in regular contact with his *familia*. In this way, misunderstandings – such as those between Jayne and Darby – were avoided. The bishop's chapel was properly the cathedral, where he should pray and celebrate with his *familia* about him. He ought, too, to live near his cathedral, not in some remote 'Palace'. All this was realised at Chester in Bennett's day. How influential, in the long run, were Bennett's writings, and the example of Chester?

Conway presents an overview of the relationship between bishops and their cathedrals, as he saw it in 1989. He reports as follows.

> Frank Bennett complained that although he had personally visited almost every Cathedral, he had never found the Bishop there, except when there was a Diocesan service. I did a little better than that! I visited every Cathedral twice, and when present at the Daily Office I actually found one Diocesan Bishop saying Evensong with his 'Familia' – (actually half of his 'Familia' as the other half were busy interviewing for an administrative post at the time!); and at Truro I attended early Mattins and the Eucharist, both of which were conducted by the Diocesan Bishop. It was reassuring to see, and yet both these Bishops lived several miles away from their Cathedrals. In fact, only sixteen Diocesan Bishops have their official residences close to their Cathedrals, something that would depress Frank Bennett were he alive today; but even more depressing would be that, of those who live as it were next door to the Cathedral, very few use their own Cathedral church as their spiritual home. They use their own private chapels instead.[3]

Thus, despite the lip service paid to Bennett's advocacy, two-thirds of the bishops live away from their cathedral. Conway's ideal is the cathedral as 'what it was intended to be' – an echo of Bennett. Its 'basic *esse*' is that it is the bishop's church, and must be perceived to be such, with Dean and Chapter and Greater Chapter as his 'Familia'. But Conway regrets that in some places the bishop plays little part in the life of the cathedral, though 'in the majority of cathedrals' the bishop was 'on the whole' felt to be 'supportive'.[4] As Conway's Report is based not merely on personal observations when he visited particular cathedrals but also on the responses to his questionnaire, his conclusions may be deemed valid.[5]

Because the purpose of the *Report* of the Archbishops' Commission is different, it approaches issues from a more formal, and hence a non-Bennett standpoint. It notes and endorses the view held by 'most people' that cathedrals are 'where the bishops belong', and considers that relations with their deans and chapters should 'be seen as one of interdependence' – no reference here to '*familia*'. It is 'desirable' [*sic*] for the bishop, 'as practically or as frequently as possible', to be part of the worshipping community of the cathedral.[6]

The *Report* focuses on the need for the cathedral's strategy in responding to the general mission of the Church to be integrated with diocesan strategy, and sees the bishop's co-ordinating role as vital. Hitherto, cathedral and diocesan plans have not always proceeded in harmony. In carefully coded language, it comments that though 'this of itself' had not produced conflict, there have been 'a small number of well-publicised cases'.[7] All this contrasts markedly with Conway's realistic view of the cathedral as being in the forefront of the Church's mission, because able to reach millions who are strangers to parish churches.

How far is the 1989 parochial perception of the 'Mother Church' in line with what Bennett was striving for? This is not an aspect which can readily be analysed in numerical terms, and so Owen Conway's comments are inevitably impressionistic. On the negative side, he reports criticisms of the cathedral voiced by both clergy and lay people, 'which indicate a total lack of understanding on the part of the cathedral authorities of the concerns and stresses of parochial life and work', and in some instances 'positive antagonism'. He admits, however, that those who live and work at some distance from the Cathedral 'are often guilty of too glib and superficial a reaction', and 'fail to appreciate Mother's problems'. He notes, also, that in a 'recent' debate in General Synod on the 'Decade of Evangelism', the role that cathedrals might play was never mentioned. Does this indicate that we have no latter-day Bennett in any of our deaneries? Finally, Conway found that the Greater Chapter was not taken sufficiently seriously, and, echoing Bennett, in the rhetoric of 1989 urges that greater use be made of this 'structured resource' to link diocese and cathedral.[8] Again, on the positive side, Conway names nine cathedrals which are well integrated into the life of their diocese, and reports also that most of the 'parish church cathedrals' are similarly well integrated with their dioceses. Bennett, we remember, had not been in favour of a cathedral retaining a parish, but it may be that the parochial element promotes greater awareness of other parishes.

The *Report*, in contrast, merely gives examples of 'good practice' encountered by the Commission.[9] Otherwise, the *Report* is concerned with integration of cathedral and parochial 'strategy' through a new administrative body, the Cathedral Greater Council, discussed below. On evangelism, it believes that 'most cathedrals could be more active in their evangelistic mission' and offers suggestions and recommendations. One suggestion, in the spirit of Bennett, is that cathedrals should make provision for those visitors whose religious feelings have been stirred by their visit and wish for more sustained experience to be put in touch with a local church.[10]

Finally, Conway suggests an imaginative up-dating of Bennett's use of cathedral chapels. These could be used 'with special prayers, cards and candles to focus on areas of deep spiritual concern in the world and the Church's mission to it', home and family, sickness and healing, peace and justice, the environment, and so on.[11] The *Report* gives no attention to the updating of chapels, but approves as 'good practice', the provision of prayer cards and intercessions cards.[12]

2

Bennett had seen the residentiary canons as constituting the Executive to the Greater Chapter. As such, they had an administrative role, with the dean, in a sense, as the Chief Executive. They were, at the same time, priests, and Bennett always thought of himself as a parish priest. The dichotomy between the two roles was perhaps less apparent in Bennett's day, but it was there, nevertheless. It was made explicit to Conway. The Chapter Clerk of Lincoln highlighted it. 'I am in effect' he said, 'the General Manager of what is tantamount to a medium-sized company – with diversified concerns – and my Board of Directors are all clergymen'.[13] Conway takes the problem of combining cathedral aministration with pastoral responsibility a stage further. Chapters must 'delegate their administrative authority and executive responsibility, rather than their priestly, pastoral and teaching roles'.[14] Bennett had in effect combined a major priestly role with that of General Manager, dealing directly with architects, designers, refectory manager, and a host of others. To him this was the only way to operate. It is not fruitful to speculate about how he might have worked in the quite different climate of the final decades of the twentieth century, but it is safe to guess where he would have put the emphasis in any conflict between a priestly and an administrative role.

The *Report* formalises, at length, what Conway suggests. The proposed structure emphasises accountability, with lay and community involvement. It also notes that by 1994 many cathedrals had appointed a professional administrator (the actual title varied) and recommends this practice to all cathedrals.[15] Executive responsibility for finance would rest with the administrator, to whom a head of finance (an accountant) would report. The Chapter (now the Administrative Chapter), chaired by the dean, and akin to a Board of Directors, would include up to three independent members (some lay), appointed by the bishop.[16] Provosts would (as Bennett had wanted) become deans. The Administrative Chapter would be responsible for the execution of its duties to a policy-making body, the Cathedral Greater Council of about 24 members, chaired by the bishop, typically with members representing the cathedral community, the wider diocese, the local community, the 'Regional/National/International Dimension' [*sic*] (up to two members). The dean and Administrative Chapter would be members.[17]

It is too early to say whether the proposals will be comprehensively accepted by cathedrals, let alone how any of the changes will work. Since the operational activity of cathedrals has not changed since Bennett's day, we may surmise that he would have been astonished that tasks he performed more or less singly had to be divided and operations multiplied; though he would doubtless have approved the closer involvement of the laity.

3

Owen Conway's report gives a useful overview of various other aspects of modern cathedral activity, some of which may be regarded as developments of Bennett's initiatives. The 'ministry of welcome', as Conway calls it, is one such and the link with Bennett is obvious, though he does not make this point.

EPILOGUE: TODAY   249

The abandonment of admission charges was only the precondition for welcoming pilgrims, and for making the cathedral into 'what-it-was-to-be'. Yet it was the physical presence of Bennett himself which made the welcome real. Vergers and volunteers who assisted took their cue from him. Conway reports that, today, schemes for visitors' care, with paid staff, are evident at many cathedrals. He talked with some of those employed specifically to organise and develop this ministry. This, in a near paraphrase of Bennett, he holds to be 'not an optional extra, but of the very essence of what a cathedral is'. As we noted earlier, Bennett is said to have transformed Chester Cathedral from a museum into the welcoming House of God, and others copied him.[18] Conway notes, however, the lack in very many cathedrals of a member of the Cathedral Chapter to show visitors round, as Bennett had prescribed, 'RELIGIOUSLY' (*sic*). He found, too, that by 1989 some cathedrals were in danger of becoming noisy centres of tourism, and considered reluctantly that charges might act as a control. Interestingly, at Canterbury and Ripon he found incense being used non-liturgically, and this, he reports, 'has a marked effect on the volume of sound ... as we know that it is only in Christian places of worship that it is so used'. The link with Bennett's thinking and practice is obvious and Conway makes the point explicitly.[19]

The *Report*, with a different emphasis, discusses visitors in the context of tourism and in effect reports the development of Bennett's initiatives in a late twentieth century milieu, but does not speak in Bennett terms of 'pilgrims', but realistically of 'casual visitors'.[20] The current provision of literature, guide-books, exhibitions, refectories, up-dated by post-Bennett electronic devices such as walk-around guides, audio-visual presentations, etc., which 'augment the personal guides', are noted. Bennett, who was always keen to use the latest technology would have been impressed, and pleased to read that 'improved interpretation of the spiritual aspects of cathedrals is also very apparent'.[21] That there was still scope for improvement 'in the spiritual interpretation of the cathedral', in the context of witness, education and evangelism, would have chimed with the thinking of one who would gently (or, if he deemed it necessary, not so gently) prod laggards into action. Perhaps in this instance to endeavour to convert 'casual visitors' into 'pilgrims'. For Bennett (and Conway) the spiritual was (and is) central.[22]

Bennett had aimed to attract children into the cathedral. Provision for youth groups, visits by school parties, with teacher supervision, hymn-singing during visits, use of the Children's Corner, were, perhaps, appropriate to the 1920s and 1930s. Chester, however, is now turning back to this Bennett strategy, and is developing a Children's Chapel. Conway reports on contemporary methods, and notes 'the potential scope of all cathedrals ... as a resource in education'. St Albans has an education centre for humanities and science subjects; GCSE projects operate there and elsewhere; cathedrals provide literature, and learning modules are available. His conclusion would surely have met with Bennett's approval: 'All this brings young people who would otherwise hardly ever visit a church, let alone worship in one, into a critical appreciation of what a cathedral stands for and what it does'. The official *Report* provides a broad survey of practices current five years after Conway.[23]

Ecumenism is another area of development, although the official *Report* adds little.[24] Conway 'found that cathedral authorities generally welcomed this ecumenical role of the cathedrals and encouraged it'. The attractiveness of cathedral churches, 'with their long links with locality and nation alike' makes them 'a neutral ground for christians of all denominations to meet', where clergy of other denominations could also officiate. Bennett did not specifically address the part the cathedral could play in ecumenism. His objectives were, in the context of the 1920s and 1930s, inevitably more limited, but his initiatives at Hawarden, and later as dean, in forming and leading a 'Societas Fratorum' of local clergy indicated where his sympathies lay. In Chester Cathedral he set up a display showing the distribution of world-wide missionary activity by the various denominations. Bennett's proposal to lend the cathedral nave to the Congregational Union for the opening service of their 1931 session must have seemed too radical for some of the Chapter, as it was postponed for discussion and not referred to again in subsequent minutes. His mature thoughts on 'Integration', the term he preferred to 'Reunion', were set out in his essay of that title. His focus there on baptism as the basis for integration was regarded by some contemporary commentators as daring, but transposed into the context of today, and combined with Bennett's approach to the cathedral 'as-it-was-to-be', it could issue logically in the ecumenical initiatives which Conway located in many (though by no means all) cathedrals in 1989.[25]

As Dean of Chester, Bennett had demoted Mattins from its position as principal service of the day and established the Eucharist as the central act of worship. In *The Nature of a Cathedral* he had asked, 'Are we any longer justified in keeping the Eucharist out of its proper place as the principal service for the day?'. Conway, listing the cathedrals he had visited, reports the arrangements he found in operation for week-day services, and concludes that 'Frank Bennett's vision from the 1920's standpoint has come about'.[26]

Bennett had lightened the load of boy-choristers, to give more time for school lessons, and had stressed that their spiritual care was 'paramount', especially after their voices had changed. It was unfair and unwise that a boy who had held an important official position from the age of ten to fifteen should be then dropped. He favoured a Servers' Guild; and ex-choristers should be one of best sources of supply for ordinands.[27] By 1989, girls were appearing in parish choirs. Conway recommended chorister education for girls as well as boys. He was impressed with the pastoral care of choristers and lay clerks, and the deep sense of mission of cathedral organists and masters of choristers; those 'blessed with Choir Schools or the equivalent' recruited lay clerks and scholars who reach standards of which the Church could be proud.[28]

Finally, as the abandonment of admission charges had been the starting point for Bennett, it is appropriate to call Conway as witness to the present situation. Though at one with Bennett in opposing charges, on principle, Conway somewhat reluctantly concludes that they could be a method of control at St Paul's, where, 'on any day except Sunday the back of the cathedral looks and sounds more like a market than a house of prayer'. The Archdeacon had told him that tourists, who happily go along the road and pay £4.50 to visit the Tower of London, put little or nothing in the donation boxes.[29] Since 1989, it has come about that many cathedrals (but not Chester) have been reviewing and modifying their policies, in the face of mounting costs for maintenance and diminishing sources of revenue. This situation in turn highlights once more the dual role of Deans and Chapters, on the one hand as priests and custodians of the House of God, and, on the other as Boards of Directors of business and 'heritage' concerns. The *Report* of the Archbishops' Commission notes that, in 1994, only at St Paul's and Ely were charges compulsory, but a third of cathedrals charged for 'extras' (roof, treasury etc., but arguably this is not a recent development). The pros and cons of charging are rehearsed, but the official report's conclusion, that 'each cathedral has to make its own decision', would have bitterly disappointed Bennett, as marking no advance on the final views of the Commission on which he had sat in 1926.[30] It may be relevant to point out that making charges has never been contemplated either by the cathedrals of the Roman Catholic communion in Britain or by the cathedral of the Orthodox Church here.

4

In final summary, what was the nature of Bennett's achievement, and what is his legacy? His years at Chester coincided with a time when the motor-car and omnibus were opening up opportunities for travel. Chester was a popular centre which attracted visitors. With the ending of war, liners from America again docked at Liverpool, and trans-Atlantic travellers made Chester their first stopping place. Hoteliers and shopkeepers were alert to the business potential, and Bennett was well aware that the cathedral itself was an attraction to the growing influx of post-war visitors. Furthermore, he had come as dean in the immediate aftermath of a war which left a very large number of families bereaved, and, despite the post-war mood of disillusion and cynicism among survivors, the bereaved were seeking comfort in religion of one variety or another. The vast crowds attending Armistice Day services were testimony to this, as were the large congregations at churches and chapels. The boom in spiritualism and other cults and popular concern with the question of survival after death reflected the mood. On the doorstep of the cathedral were the people of Chester, to many of whom the great church was an alien place they had never entered – even for a nave service. Last, but for Bennett by no means least, there was the Diocese of Chester itself, for which the cathedral was the Mother Church. All this meant that there was – put crudely in current jargon – a market for religion, and a place in which the new dean could market Christianity.

Today, with modern travelling facilities, tourists come in vast numbers to visit cathedrals. The official *Report* counted Chester as fourth in the national league table of numbers of visitors, preceded only by York, Canterbury and St Paul's.[31] There certainly seems to be a measure of interest in religion of one variety or another, indicating a continuing potential 'market' in the late twentieth century. For many, an increasingly materially-orientated culture seems unable to satisfy deep-felt longings and leaves an unfilled void. Significantly, in the wake of collapsed Marxist regimes, traditional religion has re-emerged elsewhere in the world. In Britain, successful publishing of books on religion, many in cheap paperback, and the continued existence of the BBC 'Thought for the Day' (albeit now stretched far beyond beyond Christianity) are likely indications of public interest, though admittedly not proof of any specific commitment. The pronouncements of religious leaders on the moral dimension of current issues, usually widely reported in the media, almost invariably produce a response from politicians not unconcerned about public attitudes and electoral votes.

Another manifestation of interest in religion, perhaps related to the attractiveness of esoteric cults, is a growing enthusiastic participation in unusual and emotional do-it-yourself liturgies, condemned by Lord Runcie as dangerous worship of 'candy-floss idols' but defended by the Bishop of Wakefield as indications that the Church of England remains a 'broad church'. The innovative style of the 'Eternity' service, aimed at younger age-groups, was recently so successful at a Bradford parish church that it has been moved to the cathedral.[32] Nevertheless, more traditional sung Eucharists at cathedrals still attract those of all ages, as attendances at Christmas and Easter services amply testify. Every Sunday, Chester Cathedral's services attract large numbers of visitors as well as regular cathedral worshippers. Bennett had stressed that the cathedral should offer a variety of styles of worship, though he made his own preference clear. Music, also, should cater for all tastes. It is interesting to speculate how he might have reacted to a 'rave in the nave', which some might argue to be only a few steps beyond the Alternative Service Book. The official *Report* perceives cathedrals as 'liturgical laboratories'. Would the authors accommodate experimental 'raves' therein?[33]

The most effective promoter is one who is perceived as a firm believer in the product. Bennett, a natural pastor and effective communicator, at ease mixing with all sorts and conditions of men and women, used his opportunity with skill. Never status-conscious, he was often taken by visitors to be a verger, but it was as a parish priest that he addressed himself to individual men and women and their problems.

Chester's example was followed elsewhere, as cathedrals opened their doors and as Bennett's *The Nature of a Cathedral* came into the hands of deans and chapters. The reality of welcome depended on individual chapters, with deans in the lead. Bell, at Canterbury, was one of Bennett's readiest pupils. The Chester model, the 1926 book, followed by membership of the Cathedrals Commission and the American visit, had, by the late 1920s, established Bennett's position as the doyen of cathedral reform, and he was hailed as such when he retired. But it was characteristic of the man that he was not seduced by fame and returned happily to the pastoral work he understood so well. It is as priest and pastor who opened the great church to all comers that he is hailed on the memorial tablet in the cathedral. The inscription composed by Elma Paget is commended to all visitors to Chester today.

> Remember
> Frank Selwyn Macaulay Bennett
> Dean of Chester 1920–37
> Who for love of God and his fellow men
> Opened this Cathedral without fence or fee
> so that God's children
> Should know and love their Father's House.
> 'I was glad when they said unto me
> Let us go into the House of the Lord'.

Notes

1   Owen A. Conway, *A Cathedral Pilgrimage: Reflections and Observations on the Life and Work of Cathedrals in England Today and in the Future* (privately published, 1990). Appropriately enough, the pilgrim of 1989 has now completed his journey in the footsteps of Bennett, by becoming a resident Canon of Chester, where he is Precentor. For Conway's impressions of Chester Cathedral, written three weeks after he had joined the Chapter, see Owen Conway, 'Residentary Canon and Precentor', in D. C. Kelly (ed.), *Chester Cathedral 1992: Close Encounters in the First Person* (Lincoln, 1991), 35–41. The most recent report on English cathedrals is *Heritage and Renewal: The Report of the Archbishops' Commission on Cathedrals* (London, 1994) [hereafter, Howe, *Report*]. The Commission was chaired by Lady Howe.

2   Conway, *Pilgrimage*, 3. Pat Ames testifies to Bennett's lifelong influence on her: 'I've always loved the Cathedral, ever since my childhood encounter with Dean Bennett; I feel happy here and it is my spiritual home': for her role as Welcomer and Guide at the cathedral today, see Kelly, *Chester Cathedral 1992*, 2–5.

3   Conway, *Pilgrimage*, 6. There are, doubtless, special local circumstances which render it impossible for every bishop to live near his cathedral.

4   Conway mentions 12 cathedrals (including Chester) where the bishop regularly celebrates the Eucharist, but finds that in many other places bishops have little or no part in the life of the cathedral, attending only for statutory preaching or diocesan services. The relationship of the Mother Church to the diocese is through the bishop; a cathedral proceeding otherwise is on a 'course of isolation from its children', a lesson evident to Conway 'not only from Frank Bennett's words of wisdom' but from his own experience in visiting all English cathedrals and talking to chapters and certain bishops.

5   Conway, *Pilgrimage*, 5, 7.

EPILOGUE: TODAY

6   The official *Report* quotes the words of the 1927 Cathedrals Commission, that a cathedral 'as the place of the bishop's seat is the mother church of the diocese', and 'emphatically endorses' those of the 1990 Care of Cathedrals Measure – post-Conway – that it is 'the seat of the bishop and a centre of worship and mission'. Howe makes no mention of a bishop's place of residence but states merely that he 'should be available to give advice informally to the dean on a regular basis' and that the dean should consult him on 'strategy, policy, plans and major developments or other critical matters' (Howe, *Report*, 13–16). This cannot be quite so easy to achieve, face to face, if the bishop lives at a distance. Nevertheless, in the nineteenth century, and for historical reasons, cathedral reform and the development of diocesan administration – hardly in existence before mid-century – proceeded independently. In consequence, until comparatively recent times 'the relationship of cathedral to diocese has received little appraisal'. In contrast, 'in some other constituents of the Anglican Church and the Roman Catholic Church, cathedrals have an unambiguous and close relationship to episcopal authority' (*ibid.*, 4).

7   Howe, *Report*, 3–5, 7–8. The Commission's solution to all problems, including presumably 'well-publicised' ones, is a formal relationship of accountability by the cathedral to a Greater Council, a new structure, representing a range of interests and presided over by the bishop. The 'secular analogy', it claims, 'is with the Council of a university' (*ibid,*, 13, 60, 73). Presumably, then, the Dean and Chapter would be analogous to the Senate, though somewhat more circumscribed. Glancing at universities in the 1990s, the analogy is perhaps not a notably encouraging one.

8   Conway, *Pilgrimage*, 9–11.

9   These include regular visits by parishes or deaneries to the cathedral; visits by cathedral staff to parishes, to preach or advise; cathedral choir visits to parishes, and vice versa; chapter representatives in attendance at institutions; parochial and deanery evening pilgrimages to the cathedral; a follow-up cathedral service for confirmation candidates six months after confirmation; cathedral staff acting as confessors to clergy (Howe, *Report*, 251).

10   *ibid.*, 31–2. 39. 177.

11   Conway, *Pilgrimage*, 12.

12   Howe, *Report*, 251.

13   Conway offers no precise remedy, but aware of the risks inherent in appointing men to chapters charged with making decisions which may be potentially disastrous, points to the equal danger of limiting choice of canons to those with business and administrative experience. During the course of his pilgrimage, he had heard the complaint that some deans and chapters were becoming a kind of 'brief-case brigade' and thus failing in that 'personal availability which Dean Bennett so strongly recommended, and which to any priest must be an essential modus vivendi' (Conway, *Pilgrimage*, 15). Tony Barnard, Canon of Lichfield, who had looked at the problem in

another context, had already hinted at a possible solution. While recognising that the 'visionary leadership of Deans and Provosts will be vital', he had suggested that the 'expansion of Chapters to include non-clerical canons, expert in fields other than "the church", could well be important' (Conway, *Pilgrimage*, 15; Tony Barnard, 'The cathedral, education and the proclamation of the Gospel', in James Butterworth (ed.), *The Reality of God* (London, 1986), 202).

14 He considers Chester as 'tantamount to a medium sized company'. Eight others are in the same category; both Canterbury and York rank as large concerns. To recruit the right people, cathedrals must pay salaries to their administrators which reflect those paid to general managers elsewhere, and abandon a model for non-clerical pay based on the stipend of a residentiary canon (Conway, *Pilgrimage*, 20).

15 The person appointed would have the status of a residentiary canon, participating in all Chapter discussions (including those on worship), and have full voting powers. Residentiary canons with particular skills and talents might have line-management or oversight responsibility in appropriate fields.

16 Howe, *Report*, 63–4, 79–81, 180–1.

17 *ibid.*, 60–62. The present Greater Chapter (honorary canons or prebendaries) would become the College of Canons, comprising the Administrative Chapter, ordained honorary canons, and lay canons. Its duties would include electing two of its number to the Greater Council, and possibly two to the Administrative Chapter; the purely honorific election of the bishop; acting as a two-way link with parishes and the wider community, and providing a forum through which the Administrative Chapter could seek the views of experienced clergy and laity (Howe, *Report*, 62–3, 73–4).

18 He used to say that the inter-war fashion for seaside missions was a mistake. People went to the beach to enjoy themselves, not to be preached at. The Cathedral, where people had come deliberately to the House of God, was the proper place for mission activity (information from Guy Bennett). These words have the Bennett tone, and may not be far from those actually used by Bennett to an impressionable boy. In his more measured tones, Bennett's son recorded, 'It surprised him [Bennett] that excellent people conducted missions on the sands where they were not particularly welcome while the clamant opening offered by a cathedral with its naturally impressionable visitors was neglected' ('Memoir'). The vogue for seaside missions in the inter-war years might repay investigation.

19 Conway, *Pilgrimage*, 26–7, 28–9; for the use of incense, 27.

20 Howe, *Report*, 12. Visitors are to be welcomed by properly trained volunteers and guides, encouraged to enjoy the splendour of the cathedral 'for its own sake', receive an intimation of the religious reasons why the cathedral was built and cared for, and what it conveys about God's relationship with his people. Appointment of a 'visitor officer' (as at present in eleven larger cathedrals), preferably a clerical or lay member of the cathedral's permanent staff, is recommended (*ibid.*, 145, 147–51).

21 *ibid.*, 144.

22 *ibid.*, 145. The *Report* also indicates that there is scope for some improvement in material provision but in general finds that 'the best practices are very good, and, indeed, most cathedrals show excellence in one or more areas'. It suggests means of exchanging ideas with other cathedrals. In addition, local tourist boards could prove helpful.

23 Conway, *Pilgrimage*, 21; cf. Howe, *Report*, 28, 41–4, 45–6, 144, 252.

24 Howe, *Report*, 8–9, 20.

25 Conway, *Pilgrimage*, 23–5.

26 *ibid*, 36.

27 Bennett, *Nature of a Cathedral*, 37.

28 'Even more praiseworthy' were those cathedrals without Choir Schools, where parents transported children at all hours for rehearsals and services. He singled out St Alban's for special praise. He is concerned with the problem of boys after their voices change, and 'a whole part of their life and routine may seem to drop to pieces'. Some were trained as servers; they were a source of ordinands. He commended Liverpool's ex-choristers 'Cross Guild', whose members served and virged. They 'graced the occasion', in colourful robes and with dignity, at the 1989 Hillsborough memorial service. Cathedral choirs increasingly sing at parish churches (Conway, *Pilgrimage*, 38). Howe reports girl-choirs 'on the Salisbury model', which relieve the load on boy-choirs, but recognising that 'the subject of girls singing in cathedrals is an emotive one', merely hopes that cathedrals will 'give careful consideration to the possibility of chorister education for all children' (Howe, *Report*, 52–3).

29 Conway, *Pilgrimage*, 6; Howe, *Report*, 47–51.

30 Howe, *Report*, 147–51.

31 *ibid.*, Appendix A, 221–8

32 *The Times*, 10.2.1997, 5.

33 Howe, *Report*, 19.

APPENDIX
Was Bennett ever considered for a Bishopric?

Though much was made, both in the 'Memoir' written by Bennett's son and in the 'Family History' compiled by his grandson, of Lloyd George's alleged part in Bennett's appointment as dean, little attention was paid in the Bennett family to a casual remark in the 'Memoir', not repeated in the 'Family History, to the effect that 'it was said that Archbishop Edwards wanted to get a bishopric for Bennett'. As we have seen, the story about the deanery appointment had local currency in Chester, but there seems to have been no knowledge of any thought being given to translating Bennet to a bishopric.

If Bennett ever had any prospect of becoming a bishop, his best opportunity would have been during Davidson's tenure at Canterbury. Cosmo Gordon Lang, translated from York to Canterbury on Davidson's retirement in 1928, was antipathetic towards Bennett and, as we know from his 1930 response to Paget's request that Bennett be awarded the Lambeth Doctorate, dismissive about his scholarship. How, then, would Bennett have fared under Davidson?

The official patronage files are closed, but speculation as to whether Bennett stood any chance of becoming a bishop is in order. In appointing bishops, all four prime ministers who occupied Downing Street during the primacy of Randall Davidson (1903–1928) gave careful attention to the views of the archbishop. Even before he became archbishop, Davidson, successively Dean of Windsor, Bishop of Rochester and Bishop of Winchester, had been regularly consulted by Queen Victoria, who took a close interest in appointments to bishoprics. She trusted Davidson's judgment and sought his views on the man preferred by the Prime Minister. Davidson, however, stressed, both then and later as archbishop, the constitutional right of the Prime Minister to put forward a name or names; the Sovereign could reject, but not substitute. Communication with the Queen was via Sir Henry Ponsonby, her Private Secretary, and officially the Prime Minister was unaware of this.[1] Edward VII and George V did not attempt to invade this area of the constitutional borderland, not caring to become involved closely in church appointments.

After he became archbishop, Davidson based his advice to prime ministers on the criteria he had used before. He would give background information about the diocese and indicate the sort of man who was required. For example, business powers, preaching ability, theological scholarship, potential skill in the House of Lords, had all figured in his 1885 assessment for London. He weighed candidates against these criteria, but later referred to the value of social links with prominent political figures, style of churchmanship, and avoidance of becoming involved in public controversy on the subject of appointments.[2] Again, in 1911 Davidson told Asquith that balance of styles of churchmanship should be redressed in the Northern Province, which was 'swamped ... with "Evangelical" Bishops, making the Archbishop of York [Cosmo Lang] look like an extreme High Churchman'.[3] In 1923, in the high-tide of Anglo-Catholicism, he urged the appointment of Walter Frere to Truro, as one who could speak from the bench of bishops, responsibly and with scholarly knowledge, for this school of thought.[4]

Bennett had the background of family, school and university necessary to place him within the broad bracket of eligibility. His reputation for diplomacy and persuasive oratory had been demonstrated by 1917 in controversy about Disestablishment in Wales; the part he played in the Cardiff Convention in 1917 and his subsequent election to the Governing Body of the Church in Wales were as good recommendations for promotion to a bishopric as to a deanery. He had also demonstrated skill in administering the 'mini-diocese' of Hawarden. When dean, the lead Bennett gave in reforming cathedrals, his *Nature of a Cathedral* (1925), and his role on the Cathedrals Commission might have stood him in good stead, as might his American visit. As we have seen from Davidson's pronouncements, Bennett's High Churchmanship would not have disqualified him for an appropriate diocese. However, his somewhat quirky variety of Anglo-Catholicism would not necessarily have been agreeable to those of that persuasion, and he did not compare with Frere in theological scholarship. He was, however, tolerant of those who held to other persuasions, although the mixed reception of the unusual views propounded in his *Expecto* (1926) might not have been acceptable in a bishop. Nor did Bennett have experience in an academic institution. He had produced no theological work, and had never served on a cathedral chapter. He had had experience as secretary to a bishop, and had been a bishop's chaplain, as had George Bell, but that was at Canterbury, under Archbishop Davidson.

Davidson normally consulted Lang about appointments in the Northern

Province, and so Bennett's opportunities would have been further limited by being confined to the Southern. Finally, having been appointed as dean, it is unlikely that Bennett would have been promoted in less than, say, five years. Bell served five years as Dean of Canterbury before being appointed Bishop of Chichester, and he was personally known to Davidson, whose chaplain he had been. He was also younger than Bennett, which may have been an advantage. This suggests that Bennett's best chances of a bishopric were probably limited to two periods, 1917 (a year when no appointments were made) to 1919 (eight vacancies in the Southern Province in 1918–1919), and 1925 to 1928 (six vacancies in the Southern Province). In time, evidence may emerge to give a firm answer to the question as to whether Bennett was ever suggested for elevation to the episcopate. The possibility that he was offered a bishopric and refused it cannot be excluded. Cyril Garbett, Archbishop of York (1942–1956), who was in a position to know, pointed out that a bishopric was not always joyfully accepted. 'There are men', he wrote, 'who, though attracted by the offer of a see, have refused it for the sake of the work they felt they ought not to leave'.[5] Could Bennett have been one such, at any rate after 1920?

R. B. McDowell has analysed the composition of the episcopate from 1881 to 1945.[6] He calculates indicators of academic distinction, using as criteria the percentage of appointees who obtained first class degrees or were elected to Fellowships shortly after graduation. The figures are constant from 1881–1930, but drop thereafter (1881–1905 49%; 1906–1930 49%; 1931–1945 41%). He admits, however, that his criteria are open to criticism.[7] For the two periods when Bennett stood the best chance of promotion, 1917–1920 and 1925–1928, I have calculated in the same way figures based on the information given in *Who was Who* (for both Provinces). The sample is small (18), and only three men, Hensley Henson, W. O. Burroughs, and E. A. Burroughs, had straight firsts. None of these three seems to have had a doctorate. (McDowell took no account of doctorates, arguably an equally good or better measure of high academic quality.) Seven others of my sample had doctorates in Divinity, just under 40%, and very close to the pattern in fellowships and firsts reported by McDowell.

He notes the growing significance of headships of major public schools and states that 'between 1830 and 1945 [115 years] about eighteen public-school headmasters were placed on the bench. Six indeed became archbishops – the two Temples, Tait, Benson, Fisher and Longley ...' Of my sample of clergymen who became bishops, only one had been a headmaster, although two had been assistant masters in public schools.

To be a son of the parsonage and to have attended a public school were undoubtedly helpful to advancement. My 44% for the former stands some comparison with McDowell's 55% for 1906–1930 and 44% for 1931–1945. His percentages for public-school men are 1906–1930 79%; 1931–1945 76%. Despite my sample being again very small, it fits: thirteen of the eighteen named a public school, giving a figure of 72%. In four instances no name of a school is recorded. The one man who became an archbishop was a Portsmouth Grammar School boy.

Statistical analysis of biographical details given in *Who was Who* produces the following table. But it should be remembered that these 'biographies' were devised by the men themselves, and they may for one reason or another have omitted some detail. They are, however, unlikely to have omitted anything which cast them in a favourable light.

Select qualifications of those appointed to a bishopric in 1917–1920 and 1925–1928

headmaster	1
doctorate in Divinity	7
son of influential man	2
wife from influential family*	7
son of clergyman	8
previously canon, dean, or bishop	11
held significant office in one or more religious or secular organization	4
held academic appointment	10
public school stated (those not stating counted as non-public school)	4
chaplain to a bishop	3
royal connection	8

total of qualifications 75: average per individual 4.75

* (Randall Davidson regarded wives who were influentially connected as an asset in assisting access to key social and political figures).

The figures show general trends but cannot tell the full story. The man with the highest score (6), H. M. Burge, was appointed to the important see of Oxford in 1918, at age 56. He had been Headmaster of Repton School, and later of Winchester; he was a son of the parsonage, and his wife the daughter of a clergyman. He was already Bishop of Southwark and had been a Fellow of University College, Oxford; he had attended Marlborough School, and by 1919 was Chancellor of the Order of the Garter. As an exception to prove the rule, the lowest scorer (1) was Cyril Garbett, appointed Bishop of Southwark in 1919. Although a son of the parsonage, Garbett came from a fairly poor home and his only academic qualification was an Oxford second. He had been neither don nor headmaster, only a parish priest. Nevertheless, he was translated to Winchester in 1932, and in 1942 became Archbishop of York, where, though 'a little less clever than many other bishops, he came closer to embodying for his own generation the nation's religious judgment'.[8]

As for Bennett, on the above score sheet he achieves an average of only 3 for 1917–1920. His father was not a clergyman; his wife was not influentially connected. But he was a public-school man and had been chaplain to a bishop. As an elected member of the Governing Body of the Church in Wales he briefly held a nationally significant office, and after 1925, another as a member of the Cathedrals Commission. For the second period, 1925–1928, he therefore scores rather better, with an average of 4, much closer to the overall average of 4.75. He had, of course, administered a large benefice efficiently, and was a good preacher, but I have no measure of the record of those appointed to bishoprics with which to compare these qualities.

Had Bennett's name ever been seriously floated, there would almost certainly have been some correspondence in the Davidson and Lang files in Lambeth Palace Library, but the index to these papers contains no entry to suggest that his name ever came forward. Nor is Bennett mentioned in any of the Davidson and Lang correspondence in the Bodleian Library. However, since the Davidson files in Lambeth Palace Library alone run to more than 800 volumes, although I have looked up all entries for Bennett in the index, it would require detailed combing, which I have not undertaken, to be absolutely sure that he is never mentioned in this respect. An indexer might well have missed a passing reference.[9]

It is not surprising that there is no evidence that, for his own part, Bennett ever aspired to a bishopric. He always said that the job he was doing was the one he enjoyed most, though doubtless there was an element of the diplomatic in this. Yet the clerical vocation was a profession, and Bennett, like most professionals, welcomed advancement, to enjoy expanded opportunities for deployment of innate and acquired skills. Whether Bennett would have been as successful as a bishop as he was as a dean is an open question. But it is difficult to see how, as a bishop, he could have initiated, and seen through, the 'free and open' regime, and all that went with it. To this extent the whole Church would have been the loser.[10]

Notes

1   Davidson in a Memorandum written in 1906 (G. K. A. Bell, *Randall Davidson, Archbishop of Canterbury*, 3rd edit., Oxford, 1952, 165).

2   Davidson to Sir Henry Ponsonby (Bell, *Randal Davidson*, 167–8, 174–6). In 1890 Davidson assured the Reverend F. Gell that there was no disinclination to promote Evangelicals (Davidson to Gell, 11.3.1890, *ibid.*, 178–9). In the earlier part of the nineteenth century, allegiance to a political party, being a 'safe' candidate, pledged to maintain the *status quo* in Church and State, a high reputation for learning, noble birth, influential family connections, and the influence of a powerful patron, were all factors responsible, in one case or another, for elevation to the Bench (Francis Brown, *A History of the English Clergy 1800–1900* (London, 1953), 78). It can be seen that, in a sense, some of these still applied in Davidson's day, though the emphasis was different. Learning, being generally a 'safe' candidate, birth, connections, and even a patron (though not in the older, eighteenth-century sense) could all be factors in bringing a man to attention. For the last thirty years of the nineteenth century, see *ibid.*, 125–6.

3   Davidson to Asquith 5.10.1911 (Bell, *Randall Davidson*, 1241).

4   Davidson to Frere, 28.8.1923 (*ibid.*, 1251).

5   Cyril Garbett, *Church and State in England* (London, 1950), 193–4.

6   R. B. McDowell, 'The Anglican Episcopate, 1780–1945', *Theology*, 50, June 1947, 202–9.

7   *ibid.*, 208.

8   Adrian Hastings, *A History of English Christianity, 1920–1985* (London, 1986), 447–8, 198–9; see also *Chambers Biographical Dictionary* (5th ed., London, 1992), 565. A social historian has, however, noted 'the modesty of their backgrounds' of the six Archbishops of Canterbury between 1880 and 1945, 'the most powerful men in the Church of England', (Harold Perkin, *The Rise of Professional Society: England since 1880* (London, 1989), 264.

9 I am grateful for the advice and assistance of Claire Breay, Assistant Archivist at Lambeth Place Library.

10 Bennett's reputation probably stood at its highest after 1926, with the publication of *The Nature of a Cathedral*, the Cathedrals Commission, and the American visit behind him. Whether he would have even accepted a bishopric after such close involvement in his 'Free and Open' campaign may be doubted. Nor might a bishop who had led such a campaign have been welcomed in every cathedral close.

BIBLIOGRAPHY

Addleshaw, G. W. O., 'Architects, designers, sculptors, craftsmen whose work is to be seen in Chester Cathedral', *Architectural History: Journal of the Society of Architectural Historians of Great Britain*, 14, 1971, 74–109
Addleshaw, G. W. O., *Chester Cathedral. The Stained Glass Windows, Mosaics, Monuments* (Gloucester, 1967)
Addleshaw, G. W. O., *The Pictorial History of Chester Cathedral*, (London, 1970)
Atherton, I., et. al., (eds.), *Norwich Cathedral* (London/Rio Grande, USA, 1996)
Aylmer, G. E., and Cant, R., *A History of York Minster* (Oxford, 1977)
Baker, P. J. Noel, *The League of Nations at Work* (London, 1926)
Barnard, Tony, 'The cathedral, education and the proclamation of the Gospel', in James Butterworth (ed.), *The Reality of God* (London, 1986)
Barrett, Philip, *Barchester: English Cathedral Life in the Nineteenth Century* (London, 1993)
Bedford, Sybille, *Aldous Huxley: A Biography* (2 vols., London, 1973–4)
Bell, G. K. A., *Randall Davidson, Archbishop of Canterbury* (2 vols., Oxford, 1935, 1938, cited 3rd. ed., single vol., 1952)
Bell, P. M. H., *Disestablishment in Ireland and Wales* (London, 1969)
[Bennett, F. S. M.] *Helps to Self Examination* [leaflet, 1915]
[Bennett, F. S. M.], *How to make a Confession* [leaflet, 1915]
Bennett, F. S. M., *A Cathedral Chapter: A Paper read before the Great Chapter of Chester Cathedral, On Wednesday Nov. 24th 1920 by the Dean* (privately printed, Chester, 1920)
Bennett, F. S. M. *M. Coué and his Gospel of Health*, (London/Chester, 1922).
Bennett, F. S. M. *A Soul in the Making or Psycho-synthesis* (London, 1924)
Bennett, F. S. M. *The Nature of a Cathedral* (London, 1925)
Bennett, F. S. M. *An Open Letter to the Chairman and Council of the C.E.M.S.* (Chester and London, 1925)
Bennett, F. S. M. *Expecto: an Essay Towards a Biology of the World to Come* (Chester/London, 1926)
Bennett, F. S. M. *Faith to be Healed* [pamphlet] (Chester, n.d.)
Bennett, F. S. M. *Mary Jane and Harry John or Home the Premier School* (Oxford,

1927)
Bennett, F. S. M. *On Cathedrals in the Meantime* (London, 1928)
Bennett, F. S. M. *The Christian Ideal of Health* (London, 1930)
Bennett, F. S. M. 'Integration', in H.R.L. Sheppard (ed.), *My Hopes and Fears for the Church* (London, 1930), 83–95
Bennett, F. S. M. *The Resurrection of the Organism* (London, 1930)
Bennett, F. S. M. *This Moment of Opportunity for Religious Education* (London, 1938)
Bennett, Frank [F. L. M.], *Chester Cathedral* (Chester, n.d.)
Bennett, Frank [F. L. M.], 'Our Struggle', *Theology*, July 1944.
Bennett, Frank [F. L. M.], *Laodicea in the Twentieth Century or The Church of England in the England of Today* (London, 1946)
Benson, E.W., *The Cathedral: Its Necessary Place in the Life of the Church* (London, 1878)
Blatch, Mervyn, *Cathedrals* (Poole, 1980)
Bradbury, L., *Chester College and the Training of Teachers, 1839–1975* (Chester College, 1975)
Bridge, Arthur E., 'The nineteenth century revivication of Salisbury Cathedral: Walter Kerr Hamilton, 1841–1854', in Marcombe and Knighton, *Close Encounters*, 137–60
Brittain, F. and Manning, B. L., *Babylon Bruis'd and Mount Moriah Mended* (Cambridge, 1940)
Brown, C. K. Francis, *A History of the English Clergy 1800–1900* (London, 1953), 120
Bruce, Alex, 'War memorials', *The Historian*, Autumn, 1990, 17–20
Bruce, Alex, 'Oxford War Memorial: Thomas Rayson and the Chester connection', *Oxoniensia*, 56, 1991, 155–67
Bruce, Alex, 'A city war memorial: the Chester experience', *Cheshire History*, Autumn, 1992, 21–6
Bruce, J. A., 'Giles Gilbert Scott and the Chester War Memorial Project', *Journal of the Chester Archaeological Society*, 73, 1994/1995, 99–114
Burke, Bernard, *A Genealogical and Heraldic History of the Landed Gentry of Great Britain and Ireland*, (2 vols., London, 1898)
Burman, Peter, *St Paul's Cathedral* (London, 1987)
Burne, R. V. H., *Chester Cathedral* (London, 1958)
Burne, R. V. H., *The Monks of Chester* (London, 1962)
Burroughs, E. A., (ed.), *Education and Religion. A Course of Lectures given in Bristol Cathedral* (London, 1924)
Capek, Karel, *Letters from England* (Popular Edition, London, 1927; first publ. 1925)
Carpenter, E., *Cantuar: the Archbishops in their office* (London, 1971)
Carpenter, Edward, (ed.), *A House of Kings: The History of Westminster Abbey*

BIBLIOGRAPHY

(London, 1966)
Cathedrals in Modern Life (Church Assembly, 1961)
Chadwick, Owen, *The Victorian Church* (2 vols., London, 1966–70)
Church Association, *The Disruption of the Church of England by More than 9000 Clergymen who are Helping the Romeward Movement in the National Church* (London, 1900)
Clarke, Basil F. L., *Anglican Cathedrals outside the British Isles* (London, 1958)
Clew, Jeff, *Sparkford: Memories of the Past* (Sparkford, 1997)
Cobbett, William, *Rural Rides*, ed. G.D.H. and M. Cole (3 vols., London, 1930)
[Cobbett, W. J., *William Cobbett's Rural Rides* (2 vols., London, 1957)
Collins, Irene, *Jane Austen and the Clergy* (London, 1994)
Collinson, Patrick, *et. al.,* (eds.), *Canterbury Cathedral* (Oxford, 1995)
Conway, Owen A., *A Cathedral Pilgrimage: Reflections and Observations on the Life and Work of Cathedrals in England Today and in the Future* (privately printed, 1989)
Coulthard, S. L., *The Cestrian Lodge, No, 425, Chester, Province of Chester* (Chester, 1935)
Cox, W. L. Paige, *The Scientific Study of Theology* (London, 1893)
Cox, W. L. Paige, *Aids to Christian Belief in the Miracles and Divinity of Christ* (London, 1905)
Cox, W. L. Paige, *The Church of England as Catholic and Reformed* (London, 1910)
Cox, W. L. Paige, *Christian Ethics and Peace Problems* (London, 1919)
Cross, F. L. and Livingstone, E. A., (eds.), *The Oxford Dictionary of the Christian Church* (Oxford, 1958; rev. ed. 1983)
Cuming, C. J., *A History of the Anglican Liturgy* (London, 1969)
Curteis, G. H., *Bishop Selwyn of New Zealand and Lichfield* (London, 1889)
Davies, John, *A History of Wales* (West Drayton, 1993)
Davies, Horton, *Worship and Theology in England* (5 vols., Princeton and London, 1961–5)
Dearmer, P., *The Story of the Prayer Book in the Old and New World throughout the Anglican Church* (Oxford, 1933)
Dewey, Clive, *The Passing of Barchester* (London, 1991)
Drennan, B. St G., *The Keble College Centenary Register* (Keble College, Oxford, 1970)
Edwards, D. L., *Leaders of the Church of England, 1828–1944* (London, 1971)
Edwards, Kathleen, *The English Secular Cathedrals in the Middle Ages* (Manchester, 1949)
Eeles, Francis Carolus, *Prayer Book Revision and Christian Reunion* (Cambridge, 1923)
Ensor, R. C. K., *England, 1870–1914* (Oxford, 1936)

Evans, J. H., *Churchman Militant* (London, 1961)
Everett, Crosby, *Bishop and Chapter inTwelfth-century England* (Cambridge, 1994)
Farmer, David Hugh, *The Oxford Dictionary of Saints* (Oxford, 1987)
Felkin, E. Mary, *The Cup of the Lord* (Chester/Oxford, 1925)
Feller, Richard T. (ed. Nancy S. Montgomery), *Sculpture and Carving at Washington Cathedral* (Washington, n.d.)
Flindall, R. P., (ed.) *The Church of England 1815–1948: A Documentary History* (London, 1972)
Garbett, Cyril, *Church and State in England* (London, 1950)
Gladstone, W. E., *Studies subsidiary to Bishop Butler* (London, 1896)
Godwin, George, *A History and Description of St Paul's Cathedral* (Thames Ditton, 1837)
Goulborn, K., Welch, R., and Welch, P., *Hawarden, a Portrait in Old Picture Postcards* (Loggerheads, 1990)
Gourlay, A. B., *A History of Sherborne School* (Sherborne, 1971)
Gregory, A., *The Silence of Memory* (Oxford/Providence, 1994)
[Grosvenor, Loelia Mary], *Grace and Favour: The Memoirs of Loelia, Duchess of Westminster* (London, 1962)
[Grosvenor, Loelia Mary], *Cocktails and Laughter: The Albums of Loelia Lindsay (Loelia, Duchess of Westminster)*, ed. H. Vickers (London, 1983)
Guerdan, R., *Byzantium: Its Triumphs and Tragedy* (London, 1956)
Hadfield, J. A., *Psychology and Morals: An Analysis of Character* (London, 1923)
Harris, B. H., *Victoria County History of Cheshire volume III* (Oxford, 1980)
Harris, Brian, *Chester* (London, 1979)
Harris, Robin S., *A History of Higher Education in Canada, 1863–1960* (Toronto, 1976)
Hastings, Adrian, *A History of English Christianity, 1920–1985* (London, 1986)
Heeney, Brian, 'The beginnings of church feminism: women and the councils of the Church of England', *Journal of Ecclesiastical History*, 33, 1982, 89–109
Henson, Hensley, *Retrospect of an Unimportant Life* (London, 1942)
Hick, J., *Death and Eternal Life* (paperback edition, London, 1979)
Hobbs, Mary, (ed.), *Chichester Cathedral: An Historical Survey* (Chichester, 1994)
Hubbard, E., *The Buildings of Wales: Clwyd* (London, 1986)
Hutton, W. H., *Robert Gregory*, (1912)
Huxley, Aldous, *The Art of Seeing* (London, 1943)
Jasper, R. C., *George Bell, Bishop of Chichester* (London, 1967)
Kelly, D. C., (ed.), *Chester Cathedral 1992: Close Encounters in the First Person* (London, 1991)
Knox, Ronald, *Broadcast Minds* (London, 1932)
Knox, Ronald, *Barchester Pilgrimage* (London, 1935)

Lever, Jill, (ed.), *Catalogue of the Drawings Collection of the Royal Institute of British Architects (L–N)* (Farnborough, 1973)
Lloyd, Roger, *The Church of England, 1900–1965* (London, 1966)
Longbottom, F. W., *Chester during the Great War* (Chester, 1921)
Longden, H. Isham, *Northamptonshire and Rutland Clergy* (16 vols., Northampton, 1938–52)
Longworth, P., *The Unending Vigil* (London, 1967, rev. ed., 1985)
Machin, G. I. T., *Politics and the Churches in Great Britain, 1869 to 1921* (Oxford, 1987)
Manross, W. W., *A History of the American Episcopal Church* (New York, 1950)
Mansfield, Nick, 'Class conflict and village war memorials, 1914–24', *Rural History* 6, 1995, 68–87
Marcombe, David and Knighton, C.S., (eds.), *Close Encounters: English Cathedrals and Society since 1540* (Nottingham, 1991)
Martin, Robert Bernard, *Gerard Manley Hopkins: A Very Private Life* (1991)
McDougall, William, *An Introduction to Social Psychology* (London 1908)
McDougall, William, *An Outline of Psychology* (London, 1923)
McDougall, William, *Character and the Conduct of Life* (London, 1928)
McDowell, R. B., 'The Anglican episcopate, 1780–1945', *Theology*, July 1947, 202–9
McKibben, Ross, *Classes and Cultures: England 1918–1951* (London, 1998)
Montgomery, Nancy S., *Stitches for God: The Story of Washington Cathedral Needlepoint* (Cathedral Church of Saint Peter and Saint Paul, n.d.)
Moorman, J. R. H., *A History of the Church of England* (London, 1953)
Morgan, Kenneth O., *Rebirth of a Nation: Wales 1880–1980* (Oxford, 1981)
Moyniham, M., *God on our Side* (London, 1983)
Murray's *Handbook to Lincolnshire* (1890)
Neville-Sington, Pamela, *Fanny Trollope: The Life and Adventures of a Clever Woman*
Nicolls, O. C. C., *A Register of the Alumni of Keble College, Oxford from 1870 to 1925* (Keble Association, Oxford, 1927)
Nockles, Peter B., *The Oxford Movement in Context: Anglican High Churchmanship, 1760–1857* (Cambridge, 1994)
Norman, E. R., *Church and Society in England, 1770–1879* (Oxford, 1976)
Owen, Dorothy, (ed.), *A History of Lincoln Minster* (Cambridge, 1994)
Palmer, Geoffrey, and Lloyd, Noel, *Father of the Bensons: The Life of Edward White Benson, sometime Archbishop of Canterbury* (Harpenden, 1998)
Pannenberg, W., *Jesus – God and Man* (translated, London, 1976)
Pevsner, N. and Hubbard, E., *The Buildings of England: Cheshire* (Harmondsworth, 1978)
Pickering, W. S. F., *Anglo-Catholicism* (London/New York, 1989)
Picton-Timbervill, Edith, *Christ and International Life* (London, n.d.)

Purcell, W., *Fisher of Lambeth* (London, 1969)
Ransom, Teresa, *Fanny Trollope: A Remarkable Life* (Stroud, 1995)
Reed, T. A., *A History of the University of Trinity College 1852–1952* (Toronto, 1952)
Ridley, George, *Bend' Or, Duke of Westminster* (London, 1985)
Robbins, Keith, 'The Twentieth Century, 1898–1994', in Collinson, *Canterbury Cathedral*, 297–340
Robertson, C., 'The condition of Canterbury Cathedral at the Restoration in AD 1660', *Archaeologia Cantiana*, 10 (1876)
Robertson, J. Ross, *Landmarks of Toronto, 4* (Toronto, 1904)
Rowland, Peter, *Lloyd George* (London, 1975)
Simpson, James Y, *Man and the Attainment of Immortality* (London, 3rd. edit., 1923)
Slattery, C. L., *Certain American Faces* (New York, 1918)
Spender, J. A. and Asquith, Cyril, *Life of Lord Oxford and Asquith* (2 vols., London, 1932)
Sweeting, W. D., *The Cathedral Church of Peterborough: A Description of its Fabric and a brief History of the Episcopal See* (London, 1932)
Thompson, A. Hamilton, *The Cathedral Churches of England* (London, 1925)
Thompson, David M., 'Historical Survey, 1750–1949', in Owen, *Lincoln Minster*
Tipler, Frank J., *The Physics of Immortality* (London, 1994)
Vallance, A., *Old Crosses and Lychgates* (London, 1920)
Wakelin, M. F., *English Dialects: an Introduction* (London, 1977)
Walcott, M. E. C., *Traditions and Customs of Cathedrals* (London, 1872)
Wall, Bernard, *Tales of Chester, II, Cathedral Cameos* (Market Drayton, 1992)
Washington, Peter, *Madame Blatavsky's Baboon: Theosophy and the Emergence of the Western Guru* (London, 1993)
Wiles, M., *The Remaking of Christian Doctrine* (London, 1974)
Wilkinson, A., *The Church of England and the First World War* (London, 1978)
Williams, H. C. N., *Guide to Coventry Cathedral* (London, 1984)
Williams, H. C. N., *The Twentieth Century Cathedral* (London, 1964)
Williams, N. P., *The Ideas of the Fall and of Original Sin* (London, 1927)
Wilson, T., *The Myriad Faces of War* (Oxford/New York, 1986)
Woodruff, Eveleigh and Danks, William, *Memorials of the Cathedral Church and Priory of Christ in Canterbury* (London, 1912)

ANONYMOUS PUBLICATIONS

A Guide Book: Washington Cathedral (10th Edition, Mount St Alban, Washington, 1940)
Anglo-Catholic 1923 Conference Report

Boots Guide to Lincoln (1907 edit.)
Chester Historical Pageant, July 5–10 1937: Book of Words (Chester, 1937).
Clwyd in Old Photographs, 32 (Flintshire Record Office, 1975)
Crockford Prefaces: The Editor Looks Back (Oxford, 1947)
Crockford's Clerical Directory
Form of Thanksgiving and Prayer to be used in all Churches and Chapels in England and Wales, and in the Town of Berwick-upon-Tweed [1919]
Historical Association: Branch Reports 1932–1937
Illustrated Lincolnshire (1900)
Parish Church of St Paul's, Portwood, Stockport Centenary Brochure
Report of the First Anglo-Catholic Priests' Convention (1921)
Sherborne School Lists
The Book of Common Prayer ... according to the use of the Protestant Episcopal Church in the United States of America (New York, 1892)
The Book of Common Prayer with the Additions and Deviations proposed in 1928 (Oxford, 1928)
Trinity Church [New York] *Year Book and Register*
Who's Who in Architecture (Architectural Press, London, 1926)

OFFICIAL PUBLICATIONS

Journal of the Thirty-sixth Annual Convention of the Protestant Episcopal Church in the Diocese of Washington, 20–2 May.1931, Appendix, 'Bishop's Diary, 1930'
Heritage and Renewal: The Report of the Archbishops' Commission on Cathedrals (London, 1994)
List of Members of the First Governing Body and of the Representative Body of the Church in Wales and of Committees. 1918 [n.pl., n.d.] [copies of this and the three following items held by the Information Office of the Representative Body of the Church in Wales]
Minutes of the Governing Body of the Church in Wales [n.pl., n.d.]
Official Report of the Proceedings of the Convention of the Church in Wales [?Cardiff, n.d.]
Official Report of the Proceedings of the Joint Committee of the Church in Wales No.1 [?Oxford, ?1915]
Report of the Cathedrals Commission appointed in pursuance of a resolution of the National Assembly of the Church of England, Parts I and II: Report and Appendices (London, 1927)
Report of the First Anglo-Catholic Priests' Convention (Society of SS Peter and Paul, 1921)

Royal Commission on Ecclesiastical Discipline, *Minutes of Evidence*, Cd. 3069, 3070 (1906); *Report*, Cd. 3040, *Parliamentary Papers*, 1906, vol. xxxiii.

SERIALS

(Newspapers, journals, parish magazines, etc.)   For local, discontinued and rare serials, the library or archive in which they were consulted is indicated in [ ], with a key below.

All in One [LPL]
Architectural Review
Boston Evening Globe [BPL]
Boston Morning Globe [BPL]
Chester Chronicle
Chester Diocesan Gazette [CRO (EDA 16)]
Chester Observer
Christ Church Parish Messenger [CRO (P/17/18/8, P/18/9)]
Harvard University Gazette [HUA]
Hawarden Parish Magazine [SDL]
Lincoln Cathedral Notes
New York Evening Post [NYPL]
Peterborough Advertiser
Providence (Rhode Island) Journal [BPL]
R.I.B.A. Journal
Somerset County Advertiser
Somerset County Gazette [SRO]
Stockport Advertiser [STPL]
Stockport Express [STPL]
The Architect and Building News
The Boston Evening Transcript [BPL]
The Boston Globe [BPL]
The Builder
The Cathedral Age [WCA]
The Church Militant [MDL, WCA]
The Ecclesiologist
The Green Quarterly
The Living Church [NYPL]
The New York Times
The Outlook [MDL]
The Shirburnian

The World [CCNY]
Theology
Times Literary Supplement
Toronto Daily Star [MTPL]
Worcester Echo
BPL = Boston Public Library
CCNY = Church Club of New York Archives
CRO = Cheshire Record Office
HUA = Harvard University Archives
LPL = Lambeth Palace Library
MDL = Diocesan Library and Archives, Episcopal Diocese of Massachusetts
MTPL = Metropolitan Toronto Public Library
NYPL = New York Public Library
SDL = St Deiniol's Library, Hawarden
SRO = Somerset Record Office
STPL = Stockport Public Library
WCA = Washington Cathedral Archives

MANUSCRIPT AND EPHEMERAL SOURCES

BOSTON, EPISCOPAL DIOCESE OF MASSACHUSETTS, DIOCESAN LIBRARY AND ARCHIVES
  The Cathedral Church of St Paul, Boston: Calendar
  The Cathedral by the Bishop of Massachusetts
CANTERBURY CATHEDRAL LIBRARY AND ARCHIVES
  'Chapter Book'
CHESTER CITY RECORD OFFICE
  'City and Council of Chester, Minutes and Proceedings of Council and Committees'
  'Minutes of War Memorial Committee' (CCF 42)
  'Census, 1891, Enumerators' Returns, Chester'
  W. E. Kay, 'Queen Street Congregational Church, Chester: Historical Notes from its foundation to 1942' (typescript)
CHESTER, CHESHIRE COUNTY RECORD OFFICE AND DIOCESAN RECORD OFFICE
  Chester Cathedral, 'Chapter Act Book 1816–1894', 'Chapter Act Book 1894–1941' (EDD/3913)
  Chester Cathedral, 'Commonplace Book 1908–1922', 'Commonplace Book 1922–1932' (EDD/3913)

Chester Cathedral, 'Minutes of Fortnightly informal meetings of the Chapter' (EDD/ 3913/3/13)
DURHAM, UNIVERSITY OF DURHAM LIBRARY
Chapter Muniments, 'Chapter Acts'
HAWARDEN, FLINTSHIRE RECORD OFFICE
'Hawarden District Council Minute Book'
'Hawarden Parish Council Minute Book"
'Hawarden Parish Vestry Book'
Hawarden Parish War Memorial: The Unveiling and Dedication (printed notice)
'Preachers' Book 1911–1918'
W. Bell Jones, 'History of Hawarden Parish' (typescript)
LONDON, BRITISH ARCHITECTURAL LIBRARY
Giles Gilbert Scott Papers, GG/86, 1–4.
RIBI Scale of Official Charges
LONDON, CATHEDRALS FABRIC COMMISSION FOR ENGLAND
Correspondence, Powys/Fyfe, Bennett/Eeles
LONDON, CHURCH OF ENGLAND RECORD CENTRE
CBF/CC/D 'Returns to Cathedrals Commission Questionnaire (1926)'
LONDON, LAMBETH PALACE LIBRARY
Bell Papers
Lang Register
'C.E.M.S. Minutes' (MS 3366)
NEW YORK, CHURCH CLUB OF NEW YORK ARCHIVES
'Report of the Committee on Meetings'
PETERBOROUGH CATHEDRAL ARCHIVES
'Chapter Act Books'
'Explanatory Remarks' [printed card, 1854]
Letter, Paige Cox to unknown
STOCKPORT PUBLIC LIBRARY
J. Holmes, 'History of St Paul's Church' [typescript]
Parish Church of St Paul's, Portwood, Stockport. Centenary Brochure 1851–1951 (Stockport, 1951)
TAUNTON, SOMERSET COUNTY RECORD OFFICE
Census, 1891 Enumerators' Returns, Sparkford
D/BJ/446 Letter, Bennett/Bell Jones, 1943
Edith Bennett [attributed to G. E. M. Bennett], 'Journal: Normandy with Ida, Frank, Francis, July 1925'
WASHINGTON CATHEDRAL ARCHIVES
101.2.10 'Bethlehem Chapel' [services]
103.1.1 'The Bethlehem Chapel, Notices'

120.7.4 Correspondence, Bennett/Freeman, Pepper
'Washington Cathedral Scrapbook'
WORCESTER CATHEDRAL LIBRARY
'Chapter Minutes'
'Minute Book of the Worcester Cathedral Council'

IN PRIVATE POSSESSION

Edith Bennett, 'Recollections, etc' (typescript transcribed and held by Mr P. S. Thring of St Albans, Hertfordhire)
F. L. M. Bennett, 'Memoir' [of Dean Bennett], typescript (held by the Revd. Guy Bennett, rector of Oxted, Surrey))
R. M. Bennett, 'Family History', typescript (held by Mrs Caroline Cloutte of Ashstead, Surrey, daughter of R. M. Bennett)
Grosvenor Estate, Eaton Estate Office, Cheshire (Estate volume 912, 'Housekeeper's journal'
Sherborne School Admissions Register (Sherborne School)
The King's School, Chester, 'Minutes of Governors' meetings' (King's School)
The Queen's School, Chester , 'Minutes of Governors' meetings' (Queen's School)
Walton House Preparatory School, Clevedon, Surrey, Admissions Register (Walton School)

Index

The index has been prepared by the Series Editor. Its preparation has drawn attention to a handful of minor slips and inconsistencies in the text which the author would have corrected in proof but which cannot now be resolved; while in the index he would have supplemented, extended and perhaps occasionally corrected the details of churchmen and Bennett family members which now appear. The index refers principally to the text, but the Index of Persons includes occasional references to names in notes, where the particular note is not linked to the name in the text.

INDEX OF PERSONS

The following abbreviations have been used in this index:

dn.	dean of
bp.	bishop of
archb.	archbishop of
>	later
n	note

Anselm, St 110, 113, 211, 219
Anson, Frederick, *dn.* Chester 106
Arnold, Thomas 77
Asquith, H. H. 68, 69, 259
Austen, Jane 19n14

Bartlett, Allan L., *bp.* Pennsylvania 165n55
Baxter, Aubrey 32, 217, 233
Bell, George K. A., *dn.* Canterbury > *bp.* Chichester 89, 90, 109, 114, 123, 124, 253, 259, 260

Bennett, Frank Selwyn Macaulay
  Main events: birth 13; family background 13; school and university 14–15; first post 15–18; vicar of Portwood, Stockport 26–30; marriage and family 29–30, 232–5; vicar of Christ Church, Chester 30–4; rector of Hawarden 35–48, 60–4; dean of Chester (1920–1937) 1–5, 9–12, 100–15, 204–22, 235, 236; visit to North America 143–61; publications 123–7, 170–9; retire

ment and death 236–40; epitaph 254
Anglo-Catholic and High Church practices 28, 32–4, 44–8, 184, 185, 187, 190
Bishopric question 256–63
cathedral reforms 2–5, 11, 12, 35, 100–15, 122–7, 131–4, 213–17, 235–6
character 1, 9–11, 27, 149–50, 179, 204, 232–5
contributions to debates on national church affairs 64–7, 122–3, 127–38, 185–90
later influence 244–53
pastoral activities 26, 27, 31–3, 35, 37–9, 41, 43, 46–8
reputation xi
science and psychology related to theology 170, 175, 177–9
selection as dean 67–70
Bennett family 17 [Relationships to F. S. M. Bennett of the family members are indicated in brackets.]
Bennett, Charles William [uncle], rector of Sparkford 14, 30
Bennett, Edith [sister] 29, 110
Bennett, Emily Louisa [sister] 23n52, 29, 233
Bennett, Francis/Frank Livesay Macaulay [son; references also to 'his son'] 12, 16, 30, 37, 40, 45, 46, 75, 87, 110, 111, 115, 145–8, 155, 157, 159, 170, 185, 214, 215, 219, 220, 232, 233, 235, 238, 258
Bennett, George E.M. [brother; references also to 'his brother'] 14, 29, 30, 34, 45, 69, 238
Bennett, Guy [grandson] xii, xiii, 18n5, 20n21, 21n31, 234, 235, 238
Bennet, Harry [brother] 22n44

Bennett, Helen Frances [aunt] 7
Bennett, Henry [grandfather], rector of Sparkford (ob.1874) 14, 24n64
Bennett, Henry Edward [father], squire of Sparkford 13
Bennett, James Arthur [uncle] 14
Bennett (Livesay), Ida [wife], 30, 33, 36, 39, 48, 58, 110, 153, 159, 232–4, 238, 239
Bennett (Blain), Margaret Hilda [daughter-in-law] 22n46, 234, 235
Bennett, Marion [sister] 29
Bennett, R. L. S. xiii
Bennett, Roderick Macaulay [grandson] xii, xiii, 16, 22n46, 49n23, 67, 119n66, 238
Benson, Edward White, bp. Truro > archb. Canterbury 8, 26, 124, 130, 138, 139n16, 260
Bevan, Edward Latham, bp. Swansea and Brecon 183
Blavatsky, Madame 179
Blencowe, A. J. 216
Bodley, G. F. 158
Bridgeman, John 113
Bromley-Davenport, Sir William 114, 236
Burge, H. M., bp., 262
Burroughs, E. A., bp. 260
Burroughs, W. O., bp. 260

Capek, Karel 88
Cecil, Hugh 122, 131
Child, Arthur Gascoigne 16, 175
Church, Richard William, dn. St Paul's 7, 8
Cobbett, William 94n5
Cocklebun the parrot 10, 11, 234
Conway, Owen C. xiii, 244–51
Coombes, Jeremiah 28
Coplestone, Frederick 211, 225n49
Coplestone, Mrs 113, 211

INDEX

Coué, M. 108, 109, 144, 147, 171, 179, 180, 234
Cromwell, Oliver, 15
Crossley, F. H. 105, 183, 205

Darby, John Lionel, *dn.* Chester (1886–1919) 3, 18, 68, 69, 102, 104, 106, 125, 204, 215, 218, 236, 245
Davidson, Randall, *archb.* Canterbury 68, 184, 258–62
Davies, Horton xi
De-la-Noy, Michael xi
Downing, Stanford 122
Drew, Harry, rector of Hawarden 35, 36, 38, 40–2

Eck, Herbert Vincent Shortgrave 199n102, 214, 219
Eddy, Mary Baker 191n4
Eden, Frederick 113
Edwards, A. G., *bp.* St Asaph > *archb.* Wales 47, 58, 64, 66, 67, 69, 70, 134, 258
Eeles, F. C. 113, 186
Etches, W. *bp.* 34

Fisher, Geoffrey, *bp.* Chester (1932–1939) > *archb.* Canterbury 211, 213, 217, 220, 221, 260
Foulkes, Robert 33, 47
Freeman, E. A. 4
Freeman, James E., *bp.* New York 4, 114, 151–5, 160
Frere, Walter Howard, *bp.* Truro 28, 38, 122, 123, 128, 129, 131, 259
Fyfe, David Theodore 101–5, 106, 111, 205, 207–9

Garbett, Cyril, *archb.* York 260, 262
George, David Lloyd 58, 59, 66–70, 258
Gladstone, H. N. 114
Gladstone, Helen 41, 65

Gladstone, Mrs Henry 112
Gladstone, Stephen 38
Gladstone, W. E. 7, 35, 60, 177
Gladstone, W. G. C., squire of Hawarden 36, 41, 44, 59
Griffiths, Trevor, rector of Sparkford 29

Hadfield, J. A. 173
Hall. Arthur C. A. , *bp.* Vermont 148, 149
Hall, Herbert 80, 81
Hamilton, Walter Kerr, *bp.* Salisbury 6, 7, 82, 122, 131
Hamilton Thompson, A. 122, 131
Harris, Joseph Hemington 13
Haswell, Frank 55n97
Haswell, William 106, 111
Henson, Hensley, *dn./bp.* 8, 184, 260
Hewitt, David, 112
Hopkins, John H. jnr. 144
Howe, [Lady] 244
Howson, J. F., vicar of Christ Church, Chester 31–33
Howson, J. S., *dn.* Chester (1867–85) 4, 106, 108, 143
Hughes, Robert J. 57n116
Hume, Joseph 85
Huxley, Julian 171, 178, 179

James, M. R. 122
Jayne, Francis John, *bp.* Chester (1889–1919) 3, 15–18, 28, 30, 31, 180, 211, 212, 214, 217, 218, 245
Jones, W. Bell 38, 45, 61, 238, 239
Kelly, Gerald 236
Kirk, T. P. R. 184
Kirkpatrick, J. F., *dn.* Ely 88
Knox, Ronald 75, 178, 179

Lang, Cosmo Gordon , *archb.* Canterbury 108, 122, 123, 184, 214, 220–2, 258, 259, 262

INDEX

Lawrence, Aubrey 93, 131
Lear, Francis 82
Lethaby, W. R. 101, 103, 109
Lewis, Margaret 160
Lightfoot, Joseph Barber 15
Livesey, Clegg 12, 30, 36, 58, 233–5
Lloyd, Roger xi, xiiin1, 93
Lupus, Hugh 113

Macaulay family, 14, 232, 233
Macaulay, Louisa 13
Macaulay, Sir James Buchanan 13, 14, 245
Marston, S.J. 215
McDougall, William 173, 180, 181
McDowell, R. *bp.* 260
Milman, Henry 83
Mockridge, John 149

Nairne, Alexander 214, 215
Newbolt, Henry 122
Nicholson, A. K. 113
Nicholson, Sir Charles 41
Nicholson, Sydney H. 128, 129
Noel Baker, P. J. 226n61

Owens, John 62

Paget, Elma xi, 239, 254
Paget, Henry Luke, *bp.* Chester (1919–1932), 3, 113, 114, 188, 205, 217–21, 258
Paige Cox, William Lang, archdeacon of Chester 204, 205, 214–17, 219
Paton, A. V. 110
Paul, St 178
Pearce, E. H., *bp.* Worcester 69
Peale, Norman Vincent 191n4
Phillips Brooks, - , *bp.* Massachusetts, 149
Picton-Timbervill, Edith 226n61
Platt, Henry 41

Ponsonby, Henry 258
Prince of Wales, 69, 108, 114, 159, 160

Radcliffe, Frederick 122
Rhinelander, Philip, *bp.* Washington 143, 151, 152
Rhoades, James 14, 16
Richard of Chichester, St 183, 241n17
Robbins, Keith xi
Robinson, Howard C., *dn.* New York 151
Rousmaniere, Edmund Swatt, *dn.* St Paul's, Boston 147
Russell, Bertrand 179
Russell, Lord John 83, 179

Savage, Henry Edwin, *bp.* Lichfield 129
Saunders, Augustus Page, *dn.* Peterborough 81, 92
Scott, George Gilbert 3, 76, 100
Scott, Giles Gilbert, 44, 46, 100–3, 106, 205
Selwyn, George Augustus, *bp.* New Zealand 21n43
Sheppard, Dick 189
Sheriff-Roberts, John 206
Simon de Whitchurch 113
Simpson, J. Y. 175, 177

Tapper, Walter 122
Thorpe, John H. 104
Trollope, Anthony 6
Trollope, Frances 6
Tubbs, Norman Henry, *dn.* Chester 121n91
Turner, Philip J. 155

Vaughan, Henry 158
Victoria, Queen 26, 83, 204, 258
Walcott, M. E. C. 78
Warren, Cuthbert Leicester 114
Washington, Peter 179

Werburgh, St 11, 107, 108, 110, 113, 114, 117n37, 160
Westminster, Duke of 17, 112, 171

Wickham, J. T. 90, 101, 102, 145
Williams, N. P. 178

INDEX OF PLACES

Note the separate lists of Cathedrals, Churches and Dioceses.

Albany 149

Baltimore 144
Barchester 6, 75, 132
Bishop's Lydeard 46
Buckingham 34
Bury St Edmunds 129, 130

Cambridge: Jesus College 214; King's College 32, 217
Canada xii, 13, 143–6, 160
Canterbury 48, 59, 60, 68, 82, 85–7, 89, 90, 92, 109, 114, 123, 124, 185, 189, 211, 216, 249, 252, 253, 258–260
Carlisle 244
Carnarvon 69
Chester localities: Abbey Square 210, 218, 234; Bishop's Hostel, Abbey Square 218, 219; George-street Chapel 63; Town Hall Square 206, 207
Clevedon 14
Concord, New Hampshire 148
Crete 102

Devon 13, 232

Eccleston 17
Ellesmere Port 212

Ely 88, 92, 129, 219, 251
Ewloe 35, 42

Flint 114

Glasgow 102
Glastonbury 110
Gloucester 79, 89, 92, 93, 122

Hawarden 1–3, 9–11, 26, 27, 31–48, 58–64, 66, 67, 69, 76, 101, 102, 105, 114, 154, 156, 205, 211, 217, 220, 234, 238, 239, 250, 259
Hawarden localities: Broughton 35, 42; Garden City 35, 41; Queensferry 35; Sandycroft 35, 41–3, 60; Sealand 35, 41

Lake Ontario 146
Lampeter College 16
Leeds 16, 122
Lichfield 80, 129, 218
Lincoln 8, 29, 79, 88, 89, 247
Liverpool 75, 100, 102, 122, 134, 144, 159, 234, 252
London 11, 77, 82, 83, 86, 101, 103, 146, 160, 171, 173, 218, 219, 251, 259

Manchester 29, 93, 129

INDEX

Mancott Royal 35, 41
McGill University 155
Montreal 144, 146, 155

New England 144, 147
New York 143, 144, 148, 151, 155, 182
Newport 134
Niagara 146
Northwich 111
Norwich 5, 80, 92, 129, 130, 218

Ontario 146
Oxford: Bodleian Library 262; Keble College xii, 15, 16, 214; University College 262

Peterborough 46, 80, 81, 92, 100, 129, 216
Philadelphia 144, 149–51, 153

Salisbury 6, 82, 88, 90, 91, 92
Shotton 39, 41, 42
Somerset 7, 13, 27, 46, 238
South Africa 36
Sparkford 13, 14, 17, 29, 30, 212, 232, 233, 239
Stockport 17, 27, 28, 30, 104
Sydney 128, 129, 144

Taunton 13, 234, 238
Toronto 144–6, 182
Toronto localities: University 145, 146; Hart House 146; Wickham Lodge 145
Truro 8, 122, 124, 134, 245, 259

United States of America/USA 101, 114, 148, 154, 157

Wakefield 253
Wales 40, 47, 58–60, 62–9, 73, 76, 108, 114, 134, 150, 160, 190, 206, 207, 259, 262
Washington 94, 114, 134, 143, 144, 150–4, 156–60, 179
Waverton 47
Wellington College 8
Wells 16, 58, 79, 88
Wembley Exhibition buildings 134, 153
Worcester 69, 90–3, 112, 122, 131

York 82, 88–90, 108, 112, 114, 122, 123, 151, 185, 220, 252, 258–60, 262

Cathedrals, etc (by locality)
Albany, All Saints 149
Bangor 76
Brecon, Priory Church of St John the Evangelist 76
Boston, St Paul 146, 147
Bradford 253
Bristol 87, 88, 90, 92
Buffalo, St Paul 143, 144
Bury St Edmunds 129, 130
Canterbury 48, 82, 85–7, 89, 90, 92, 109, 114, 123, 124, 189, 249, 252, 253, 260
Chichester 78
Constantinople, St Sophia 44
Durham 79, 88
Ely 88, 92, 129, 251
Gloucester 79, 89, 92
Guildford 134, 135
Lichfield 89
Lincoln 79, 88, 89, 247
Liverpool 100, 122, 134
Llandaff 76
London, St Paul 7, 8, 82, 149, 251, 252
London, Orthodox 77
London, Westminster Abbey 69, 83–5, 122, 128, 149
Manchester 129
Montreal, Christ Church 155

New York, St John the Divine 151, 155
Norwich 5, 80, 92, 129, 130, 218
Peterborough 80, 81, 92, 129, 216
Ripon 249
Rochester 92
Salisbury 6, 82, 88, 90, 92
Southwell Minster 129, 130
St Albans 88–90, 92, 145, 159, 250
St Asaph 76
St David's 76
Toronto, Christ Church 155
Truro 134, 245
Washington 151, 152, 156, 158–60
Wells 79, 88
Winchester 6, 79, 89, 92, 182, 216, 258, 262, 263
Worcester 69, 90–2, 112
York 82, 88–90. 112, 114, 220, 252

Churches (by name)
Christ Church, Chester 9, 26, 30–5, 37–41, 43, 45, 47, 62, 220, 236
Christ Church, Philadelphia 150
Holy Innocents, Pentre/Hawarden 35
St Alban the Martyr, Toronto 145, 146
St Alban, Washington 159
St Andrew, West Kirby 159
St Bartholomew, Sealand/Hawarden 35
St Deiniol, Hawarden 35
St Ethelwold, Shotton/Hawarden 35, 60
St George, chapel, Windsor 112, 214, 258
St James, Bury St Edmunds 130
St James, Philadelphia 149
St James, Toronto 145, 146
St John, Chester 16, 218
St John, Pentrobin/Hawarden 35
St John, Providence, R.I. 148
St Mark, Washington 151, 152
St Mary, Broughton/Hawarden 35
St Mary, Bury St Edmunds 130
St Mary, Stockport 30
St Paul, Burlington, Vermont 149
St Paul, chapel, New York 148
St Paul, Portwood/Stockport xii, 17, 26–35, 38, 42, 47, 219, 232
St Thomas, Stockport 28
St Thomas, Washington 152
St Winifred, Ewloe/Hawarden 35
Trinity, New York 148

Dioceses (named)
Bangor 59, 66, 76
Bath and Wells 16
Chester 15, 28, 35, 158, 184, 238, 252
Chichester 89, 260
Gloucester 93, 122
Lichfield 129, 218
Lincoln 8
Llandaff 59 76
London 11, 218, 259
Manchester 93
Massachusetts 149
Monmouth 66, 76, 134
New York 164
Norwich 218
Oxford 122, 262
Pennsylvania 151
Rochester 258
Southwark 262
St Asaph 65, 66, 76
St David's 59, 76
St Edmundsbury and Ipswich 130, 131
Swansea and Brecon 76, 183
Truro 8, 122, 124, 259
Vermont 149
Washington xii, 160
Worcester 69, 93, 131
York 259, 260, 262

INDEX OF SUBJECTS

Admission/entrance fee/charge 11, 76–80, 83–6, 89, 91, 92, 221, 249
American church 143, 157–9
Anglo-Catholic 28, 38, 44, 45, 149, 184, 185, 187, 190, 216, 221, 259
Anti-ritualist protest 29, 33, 34, 47, 48
Auto-suggestion 171, 172, 179

Bishopric, appointment to, mode of selection 258–60
Bishops 1881–1945 analysis of credits for selection 260–2
Book of Common Prayer/Prayer Book 28, 38, 60, 172, 181, 184–90
British and Foreign Bible Society 42

Car parking 135, 159, 210
Cathedral reforms, predecessors of Bennett 5–9
Cathedral staff: canons 4, 8, 32, 35, 36, 69, 82, 85, 90, 100–2, 104, 112, 124–8, 130–8, 159, 182, 204, 207, 214–17, 219, 233, 235, 236, 239, 247, 261; chapter 2, 4, 5, 7, 8, 11, 74, 76, 78–86, 88–93, 100–8, 123–5, 127–31, 133, 135–7, 146, 157, 180, 205, 207–17, 219, 235–8, 245–51, 253, 259; choir 4, 7, 11, 32, 38, 84, 85, 104, 108, 125, 129, 133, 134, 160, 251; clerks 90, 101, 106, 129, 133, 136, 137, 247, 251; dean *passim*; guides 4, 79, 86, 127, 249; sacristans 2, 88, 124; sextons 77, 79, 81; vergers 11, 12, 77–82, 86, 89, 91, 126, 127, 188, 213, 249, 253; vicars choral 7
Cathedrals Commission (1854) 77
Cathedrals Commission (1924–27) xii, 80, 83, 88, 89, 92, 110, 113, 122, 123, 127–32, 135, 143, 253, 259, 262
Cathedrals Measure (1931) 135–7
Cathedrals report (1994) - *see* Publications/*Heritage and Renewal*
Ceremonial (church ritual): 2, 11, 28, 33, 34, 38, 41, 46, 124, 157, 158, 180, 185, 186, 211 *see also* Liturgical
Chaplains 17, 18, 40, 62, 126, 137, 211
Chester and North Wales Archaeological Society 207
Chester Cathedral: administration 2, 4, 124–6, 136, 137, 213–217; diocesan role 3, 4, 123, 124, 132, 133, 217–22; fabric 3, 100–5, 111–13, 207–9; finances 5, 106–10, 113–15, 132–4, 159, 210, 235–6; services 2–4, 123
Chester Cathedral building, select parts: cloisters 3, 74, 100, 104, 105, 110, 113, 127, 131, 211; refectory 3, 74, 100, 103–105, 108, 110, 111, 131, 145, 172, 182, 210, 211, 219, 221, 236, 239, 248; sacristry 108, 112, 113, 160; tower 100, 101, 104, 108, 111, 207, 215; vestry 88, 160, 176, 207–9
Chester [Teachers' Training] College 213
Chester Debating Society 62–3
Chester Diocesan Gazette xii, 9, 35, 76, 87, 93, 108, 114, 151, 157, 180, 186, 212
Children's corner/chapel 43, 105, 154–7, 181, 237, 249, 250

INDEX

Church Army 35, 41, 60
Church Association 29, 33, 38, 47, 186, 187, 214, 216, 218
Church Lads' Brigade/CLB 27, 31, 39, 43, 44
Church League for Women's Suffrage 65
Church of England Men's Society/ CEMS 28, 31, 33, 87, 183, 184
Church of England Temperance Society 212
Church in Wales, the xii, 40, 58, 59, 63–6, 68, 69, 259, 262
Church services: Baptism 28, 38, 147, 181, 183, 184, 189, 250; Communion 2, 32, 38, 45, 47, 59, 124, 126, 152, 186, 187, 219; Compline 126, 219; Confessions 2, 125, 185; Eucharist 2, 7, 28, 32, 38, 43–7, 123, 125, 133, 156, 180, 183, 214, 215, 219, 239, 245, 250, 253; Evensong 32, 38, 82, 93, 126, 133, 152, 236, 245; Mattins 87, 123, 125, 126, 133, 245, 250
Churchwardens 38, 39, 61, 238
Community of the Resurrection 28, 38
Confraternity of the Blessed Sacrament 38, 184
Council for the Preservation of Rural England 212
Council of Church Training Colleges 213
Crucifix 33, 47, 215
Curates 17, 29, 111, 149

Disendowment (of the Church in Wales) 5, 6, 37, 58–63 *passim*
Disestablishment – *see* Welsh disestablishment

Ecclesiologist, The 143, 144

Ecumenism 147, 250
Education – *see* Religious education
Education Act (1935) 182
English Church Union 47, 184, 186, 214
Episcopacy 143, 144, 147, 189, 190
Evangelical/s 6, 28, 47, 221, 259

Free Will Offering 35, 40
Free Church – *see* Nonconformist
Freemasonry/Masonry 3, 41, 114, 146, 183, 189, 211, 221
Friends of Chester Cathedral 114, 160

Girls' Friendly Society 31, 39
Girl Guides 236
Great War 12, 187
Guide book to Chester cathedral 4, 12, 79, 86, 127, 249
Guild of Help 32

Hackney Phalanx 6
Hawarden Parish Magazine xii, 2, 35, 40, 60
Healing and health 16, 147, 171–3, 178, 181, 182, 233, 234, 247
High Church 2, 3, 6, 28, 29, 33, 184, 186, 214, 216, 218, 259
Historical Association 210
Holy Cross Society 184

Immortality (of the soul) 174, 177–9
Industrial Christian Fellowship 184
Infants, deaths of the Bannetts' 233
Integration (of churches) 189, 190, 250

King's School, The 17, 180, 205

Lambeth doctorate 221, 237, 258
League of Loyalty and Order 188
League of Nations 157, 212
Liberal (party) 17, 33, 58–61, 63
Lighting, importance of 111, 126

Liturgical practice/concerns 35, 38, 46, 47, 157, 158, 180, 186, 189, 240, 253

Mothers' Union 31, 107, 152–4, 233
Music and singing 3, 7, 15, 29, 31–4, 38, 39, 45, 46, 75, 85, 123–7, 133, 157, 158, 185, 215, 219, 253

National Day of Prayer for the Church 61
National Mission of Repentance and Hope 45
Nonconformist/Free Church 29, 42, 58, 59, 61–3, 69, 186, 189
North Wales University College 69

'Open and free' 11, 12, 73, 77, 87, 126–32
Organism 156, 173, 176–8, 189, 190

Parents' League 33
Parish church cathedrals 127, 134, 149, 247
Parish council 33, 35, 37, 39, 40
Patriotism, war 43–5
People's Refreshment House Association 17, 212
Pilgrims/pilgrimage (to cathedrals) xi, 11, 74, 77, 91, 108, 109, 131, 138, 214, 215, 238, 239, 249
Police Court Mission 212
Protestant 5, 28, 29, 47, 186, 218
Prayer Book revision 185–9 *passim*
Publications
  by F. S. M. Bennett:
  M. Coué and his Gospel of Health (1922) 147, 171, 172, 180
  A Soul in the Making or Psychosynthesis (1924) 171–4, 180

The Nature of a Cathedral (1925) 76, 87, 110, 122–7 *passim*, 132, 134, 138, 145, 146, 149, 156, 158, 217, 219, 244, 250, 253
Expecto: An Essay Towards a Biology of the World to Come (1926) 70, 147, 149, 152, 171, 174–7, 259
Mary Jane and Harry John or Home the Premier School (1927) 180, 181
On Cathedrals in the Meantime (1928) 132, 153, 156
The Resurrection of the Dead (1929) 176–8
The Resurrection of the Organism (1930) 156, 176–8
The Christian Ideal of Health (1930) 181
This Moment of Opportunity for Religious Education (1938) 182, 222, 238
  by others:
  Essays on Cathedrals (J. S. Howson, 1872) 4
  Studies Subsidiary to Bishop Butler (W. E. Gladstone, 1896) 177
  Laodicea in the Twentieth Century: The Church of England in the England of Today (F. L. M. Bennett, 1946) 238
  A Cathedral Pilgrimage: Reflections and Observations on the Life and Work of Cathedrals in England Today and in the Future (O. C. Conway, 1989) 244–51 *passim*
  Heritage and Renewal: The Archbishops' Commission on Cathedrals (Lady Howe, 1994) 244–51 *passim*

Queen's School, The 212, 236

Reincarnation 174
Religious education 33, 42, 180, 182, 183, 222, 238
Reservation (of the Sacrament) 186–8
Rotary Club 211

Sarum Theological College 17
Scouts 27
Sherborne School 14, 15, 233, 235
Society of St John the Evangelist/ 'Cowley Fathers' 149, 184
Society for the Protection of Ancient Buildings 206
Spiritualism 176, 252
St David's Day 42
St Werburgh's Day Festival 107, 110
Sunday School 32, 33, 39, 41–3, 45, 180, 182, 220, 236

The Times 15, 17, 74, 80, 89, 109, 134, 153, 176, 188, 207, 208, 211, 237, 238
The Times Literary Supplement 123, 177
Theology 152, 170–9 *passim*, 184, 185, 187, 189, 214, 219, 235, 238, 259
Tractarianism 6, 194
Transfiguration, the 175, 176

War memorial 46, 100, 104, 204, 206
Welsh Disestablishment xii, 37, 58–70 *passim*
Welsh Education Department 42
Welsh language 41, 42
Women, inclusion of 64, 65
Women's Auxiliary 153
Women's Help Society 31

YMCA 218